SEVENTY DAYS TO SINGAPORE

Other books by Stanley L. Falk
The March of Death
Decision at Leyte
Liberation of the Philippines
Bloodiest Victory: Palaus

SEVENTY DAYS TO SINGAPORE

The Malayan Campaign,
1941-1942

STANLEY L. FALK

ROBERT HALE · LONDON

Filmset by Specialised Offset Services Limited, Liverpool
and printed in Great Britain by
Compton Printing Limited
Aylesbury, Bucks

Contents

Illustrations

MAPS

The above maps are based on maps and sketches contained in *The War Against Japan*, Volume 1, by S. Woodburn-Kirby (H.M.S.O. 1957) by permission of the Controller of Her Majesty's Stationery Office.

PICTURE CREDITS

Robert Hunt Library, 1,4,12,21; Imperial War Museum, 2,3,5,6,7,8,10,11,13,14,15,20; Associated Press, 9,16,17,18,19.

Preface

By the end of the year 1971 Great Britain completed the withdrawal of all military and naval forces from Singapore and turned over the last of her installations on the island to the government of the young republic that replaced British rule there. Even before that date a portion of the great naval base had passed into the hands of workmen for conversion into a commercial shipyard, auxiliary port, and industrial park. A century and a half of British presence at Singapore, the crossroads of the Far East, thus reached its end.

The only interruption in that long presence came during World War II, when for three and one half years the Japanese held Singapore, and indeed all of Malaya, in their grasp. Many observers trace the final British evacuation directly to this brief but all too painful and forcible interruption. Japan's conquest of Malaya and Singapore, they suggest, brought with it not only the beginning of the end of the British Empire, but also the death of colonialism and white supremacy in the Far East. The Japanese victory at once discredited the white man and created a power vacuum into which the rising tide of Asian nationalism might surge once the war was ended.

This interpretation, while persuasive, is not really convincing. The British Empire would have dissolved even if Singapore had never fallen, even, in fact, if the war had never touched Malaya. The causes for change were too strong, the forces of nationalism too mighty, to require anything so transitory as a battle to bring them into full effect. No, the fall of Singapore did not, as someone put it, change the world. It is doubtful if it even hastened significantly whatever developments would have occurred in any event.

Why then is the Malayan campaign important? There are two reasons. First of all, Singapore was a symbol: a symbol of imperial might and invincibility, of nineteenth-century colonial prestige, and of a kind of international political relationship that had outlived its time. Its fall so clearly signalled a change already inevitable for other reasons that it has sometimes been difficult to distinguish cause and effect. Japan's conquest of Malaya thus appeared to be more meaningful than all of her other great victories. More than any other Western defeat, it represented a shift in the tides of power. In this sense, it is fitting to examine the Malayan campaign, not as a decisive battle like Marathon or Hastings, but rather as a clear benchmark on the rough terrain of Asian history.

A second reason for studying this campaign, closely linked to the first, is the fact that for much of the world Singapore not only symbolised Western strength and grandeur, but it stood as an impregnable fortress against which no enemy could prevail. When it fell, in only seventy days, to a foe whose military prowess had been somewhat lightly regarded, the event was a shock, a stunning blow to complacency and almost every military misconception held by man. It is this tumultuous fact, perhaps more than anything else, that makes the story of Singapore worth telling. Certainly, for both vanquished and victor in Malaya, the campaign underlines the wisdom of Admiral Mahan's observation that 'defeat cries aloud for explanation; whereas success, like charity, covers a multitude of sins'.

The pages that follow are less an explanation of *why* Singapore fell — this should become clear in the first few chapters — than an attempt to tell *how* it fell. They contain the story of a military campaign and thus tend to emphasise military matters: strategy and tactics, logistics and movements, arms and equipment, the soldier in the field and the officers who led him. They seek to tell the story of both conqueror and conquered, assessing credit and blame where these sometimes elusive responsibilities appear evident. Where they differ from other interpretations, they follow what seems to me to be the clear direction of the evidence.

Of those who have been particularly helpful, I owe special thanks to Miss Hannah M. Zeidlik of the Office of the Chief of Military History, Department of the Army, and Mrs Lois Aldrich, Modern Military Records Division, National Archives, for their assistance in locating certain documentary materials; to Mr Louis Allen, Senior Lecturer in French at the University of Durham, England, and Japanese military scholar, for his generosity in providing material from several Japanese sources, for obtaining for me a copy of Major Wild's personal account of General Percival's surrender, and for other valuable suggestions; to the Very Rev. John H.S. Wild, D.D., Dean of Durham, for allowing me to quote from his brother's memoirs; to Dr. E.R. Lewis, of Washington, D.C., for helping me to unravel the sometimes confusing story of the

Singapore guns; and finally to Mr. Hanson W. Baldwin, who suggested this work and encouraged its writing.

Permission to quote from the following books has been generously granted by: Houghton Mifflin Company, for Winston S. Churchill, *The Second World War*; Angus & Robertson Ltd., for Lieut.-General H. Gordon Bennett, *Why Singapore Fell*; David Higham Associates, for Lieut.-General A.E. Percival, *The War in Malaya*; Her Majesty's Stationery Office, for Maj.-General S. Woodburn Kirby, *et al., The Loss of Singapore*; Mrs. Maria Therese Morrison, for Ian Morrison, *Malayan Postscript*; Frederick Muller Ltd., for Lieut.-Commander T.J. Cain, *H.M.S. Electra*; and the Ann Elmo Agency, for Lieut.-Commander P.K. Kemp, *Key to Victory: The Triumph of British Sea Power in World War II.*

Stanley L. Falk

Alexandria, Virginia

TO LISA AND KAREN

1
Rendezvous

At nine o'clock on the morning of December 7th, 1941, three Japanese convoys came together near the centre of the Gulf of Siam.* Soon they would split again and proceed to more than half a dozen previously chosen landing points along the western shoreline of the Gulf. The invasion of Thailand and Malaya was about to begin.[1]

The largest of the convoys, carrying Lieutenant-General Tomoyuki Yamashita, commander of the Japanese Twenty-fifth Army and nearly 27,000 of his men, had been at sea for three days. It included nineteen slow transports, all under 10,000 tons, a small hospital ship, minesweepers and subchasers, and an escorting destroyer squadron. Sailing with the convoy aboard the heavy cruiser *Chokai* was Vice Admiral Jisaburo Ozawa, naval commander for the Malayan operation. General Yamashita was on the transport *Ryujo Maru*, prepared to go ashore with troops of the 5th Division.

The convoy had left the port of Samah on Hainan Island early on the morning of December 4th. As it steamed south along the Indo-Chinese coast, a heavy cruiser squadron shielded its seaward flank, while still more of the powerful units of Vice-Admiral Nobutake Kondo's Southern Force — supporting both the Malayan and the Philippine invasions — sailed from Formosa at noon and moved into the South China Sea to provide distant cover. Minelayers and submarines were already shifting to block British naval movement north from Singapore. In Indo-China, Japanese army and naval air units were completing a southern deployment, and the Twenty-fifth Army convoy

* Malayan time is given here, seven and a half hours ahead of Greenwich mean time. Unless otherwise indicated, Malayan time will be used throughout this book. Determining exactly when events took place during the Malayan campaign is sometimes difficult, since Japanese forces operated on Tokyo time (an hour and a half ahead of Malayan time) and it is seldom clear whether Japanese sources are using Tokyo or Local time. British forces went by Malayan time throughout the campaign, and used it in contemporary and later reports — including those describing events in nearby but different time zones. Wide variations in time thus appear in many sources.

hugged the shoreline to remain well within range of this land-based air cover and out of sight of unfriendly air reconnaissance. Even if the convoy were spotted from the air, its course and the relatively small naval force travelling with it might prove deceptive. Perhaps it was merely carrying supplies or reinforcements to Japanese troops in southern Indo-China? With luck and a little help from the weather, the true objective of the movement might be concealed until it was too late for the enemy to intercept it.

On December 4th, the weather was bright and clear. As the convoy slid out of Samah harbour, General Yamashita noted that the rising sun shared the cloudless sky with a half-moon not yet set. He regarded this as a good omen.[2] But he would have preferred the more real protection of clouds or rain. Along with practically everyone else aboard, he maintained an anxious lookout for signs of hostile planes or submarines.

The day remained clear, but passed without incident. Black funnel-smoke stained the unbroken blue of the sky as the ships pushed south, 'plowing up angry billows'.[3] The troops sprawled on the decks under the hot tropical sun, trying to accustom themselves to the rolling, pitching movements of the vessels. Many were stiff from inaction, having spent as much as a week on board their transports before leaving Samah.[4] The cramped accommodations at sea did not help matters, nor did the unsatisfactory shipboard fare: boiled rice and barley, pickled radishes, and an all-but-tasteless bean soup. Some of the men took packets of dried eels from their knapsacks, heated them on deck over tiny field stoves, and munched them along with their other rations.

Most of the troops were leafing through a most remarkable document, a pamphlet entitled *Just Read This and the War is Won*, which they had received as they embarked.[5] Written in simple, informal language, it was a detailed summary of Japan's reasons for going to war, a manual for behavior on shipboard, while landing, and during the forthcoming campaign, and an exhortation to victory. It's content ranged from a description of Southeast Asia as a treasury being looted by the White Man to a discussion of the proper way to descend into a landing craft, from a warning against snakes and insects to instructions for the care of horses and weapons. It covered, among other things, war aims, tactics, communications, and personal hygiene. It closed with a bold declaration that peace and freedom rested on Japanese shoulders, reaching a crescendo with the classic lines of *Umi Yukaba*, a famous eighth century poem by Yakamochi Otomo, very popular as a song after the start of the Sino-Japanese war in 1937:

Across the sea, corpses in the water;
Across the mountain, corpses heaped upon the field.
I will die only for the Emperor.
I will never look back.

The first night at sea was uneventful. But as day broke on December 5th, a ship appeared on the southern horizon and slowly approached the convoy. It proved to be a Norwegian steamer. A boarding party from the destroyer *Uranami* searched the ship and released it after telling its captain in no uncertain terms what course to take. No other vessels nor any planes were sighted during the rest of the day, but that afternoon hostile submarines were reported to be in the area and the ships began to zigzag. A few hours later, as the convoy turned west into the Gulf of Siam, its passengers were relieved to see the sky blacken with clouds. The ships were entering the cover of the north-eastern monsoon which dominated these waters during the autumn and winter, reducing visibility and making navigation difficult for hostile reconnaissance planes. Until the convoy reached its destination it would be assured of rainy afternoons and, throughout the day, sudden violent squalls and periodic downpours. It made for rough sailing in the small, slow transports, but it lengthened the odds against the force being discovered. And heavier weather was doubly important now, for early that evening a second and much smaller convoy had left Saigon for the Gulf of Siam rendezvous.

Discovery came, nevertheless, the next day. During the morning of the 6th, the Twenty-fifth Army convoy caught up with two slow transports and an escorting minelayer that had left Samah on the night of December 3rd. Then, shortly after noon, when the ships were about eighty miles south of Cape Cambodia, a large British aircraft emerged from the clouds.[6] One of the nearby cruisers launched a float-plane and the intruder fled. But the convoy had been sighted and there was no way of knowing how soon it might be attacked. Reports of other British planes in the area did nothing to lessen Japanese apprehensions, despite the increasing heaviness of the weather.

To meet the growing threat of interception Admiral Ozawa ordered four Japanese submarines that had left Samah the previous evening for Malayan waters to shift their course to the west. Cruising on the surface to make their best speed, they were to go to a point some twenty miles south of the convoy route and lie in wait for any enemy fleet that might venture into the area. Japanese army and naval aircraft now completing their concentration in southern Indo-China were also directed to increase their surveillance over the Gulf of Siam and shoot down any planes they encountered. During the night the invasion convoy turned north-west to give the impression to any hostile eye that it was proceeding up the Thai coast, perhaps towards Bangkok.[7]

Some time after midnight on December 6th-7th, the third and smallest of the three Japanese convoys left Phu Quoc Island, off the south-west coast of Indo-China, and started toward the centre of the Gulf of Siam. A few hours later, five army fighter planes of the 3rd Air Group took off from a newly constructed field on Phu Quoc. Flying south-west through intermittent rain squalls, they came upon a lone reconnaissance plane, a Singapore-based Catalina flying-boat of the Royal Air Force. The big, lumbering British craft was no match for the speedy fighters. The nearest plane, piloted by a first lieutenant named Tsubotani, put a burst of gunfire into one wing, setting the Catalina aflame. Hit quickly again and again by the other fighters, the flying-boat exploded and plunged into the sea before its startled crew could radio a message to Singapore.[8]

This brief moment of execution, high above the waters of the Gulf of Siam, came some twenty hours before the Japanese attack on Pearl Harbour. It was the first act of war in the great Pacific conflict then unfolding. Lieutenant Tsubotani had fired the initial shot.

Word of the aerial encounter reached General Yamashita a few hours later, at about the same time that he received a report that British warships had left Singapore. By now the assembly of convoys near the middle of the Gulf of Siam was complete. Yamashita and Admiral Ozawa held a hasty conference to decide whether the possible enemy naval threat required them to make any changes in the landing plan. But this hardly seemed necessary. Rain, fog, and heavy cloud shielded the invasion force from hostile eyes, and Japanese fighter planes 'were continually diving through breaks in the clouds and flying between the patches of fog, giving the convoy continuous protection'.[9] There could be no hesitation. The landings would take place as planned. Each unit was thus informed. A few hours later, Ozawa, with *Chokai* and a destroyer, left the escort group and turned south, a small, brave force bent on intercepting any British warships that might threaten the invasion.

At Singapore, meanwhile, there was no report on the fate of the missing Catalina, and other reconnaissance planes had failed to make new contacts with the Twenty-fifth Army convoy. The British high command was still trying to guess the destination of the Japanese force, still unaware that each passing hour brought the invasion of Malaya closer and with it the inevitable fall of Singapore.

Notes

1. Basic sources for this chapter: U.S. Army Forces, Far East, Japanese Monograph Series: No. 54, *Malay Operations Record, November 1941-March 1942*, pp. 20-24; No. 55, *Southwest Area Air Operations, November 1941-February 1942*, pp. 37-42; No. 105, *General Summary of Naval Operations, Southern Force*, pp. 3, 7-9; No. 107, *Malaya Invasion Naval Operations (Revised Edition)*, pp. 11-19; Colonel Masanobu Tsuji, *Singapore, The Japanese Version* (New York: St. Martin's Press, 1960), pp. 72-78.

2. John Deane Potter, *The Life and Death of a Japanese General* (New York: The New American Library, 1962), pp. 49-50.

3. Southwest Pacific Area, Allied Translater and Interpreter Section (ATIS), Enemy Publications, No. 278, *Malaya Campaign 1941-1942*, January 11th, 1945, p. 4.

4. ATIS, Research Report No. 131, *Japan's Decision to Fight*, Dec. 1, 1945, pp. 12-13, 27-28.

5. App. I, Tsuji, *Singapore*. Also see 4 above, pp. 13-15.

6. *Malaya Invasion Naval Operations*, p. 19. For British activities, Air-Chief-Marshal Sir Robert Brooke-Popham, *Despatch: Operations in the Far East, from October 17th, 1940 to December 27th, 1941*, May 28th, 1942, Supplement to the *London Gazette* of January 20th, 1948, *p. 555;* Air-Vice Marshal Sir Paul Maltby, *Report on the Air Operations During the Campaigns in Malaya and Netherlands East Indies from December 8th, 1941 to March 12th, 1942*, July 26th, 1947, Third Supplement to the *London Gazette* of February 20th, 1948, pp. 1363-64; Douglas Gillison, *Royal Australian Air Force, 1939-1942*, Australia in the War of 1939-1945, Series 3, *Air*, Vol. I, (Canberra: Australian War Memorial, 1962), pp. 199-202; Denis Richards and Hilary St. George Saunders, *Royal Air Force, 1939-1945*, Vol. II, *The Fight Avails*; (London: Her Majesty's Stationery Office, 1954), pp. 15-17.

7. Takushiro Hattori, *The Complete History of the Greater East Asia War* (4 vols.; Tokyo: Masu Publishing Company, 1953) (Translation by U.S. Army Forces, Far East, 500th Military Intelligence Service Group, on file in Office of the Chief of Military History, Department of the Army), II, 25.

8. For a somewhat romanticised account, see ATIS, *Malaya Campaign*, p. 12.

9. Tsuji, *Singapore*, p. 77.

2
The Thief at the Fire

The fate of Singapore was sealed in Tokyo on a hot and humid day in the summer of 1941. On Wednesday, July 2nd, five months before the first Japanese combat troops set foot in Malaya, Japan's leaders made a momentous decision.

Japan in that fateful summer stood at the crossroads of fortune. The long years of development that had transformed her from an isolated feudal state into a major world power were now reaching their climax. Either the Japanese would achieve their self-proclaimed destiny as the leaders of Asia or they would have to admit that they had come as far as they could and that any further success must depend on the assistance and good will of the rest of the world.

During the 1930s Japan had gained a dominant position in the Far East. But her relative poverty in mineral resources, especially in the oil and other basic materials so necessary to twentieth-century technology, was a growing threat to the maintenance of Japanese power. As the decade of the forties began, rising military expenditures and the development of a completely war-focused economy underlined a national determination to seize those bases and raw materials that would make Japan economically strong and self-sufficient. Thanks to German military victories, the ability of European colonial powers to defend their Far Eastern possessions had been sharply reduced. For Japan, the chance to 'play the thief at a fire', as the Emperor reportedly put it, was becoming increasingly attractive.[1]

While the Japanese army, which had so far been mainly responsible for the nation's militaristic adventures, looked to further conquests on the Chinese mainland, the navy turned elsewhere. Naval strategists had always viewed the vast reaches of the Pacific as a fitting arena for war and national expansion. With the growing importance of oil to modern arms, the navy saw in the rich and vulnerable mineral resources of the Netherlands Indies the key to Japan's future. The army, too, despite its preference for an attack on the Soviet Union, was aware that without oil the entire Japanese war machine might grind to a standstill. Stringent rationing and the manufacture of synthetics could not solve the problem. The answer lay in the willingness of American, Dutch, and British suppliers to provide Japan with the necessary oil to continue her war in China, and to support her in whatever other ventures she initiated.

By the summer of 1941, it was clear that Western economic sanctions would soon strangle Japan's aspirations to empire. Only by surrendering her ambitions in China – a sacrifice she was unwilling to make – could she gain the removal of these restrictions. There was of course another alternative: to seize for herself the mineral-rich resources of South-east Asia. And it was this alternative that in mid-1941 seemed to the Japanese leaders to be less and less a choice and more and more a necessity.

The situation had become critical. Oil reserves were falling lower. The war in China seemed no closer to an end. The Tripartite Pact with Germany and Italy had increased rather than weakened American hostility. And negotiations with the Dutch for oil from the East Indies had broken down. Now, with the Soviet Union, the traditional enemy, engaged in a life-and-death struggle against Germany, Japan's northern flank was no longer threatened by a possible Russian attack. The time seemed ripe to move south and seize the oil that the west withheld.

On July 2nd, 1941, an Imperial Conference – a meeting of Japan's top military and political leaders in the presence of the Emperor – agreed to put aside thoughts of an attack on the Soviet Union and to concentrate instead on achieving Japanese objectives in the south. The Empire would 'continue all necessary diplomatic negotiations', but meanwhile prepare for war. As a first step, Japan would implement previously-made plans for the domination of French Indo-China and Thailand 'with the purpose of strengthening our advance into the southern regions'. In carrying out this policy, the Japanese would 'not be deterred by the possibility of being involved in a war with Great Britain and the United States'.[2]

Present at this important meeting were the civil and military chiefs of the Japanese government and armed forces, facing each other stiffly across two long brocade-covered tables. The forty-year-old Emperor presided, sitting silently before a gold screen on a dias at one end of the parallel tables. As usual, he listened impassively while the others described and explained decisions they had already made at less formal meetings during the previous weeks. The Emperor's approval of such decisions, while legally necessary, was in practice only a matter of form, since he customarily followed the advice of his counsellors and rarely exercised his constitutional authority to change or disapprove governmental policies. On July 2nd, as usual, he asked no questions. Whatever doubts he had were expressed by the President of his Privy Council, Yoshimichi Hara, who was troubled by the willingness of the others to risk war with Great Britain and America. 'I think', Hara stated bluntly, 'that such a war will occur if we take action against Indo-China'.[3] No one else, however, seemed over concerned, and even the Emperor appeared to be satisfied. In the end, he gave his assent, 'at one-thirty, immediately after lunch'.[4]

There was not a single mention of Singapore at this conference. But several of those present must have been thinking of it. For some time now, Germany had been urging its Japanese ally to attack the British naval base — although with no success as far as the Germans could tell. Now that Germany had invaded the Soviet Union and, indeed, had requested similar action from Japan, the Japanese had finally decided on a step that might well involve them in war with Britain. They would make all necessary preparations for this conflict and if it came Singapore would be an obvious target for early seizure. As the army Chief of Staff, General Gen Sugiyama, put it, 'Our occupation of Indo-China will certainly provoke Great Britain and the United States'.[5] Barring some sort of negotiated settlement, the die was cast for a push south: to Singapore and beyond.

The Japanese were actually already in control of northern Indo-China. In the previous summer, as part of an effort to tighten their blockade of China, they had forced the helpless Vichy French government to permit Japanese 'military observers' to operate out of Hanoi. By late September, the Japanese had established ground and air bases in Tonkin, occupying virtually the entire province. When Thailand also sought to take advantage of French weakness and satisfy some old border claims, the Japanese saw to it that the Thais got what they wanted. The price was a drastic increase in Japanese influence in Thailand. By early 1941 a large part of Indo-China was in Japanese hands, and the rest of the country isolated and ripe for the taking.

It was with little difficulty that in late July 1941 Japanese troops implemented the policy decision made earlier that month in Tokyo. The French were forced to sign a mutual security pact and accept the occupation of the rest of Indo-China. Japan now held a key area from which to dominate all of South-east Asia.

The Western reaction was as General Sugiyama had predicted. The United States, Britain, and the Netherlands Indies promptly froze

Japanese assets. This far-reaching move brought a quick review of the national economy by Japan's leaders and the ominous conclusion that the new economic blockade would topple the Empire within two years. Japan continued to prepare for war, with the full knowledge that a decision could not be postponed much longer.

Within the next few weeks, Japanese military planners examined alternative strategies for the destruction of Western forces in the Far East and the seizure of the Netherlands Indies. The most obvious course was a direct attack on the Indies, followed by the invasion of the Philippines and Malaya. This was discarded as too risky, since in its initial stages it would leave the Japanese flanks open, subject to attack from both American and British bases. A second plan, favoured by the navy, called for a step-by-step campaign through the Philippines to the Indies and finally to Malaya — a careful advance with no serious problems. The army, however, rejected this, pointing out that by the time the main objectives were reached their defenders would have had ample time to strengthen them. The army planners were intrigued with the concept of attacking primarily overland through Malaya to the Indies, by-passing the Philippines altogether. This would avoid hazardous long-range amphibious operations, ensure the rapid seizure of South-east Asia, and delay American entry into the war. But, as the navy was quick to object, this would also leave American air and naval forces in the Philippines free to attack and cut the Japanese line of communications to the south; an unacceptable risk.

In the end, the plan adopted was a compromise: a simultaneous advance along both axes of attack, through Malaya and the Philippines, to the Indies. The scheme was an imaginative but highly complicated one. It called for the utmost skill in co-ordination and timing, in the shuttling of troops and supplies, and in the allocation of shipping. It made for a dangerous dispersal of forces, and in its magnitude was as risky as any other strategy. Yet it was the only one that all the planners could agree upon. They did not discuss a separate naval plan to destroy American seapower by a surprise attack on Pearl Harbour. This project, under study since January, had no place in the summer high-level inter-service talks at Imperial General Headquarters. Adopted shortly thereafter by the naval general staff, it was regarded as a tactical naval operation, of no concern to the army.

It was mid-August before army and navy strategists reached agreement on the general scheme of offensive operations in the south. Diplomatic negotiations, meanwhile, showed little indication of success. On September 6th another Imperial conference decided on war at the end of October, if Japanese objectives could not be achieved through diplomacy before that time. Military planning and other preparations were accelerated, and although the deadline passed without a final decision to open hostilities all was in readiness by late October.

The primary goal was the Netherlands Indies, with Malaya and the Philippines to be captured as initial stepping stones. To seize these objectives, the Japanese would undertake simultaneous attacks against widely separated targets in the first days of war. Carrier-based aircraft would destroy or neutralise the American Pacific Fleet at Pearl Harbour, while other air strikes would hit Malaya and the Philippines. Guam and Wake would be captured to cut the American line of communication across the Pacific, Hong Kong attacked to eliminate that British outpost, and Thailand occupied to provide forward bases for the invasion of Malaya and Burma. Then advance units would land in the Philippines and northern Malaya to secure air and sea bases for further moves. Barely pausing for breath, the Japanese would next launch major invasions of the Philippines and Malaya, and press on to occupy the Bismarck Archipelago and key points in Borneo and Celebes. With all of this accomplished, Japanese forces would advance south to seize Singapore, Java, and Sumatra in a gigantic pincer movement. Burma, too, would be occupied if the situation proved favourable. The time-table for this remarkably ambitious and difficult scheme of manoeuvre required the capture of the Philippines in 50 days, of Malaya in 100 days, and of the Netherlands Indies in 150 days.

The forces allocated were surprisingly light. The bulk of the Japanese army was engaged in China or tied down in Manchuria and Korea for defence against the Soviet Union. Thus, only eleven infantry divisions, and two army air groups comprising some 700 planes – the Japanese had no separate air force – were available for operations in the south. Opposing this force, the Japanese estimated, were almost half a million Allied troops supported by nearly 1,300 aircraft. But this strength was widely dispersed over thousands of square miles of land and ocean with little chance of being efficiently concentrated to meet a forceful attack. The bulk of the defenders, moreover, did not appear to be well trained or equipped, and their airpower, while formidable in numbers, consisted largely of obsolescent planes. By bringing superior forces to bear at strategic points and striking swiftly and relentlessly, the Japanese hoped to catch their enemies off balance and drive through to victory before the Allies could react. The key element would be the powerful Japanese fleet and naval air arm, particularly the fast carrier task-forces that had reached a peak of strength and mobility. Japan's navy, most of which would be committed to the operation, was capable of handling whatever the Western powers could throw together initially from their own widely separated and dispersed naval elements. Japanese naval air strength, some 1,600 land- and carried-based planes flown by skilled, experienced pilots, was more than a match for anything in the Pacific and would carry the main burden of the opening attacks.

The Japanese plan placed a premium on speed and co-ordination. But there were two other reasons why rapid success was essential. The first was the ever-present Soviet threat from the north. Operations in the south would have to be completed during the winter in order to free troops and aircraft for rapid redeployment to meet any Russian spring offensive or, if luck would have it, to take advantage of a Soviet military collapse in Europe. The weather, the same element that would keep the Manchurian border area frozen until spring, was also an important factor in the south. The January north-east monsoon would prove a serious bar to amphibious operations in the South China Sea, while heavy gales at the same time would limit naval operations in the north Pacific. The entire southern operation, would have to be launched early, carried out rapidly and efficiently, and completed by spring.

If successful, it would give Japan all she desired. Incorporating new conquests within the already established Empire, the Japanese would hold a powerful defensive perimeter from the Kurils in the north, through the Marshall and Gilbert Islands of the central Pacific, and west through New Britain and along the Malay Archipelago to the mainland of South-east Asia. Within this area would lie the oil, rubber, bauxite, and metals of the Indies, the Japanese home islands themselves, and the vital shipping lanes that linked them. Perhaps later, if all went well, the area of conquest might be somewhat extended. But the Japanese contemplated no all-out defeat and ultimate abject surrender of their enemies, never, indeed, planned to fight more than a limited war with limited objectives. Once these had been achieved, they would hold fast within their huge perimeter, beating off Allied attacks until at last, when the futility of those blows had been demonstrated, a negotiated peace would be reached that would leave to Japan those means and resources for which she had begun hostilities. Implicit in Japanese planning was the assumption that Germany would either win the war in Europe or else so incapacitate Russia and Great Britain that neither would be able to affect the outcome of the Pacific conflict. Implicit also was the fact that, however desperate the Japanese plan might appear, few in Tokyo believed the Empire had any other alternative.

For the Japanese army, the occupation of Malaya and Singapore was the most important part of the entire southern operation. Indeed, plans and preparations for the Singapore campaign had been under way ever since the occupation of northern Indo-China in the late summer of 1940. At that time, the army high command knew little about the defences and military geography of Malaya, and even less about the problems of conducting a major campaign in the tropical jungles of the south. Intercepts of British diplomatic communications when decoded indicated that Singapore's defences were considerably weaker than the world had been led to believe,[6] but much research, study, and training would still be necessary to ensure a speedy victory.

In mid October 1940, even as the army staff undertook its initial appraisal of the geography, terrain, and climate of the whole southern area, the 5th Division began amphibious training near Shanghai. In early December, three other divisions in south China started training for tropical warfare and, in particular, for landing operations. A few weeks later the so-called Taiwan Army Research Section was established at Taipeh, Formosa, to undertake a detailed examination of the southern area and the problems of occupying it. Colonel Yoshihide Hayashi, the section commander, had orders to complete his studies, and prepare draft plans for operations, by the end of June.

Hayashi's small group – it numbered at most some thirty intelligence specialists – set to work at once to answer the many questions at hand. What new tactics and equipment would be necessary for jungle operations? Should units, organised for winter combat against Russian troops, be re-structured to fight in the tropics against British and American forces? What had to be done to cope with health and sanitation problems not previously encountered? By what means could Japanese forces be assured of adequate supplies and communications across the vast, watery distances of the southern area? How should the troops be instructed to handle the diverse populations in the regions to be occupied? And, finally, how much could be learned in the short time available about terrain, weather, landing beaches, roads, and military strengths and weaknesses in the south?[7]

Responsibility for Singapore and Malaya fell to Lieutenant-Colonel Masanobu Tsuji, Hayashi's dedicated and aggressive second in command. While others turned their attention to the Philippines, the Netherlands Indies, and Burma, Tsuji and a few subordinates concentrated on the Malayan Peninsula. They embarked on a crash research programme, studying reports and publications, interrogating specialists, pestering sea captains, mining engineers, bankers, university professors, diplomats, Buddhist priests – in short, anyone and everyone in Japan and Formosa who knew anything at all about the tropics. Nor were more dangerous forms of research neglected. In the early months of 1941, Japanese agents slipped ashore at several points in the vast area of the southern region. In the skies above, Japanese pilots made clandestine flights to photograph coast sectors, airfields, and other points of interest. Tsuji's spies began operating in January, moving into southern Thailand, down the Malayan Peninsula, and across the great causeway onto Singapore Island itself. They roamed at will, tracing roads and rivers, checking bridges, airfields, and beach defences, and estimating military engineering and transport requirements. At the same time, army pilots photographed landing areas along the north-east Malayan coast. One enterprising Japanese resident of Malaya even managed to fly his own plane over Singapore and take pictures, which he then passed on to Colonel Tsuji.

In March 1941, selected army staff officers began amphibious training, and at the end of the month large-scale army and navy manoeuvres got under way. The 5th Division, escorted by elements of the Combined Fleet and protected by army air units, crossed the East China Sea from Shanghai in the face of simulated enemy air and naval attacks, made an assault landing on the shores of Kyushu, and went through the motions of capturing local coastal defences. The two-week exercise was planned to resemble an assault on Singapore after a landing on the Malayan peninsula. The attackers concentrated on developing anti-aircraft and anti-submarine defence for convoys, on the tactical problems of assault landings, and on the speedy establishment of airstrips on newly-captured territory. The operation was a vast success, with important lessons learnt for the actual campaigns ahead. Lieutenant General Sosaku Suzuki, who commanded the manoeuvre, later became Yamashita's chief of staff in Malaya, and many of the other participating officers would hold important positions throughout the southern theatre of operations.

A second field exercise took place in June in south China. For ten days officers and men sweated and strained under the hot sun as they tested tactical and logistical innovations suggested by the findings of the Taiwan Army Research Section. The climax of the manoeuvres was the landing of a reinforced infantry battalion on Hainan Island. Hainan's circumference, something over 600 miles, approximately equalled the distance from proposed landing sites on the Kra Isthmus of southern Thailand to Singapore, and the assault force moved around

Hainan to simulate an advance on the British naval base. The troops destroyed and repaired bridges, made practice attacks, and carried out other useful tests. As a result, the Japanese knew a great deal more at the end of June about tactics, organisation, equipment, and rations for tropical warfare than they had six months earlier. Colonel Tsuji, who had participated actively in both manoeuvres, was particularly pleased with what he had learned. He and his staff immediately set about assessing their research and observations and writing out the results. One of their products was the detailed and valuable manual, *Just Read This and the War is Won*, which would be distributed to General Yamashita's invasion troops as they embarked for Malaya.

The decision of the Imperial Conference on July 2nd accelerated preparations for the invasion of the southern area. As Japanese forces moved into southern Indo-China at the end of the month, the army section of Imperial General Headquarters set about translating Colonel Tsuji's recommendations and drafts into comprehensive operation plans. Despite the preliminary work already accomplished, much still remained to be done. Troop and shipping lists had to be drawn up, commanders selected, landing sites chosen, time-tables developed, priorities established, air and naval co-ordination worked out, and a host of other details taken care of. Not the least of these was the preparation of special tropical rations and supplies and the publication of maps, Japanese-Malayan dictionaries, and manuals on jungle warfare, landing operations, and other useful subjects.

On August 20th, the Army Section issued a broad training directive for the Malayan campaign.[8] It was a revealing preview of the tactics and techniques later so brilliantly applied during the course of operations. The aim of the training was to 'enable the troops to adjust themselves to tropical surroundings, overcome the hardships awaiting them in undeveloped lands, and engage in combat for days on end'. The focus was on small-unit exercises, usually two or three infantry battalions supported by a battalion of artillery, two or three tank companies, and one or two engineer companies. During manoeuvres, these forces would advance 'along a good road, launch sudden attacks and break through the enemy, and carry out extended operations'. They would get practice in 'fighting in wooded areas and rubber-tree forests on both sides of the road, the securing and repairing of bridges ... and particularly in capturing bridges to the rear of the enemy by raiding parties sent out before the major engagement'. The directive also emphasised training in landing operations, in the rapid unloading of vehicles under enemy fire, and in the use of small craft for shore-to-shore advances down the coast. Special stress, finally, was laid on 'training and research concerning the prevention of epidemics, and the preservation and improvement of the health of men and horses in tropical areas'. In recognition of Malaya's many rivers and bridges, other directives called for special training of engineer units. One engineer regiment later reported that in anticipation of the assault on Singapore Island, its men had spent months practicing 'attacking pill-boxes, and operations with flatbottomed boats with outboard motors attached'.[9] Nor were air units neglected. Still another training order emphasized long-distance overwater flights and night flying, as well as the necessity for close liaison with naval air elements.

During September and October, Japanese army planners agreed on the troops and commanders for the Malayan campaign, and on the general scheme of manoeuvres. In deference to its importance, they assigned to the campaign the best ground forces, with the most experience in amphibious operations, the strongest air units, and the fastest transports available. Colonel Tsuji and his staff were transferred to Indo-China, and set about overseeing the construction of airfields there and drawing up final detailed operational recommendations. They still lacked large-scale maps of Malaya. Despite a major effort, the best the Japanese could collect were on too small a scale for tactical use on the ground. Their knowledge of topography, key terrain features, and roads was based primarily on research and agents' reports. Now, two of Tsuji's officers undertook on foot a careful reconnaissance of landing sites and airfields on the Kra Isthmus and in northern Malaya. Tsuji himself made a dangerous reconnaissance of the area in an unmarked plane, to check on the capabilities of the northern British airfields. He returned convinced that the success of the invasion rested on the speedy capture of these airfields in the first days of hostilities. But no one could discover any good maps, and the Twenty-fifth Army would later go into battle with nothing better than sketches, and 1/100,000 scale maps.

Colonel Tsuji was also in touch with Major Iwaichi Fujiwara, in Bangkok, Thailand. Fujiwara had some spies working for him, but he was more concerned with an entirely different type of project. For some time now the Japanese had been making efforts to exploit the nationalist movement in India to their own advantage. They hoped to utilise the so-called Indian Independence League — a secret nationalist organization with branches all over eastern Asia — not only as a source of intelligence but also, once hostilities began, as a means of subverting Indian formations in the British army. On the outbreak of war,

Fujiwara would infiltrate representatives of the Indian Independence League through British lines in Malaya in an effort to disaffect Indian troops. Since the Japanese believed that Indians constituted a large proportion of the British forces in Malaya, they thought that Fujiwara's work could be of great importance.[10]

Meanwhile, in Tokyo the newly formed government of General Hideki Tojo had all but given up hope of achieving Japanese aims through diplomatic negotiations. An Imperial Conference on November 5th approved a decision to go to war if no agreement could be reached by the end of the month. Imperial General Headquarters promptly issued mobilisation orders and general operational plans for the seizure of British, American, and Dutch possessions in the Far East. Japan would attack in early December.

The operation was the responsibility of Field Marshal Count Hisaichi Terauchi's newly formed Southern Army, supported by Admiral Kondo's Southern Force. For the Malayan campaign, under Terauchi's general control were Yamashita's Twenty-fifth Army and the 3rd Air Group of Lieutenant General Michio Sugawara.

Yamashita, a forceful and imaginative officer with extensive experience in command but little in combat duty, had just come from a quiet post in Manchuria. A large, heavy man, his round face was set off by dark, closely cropped hair and a neat moustache. Self-disciplined in thought and manner, he often seemed passive, but underneath this apparent stoicism lay ruthless energy and ambition. He received his new assignment a few days before his fifty-sixth birthday, and welcomed it as a challenging mission of the greatest importance.[11]

The Twenty-fifth Army included three infantry divisions totalling 50,000 men, a tank group of at least 80 medium and 100 light tanks, and strong artillery elements. To meet special requirements imposed by the Malayan terrain numbers of support units were assigned to the campaign. These included not only additional heavy engineer elements, but also several units specifically organised and equipped to replace or repair bridges, and otherwise assist in getting troops and tanks across the many rivers that flow through Malaya. A fourth infantry division assigned as Yamashita's reserve, along with some of the other units, never joined the Twenty-fifth Army. The actual strength of the force committed was probably about 80,000 combat and combat support troops, and approximately 30,000 'line of communication' troops. The 3rd Air Group totalled some 450 planes. Naval strength included more than a score of cruisers and destroyers, and two-thirds as many submarines, in Admiral Ozawa's escort forces, with Admiral Kondo's main body — two battleships, two heavy cruisers, and ten destroyers, supporting both the Malayan and Philippine campaigns — also available if necessary. About 200 naval aircraft were in Rear Admiral Sadaichi Matsunaga's reinforced 22nd Air Flotilla.*

The three divisions assigned to the Malayan campaign exemplified an organisational change taking place within the Japanese army. Until 1937 Japanese infantry divisions included two brigades, each consisting of two regiments of three battalions each. After the start of the war in China the Japanese army began to drop this 'square' organisation in favour of a 'triangular' division, of three infantry regiments formed into an 'infantry group' that replaced the former brigade structure. Both types of division included artillery, engineer, reconnaissance, transport, signal, medical, and other miscellaneous support units, of which the exact 'mix' often varied during operations. Japanese field artillery — 75-mm. guns and 105-mm. howitzers — did not normally include as many pieces as did similar units in other armies, but there were more light guns and mortars in the Japanese infantry than elsewhere. In the Twenty-fifth Army, the 5th Division was of the old 'square' type, the Imperial Guards Division was 'triangular', while the 18th Division, nominally 'square', would operate in Malaya with only three regiments and a single brigade headquarters, thus assuming a 'triangular' form. The 5th and Imperial Guards Divisions were mechanised, the 18th Division still relied primarily on horses. Japanese armour in Malaya included 16-ton medium tanks, each armed with a 57-mm. gun and two machine-guns, and 10-ton light tanks, each with a 37-mm. gun and two machine-guns.

Most of the Japanese aircraft assigned to the Malayan campaign were late-model machines, fast, manoeuvrable, well-armed. This was particularly true of the fighters. The thirty-six naval fighters were called Zeros — the Zero corresponding to the year 1940, when the plane was adopted — a truly remarkable new aircraft possessing speed, agility, range, and power beyond the capacity of any Allied plane then in the Pacific. Approximately one-third of the army fighters were Type 1's (model year 1941), which had performance characteristics similar to the Zero, while most of the others were fairly recent models.

The supporting naval surface and submarine forces were also powerful. The bulk of their strength lay in fast, heavily-armed cruisers and destroyers, whose newly-developed torpedoes were probably the

---

* Most strength figures are at best an estimate, based on the Japanese sources cited earlier in this chapter, not all of which agree. Naval aircraft figures include last-minute reinforcements.

best in the world. And if Admiral Kondo's two battleships were old vessels, their eight 14-inch guns had the range and punch to handle any enemy force then in Far Eastern waters.

The plan for the capture of Singapore was based on an accurate assumption of British weakness in Malaya. Thanks to the work of men like Colonel Tsuji, the Japanese were well aware that the forces they would encounter lacked strength, cohesion, and modern weapons. They estimated that the British army, widely scattered throughout Malaya or garrisoning Singapore Island, totalled between 80,000 and 100,000 men, of whom less than half were British or Australian, and the rest poorly trained Indian and Malay troops. British air strength seemed to be about 265 planes, mostly obsolescent types. Naval strength also appeared negligible – a handful of cruisers, destroyers, and submarines – but the British were believed capable of shifting stronger elements from the Indian Ocean to Singapore. The most important piece of information in Japanese hands was that the vaunted 'impregnable fortress' of Singapore, while capable of withstanding the heaviest naval attack, was all but defenseless against assault from its landward side.

Awareness of the chinks in the British armour enabled the Japanese to assign a minimum of military resources to the invasion of Malaya. Air power, for example, while less impressive than that thrown against Pearl Harbour or the more dangerous Philippine-based American air · units, was still strong enough to overcome the estimated British air strength. Naval forces were widely spread and lacked aircraft carriers, but would be hard pressed only if the enemy brought modern capital ships into Malayan waters. And ground forces, while formidable, could be employed somewhat piecemeal and, if necessary, utilised elsewhere.

The operation would begin with surprise landings at three points: Singora and Patani in Thailand, on the eastern shore of the Kra Isthmus, and further south Kota Bharu, on the north-eastern Malayan coast. The choice of these targets had been practically dictated by Malaya's terrain and road-network, which admitted of no other point of entry for military forces within the protective range of Japanese land-based aircraft. Singora, the northernmost point, was at the upper terminus of the main road to Singapore, and was linked by a branch line to the Singapore-Bangkok railway. Patani and Kota Bharu were the only other coastal points in this area providing road access inland, and Kota Bharu was also on a branch line of the main railroad. Furthermore, all three towns boasted airstrips, the largest at Kota Bharu, and no less important had excellent landing beaches.

The 5th Division (less one regiment) would make the main landings at Singora and Patani, strike across the Kra Isthmus to seize airfields in northern Malaya, and then drive south along the west coast. A regiment of the 18th Division would land simultaneously at Kota Bharu, on the north-east coast of Malaya, take the airfield there, and move south. At the same time, elements of the Fifteenth Army — responsible for occupying Thailand and invading Burma — would land at four points further north along the Kra Isthmus to shield Yamashita's northern flank and capture local airfields.

During the initial stages of the attack, Japanese aircraft would operate from bases in southern Indo-China. The army's 3rd Air Group would destroy British air power in northern Malaya, with the secondary mission of covering the invasion convoys. Naval planes would be primarily responsible for convoy protection and, with their longer range, would also hit Singapore. In the absence of Japanese aircraft carriers, however, the early seizure of air bases was vitally important in order to enable land-based air-power to move forward and cover the advance of the troops.

While all this was being accomplished, the Imperial Guards Division, the third division assigned to the Twenty-fifth Army, would be moving over-land into Thailand from Indo-China. After occupying Bangkok and seizing local airfields, it would shift south along the railway in stages to join the Twenty-fifth Army. Then it would support the 5th Division in the main drive down the west coast of Malaya toward Singapore. By this time the remaining regiment of the 5th Division would also have landed and joined in the advance. The remainder of the 18th Division, however, would not arrive until January, at which time it would either participate in the attack on Singapore or make ready to invade Sumatra. The 56th Division, Yamashita's reserve, was available in Japan if needed to crush British resistance in southern Malaya.

The Japanese would thus throw small but locally superior forces against widely scattered points along the thin British defence line. Once assured of air supremacy, they would drive for Singapore as fast as possible. They would make their primary effort in western Malaya, taking advantage of the better road and rail network there; and, no less important, of the fact that this area was shielded from the torrents of the north-east monsoon by the central mountain range that formed the backbone of the peninsula. The advance south would be protected on both flanks and overhead by Japanese sea and air power, also ensuring Japanese ability to bring in reinforcements while preventing help from reaching the defenders. The entire operation would take 100 days.

These plans and the orders for their execution were put into final shape and issued to the invasion forces during November. Three points however remained in doubt until almost the last moment. The first was the exact date on which operations would begin. This would depend as much on the outcome of diplomatic negotiations as on last-minute weather and tactical considerations. The second was the possibility of a pre-emptive British advance into Thailand to seize airfields and landing sites before the Japanese could capture them. An intercepted and decoded British radio message had suggested this possibility as early as January 1941 and, in view of the importance of Thailand as a staging area, it could not be overlooked now. After considerable discussion, Japanese army and navy planners decided that should the British move into Thailand, the Fifteenth Army would attack immediately to capture Bangkok and the southern Thai airfields. If the invasion force for Malaya was already at sea, it would proceed as planned. But if not, the main landings would be postponed, and part of the 5th Division would go ashore with Fifteenth Army troops along the northern Kra Isthmus to ensure the capture of the airfields there. The assault on Malaya would be delayed until British air-power was destroyed.

The third point at issue was partly related to the second. The landings at Singora, Patani, and Kota Bharu would be made at extreme fighter range from Japanese air bases in Indo-China. Japanese naval officers feared that any last-minute reinforcement of British air strength might enable the defenders to gain air supremacy over the landing sites, with dangerous consequences for the invasion forces and their naval escorts. Better, they argued, to put only a small advance force ashore and delay the main landings until British air units could be eliminated and Japanese supremacy in the skies assured. Otherwise, heavy casualties among the Twenty-fifth Army assault troops, and serious losses in transports and warships, might jeopardise the entire Malayan campaign before it could be launched.

Army planners, however, urged that the three landings be made as early as possible, relying on surprise and speed to ensure the seizure of airfields, thus denying their use to the British and at the same time making them available to Japanese air units. Based on their belief that the invasion forces would have little to overcome in the way of land defence, and their knowledge that each day's delay into the monsoon season increased the possibility of choppy seas and high winds, they pressed for the landings and air strikes to be carried out simultaneously and as early as possible.

In the end, the army view prevailed, thanks in large measure to the backing of Admiral Ozawa, who announced his willingness to take whatever risks might be necessary to support the plans of the men actually making the invasion. To minimise these risks, however, the construction of airfields in southern Indo-China was hastened, with special priority given to work on a fighter strip on Phu Quoc Island, just across the Gulf of Siam from the Kra Isthmus. It was also agreed that the Twenty-fifth Army landings would begin under cover of darkess. At Kota Bharu, the southernmost invasion point, unloading would take place only at night, with the transports moving north to safer waters just before dawn and returning the following evening to complete the disembarkation of troops and supplies. If, despite all precaution, British air power proved too strong, the Kota Bharu landing might be postponed for twenty-four hours. Given the worst circumstances, the plan conceived to meet a British invasion of Thailand would be followed, part of the 5th Division landing further north with the Fifteenth Army, and main landings being delayed until Japanese air units could move forward to the northern Kra Isthmus.

General Yamashita was appointed commander of the newly-organised Twenty-fifth Army on November 6th. From Manchuria, where he had commanded the Kwantung Defence Army, he flew to Tokyo and joined other Southern Army commanders for a week of conferences and briefings with Marshal Terauchi and his staff. Yamashita knew little about the southern area and had no experience in amphibious and jungle warfare. But the operational plans appeared sound, and he was pleased by the calibre of the forces assigned to him. On November 15th he landed at Saigon. Colonel Tsuji and other Twenty-fifth Army staff officers submitted their detailed plans for his approval, and they and Yamashita plunged almost immediately into final planning sessions with airforce and naval officers. By the 25th, final agreement had been reached on almost all details, orders had been issued, and all that remained was for Tokyo to give the word to start operations. 'I know I shall be able to carry out the landing plan without much trouble', Yamashita wrote in his diary. 'I also believe we shall win, but it will cost us a great effort'.[12] That night he and his staff left Saigon for Samah, on Hainan Island.

Meanwhile, the forces for the Malayan campaign were completing their assembly. Most of Admiral Ozawa's escort and support units had already reached Hainan, and Admiral Kondo's heavier units were steaming toward Mako in the Pescadores. Naval air elements were moving into Indo-China, while General Sugawara had established his 3rd Air Group headquarters at Saigon, and his units were on the move from China to Indo-Chinese bases. Yamashita's troops were also in position: most of the 5th Division, and a regiment of the 18th, at Samah; the remainder of the 18th at Canton; and the Imperial Guards Division in Indo-China. Fifteenth Army forces were also in Indo-China. And great quantities of supplies, munitions, rations, and equipment were being assembled on Hainan and Formosa and in south China and Indo-China.

The movements of the 41st Infantry Regiment of the 5th Division, scheduled to land at Singora, are perhaps typical of this concentration. The regiment had been fighting in China at least since 1939. Early in October 1941 it assembled in Shanghai and for a month practiced jungle fighting and assault landings. On November 13th, the men received tropical clothing, rations, and medical supplies, and on the 17th took part in a review to celebrate their impending departure for the field. 'Orders have finally come', wrote one soldier in his diary. 'We will have action'.[13]

During the next few days, the men of the 41st Infantry Regiment boarded transports and began to journey to Hainan Island. The first contingent reached Haikow, on the north side of Hainan, as early as the 20th. Here the men practiced disembarking and climbing down rope ladders into landing craft, and reloaded supplies and equipment for the invasion. By December 2nd, the transports carrying the regiment – and, indeed, the entire Twenty-fifth Army landing force – were anchored off Samah. That afternoon the troops rehearsed the planned assault landing. Their performance was somewhat discouraging, but no major disasters occurred, and in any event it was too late for further training.

The Japanese decision for war came at an Imperial Conference on the afternoon of December 1st. Diplomatic negotiations had finally failed; and indeed Japanese military and civil leaders had already made up their minds. The conference on the 1st was merely to secure the Emperor's approval, a necessary but almost routine procedure. A previous army-navy agreement had set December 8th as the last favourable date for opening hostilities. After the 8th, weather and tide conditions would make amphibious assaults in the Malayan area extremely hazardous. The 8th, also, was the best date for the attack on Pearl Harbour. This choice of date was confirmed on December 1st.

That very night, however, a disturbing message reached Tokyo from army headquarters in China. A transport plane carrying warning orders for the attack on Hong Kong had crashed during the day in enemy territory near Canton. It seemed doubtful that those aboard the plane would have been able to estroy the incrimating documents, and the scene of the accident was too far from Japanese lines for patrols to

9. ATIS, *Japan's Decision to Fight*, p. 31.

10. Japan Defence Agency, War History Section, *Mare Shinko Sakusen (Operations of the Malaya Campaign)* (Tokyo: Asagumo Shimbunsha, 1966), pp. 66-68. I am indebted to Mr. Louis Allen for alerting me to Major Fujiwara's activities, and for providing me with translations of relevant portions of *Mare Shinko Sakusen.* See also Maj.-Gen. Shahnawaz Khan, *My Memories of I.N.A. & Its NETAJI* (Delhi: Rajkamal, 1946), p. 13.

11. Potter, *Life and Death of a Japanese General*, chaps. i-iv; Arthur Swinson, *Four Samurai* (London: Hutchinson, 1958), chap. iii.

12. Potter, *Life and Death of a Japanese General*, pp. 45-46. Also pp. 41-47.

13. Diary of Superior Private Yamashita, 3rd Battalion, 41st Infantry, in ATIS, Current Translations, No. 45, June 1st, 1942, p. 27. Extracts from this and other diaries on which most of this paragraph is based are also quoted in ATIS, *Japan's Decision to Fight, passim.*

14. Hattori, *The Greater East Asia War*, I, 364.

15. Masatake Okumiya and Jiro Horikoshi, with Martin Caidin, *Zero* (New York: Dutton, 1956), pp. 92-93; Masanori Ito with Roger Pineau, *The End of the Imperial Japanese Navy* (New York: Norton, 1962), pp. 45-46; Captain Russell Grenfell, *Main Fleet to Singapore* (New York: Macmillan, 1952), p. 98.

16. Tsuji, *Singapore*, p. 71.

17. Hattori, *The Greater East Asia War*, I, 366.

3

Impregnable Fortress

The Malay Peninsula forms the southernmost extension of Asia. It hangs down from the south-east corner of that continent like a giant arm, pointing toward the islands of Indonesia and Australia, and separating the Indian Ocean from the South China Sea. But for Malaya, and the narrow Kra Isthmus that links it to the mainland, the trade route from Europe to the Orient would be shorter and simpler. As it is, most seagoing commerce must follow the Strait of Malacca, between the southern tip of Malaya and the huge island of Sumatra. It is this accident of geography that gives Singapore, at the eastern exit of the strait, its great strategic and commercial value. A small nearly elliptical island of just over 200 square miles, separated from the mainland by the tiny Johore Strait, and on the south from several other islands by the narrow Singapore Strait, it commands the sea-lanes east, west, and south, and in 1941 it was a great trading centre and an entrepot for all of South-east Asia.

The island itself consists primarily of mangrove swamps and rubber plantations; the impressive naval base was on its northern shore, and a huge teeming metropolis, the city of Singapore, in the south. A jungled haunt of Malay pirates when Sir Stamford Raffles acquired it for England in 1819, a marshy, fever-infested stretch of ancient trees and rank vegetation, in less than a century and a quarter it had become a thriving modern port and the centre of British power in the Far East. In 1941, the city was a mixture of old and new, of baroque beauty and uncontrolled squalor. Stately white Western buildings along broad avenues contrasted sharply with low native houses in filthy, crowded back streets. Fashionable limousines and solid-looking buses jockeyed for position with oxcarts, bicycles, rickshas, and thousands of pedestrians, including porters straining under heavy loads piled on their backs and shoulders or hanging in balance from the ends of long poles – the whole presided over by imposing, bearded Sikh policemen in turbans and military dress. Huge modern billboards advertised the delights of

canned pineapple, condensed milk, or the latest movie, while in countless tiny shops an age-old litany of bargaining repeated itself endlessly as myriads of wares were bought, sold, or bartered in a time-tested routine. Modern air-conditioned restaurants and cinemas vied for attention with tiny dance-halls, out-door eating places, Chinese theatres and amusement parks, and, further out, fine golf and swimming clubs where once grew heavy jungle. Still visible, too, were the remains of the ancient Malay citadel, Singapura, the City of the Lion.

Three quarters of a million people lived in Singapore. Nearly 600,000 were Chinese, with Malays, Indians, Europeans, and a broad mixture of other races making up a varied minority. The Chinese — some owing allegiance to the Kuomintang, others to the Communists — were the most evident, swarming through bright, noisy residential areas, with their colourful temples, ubiquitous merchants, and gaily dressed girls in narrow, slit skirts. The Malays lived mostly in the suburbs, and by comparison were very quiet. The Indians, too, seemed mute and retiring next to the energetic Chinese — except, that is, when frenzied fakirs pushed kives or skewers into their flesh or walked across burning coals, before shouting mobs of religious devotees and fascinated tourists. The Europeans, primarily British, kept mainly to themselves, living an English-away-from-home existence, with their exclusive clubs, rigid social customs, cocktails, tennis and golf, and the white linen suits which seemed inappropriate in the sweltering heat when contrasted with the looser Malay and Indian garb.

North of the city, on the Strait of Johore, was the great £63,000,000 naval base, twenty-one square miles in area and capable of sheltering the entire British fleet. Its neat whiteness stood out clearly from the dark green jungle that surrounded it. Amidst the piers, cranes, store-houses, repair-shops, power-stations, and other structures, two great 50,000-ton dry docks caught the eye. One, the King George VI Graving Dock, had only recently been completed. The other, a huge floating dock, had been built in England in 1928 and towed half way around the world to Singapore; an outstanding feat of seamanship. West of the base was the long white Johore Causeway, straight as an arrow, linking the island with the mainland. Nearby were also the dull-looking oil tanks, the colour of unpolished pewter, the Singapore airfields, and the giant lake-like reservoirs that held the island's water supply.

From Singapore, the Malay Peninsula runs north for some 400 miles to the Thai border. For most of this distance it is fairly wide, roughly 200 miles across at its broadest and narrowing to about 60 miles at

both ends. Its total area, over 52,000 square miles, is a little more than that of England (not including Wales). Malaya is dominated by a long central mountain range covered with jungle, some 4,000 feet high and rising to more than 7,000 feet in the north. Between the mountains and the sea are low plains, narrower on the western side of the peninsula, with deep swamps and heavy vegetation. Central Malaya is the source of many swift mountain streams that broaden into deep rivers as they seek an exit to the sea. Fed by heavy rains and frequently choked by jungle growth, they are serious obstacles to movement up and down the peninsula.

The greatest barrier to mobility, however, is the jungle. A thick, humid carpet of bamboo, flowering plants, tangled vines and undergrowth, under huge trees that tower 200 feet above the earth, it covers nearly three-quarters of Malaya. Its floor is dark and dank, shielded from the sun by a heavy natural canopy, and full of the damp, pungent odour of decaying leaves and vegetation. Except where man has carved out roads and rubber plantations or other cultivated areas, the jungle is a thick, almost solid mass of growth, limiting passage and visability to all who seek to penetrate it. In 1941, few did. Aside from a wild tribe of natives, the jungle belonged to a population of monkeys, snakes, strange birds and marvellous butterflies, spiders, hornets, an occasional tiger or elephant, and the ubiquitous leeches and mosquitoes. It was not, in the words of one Australian officer, 'a place where normal men would go for a holiday'.[1]

The Malayan climate is equally uninviting. With the equator less than 100 miles away, temperatures are uniformly hot, offering no seasonal changes to relieve the tropical monotony. The warm seas surrounding the peninsula, and the heavy rainfall it has during much of the year, keep the humidity unbearably high. Thus, while the steady temperatures of 90°F. during the day and 70°F. at night are not in themselves too unpleasant, when combined with the pervasive humidity they become enervating and depressing, particularly for those who have not had two or three months to acclimatize themselves. After a few moments of mild exertion in this hothouse, they are overwhelmed with perspiration and fatigue. Troops attempting to operate in Malaya's humid jungles and malarial marshes are much handicapped.

The weather affects both ground and air operations. During the winter monsoon from the north-east, the lowlands east of the mountains are often flooded and movement is fairly well restricted to the few roads and railways in the area. Troops can move more freely in the more sheltered and better developed western coastal area, but the

narrowness of this corridor and the constricting effect of jungle, swamps, and rubber plantations also limit most movement to the good road and rail system. Rainstorms and thunder-showers, meanwhile, combine to cover much of the peninsula with heavy, low-lying clouds – difficult, in 1941, to fly through or over, and severely cutting visibility in the air. The monsoon itself is a serious obstacle to air operations and makes air-ground co-ordination extremely difficult.

Most of the five and a half million inhabitants of pre-war Malaya lived in the western coastal area or on Singapore Island. Several races were represented, dwelling together in relative harmony but sharing no common citizenship, national spirit, or other unifying ties to hold them together in time of stress. Malays and Chinese, some two million and more of each, constituted about eighty-five percent of the people. Nearly three quarters of a million Indians made up the third largest group. The remaining population included roughly 30,000 Europeans, 20,000 Eurasians, 6,000 Japanese, and 55,000 others.

Of all these groups, only the Malays, less than half the total, were indigenous to the peninsula. A gentle, easy-going people, inclined to accept life as it came, and without apparent ambition, they were primarily small farmers and fishermen. Their lack of interest in trade and commerce left a vacuum that the enterprising and industrious Chinese were quick to fill. The latter, drawn to Malaya by the lure of ready business profits, controlled most of the peninsula's commercial activity but wanted no part in administrative or political matters. In 1941, only a third of them had actually been born in Malaya. The rest, immigrants, had every intention of returning to China after making their fortune. The Indians, too, were primarily immigrants, rubber plantation workers who usually went back to their native Madras after a few years, to buy farmland with their earnings. Many Punjabis and Sikhs became valuable members of the Malay Police Force, but most of the Indians had no strong attachment to Malaya. Nor did the Japanese. Spread throughout Malaya, they could not have been better dispersed for potential espionage than if their locations had been carefully planned. They were businessmen, photographers, bankers, or owners of rubber plantations, iron mines, or shipping services, and could be found in every town or city. Many had seen military service and some, indeed, were spies. Their presence worried the British authorities, who of course had every reason to be concerned.

The lack of cohesion among Malaya's varied peoples was matched by the decentralised political organisation of the country. Directly under British rule was the Crown Colony of the Straits Settlement, consisting

of the earliest British settlements in Malaya: Penang Island at the
north-east entrance to the Strait of Malacca, Malacca itself on the
mainland further south, and the island of Singapore. Perak, Selangor,
Negri Sembilan, and Pahang, four central Malayan principalities, were
known as the Federated Malay States. They shared a federal government at Kuala Lumpur, but otherwise ruled themselves with the advice
of British Residents. Five so-called Unfederated Malay States – Johore,
Trengganu, Kelantan, Kedah, and Perlis – were self-governing parts of
the British Empire, ruled by their own Sultans with the assistance of
British Advisers. The Governor of the Straits Settlements also doubled
as High Commissioner for the Federated and Unfederated States and
had the unenviable task of co-ordinating policy and activity throughout
all of Malaya. That to do so meant working with as many as eleven
different administrative organs only made more difficult his job of
developing some sort of unity in a country of such disparate and widely
motivated peoples.

The uncertainties of civil co-ordination, serious as they were, paled
in significance beside the greater problem of devising an effective
military defence of British Malaya. For this, three basic questions had
to be answered. First, how much and what areas of Malaya must be
defended? Second, what was the best means of doing this? And, finally,
what forces could be provided for the task?

Although the British had been in Malaya since the early nineteenth
century, problems of defence did not really arise until after World War
I. The growth of Japanese power during that conflict and the disturbing
indications that Japan intended to use this power aggressively raised a
potential threat to Great Britain's Far Eastern possessions. The
subsequent British decision to scrap the nearly twenty-year-old Anglo-
Japanese alliance in favour of a closer association with the United
States further underlined the need for improved security in the area.
The initial answer to this requirement, proposed by Admiral Jellicoe in
1919, was to create a permanent and formidable Far Eastern Fleet,
capable of meeting any Japanese naval force, and a major base to
handle the fleet. But fiscal considerations, the assumption that major
war was unlikely for at least a decade, and the restrictions of the 1922
Washington naval armaments limitation treaty, ruled out any possibility
of establishing a separate Far Eastern Fleet. The alternative, perforce,
was to keep the main British fleet in European waters, prepared to shift
to the Far East if need arose. When it arrived it would require a
substantial base to accommodate it, with large dry-docks, powerful
cranes, extensive shore installations, a full stock of supplies, and, of

course, sufficient defences.

The location of this base was subject to some debate. Hong Kong, already a small naval base, was eliminated by the terms of the Washington Treaty, and in any event was vulnerable to Japanese attack. Sydney in Australia, another suggestion, was more secure but offered protection to only a portion of the British Far East, and it could not prevent the loss of the important trading port of Singapore. Singapore itself was well located to guard the approaches to both Australia and India, was already a major refuelling and resupply point on the British line to the Orient, and could be made relatively immune from attack. In June 1921, therefore, the British government decided to build a major naval base at Singapore.[2]

Planning for the base proceeded on the assumption that it would have to be defended against only naval assault. An overland attack through Malaya was ruled out on the grounds that the swamp and jungle there would frustrate any large-scale approach by way of this venue and that, in any event, British naval forces could prevent major landings on the peninsula or, failing that, could certainly thwart attempts at supply and reinforcement. Air attacks also seemed improbable because of the distances involved and the vulnerability of hostile aircraft-carriers to surface or submarine attack. By early 1923, the Cabinet had approved a scheme to build a new base on Singapore Island, on the protected shore of Johore Strait, with strong enough defences to repel a naval attack until the main battle fleet could arrive, a period estimated at seventy days after the start of war.

Construction of the Singapore base proceeded slowly. That it did not move faster was due primarily to considerable opposition in the British parliament and press. Critics of the plan included pacifists, financial conservatives decrying the heavy expenditure, reformers who argued that the money would be better spent to satisfy economic and social needs at home, and still others who, while urging military preparedness, disagreed with the strategic basis of the decision. Work was actually halted for six months under the short-lived Labour Government of 1924, and slowed down considerably at the end of the decade by the second Labour Government. Indeed, the London Treaty of 1930 to limit naval armaments might well have aborted the entire project had not Japanese aggression in Manchuria the following year alerted the British to the potential dangers ahead.

Work on the base was now accelerated. But first it was necessary to settle a controversy which had been under way for nearly a decade between the advocates of airpower for the primary defence of

Singapore and those who maintained that heavy guns could best fill this requirement. It was strictly an inter-service argument, with the Air Ministry holding out for the flexibility, longer range, and economy of aircraft, and the Admiralty and War Office expounding the proven quality and greater reliability of permanent heavy guns over untried airpower that might not, in any event, be available when needed. In the end a compromise was reached. Guns would retain their primary importance, but aircraft would also play a valuable and essential role in the security of Singapore.

By 1937, Singapore seemed almost ready. Work on the naval base was just about done – it would be opened formally on February 14th, 1938 – and the island's heavy gun defences were well along, military airfield construction was all but complete, and a small defensive garrison was in place. Singapore seemed reasonably capable of holding out for seventy days until the arrival of the fleet. It was, indeed, beginning to be thought of as an impregnable fortress, a bastion of British power in the Orient. Newspapers called it 'the Gibraltar of the Far East'.

Unfortunately for its defences, however, there had been significant changes in the decade and a half since the base was planned. For one thing, the rise of German and Italian naval power made it very doubtful that a sizeable portion of the British battle fleet could be spared to be sent to the Far East. While it was hoped that Japan would not attack unless a major European war began, and that a powerful British naval force at home would have a deterrent effect in Europe, there was no guarantee that Britain's potential enemies would adhere to this formula. Independent Japanese action could come in any event, or the simultaneous outbreak of war in both Europe and the Orient might well make it impossible to send a relief force to Singapore. The growth of the Japanese fleet, especially in carrier-based air-power, thus increased the danger to Singapore at a time when the speedy arrival of the main battle fleet seemed open to serious question.

These developments added force to the arguments of those who championed air-power as Singapore's primary defence. It now seemed more important than ever to discover and destroy attacking forces as far out to sea as possible, well beyond the range of Singapore's heavy guns. To provide better coverage over the South China Sea and the Gulf of Siam, the Air Ministry therefore decided to build three additional airfields on Malaya's east coast: at Kahang, in south-east Malaya; at Kuantan, half-way up the peninsula; and at Kota Bharu, just below the Thai border. In what was perhaps a typical case of lack of inter-service co-ordination at this time, however, air force officers chose the location of the fields without checking with the army. As a result, the airfields were built in places where they could not be defended against strong enemy landing forces. And the army, preoccupied with the assumption that an attack could only be seaborne and directed against Singapore Island, was unwilling to send part of the small Singapore garrison to defend indefensible airfields.

At the same time it was becoming evident that defending Singapore alone would not be enough to protect the naval base. In the fall of 1937, the British army commander in Malaya, Major General William Dobbie, and his chief of staff, Colonel Arthur Percival, made a study of the entire defence problem and concluded that Singapore's security depended on holding the greater part of the Malay peninsula. On the assumption that the British fleet might not be able to reach the Far East in the projected seventy days, Dobbie submitted to the War Office an estimate of probable Japanese strategy. He foresaw an initial seizure of bases in southern Thailand, followed by a landing in force along the east Malaya coast. The expanded capabilities of air-power and the development by the Japanese of special landing craft made this all the more probable. And while amphibious assaults along the east coast of Malaya had been generally thought to be impossible during the winter (northeast) monsoon, tests run by Dobbie indicated that they could in fact be made. The stormy weather would do less to impede the landings than it would to thwart the defenders' air reconnaissance. Singora, Patani, and Kota Bharu were among the possible landing points that Dobbie listed. From them, the Japanese could advance rapidly on Singapore, since the local forces, intended only for limited operations during a seventy-day period, would be unable to maintain a protracted defence. As Dobbie summed it up in a subsequent report in early 1938:

It is an attack from the northward that I regard as the greatest potential danger to the fortress. Such attack could be carried out during the period of the north-east monsoon. The jungle is not in most places impassable for infantry.[3]

By now, however, Dobbie was no longer thinking of defending all of Malaya. The presence of the French in Indo-China would probably rule out Japanese landings in Thailand or northern Malaya. But Japanese forces supported by aircraft-carriers might well land in eastern Johore, the southernmost state on the Malayan mainland, and strike along a good road directly toward Singapore. Once they reached the north shore of Johore Strait, they could effectively neutralize the naval base without even having to capture it. Since the whole idea of securing the base was to permit the battle fleet to use it, it seemed clear that the only sensible defence of Singapore was one that kept the enemy at a reasonable distance from the naval base. Dobbie recommended the construction of defensive positions in southern Johore.

For this he was granted additional funds and plans were made to strengthen British forces in Malaya. But nothing was done to solve the basic problem of ensuring the arrival of the battle fleet within the planned seventy days. Australia and New Zealand had argued strongly that the best defence against the Japanese was to station the fleet in the Far East at once, as a deterrent. But the British Chiefs of Staff pointed to the growing menace of Germany and Italy, and reiterated that the fleet must be kept at home. They agreed however that Singapore was a key position, no less important than the British Isles themselves for the security of the Commonwealth. In the event of a major war only the defence of the United Kingdom itself would have priority over that of Singapore. If hostilities broke out in the Far East, then, the security of the Mediterranean would have to be left to the French, and barring some unforeseen delay a battle fleet would reach Singapore in seventy days.

By early 1939 the position of Germany and Italy in Europe, and indeed of Japan in Asia, had become so strong that the Chiefs of Staff were forced to take another look at priorities. Despite the increased danger in the Far East, the threat at home was far greater. Just how large a fleet could be spared for Singapore was becoming increasingly problematical. Hedging their bets considerably, the Chiefs of Staff stated that while a fleet would certainly go to the Orient, its actual strength would have to 'depend on our resources and the state of the war in the European theatre'.[4]

In May 1939, the Committee of Imperial Defence – the Prime Minister, appropriate Cabinet ministers, and the Chiefs of Staff, charged with determining strategy for the security of the Empire – concluded that they were no longer able 'to state definitely how soon after Japanese intervention a Fleet could be despatched' and that it was impossible 'to enumerate precisely the size of the Fleet that we could afford to send'. The following month, in answer to an Australian request for an assurance that a fleet would be sent to Singapore strong enough and early enough to handle the Japanese, the Prime Minister, Chamberlin, responded encouragingly. While the timing and strength of the fleet would depend on several factors, he said, it was still the full intention of His Majesty's Government to despatch a fleet to block major operations against Australia, New Zealand, or India, to keep open sea communications and 'prevent the fall of Singapore'. But even as this exchange took place the British Admiralty reported that no more than two capital ships could be included in any Far Eastern fleet. And in July, the Committee of Imperial Defence increased the critical time-period from seventy to ninety days. They recognised, furthermore, that the actual time required might be as long as six months. To help carry the extra burden imposed on Singapore's defenders, additional ground and air reinforcements reached Malaya that summer.

By the time war broke out in Europe in September 1939, the Singapore naval base and its coastal defences were believed to be just about ready.[5] The number of troops assigned to Malaya was greater than ever before and additional aircraft were on the way. Singapore's reputation as an impregnable fortress – stronger, some said, than Gibraltar – continued to grow. This reputation was based primarily on the widespread publicity accorded the heavy naval guns of the island's defences. These guns, five 15 inch/42 calibre/rifles of the kind mounted on almost all modern British capital ships, as well as several medium and light batteries – 'more guns', wrote an Australian newspaperman, 'than plums in a Christmas pudding'[6] – were generally believed to be the most powerful in the world. Their size was exaggerated – they were usually identified as 18-inch monsters originally built for the old battle cruiser *Furious* – and their potency was universally accepted as guaranteeing Singapore's invincibility.[7] Few indeed questioned the impregnability of this Far Eastern bastion of the British Empire.

But well they might have. There were still not enough troops in Malaya to meet a major ground attack, and promised reinforcements were not sent. Work on General Dobbie's Johore defence positions was suspended for lack of funds. There were pitifully few first-line aircraft in the area, and the number of new squadrons arriving was only half that already approved. The comparatively puny British naval forces in the Far East were also weakened when the Admiralty began to transfer major units of the China Squadron to convoy duty in the Indian Ocean. And at a time when Germany was demonstrating the terrible and destructive force of air-power against ground targets, there was no air raid warning system nor, for that matter, any effective civil defence organisation in all of Malaya. Yet, in both London and Singapore, no one seemed over concerned. The island fortress, after all, was impregnable. And besides, no matter what happened in Europe, Japan would hardly dare to attack now that it appeared she would also have to face the United States in any Pacific showdown. These thoughts may have been of some comfort when, at the end of September, the Chiefs of Staff extended to 180 days the period before the arrival of the fleet at Singapore.

The implications of this decision were fairly evident. However impregnable Singapore might be, many doubted that she could hold out for six months. The additional delay in despatching the fleet would allow the Japanese ample time to develop advance bases in southern Thailand, move into northern Malaya, and support their attack on Singapore with heavy air raids from nearby bases. Under such pressure, the naval base might well be lost before the relief force could reach Malayan waters.

The solution proposed by Air-Vice-Marshal John Babington, the Malayan air-force commander, was to rely primarily on air power for defence. Babington recommended building up a strong air force in Malaya. The Governor of the Straits Settlement, Sir Shenton Thomas, enthusiastically supported this view. He did so primarily because he realised the small chance there was of augmenting Malaya's ground defence force in time of emergency. London had decreed that Malaya's first mission was to produce the rubber, and tin, and through trade the foreign currency, so vital to the British war effort. So no attempt had been made to create a military force out of the native Malayan population – which, in any event, had little interest in problems of defence – and arming and training civilians at short notice was clearly impractical. Of the relatively few Englishmen of draft age in Malaya, almost all were fully engaged in running the country and trying to increase its production of valuable resources. A few had joined the Volunteer Forces and the newly-organised civil defence services, but little more could be expected from this source.[8] So Sir Shenton Thomas, like Air-Vice-Marshal Babington, called for heavy air reinforcements to be sent swiftly – not only to defend Malaya but also as a very possible deterrent to a Japanese attack in the first place.

In these recommendations, Babington had also stressed the necessity of holding all of Malaya – not just Singapore and southern Johore – as a means of protecting the northern British airfields from which the airforce could be expected to frustrate Japanese invasion efforts. When it became clear, during the winter of 1939-1940, that the war against Germany ruled out air reinforcements for Malaya, Babington's point became even more imperative. In April 1940, the new army commander in Malaya, Major-General Lionel Bond, reiterated to the War Office in no uncertain terms that all of Malaya would have to be held, and for this he needed three reinforced divisions, including tank units –

somewhat less if sufficient air power could somehow reach Malaya to take over the primary defensive role.

The fall of France in June made matters worse. The loss of French naval power in the Mediterranean increased British naval requirements there and reduced even more the chances of a sizeable British fleet being able to rush to Singapore. Nor did there seem much hope that major ground reinforcements could be spread. To darken the situation further, Bond and Babington were continuing the old army/air argument over Singapore's defences. To Bond, the only reason for defending Singapore was to preserve the naval base for the arrival of the fleet. While he agreed that airfields in northern Malaya should be held, he was unwilling to reduce his limited forces on Singapore Island and in southern Johore. To do so, he reasoned, would leave Singapore vulnerable to a direct attack; the British might well end up holding the northern airfields while the Japanese occupied the naval base – which would not help matters at all when the fleet arrived. Babington, on the other hand, argued that the only way to defend Singapore was by destroying the invaders from the air. If the northern airfields fell to the Japanese, the naval base would follow in short order. It was thus more important to defend the airfields, even at the risk of reducing Singapore's garrison.

The British Chiefs of Staff reviewed the situation during the summer of 1940. Given the changed strategic situation the threat to Singapore was clear, as was the need to defend all of Malaya and not just the naval base. They agreed that this was primarily an air-force responsibility, and that army units should concentrate on the close defence of the naval and air bases, internal security, and handling any Japanese troops who succeeded in getting ashore. In August they concluded that the British air-force then in Malaya, eighty-eight aircraft most of them obsolete, would have to be expanded to 336 first-line planes, and that the size of the army garrison would have to be doubled, from three reinforced brigades (nine battalions) to six. The Chiefs hoped to complete the air reinforcement programme by the end of 1941. Until that time, even six brigades would be inadequate to make up for the shortage of planes, so the additional three divisions requested by General Bond would have to be sent to Malaya. This would provide Malayan defences with a total of thirty-six infantry battalions plus supporting troops.

These recommendations were approved by the Cabinet. But there was a serious disagreement between the Chiefs of Staff and the Prime Minister, Winston Churchill, who accepted neither the imminence of the threat to Singapore nor the Chiefs' strategy for defending it.

Churchill held that Japan was not on the verge of war, and even if she were would scarcely undertake so major a venture as an attack on Singapore. In any event, the danger in the Orient was hardly as great as in the Middle East, where an Italian army had already entered Egypt. Should Japan attack nevertheless, he said, 'the prime defence of Singapore is the Fleet'. That defence 'must, therefore, be based upon a strong *local* garrison and the general potentialities of sea-power. The idea of trying to defend the Malay peninsula and of holding the whole of Malaya . . . cannot be entertained.'[9] There was continued confusion over how to defend Singapore.

In October 1940 Singapore was the scene of a general defence conference attended by British representatives from all over the Far East. They had before them a tactical appreciation prepared by the military, naval, and air-force commanders in Malaya which called for a minimum air strength there of 566 planes, as well as more ground reinforcements. The conference readily endorsed these conclusions, indeed raising the air requirements by an additional squadron.

At about the same time, in an effort to unify British forces throughout the Far East, the position of Commander-in-Chief Far East was created, to control all land and air forces in Malaya, Burma, and Hong Kong. Air-Chief-Marshal Sir Robert Brooke-Popham assumed this important post with the dual injunction that British policy was to avoid war with Japan, and that Far Eastern defences would be based primarily on air power until a fleet could be dispatched.

'Brookham,' as he was called by the Air Force, was an able officer with a distinguished record. Unfortunately, as one newspaperman wrote, he was 'not the type to inspire confidence'.[10] A lanky man, with thinning blonde hair and a straggly, reddish moustache, at sixty-two he was relatively old for active command. He had, furthermore, a disturbingly high-pitched voice, a giggling laugh, and a shy, though friendly, manner. Despite appearances, however, he approached his broad task with brisk vigour.

Brooke-Popham quickly accepted the view that all of Malaya, and not just Singapore, would have to be held. He believed that a strong British Malaya might well deter a Japanese invasion, and supported the earlier recommendations for reinforcements. He also endorsed a proposal made by the three service chiefs in Malaya that if the Japanese entered Thailand, British forces should move immediately into the Kra Isthmus to seize air and sea bases there before the invaders could occupy them.

The Chiefs of Staff in London received these recommendations with a considerable amount of sympathy, although Churchill continued to feel that the dangers in the Far East were relatively slight in comparison with those closer to home. British policy, as he wrote to the Australian Prime Minister, Menzies, was to build up forces in the Mediterranean rather than the Far East. In case of a serious threat to Australia, however, 'we should not hesitate to compromise, or sacrifice the Mediterranean position, for the sake of our kith and kin'.[11] The Chiefs of Staff told Brooke-Popham in January 1941 that while the aircraft levels recommended for Singapore might be desirable, they were clearly out of the question in view of what was available and what was needed elsewhere. Even the total of 336 planes approved earlier for the end of 1941, which they felt would provide a reasonable degree of security, could not now be achieved on schedule, despite all efforts to send reinforcements. They did, however, hope to have the equivalent of four divisions in Malaya by June, although tanks and additional artillery could not be sent. The Chiefs did not commit themselves on the proposal to move into the Kra Isthmus if necessary.

Churchill's relative optimism about a Japanese attack was based in large measure on his belief that Japan would not dare to move against Singapore as long as the American Pacific Fleet remained a threat on her flank. To make good this threat in case of necessity, British and American planners had held, and would continue to hold, a number of talks aimed at developing joint war plans for the Far East.[12] But these talks had only limited success. The British and Americans were agreed that should both countries become involved in a war against all three Axis powers – Germany, Italy, and Japan – then the primary effort would be made in Europe, with Allied strategy in the Far East being essentially defensive. Offensive operations in the Pacific would be restricted to those carried out by the American fleet; these would, among other things, be aimed at diverting Japanese power from the south-west Pacific.

General agreement on this scheme of operations was reached by the spring of 1941. But the details were never really worked out. The main problem was that the British wanted at least a portion of the American Pacific Fleet to be based at Singapore. The Americans not only refused to go along with this, but also had some doubt whether Singapore was worth defending, or could even be held if the Japanese used air-bases in Indo-China. No agreement for joint command or operations could be achieved, and plans for co-ordination with the Dutch and Australians also remained more tentative than actual. It was clear that the Allies would work together in the Pacific, and that the increasingly anti-Japanese attitude of the United States would probably bring America into the war if Japan undertook a southern advance. But when and how the United States would join the fight, and what joint Anglo-American action would be taken, remained an unsolved problem. For Brooke-Popham, certainly, there was no assurance that American support would in any way ease his own defence burdens.

These grew heavier as 1941 progressed. The Russo-Japanese neutrality pact, Germany's invasion of the Soviet Union, and Japan's growing power in Indo-China and Thailand increased the danger of a Japanese push to the south. At the same time, the requirements of the Middle East and of aid to Russia continued to limit the men and equipment that could be sent to reinforce Singapore. For while the threat to Singapore grew more and more ominous in the minds of those most concerned with her defence, Winston Churchill was forced to regard his problems in broader prospective. 'I confess', he wrote later, 'that in my mind the whole Japanese menace lay in a sinister twilight, compared with our other needs'. If Japan struck, he felt, the United States would stand alongside Britain, otherwise there was no way to defend any part of the Far East, no matter what the British did. But if a Japanese attack brought America into the war, Britain's gain would outweigh her loss. Thus, Churchill set British priorities in 1941 as 'first, the defense of the Island . . .; secondly, the struggle in the Middle East and Mediterranean; thirdly, after June, supplies to Soviet Russia; and, last of all, resistance to a Japanese assault'.[13]

The Middle East and Russia thus received the bulk of what Britain could spare from home defence. Russia alone received 676 planes and 446 tanks, more than enough to satisfy Malaya's needs.[14] Whether this equipment was the key to keeping the Soviet Union in the war, and whether it could have saved Singapore in any event, may be argued indefinitely without conclusion. Clearly, though, Malaya's defences were the weaker for not having it.

By late 1941 a considerable number of Indian and Australian troops and a few air units had reached Malaya. These reinforcements, especially in aircraft, were far less than Brooke-Popham desired. That they represented a significant increase over what had been available in mid-1940 was only partially reassuring.

Changes in command in the spring of 1941 had brought back as the British army commander in Malaya Lieutenant-General Arthur Percival, the former chief-of-staff there. A tall slender man, his slight build, soft voice, and almost boyish face gave no hint of his energy, athletic ability, and personal courage. He wore his grey hair parted on the side, and his most obvious characteristic was a pair of protruding upper teeth. With his red cheeks and small dark moustache, they gave him an almost rabbit-like appearance. Now fifty-three, with a fine World War I and post-war record, he had served in France in 1939-1940 and then on the Imperial General Staff. He was pleasant, intelligent, and well prepared for senior command, but many felt that he lacked the special brilliance and hard drive necessary for top military leadership. A few weeks before Percival reached Malaya, Air-Vice-Marshal Conway Pulford replaced Babington as the Far East air commander. Neither Percival nor Pulford was satisfied with the strength of his command and both, as well as Brooke-Popham, continued to press London for additional reinforcements.

By late autumn Percival's forces — known as Malaya Command — totalled about 88,600 British, Australian, Indian, and Malayan troops: in all, thirty-one battalions and their supporting elements. They were organised into one Australian and two Indian divisions, reserve and supporting units, and the Singapore Fortress, as the island's defences were called. These forces were not only well below the strength considered necessary in the absence of strong British air units — Percival that summer had put the minimum requirement at forty-eight battalions — but they also lacked tanks and sufficient anti-tank and anti-aircraft artillery. Furthermore many of the troops had received only a minimum of training, and some had not been in Malaya long enough to get used to the climate or to the problems of fighting in the jungle.

Of the 37,000 Indian troops, many were scarcely better than raw recruits, few had had more than a brief exposure to jungle-warfare training, and most of their officers and non-commissioned officers were new or inexperienced. The 15,200 Australians also lacked experienced leaders and, while considerably better trained than the Indians, still had a good deal to learn about fighting in the jungle. British units, 19,600 troops in all, could boast of better training, but they too were short of experienced officers and were relatively unfamiliar with jungle warfare. The remaining 16,800 troops were local forces whose primary commitment in their civilian capacity to maintain rubber and tin production, had kept them from being called up soon or often enough to receive more than a bare introduction to training. The British need for Malayan resources — coupled with an unrealistically low peace-time rate of pay for military labour — also crippled efforts to organise civilian labour units to support the troops; a failure no less significant than the other inadequacies of Malayan defence.

British, Australian, and Indian divisions were organised somewhat differently from comparable Japanese forces. All employed the batalion as the basic unit of infantry, but the regiment, which might contain any number of battalions, was merely a housekeeping parent organisation that remained at home and had no combat or field function. In the field three infantry battalions, usually from different regiments, were grouped together in an infantry brigade. A division normally consisted of three brigades, but those in Malaya had only two brigades. Each division had the usual supporting arms and services. British and Australian — but not Indian — field artillery included more weapons than the Japanese. The standard field piece was the 25-pounder (88-mm.) gun-howitzer, although some units still had the World War I 18-pounder (85-mm.) gun and 4.5-inch howitzer.

There were no British divisions in Malaya. Of the six British battalions, three were in the Singapore Fortress and the others were assigned to Indian brigades. Indian units in Malaya were part of the Indian Army, a separate force within the British military system, trained and organised along the same lines as the British army. Equipment, however, tended to be somewhat lighter and there was less artillery and fewer anti-tank and anti-aircraft weapons. Officers were both British and Indian, most of the senior ranks going to the former, and all held their commissions in the Indian, not the British, army. In normal circumstances, one of the three battalions in an Indian brigade was British, but half the Indian brigades in Malaya contained no British units at all.[15]

The only non-Indian division in Malaya was the Australian 8th Division, organised and equipped much like a British unit. While subject to Percival's operational control, the 8th Division occupied a somewhat unique position. Its commander, Major-General Henry Gordon Bennett, was under instructions from his government to see that the division maintained its identity as an Australian force, and was not split or used piecemeal by Malaya Command without Bennett's approval. Bennett, moreover, was authorised to have direct communication with Australia, which gave him a means of going over Percival's head if he desired. This situation, while understandable from the Australian point of view, nevertheless limited Percival's freedom to employ subordinate units as he saw fit. Although not a regular soldier, Bennett was a veteran of World War I, where he had earned a brilliant reputation as the youngest brigadier in any British army of that period. Now fifty-two, he was tough, aggressive, and popular with his men — who called him 'Ginger' because of his thin red hair and moustache and pink cheeks. Outspoken to the point of rudeness, sarcastic and impatient, he did not get along well with regulars or, for that matter, with anyone else with whom he disagreed. His rasping personality did nothing to improve command relationships.[16]

If Percival's ground defences were shockingly weak, Air-Vice-Marshal Pulford's resources were even less.[17] Instead of the nearly 600 planes urgently recommended by his predecessors and the 336 approved by the Chiefs of Staff, there were in Malaya on the eve of the Japanese attack the sum total of 158 operational aircraft, most of which were obsolescent or worse. These were divided among nine Royal Air Force, five Australian, and two New Zealand squadrons, not one of which could match in experience and equipment what the Japanese were to throw at them. The four regular fighter squadrons were equipped with slow, awkward, and short-ranged American Brewster Buffaloes, which had given their pilots and maintenance crews nothing but trouble since their arrival earlier in the year. The one night-fighter squadron had to be satisfied with the even less adequate British Blenheims, obsolescent bombers modified as fighters, while the two torpedo-bomber squadrons flew lumbering Vildebeestes, declared obsolete more than a year earlier. The Blenheims and Hudsons in the light bomber and reconnaissance squadrons were not much better. There were few reserve aircraft or spare parts available, and no dive-bombers, transports, long-range bombers, or photo-reconnaissance planes. Radar and communication links were poor, and repair and maintenance facilities inadequate. Airfields, some of which were still incomplete, lacked sufficient anti-aircraft guns, not to mention an adequate warning system against surprise attack. Some of the pilots were reasonably well trained; many were not, and none had seen combat.

The weakness of the British in the air was particularly reflected in fighters. This was due as much to the low priority assigned to Malaya as to a failure to appreciate the qualities of new Japanese fighter-planes like the Zero. In May 1941, the Chinese had shot down a Zero and had been able to examine it carefully. Their report, and a subsequent evaluation by the British air attaché at Chungking, provided full data on the performance, armament, and range of this highly capable aircraft. This important technical information reached Singapore, London, and other British headquarters, but British air intelligence in the Far East was in such organisational disarray at this time that the vital data remained hidden in the files and was never acted upon. As a result, the air staff were convinced that the Brewster Buffaloes were more than a match for Japanese fighters, and the British pilots were completely unprepared for the performance qualities they would meet in the Zero and similar planes.[18]

On the eve of war, the state of British ground and air forces in Malaya reflected a curious irony. Air power was to have constituted the primary defence. But since it was clearly inadequate for this task the major responsibility fell to the troops on the ground. They had been heavily reinforced to offset the lack of air power, but they were still dangerously weak. And, of course, they would now have to defend themselves without sufficient air support.

The original Singapore defence plans had also visualized the arrival of a strong British fleet to thwart any attack. These plans had gone through many modifications which by late 1941 had brought them full-circle. For so fragile were the ground and air defences that only the presence of a strong battle fleet could possibly have redressed the balance against a powerful and determined enemy. Yet this presence was not to be.

In mid-1941, Malaya's naval defences had depended on a handful of old cruisers and destroyers at Singapore and the tiny, obsolete aircraft-carrier *Hermes*, 1,500 miles away at Ceylon.[19] The old battle cruiser *Repulse*, also scheduled to go to Ceylon, was being refitted in England. It is not surprising then that despite the conclusion in September 1940 that no battle fleet could reach Singapore until six months after the start of hostilities in that area, the Admiralty had been considering plans to establish a strong Eastern Fleet. These plans contemplated the deployment in the Indian Ocean of a balanced force of seven capital ships, an aircraft carrier, ten cruisers, and about two dozen destroyers. So pressing, however, were British naval requirements in the Atlantic and Mediterranean, and so badly damaged were many of the British squadrons, that little of this proposed force would be available before March 1942. The Admiralty hoped to send one modern battleship in September 1941 and four older ones by the end of the year.

By August 1941, however, the situation in the Pacific had become critical. The United States had drawn the line more sharply, in the face of Japanese ambition, and appeared more than ever to have cast her lot with Great Britain. To the Prime Minister, Churchill, it seemed essential to back the American Pacific Fleet with a powerful British naval deterrent. The proposed slow build-up of a large but obsolescent fleet in the Indian Ocean did not appear to him to meet this need. It would neither deter the Japanese nor, for that matter, fight them effectively in case of war. He proposed instead to place a small, but 'formidable, fast, high-class squadron', including at least one of Britain's best battleships, in the Indian Ocean by the end of October.[20] This force, he believed, would have a strong deterrent effect. It would be potentially offensive rather than merely capable of protecting shipping, which, he felt, was all that could be expected from the force planned by the Admiralty.

The impasse between the Prime Minister and his naval advisers dragged on into October, the Admiralty insisting that the Japanese had little to fear from a small deterrent, Churchill that a larger but mainly obsolescent force was no deterrent at all. By now the *Repulse* was well on her way to the Indian Ocean, but no other capital ship was under orders to join her. Late in the month, however, the darkening Pacific war clouds forced a decision. Britain's newest battleship, the swift and powerful *Prince of Wales*, sailed for Capetown. From here she would continue east, pick up the *Repulse*, and the two mighty warships, with four destroyers, would go on to Singapore. The new aircraft carrier *Indomitable*, then making her trial run in the West Indies, was also scheduled to join this force. This new Eastern Fleet, small but strong and balanced, would it was hoped help to deter the Japanese war-lords.

Unfortunately for British intentions, the *Indomitable* ran aground off Jamaica and effectively removed herself from the picture. The other warships reached Singapore on December 2nd. Their arrival was marked by great publicity, as their deterrent role required, but there was no gain-saying the fact that the absence of the *Indomitable* left them with practically no air cover. By spring a large force, including an aircraft carrier, could be based on Singapore; but at the moment, nothing else was available. The *Prince of Wales* and the *Repulse* stood virtually alone. If their presence failed to deter a Japanese attack, the odds in battle would be heavily against them.

British inability to base a strong fleet at Singapore thus made land-based airpower, however weak, the first line of defence. General Percival's ground dispositions were aimed at protecting the airfields, and these, thanks to pre-war service rivalries, had not been sited with any particular regard for ground defence. The ones in the north were especially vulnerable to a Japanese attack through Thailand, or a landing at Kota Bharu. Their loss would not only seriously weaken British air capabilities but would also greatly increase those of the enemy. But the Japanese might prefer to by-pass northern Malaya by landing at Kuantan, with its airfield and ready access to central Malaya, or in Johore, or even on Singapore Island itself. They might even attempt operations at a number of place simultaneously. The choice lay with the Japanese. Percival, in addition to his concern for these widely scattered threats, also had to be ready, if necessary, to make a swift advance into southern Thailand to forestall Japanese landings there.

His solution, an unhappy one at best, was to put the bulk of his troops in the north and trust that they could move forward if called upon to do so or, if the worst came to the worst, could fall back without undue loss to help in the close defence of Singapore. This northern force, the III Indian Corps under Lieutenant-General Sir Lewis Heath (fresh from a brilliant command in Africa), consisted essentially of two divisions and a reserve brigade. The defence of Johore was the responsibility of General Bennett's 8th Australian Division. Two brigades held Singapore Island, while a third constituted Percival's reserve.

As these defences were forming, during the autumn of 1941, it was still not clear just when and where Japan would strike or even — given the presence of the American battle fleet at Pearl Harbour — whether she had the courage and the capability to strike at all. Some, like Churchill, were inclined to emphasize the limitations of Japanese power, while others, like Brooke-Popham, felt that the beleaguered Soviet Union was the most attractive target for Japanese attack. It was not until late November that persistent reports of Japanese air, ground, and sea movements southward convinced the Far East commander that an assault on Malaya might be imminent. Even then, there were those at Singapore who still felt that the force of the north-east winter monsoon in the South China Sea and Gulf of Siam would prevent a Japanese blow until spring. Others remained unconvinced of the fighting qualities of the Japanese troops, who after all had faced no stronger foes than the Chinese, and of the Japanese pilots, most of whom were thought to be myopic amateurs flying rickety crates.

Nevertheless the portents were clear. Japanese aircraft were moving in force into Indo-China. Some were even making reconnaissance flights over Malaya; too high and fast for positive identification, but leaving little doubt about their mission. Shipping was increasing around Hainan and at the Indo-Chinese ports of Saigon and Camranh Bay. Japanese troops were reported to be undergoing jungle-warfare training, and landing craft were seen being moved south from Shanghai. By the end of the third week in November, Brooke-Popham was reasonably certain that the Japanese were about ready to strike.

On the 21st, he asked London for specific instructions on the circumstances in which he could launch *Operation Matador*. This was the scheme, developed in great secrecy, to move into the Singora-Patani area of the Kra Isthmus if the Japanese entered Thailand. Percival's staff had worked out detailed plans for *Matador*, prepared maps and propaganda pamphlets, gathered up Thai currency, and arranged to distribute rice in occupied areas. To collect information on terrain and other important matters and to familiarise troop leaders with the countryside, thirty officers, in groups of two or three at a time, crossed into Thailand wearing civilian clothes. They sometimes encountered Japanese, obviously on a similar mission, and on occasion even stayed at the same tiny Thai rest-houses as their potential foes. They brought back much useful information. But there was no way of discovering how the Thais might react to a British invasion, whatever the pretext, and the *Matador* plans had to cover all contingencies. Even more vital was the need to have ample warning of the Japanese intent to move into Thailand; for to prevent enemy seizure of the Singora area, with its important road and rail links, it was necessary to begin *Matador* at least twenty-four hours before the Japanese landed. And Brooke-Popham would need thirty-six hours to launch the operation once he had been authorised to do so.

In the fall of 1941 the Chiefs of Staff had emphasised to him that the policy of trying to avoid war with Japan ruled out any crossing of the Thai border before Japanese entrance into that country, lest the Japanese themselves use this as a cause to start the war. On November 25th, in answer to his request for detailed guidance, the Chiefs told Brooke-Popham that the British government could not commit itself in advance to *Matador*. If the Japanese seemed on the verge of entering Thailand, he should immediately get ready to move. London would give him a decision within thirty-six hours – which, after all, was the period Brooke-Popham had indicated as necessary to get *Matador* under way.

Brooke-Popham, however, had already alerted his forces in Malaya and had ordered General Percival to begin preparations for *Matador*. On the 27th, he reiterated to the Chiefs the necessity for beginning the operation in time to beat the Japanese to Singora. Since a convoy could reach the Kra Isthmus from Saigon in less than thirty-six hours, the Japanese could obviously land before Brooke-Popham could get permission to forestall them. Clearly he needed some prior authorisation. On the 28th, he asked for authority to launch *Matador* as soon as escorted Japanese convoys were spotted approaching the Thai coast.

The urgency in Brooke-Popham's pleas was stimulated by continuing reports of Japanese activities. His request of the 28th, for example, was provoked by information that the American consul at Hanoi had reported on the 26th that the Japanese would invade the Kra Isthmus and northern Malaya without warning on about December 1st. On the

29th, word reached him that American-Japanese negotiations might break off at any time, and that as a result Japanese attacks on the Philippines, Thailand, or even Borneo could be expected. He immediately ordered Percival to place General Heath's III Corps, in northern Malaya, on twenty-four-hour alert and to have it ready for *Matador*. Heath, in turn, aware of the need for a swift advance on Singora, put the troops assigned to *Matador* on six-hour alert.

In London, the Chiefs of Staff were as concerned as Brooke-Popham. Yet bearing in mind the necessity of avoiding war with Japan if at all possible, they were unable to grant their Far East Commander the authority to start a fight on his own. The presence of an escorted Japanese convoy in the Gulf of Siam, they told him, could not in itself be interpreted as an attack on Thailand. And moving into the Kra Isthmus on the basis of this threat alone would mean that Britain, rather than Japan, would be the first to violate Thai neutrality — at the risk of starting the very war she still hoped to avoid. Only a prior guarantee by the United States to join in the struggle, they concluded, would allow them to grant Brooke-Popham the freedom to act that he so badly needed.

Two days later, on December 1st, the Chiefs informed him of the breakdown in American-Japanese negotiations, warned again that Japan might suddenly attack, and added that Washington had been asked to guarantee military support if the British acted to forestall a Japanese assault on the Kra Isthmus. Brooke-Popham immediately mobilised the Volunteer Forces and put his entire command in a tighter state of alert. And well he might. Among the increasingly threatening reports that reached him in the next few days was a story from Thailand that pro-Japanese leaders there had suggested a Japanese attack on Kota Bharu as a means of provoking a British advance into Thailand, thus making Britain the aggressor and providing the basis for a Thai declaration of war. Passing this on to London on the 4th, Brooke-Popham pointed out that a Japanese landing at Kota Bharu would eliminate the need for further efforts to avoid war, that the Japanese would probably land at Singora in any event, and that *Matador* would still be necessary. He asked for permission to order *Matador* if the Japanese struck Kota Bharu.

On December 5th, the word finally came. The Chiefs of Staff authorised Brooke-Popham to begin *Matador* without reference to London if he learned that a Japanese force 'was advancing with the apparent intention of landing on the Kra Isthmus', or if Japan 'violated any other part of Thailand'.[21] This did not answer Brooke-Popham's question about undertaking *Matador* in case of an attack on Kota Bharu alone, but it gave far more authority than he had previously enjoyed. The Cabinet had granted this to him, said the Chiefs, because Washington had at last promised military support if the Japanese attacked British or Dutch territory or if the British undertook *Matador*, either to forestall a Japanese landing on the Kra Isthmus or in response to the invasion of any other part of Thailand.

This American assurance was the culmination of months of co-operative military talks between Britain and the United States. For some time now the two nations had shared intelligence information about the Japanese, including the products of that marvellous American decoding process known as 'Magic', which could read and interpret some of Japan's most secret messages. There were, indeed, 'Magic' machines at both London and Singapore.[22] But the potential allies had been unable to agree on a detailed joint plan of action in the Far East and, in particular, differed over the value and future role of Singapore.

During the tense days of late November British, American, and Dutch planes were reconnoitering the waters of the South China Sea through which a Japanese amphibious force would have to pass on its way to invade Malaya, the Philippines, or the Netherlands Indies. British aircraft covered the area off eastern Malaya and flew as far north as the southernmost tip of Indo-China. But they lacked the range necessary to penetrate far into the Gulf of Siam. American naval flying boats from the Philippines were operating over the South China Sea, east and north of the Philippines. On December 1st their area of surveillance was extended west to the Indo-Chinese coast, while the speedier army Flying Fortresses, with their higher ceiling, moved to cover the waters around Formosa. On that date, also, Brooke-Popham asked General Douglas MacArthur, the American army commander in the Philippines, to send a Flying Fortress on a photo-reconnaissance mission over Camranh Bay. He was sure Japanese shipping was massing there, but he had no specific information and he lacked planes capable of flying fast or high enough to reconnoitre without being intercepted. But MacArthur, like Brooke-Popham, was under orders to avoid starting a fight, so he explained that he was unable to help the British Far East commander. Brooke-Popham was apparently unaware — although the British mission in Washington had been told — that extended American naval air reconnaissance was now covering Camranh Bay.[23]

In Washington, meanwhile, President Roosevelt and the British Ambassador, Lord Halifax, were discussing possible joint Anglo-American action in case of a Japanese attack. The President had in his hands a message from Churchill urging a strong warning to the Japanese against further aggression, a message given some urgency by Halifax's announcement that a Japanese assault on Thailand and the Kra Isthmus was expected any day. Roosevelt, however, was still hoping to play for time. He was not certain what the Japanese were up to and he wanted to be sure before taking an irrevocable step. If it became clear that the Japanese were indeed launching a southern aggression, he told Halifax on December 1st, then 'we should obviously all be together'.[24]

It was perhaps with this in mind that the President late that evening ordered a special reconnaissance of Indo-Chinese waters to supplement the aerial surveillance already being maintained. Admiral Thomas C. Hart, commander of the American Asiatic Fleet based in Manila, was directed to charter three small vessels, outfit them sufficiently to establish their identity as American, and despatch them 'to observe and report by radio Japanese movements in the west China Sea and Gulf of Siam.'[25] This was to be done as soon as possible, preferably within two days. The ships were to take station at the entrance to the Gulf of Tonkin, off the Indo-Chinese coast south of Camranh Bay, and below the southern tip of Indo-China. Any major Japanese convoy headed south could hardly evade observation by these vessels. Its sighting would give Roosevelt time to make up his mind about American action and, of course, would do the same for the British as far as *Matador* was concerned.* Unfortunately for the Allied cause, the Japanese struck before any of the three ships could get on station, and aerial reconnaissance was unable to provide a sufficiently early or adequate warning for the British.[26]

Roosevelt, in any event, did not wait for the results of the tiny naval patrol. Hart's aerial reconnaissance on December 2nd found twenty-one transports in Camranh Bay and a force of nine Japanese submarines headed south along the Indo-Chinese coast.[27] Other intelligence was no

---

* Rear-Admiral Kemp Tolley, who as a young officer commanded one of the three vessels, makes much of the fact that the message from the Chief of Naval Operations to Hart authorised the use of Filipino crews. He charges Roosevelt with setting up the whole operation in the hope of provoking a Japanese attack and rallying the Philippine people to the American cause. But Hart was not actually directed to use Filipino crews, and it is not clear from the message whether the idea was Roosevelt's or that of the Chief of Naval Operations. It is also possible that the use of Filipino crews was authorised because Hart's American naval personnel were already rather thinly spread. The reconnaissance mission entailed risks, but no more than were already involved in aerial reconnaissance. Roosevelt was anxious for full and accurate information, and two of the reconnaissance vessels, those in the north and the south, would be stationed in areas not covered by Hart's planes. Finally, identifying the ships as American was probably intended to prevent a Japanese attack on them rather than, as Tolley implies, provoke one.

less threatening. On the evening of the 3rd, Roosevelt told Halifax that his assurance of support meant armed support.[28] He had not yet decided just what sort of warning to give the Japanese, but in any event he would back *Matador*. It seems clear, incidentally, that both Halifax and Roosevelt were aware of the President's constitutional limitations. Roosevelt pointed out that American support might be delayed for a few days, while the British had already become familiar with what a United States President could or could not do without the approval of Congress. Nevertheless, it was Halifax's report of this conversation with Roosevelt that enabled the British government to untie Brooke-Popham's hands.

Three days before Brooke-Popham received his qualified authority to order *Matador*, the *Prince of Wales* and the *Repulse* and their escorts reached Singapore. The commander of the new Eastern Fleet, Admiral Sir Tom Phillips, previously Vice Chief of the Naval Staff and now taking over the British Far East naval command, had actually arrived by air two days earlier. He had little time for conversation with Brooke-Popham, for he was under orders to go on to Manila to co-ordinate plans with Admiral Hart. He did, however, talk with Air-Vice-Marshal Pulford, and was seriously disturbed to learn exactly how weak British air strength in Malaya was. Without an aircraft-carrier to provide cover for the fleet, Phillips knew he would have to depend on Pulford's force to protect him against Japanese air attack.

In London, meanwhile, all the doubts that had first assailed the Admiralty about sending out the *Prince of Wales* and the *Repulse* now arose again. The news of Japanese activity seemed to indicate clearly that the two warships had failed in their deterrent mission and that they were now exposed to sudden and possibly fatal attack. On December 1st, then, even before the vessels reached Singapore, the Admiralty suggested to Phillips that he might send them to sea again for their own security. Phillips, indeed, was himself considering such a move, with the thought of perhaps shifting his base to Darwin, Australia. On the 3rd, he received a second message from London, this time suggesting that he should try to get some additional destroyers from Admiral Hart, and move *Prince of Wales* and the *Repulse* eastwards to join the American Asiatic Fleet. Phillips had by now decided that he must talk to Hart before taking any final action. He directed the *Repulse* to pay a short visit to Darwin and on the 4th he himself flew to Manila in one of the only three planes at Singapore capable of making the 1,500-mile trip. *Repulse* and two destroyers sailed the next day, under orders 'to proceed for the first 48 hours at comparatively slow speed'.[29]

At Manila, Phillips conferred with Hart and General MacArthur and reached general agreement on naval policy — most of which was to be overtaken by the events of the next week. While they were talking, on December 6th, a message arrived from Singapore. A large Japanese convoy had been spotted well down the Indo-Chinese coast, headed either for Thailand or for Malaya. Phillips said goodbye to his American hosts and that evening took off to rejoin his command. The battle-cruiser *Repulse* had already returned.

NOTES – Chapter Three

1. Lieut. Gen. H. Gordon Bennett, *Why Singapore Fell* (Sydney: Angus and Robertson, 1944), p. 8. Most of the sources listed in the bibliography contain material about Malaya's geography. Particularly useful for Singapore itself are R.C.H. McKie, *This Was Singapore* (London: Robert Hale, 1950), and H. Gordon Minnigerode, Life Grows Grim in Singapore, *National Geographic Magazine*, LXXX (November 1941), 661-86.

2. For the background and building of the Singapore base, see Eugene H. Miller, *Strategy at Singapore* (New York: Macmillan, 1942), Woodburn Kirby, et al., *The War Against Japan*, Vol. I, *The Loss of Singapore* History of the Second World War: United Kingdom Military Series (London: Her Majesty's Stationery Office, 1957), chap. i; C. Northcote Parkinson, The Pre-1942 Singapore Naval Base, *United States Navl Institute Proceedings*, Vol. 82 (September 1956), pp. 939-53; Robin Higham, *Armed Forces in Peacetime* (Hamdon: Archon Books, 1962), pp. 106-109, 272-78; Richard Hough, *Death of the Battleship* (New York: Macfadden-Bartell, 1965), chap. vi; Grenfell, *Main Fleet to Singapore*, chaps. iii, v.

3. Lieut. Gen. A.E. Percival, *Despatch: Operations of Malaya Command, From December 8th, 1941 to February 15th, 1942*, April 25th, 1946, Second Supplement to the *London Gazette* of February 20th, 1948, p. 1250. Also *ibid.*, App. A; Percival, *The War in Malaya* (London: Eyre & Sportiswoode, 1949), pp. 13-17, 36-45.

4. This, and the quotations in the following paragraph, are given in Kirby, *The Loss of Singapore*, pp. 19-20.

5. For Malayan defence plans and preparations, 1939-1941, see *ibid.*, chaps. ii-iv; J.R.M. Butler, *Grand Strategy*, Vol. II, *September 1939-June 1941* History of the Second World War: United Kingdom Military Series (London: Her Majesty's Stationery Office, 1957), chaps. xiv, xxi; J.M.A. Gwyer and Butler, *Grand Strategy*, Vol. III, *June 1941-August 1942* (London: Her Majesty's Stationery Office, 1964), chaps. i, v, x-xii; Brooke-Popham, *Despatch*, pp. 535-55; Percival, *Despatch*, pp. 1245-67; Maltby, *Report*, pp. 1347-65; Grenfell, *Main Fleet to Singapore*, chaps. vi-vii; Percival, *The War in Malaya*, chaps. ii-vii.

6. Lionel Wigmore, *The Japanese Thrust*, Australia in the War of 1939-1945, Series I, *Army*, Vol. IV (Canberra: Australian War Memorial, 1957), p. 47. Col. K.W. Maurice-Jones, *The History of Coast Artillery in the British Army* (London: Royal Artillery Institution, 1959), pp. 215-18.

Air Chief Marshal Sir Robert Brooke-Popham (*extreme right*) on a tour of the naval and air bases at Singapore with General Sir Archibald Wavell

(*left*) Air Vice Marshal Pulford and (*right*) Lieutenant General A. E. Percival

Japanese forces landing at Singora on the Kra peninsula

7. See for example: John Gunther, Singapore – A warning to Japan, *The Saturday Evening Post*, June 18th, 1938, p. 92; Minnigerode, Singapore, *loc. cit.*, pp. 682-84; and, especially, the knowledgable comment by Lewis, Dreadnought, *United States Naval Institute Proceedings*, Vol. 92 (January 1966), pp. 120-21.

8. Sir George Maxwell, *The Civil Defence of Malaya* (London: Hutchinson & Co. [1944?]), Part I.

9. Prime Minister to General Ismay, September 10th, 1940, Winston S. Churchill, *The Second World War*, Vol. II, *Their Finest Hour* (Boston: Houghton Mifflin, 1949), pp. 667-68.

10. Edwin Maurice Glover, *In 70 Days: The Story of the Japanese Campaign in British Malaya* (2nd ed.; London: Frederick Muller, 1949), p. 123; Cecil Brown, *Suez to Singapore* (New York: Random House, 1942), pp. 149-50; Wigmore, *The Japanese Thrust*, pp. 46-47.

11. Winston Churchill to Prime Minister of Australia, December 23rd, 1940, *ibid.*, pp. 704-705.

12. For American strategic conditions, see Maurice Matloff and Edward M. Snell, *Strategic Planning for Coalition Warfare, 1941-1942* United States Army in World War II: The War Department (Washington: Office, Chief of Military History, 1953), pp. 32-78; Louis Morton, *Strategy and Command: The First Two Years* United States Army in World War II: The War in the Pacific (Washington: Office, Chief of Military History, 1962), pp. 79-91; Samuel Eliot Morison, *History of United States Naval Operations in World War II*, Vol. III, *The Rising Sun in the Pacific, 1931-April 1942*, (Boston: Little, Brown, 1951), pp. 48-56.

13. Winston S. Churchill, *The Second World War*, Vol. III, *The Grand Alliance* (Boston: Houghton Mifflin, 1950), pp. 587-88.

14. Wigmore, *The Japanese Thrust*, p. 103.

15. Kirby, *The Loss of Singapore*, App. 11, Brigadier Cyril N. Barclay, The Indian Army, *Army*, July 1967, pp. 52-58.

16. Wigmore, *The Japanese Thrust*, pp. 32-35, 65; Percival, *The War in Malaya*, pp. 34-35; Kirby, *The Loss of Singapore*, App. 12; Brown, *Suez to Singapore*, pp. 211-13; Ian Morrison, *Malayan Postscript* (London: Faber and Faber, 1942), Frank Legg, *The Gordon Bennett Story* (Sydney: Angus and Roberton, 1965).

17. Richards and Saunders, *The Fight Avails*, pp. 1-13; Gillison, *Royal Australian Air Force*, chap. vii.

18. Kirby, *The Loss of Singapore*, p. 240.

19. For the naval situation, see also Captain S.W. Roskill, *The War at Sea, 1939-1945*, Vol. I, *The Defensive* History of the Second World War: United Kingdom Military Series (London: Her Majesty's Stationery Office, 1954), pp. 553-62; Hough, *Death of the Battleship*, chap. vii.

20. Prime Minister to First Lord and First Sea Lord, August 25th, 1941, in Churchill, *The Grand Alliance*, p. 854.

21. Brooke-Popham, *Despatch*, p. 546.

22. Farago, *The Broken Seal*, chap. xx.

23. For American. reconnaissance activities, see also Lewis H. Brereton, *The Brereton Diaries: The War in the Air in the Pacific, Middle East and Europe* (New York: William Morrow, 1946), pp. 34-35; Wesley Frank Craven and James Lea Cate (eds.), *The Army Air Forces in World War II*, Vol. I, *Plans and Early Operations, January 1939 to August 1942* (Chicago: University of Chicago Press, 1948), p. 191; U.S. Congress, Joint Committee on the Investigation of the Pearl Harbour Attack, *Pearl Harbour Attack* (39 Pts.; Washington: U.S. Government Printing Offices, 1946), Part XV, pp. 1768-69.

24. Sir Llewellyn Woodward, *British Foreign Policy in the Second World War* History of the Second World War (London: Her Majesty's Stationery Office, 1962), p. 186. For the Roosevelt-Halifax talks and FDR's agreement to support the British, see *ibid.*, pp. 185-88. Also Churchill, *The Grand Alliance*, pp. 599-601. A thorough analysis appears in Raymond A. Esthus, President Roosevelt's Commitment to Britain to Intervene in a Pacific War, *The Mississippi Valley Historical Review*, L (June 1953), 28-38.

25. OPNAV to CINCAF, 012356, December 2nd, 1941, as paraphrased in *Pearl Harbour Attack*, Part XIV, p. 1407.

26. See also Admiral Hart's testimony in *ibid.*, Part X, pp. 4807-4808; testimony of Admiral Harold R. Stark, former Chief of Naval Operations, *ibid.*, Part V, pp. 2190-91, 2416-18; and of Admiral Royal E. Ingersoll, former Assistant Chief of Naval Operations, *ibid.*, Part IX, pp. 4251-54; and Rear Adm. Kemp Tolley, The Strange Assignment of the USS *Lanikai*, *United States Naval Institute Proceedings*, Vol. 88 (September 1962), pp. 71-83.

27. *Pearl Harbour Attack*, Part XV, p. 1769.

28. Woodward, *British Foreign Policy in the Second World War*, p. 187.

29. Brooke-Popham, *Despatch*, p. 557.

4

Matador Defeated

At 10.30 a.m. on December 6th, three Hudsons of No. 1 (Reconnaissance) Squadron, Royal Australian Air Force, splashed down the water-soaked runway at Kota Bharu and took off over the South China Sea. The heavy northeast monsoon had washed out the airfield for two days and now even on the 6th intermittent tropical downpours still made navigation difficult and limited visibility. At about 12.15, nevertheless, some 185 miles northeast of Kota Bharu, Flight Lieutenant J.C. Ramshaw and his crew sighted three Japanese vessels – possibly part of the convoy that had left Saigon the night before, more likely some of the smaller escort ships in the main Twenty-fifth Army convoy carrying General Yamashita. Fifteen minutes later, further east, Ramshaw came upon the rest of the convoy spread over the ocean like toy ships on a dirty blue-green rug. He barely had time to count and identify the vessels when a Japanese float plane arose. Ramshaw wisely sought cover in the clouds and radioed home a report. Approximately a quarter of an hour later, in the same general area, a second Hudson, commanded by Flight Lieutenant J.G. Elberton, also discovered a large Japanese force, either part of Yamashita's convoy or, probably, the smaller group of vessels coming from Saigon. Elberton, too, flashed a message to Kota Bharu.[1]

Word of the sighting reached Brooke-Popham in Singapore at about 2 p.m. It was not clear from the reports, nor from subsequent pilot interrogations, whether two or three separate convoys had been sighted; more important, it was not clear just where the Japanese ships were heading. The first group of three small vessels had been moving north-west, the other ships, west. It was apparent, however, that a large force was involved, with a strong naval escort. Admiral Phillips was still in Manila, so Admiral Arthur Palliser, his chief of staff, and Vice-Admiral Geoffrey Layton, the former Far East naval commander who still retained some responsibility in the area, joined Brooke-Popham to discuss the Japanese movements. Already in their hands were reports that Japanese convoys had left Camranh Bay and Saigon and that Thai border-guards were throwing up blocks across the Singora and Patani roads. Clearly something was afoot. But what? Should Brooke-Popham order *Matador*?

Lieutenant Ramshaw had requested permission to shadow the Japanese force, but this had been denied in favour of his continuing on patrol over a wide area. The reason for this is not clear. Brooke-Popham later stated that the Hudsons could not maintain contact because they were at the limit of their patrolling range.[2] Yet both Ramshaw and Emerton actually had a good two hours' fuel remaining, over and above that needed to return to base. One or both could have stayed in sight of the Japanese until relieved. They would, of course, have risked being shot down, but they might have provided Brooke-Popham with a little more information on which to make a decision.

As it was, the Far East commander and his advisers could only conclude that the larger Japanese convoy or convoys would follow the three small vessels into the Gulf of Siam and assemble in a convenient bay. From there they could make a final approach to Kota Bharu, the Kra Isthmus, or, very possibly, Bangkok. It was also not beyond belief that the Japanese were simply manoeuvring to test British nerves. 'Bearing in mind the policy of avoiding war with Japan if possible', Brooke-Popham wrote later, 'and the situation in the United States with the [diplomatic] talks still going on in Washington, I decided that I would not be justified in ordering *Matador* on this information'.[3] Instead, he put all forces in Malaya on full alert and directed Air-Vice-Marshal Pulford to re-establish and maintain contact with the Japanese convoy.

This was easier said than done. Pulford's searches were unable to find any Japanese ships that afternoon, either because of the continued cloudy and rainy weather or because of the inexperience of the pilots. Japanese planes were observed over Malaya, however, and anti-aircraft gunners had authority to open fire on any unidentified aircraft. British planes, meanwhile, moved forward to northern airfields. At Kota Bharu, seven Wildebeestes were armed with torpedoes. But there was still no sight of the Japanese convoys, although, ominously, two Royal Air Force Catalina flying boats sent out during the night – the first that evening, the other at 2 a.m. – failed to return. It was probably the second one that fell victim to Japanese fighter-planes early on December 7th, in the first act of violence of World War II in the Pacific.

During the 7th, Pulford kept as many reconnaissance planes as possible in the air. They covered all the waters east of Malaya, lest the Japanese attempt a sneak landing in Johore, and swept the Gulf of Siam in an effort to re-locate the Japanese convoys. But the thick clouds, intermittent storms, and occasional fog, which General Yamashita had been so glad to see, effectively blinded the British searches. Not until 1.45 in the afternoon did one of Pulford's aircraft come upon a lone cargo-ship, steaming west, in the Gulf of Siam. By this time, the Japanese convoys assembled in the middle of the gulf had split up and begun their approaches to seven landing-points along the Kra Isthmus and an eighth at Kota Bharu. At 3.45, a Hudson spotted another merchant-vessel sailing south, apparently all by itself, with its deck full of soldiers. And shortly before 6 p.m. another Hudson was nearly shot down by what looked like a Japanese cruiser escorting a transport toward Kota Bharu. Follow-up searches on these sightings discovered at about 6.45 four more large ships, evidently headed for Patani, but heavy weather, and nightfall, successfully masked this force from closer scrutiny.

None of this information reached Brooke-Popham until approximately nine that evening, when he received word of the 6.45 sighting only. The reason for this cannot be determined and, because of the destruction of British records, will probably never be known. But the results are clear. For nearly a day and a half, at a time when accurate, current information was of the utmost importance, the British Far East commander was practically ignorant of Japanese movements.

Soon after he learned of the vessels approaching Patani, Brooke-Popham met General Percival and Admiral Phillips, just back from Manila, to consider again what to do about *Matador*. Despite all the indications of an imminent Japanese attack, there were strong arguments against ordering the advance into Thailand. That afternoon Brooke-Popham had received an almost frantic message from the British Minister in Bangkok. 'For God's sake', it read, 'do not allow British forces to occupy one inch of Thai territory unless and until Japan has struck the first blow at Thailand'.[4] The Thais would side with Britain, the message continued; but would not do so — and would, indeed, join the Japanese — if the British invaded first. Whatever Brooke-Popham thought of this, he still had no proof that the Japanese were definitely about to strike. Perhaps they were simply attempting to provoke a British violation of Thai territory. In any event, if the Japanese were intent on landing on the Kra Isthmus, they could be there in about three more hours — and it would take British troops twenty-four hours to reach Singora and Patani, after *Matador* was ordered. There was still time for an air strike at the approaching vessels, but until the Japanese actually attacked British, Dutch, or American territory, Brooke-Popham had no authority to hit a Japanese force at sea. Nor had he heard anything further from London. His report of Japanese convoy movements had precipitated anxious meetings of the Chiefs of Staff and the Foreign Office, but these discussions produced no new decision about *Matador*.[5]

Shortly before midnight on December 7th-8th, Brooke-Popham decided not to initiate *Matador* at this time. But on the assumption that it might still be necessary or desirable, he ordered a dawn air-reconnaissance of the Singora area and directed General Heath's III Indian Corps to be ready to execute *Matador* at the same time.

The III Corps had been on full alert since about 3.15 p.m. on the 6th, when the first reports of Japanese convoys reached General Heath. 'Piggy' Heath, as his troops called him, was a large, competent man with a sharp mind and a strong personality. Despite a left arm crippled in World War I, he looked and acted as every inch a soldier. He remained calm now as always despite the heavy responsibility he carried: defence of all of Malaya north of the states of Malacca and Johore and, if necessary, the execution of *Matador*.

Heath's headquarters were at Kuala Lumpur, in south-western Malaya, and his units were scattered in a desperate effort to fulfil his all-but-impossible mission. Given the large area he had to defend, and the fact that he had for this task the equivalent of only one division and two-thirds of a second, he might well have established a strong line across the centre of the peninsula and left it to delaying units, and the air-force, to contest any Japanese entry into northern Malaya. Unhappily for Heath, the requirement to hold the northern airfields, the possibility of *Operation Matador*, and the unfortunate configuration of the Malayan Thai border denied him the advantage of a sound defensive position.

From the South China Sea, just north of Kota Bharu, the Malayan border runs inland in a direction generally west by south. Two-thirds of the way to the Strait of Malacca, above the town of Kroh, it suddenly turns north, proceeds in that direction for a while, and then meanders off to the north-west until it reaches the coast. The effect is to create a salient — the states of Kedah and Perlis — projecting up the Kra Isthmus from north-western Malaya. To defend the important Kedah airfields at Alor Star and Sungei Patani, and to launch, if ordered, an offensive into Thailand, General Heath had deployed a large portion of his corps in this salient. By so doing, of course, he exposed them to a Japanese flanking drive down the road from Patani through Kroh. And the necessity of being prepared, either to advance rapidly into Thailand or to fall back and defend the airfields and their exposed flank, placed a difficult burden on the troops in this forward area.

The primary responsibility belonged to Major-General D.M. Murray-Lyon's 11th Indian Division, which had reached Malaya in late 1940 with only two of its three brigades. Despite this weakness, Murray-Lyon, a handsome, graying, small but solid-looking man, was quite confident that his troops could do the job. Both the 6th and 15th Brigades had most of their strength in northern Kedah, either to strike for Singora or to occupy a defensive position eighteen miles south of the border at Jitra, covering the Alor Star airfield. The key to either mission was Murray-Lyon's ability to hold the Singora-Jitra road. Protecting his vulnerable east flank, a battalion of the 15th Brigade at Kroh supported by a battalion to be drawn from Penang Island made up an improvised column called Krohcol, with the important task of holding the Patani-Kroh road. Whatever the mission of the 11th Division, offensive or defensive, Krohcol was to advance some thirty miles into Thailand and occupy a position called 'The Ledge' which dominated the road.

The 9th Indian Division, under Major-General A.E. Barstow, also had only two brigades. Barstow was tall, slim, and blue-eyed, a no-nonsense type of officer whose men admired his toughness and obvious courage. Faced with the necessity of defending exposed airfields, either for use by the British or in order to deny them to the Japanese, he had no choice but to place his units in tactically undesirable positions on the east coast. The 8th Brigade, with a battalion from the 22nd, held Kota Bharu. The rest of the 22nd Brigade defended Kuantan and the important east-west road running inland from that town.

Four of Heath's five brigades were thus in forward exposed positions, where they could be cut off or simply overwhelmed piecemeal by superior enemy forces. His only reserve, in effect defending all of central Malaya, was the 28th Indian Infantry Brigade at Ipoh, mid-way up the main road in western Malaya. From here it could move easily to support the 11th Division, but since there were no east-west roads at this point it could shift only with difficulty to assist the 9th Division. To add to Heath's problems, his beach defences along the extensive Malayan coastline were barely organised and neither they nor the positions at Jitra or Kroh were constructed in depth. He had no tanks in his command, and his anti-tank defences were incomplete or non-existent. Despite these weaknesses, it was III Corps nevertheless that constituted the bulk of Percival's army, and on whom would fall the heavy initial burden of meeting the enemy thrust.

The first contact came on the night of December 7th-8th, less than half an hour after Brooke-Popham had decided against initiating *Operation Matador*. At about 11.45 p.m., Indian troops on the beaches north-east of Kota Bharu discovered that several ships were anchoring offshore. This news reached Singapore shortly after midnight, to be followed by reports of artillery fire and a Japanese landing. Brooke-Popham held a hasty conference with Air Marshal Pulford and General Percival, and ordered air attacks on the landing-force as soon as possible.

At 3.30 a.m., while the British commanders and their staffs were still reacting to the news from Kota Bharu, radar watchers in Singapore's Fighter Control Operations Room picked up approaching unidentified aircraft some 135 miles to the north-east. These were twin-engine bombers — called 'Nells' by Allied forces — of Admiral Matsunaga's 22nd Air Flotilla. Shortly before midnight, thirty-two Nells of the Genzan and Mihoro Air Groups had taken off from bases in southern Indo-China and flown south into increasingly stormy weather. Sheets of rain and heavy winds battered the planes, reducing visibility to close to zero, and pushing the bombers almost down to the wave-tops. The raging storm finally broke the Genzan Group's formation and forced it to turn back. The Mihoro force continued toward Singapore and discovered clear weather as it approached the island.[6]

Singapore's military defences had gone on full alert at the first radar sighting. Anti-aircraft gunners manned their blacked-out positions and night fighters warmed up on the runways. But for some reason never completely clear no one was on duty at the civil Air Raid Precautions headquarters. Warning of the impending attack could not reach civilian authorities until the first Nells roared overhead at about 4 a.m. on December 8th. The Japanese pilots found the city still brightly lit; although the full moon and the unmistakeable outline of Singapore's harbour would have given them all the guidance they needed anyway.

A few minutes later, almost simultaneously with the sound of exploding bombs, the residents of Singapore were awakened by the chilling wail of a siren. 'Rising and falling, rising and falling', one of them wrote later, 'it cut across the stillness of the tropic night like some frightful oath uttered in a polite drawing-room. One after the other the sirens from different parts of the city chimed in until they formed one shrill cacaphony'.[7] Sleepy civilians struggling from their beds, or groping nervously out into the streets, heard the powerful blast of anti-aircraft fire and saw the long probing fingers of searchlights criss-crossing the skies. No planes rose to meet the attackers, however. Air Command kept its fighters grounded for fear that the combination of guns, lights, and aircraft would be too much for the confused and inexperienced defenders, who might well have shot down their own planes – although they hit none of the Japanese. Nor did the city's lights go off until nearly 5 o'clock, after the raiders had left and the all-clear had been given.

Fortunately for Singapore's residents, the Nells had concentrated their attacks on the Tengah and Seletar airfields, west and north of the city, where they did little damage. A few bombs fell in the centre of the city and in the eastern part of the waterfront, probably aimed at the Kallang airfield. They destroyed or damaged a number of buildings, killed some sixty civilians, and wounded twice as many more, mostly Chinese shopkeepers and a few Sikh watchmen The biggest blow, however, was to the confidence and peace of mind of the civilian population. Secure in their understanding – so often repeated by official spokesmen – that Singapore was well defended and that the Japanese would never dare attack, both British and Asiatic residents of the city had now been seriously shaken.

They were hardly reassured later that morning when Brooke-Popham issued an Order of the Day, drawn up some time previously to allow for its translation into the many different languages of the British Far East, and for distribution throughout the entire Far Eastern command. Characteristically optimistic, it spoke of British preparedness and strength, of a weakened Japan, 'drained for years by the exhausting claims of her wanton onslaught on China', and of the final and complete victory that could be expected.[8] The order was aimed primarily at raising the morale of the Indian soldiers in Malaya. But it had the opposite effect on civilians in Singapore. Having witnessed the inability of British defences to prevent a Japanese air attack on the city, and with the news of Kota Bharu just reaching them, Singapore's residents could only be profoundly shocked.

Brooke-Popham, meanwhile, had more immediate problems. Beginning at about 7.30 a.m. on December 8th, Japanese planes flew over airfields in northern Malaya, striking at aircraft and ground installations alike as they sought to destroy the small British air-force before it could get into action. Half an hour after this attack began, the Far East commander received from London the authority to launch *Matador* in reply to a Japanese landing at Kota Bharu, authority he had requested four days earlier. By now, of course, the enemy had been ashore at Kota Bharu for several hours. *Matador* might still forestall a landing at Singora, but it was obviously too late to begin the operation if the Japanese were already established on the Kra Isthmus. Brooke-Popham decided to await the report of a dawn aerial reconnaissance of that area.

For some strange reason – perhaps because he had had little or no sleep since the first enemy sightings on the 6th, perhaps because he was distracted by news of other Japanese offensives in the Far East – he failed to realise that he was now free to order British forces into Thailand, that defence plans called for Krohcol to cross the border whether *Matador* was undertaken or not, and that there was no point whatsoever in delaying Krohcol's seizure of the tactically important 'Ledge' position. At 8.20 a.m. he told General Percival of the message from London but, curiously, added the injunction, 'Do not act'.[9]

Not until 9.45 a.m. did Brooke-Popham receive definite news that Japanese troops were landing at Singora and Patani. Only then did he send word to Percival that the 11th Division should proceed with its defensive mission, holding the Jitra position and sending Krohcol forward. But now came another inexplicable delay. Percival had left his headquarters for a previously scheduled meeting of the Straits Settlement Legislative Council, to which he felt it would be desirable to present a first-hand report. Apparently no one in Malaya Command had authority to transmit Brooke-Popham's decision to III Corps, and not until after Percival's return at 11 a.m. did the command prepare orders for Heath. These did not reach him, again inexplicably, until 1 o'clock. Heath immediately telephoned Percival for confirmation that he was actually to cross into Thailand. The ensuing conversation made clear, finally, that *Matador* was definitely off and that III Corps was to occupy Jitra, send a delaying force up the Singora road, and push off with Krohcol for the Ledge. Heath called 11th Division headquarters at 1.30 and gave General Murray-Lyon the necessary orders.

Nearly four hours had passed since Brooke-Popham had received definite word of the enemy landing on the Kra Isthmus, some five and a half hours since he had been authorised to enter Thailand, and nearly twice as long since Japanese troops had gone ashore at Singora and Patani. The time lost in reacting could never be regained. It would cost the British dearly.

Already a heavy and sustained Japanese air offensive had all but destroyed Air-Vice-Marshal Pulford's capability to support Percival's ground operations. Despite bad weather, which delayed or aborted several missions, General Sugawara's 3rd Air Group had attacked northern Malayan airfields again and again throughout the day. The initial blows, by nearly 100 bombers and fighters, were launched from southern Indo-China, and the swift capture of airfields at Singora and Patani significantly shortened the distance to targets for later flights. In formations including as many as sixty planes, the raiders struck repeatedly at Kota Bharu and other fields in north-eastern Malaya and even more fiercely at those in the north-west: Alor Star, Sungei Patani, Butterworth, and Penang. While Japanese fighters swept low to strafe their targets or flew effective cover overhead, the bombers dropped mainly fragmentation and anti-personnel bombs, deadly against men and machines but practically harmless to the runways which Sugawara hoped to use himself once the fields were captured.

The steady, intense tempo of the attacks, the inadequacy of the air-warning system and fighter defence organisation, and the lack of sufficient anti-aircraft guns, frequently allowed the Japanese to catch British aircraft on the ground refuelling and rearming between flights. Many of Pulford's planes were thus destroyed when they were most vulnerable, while their pilots crouched helplessly in slit-trenches or shelters to avoid the lethal bomb fragments. Fighter-pilots who did get aloft discovered the Japanese to be skilled and courageous adversaries. So effective were the Japanese 3rd Air Group attacks that of 110 British aircraft available for combat in Malaya on the morning of the 8th, only fifty were still operational by nightfall. For all practical purposes, Brooke-Popham no longer had an air-force. This magnificent victory cost General Sugawara only a handful of planes.

Brooke-Popham sent a message to General MacArthur in the Philippines asking him to attack Japanese airfields in Indo-China with his long-range bombers. But half of MacArthur's bomber force lay smouldering in the wreckage of Clark Field, while the rest were frantically preparing to defend the islands against an expected Japanese invasion force.[10] The British Far East commander also made an urgent request to London for immediate air reinforcements. If these were sent, it would be a while before they could reach Malaya.

On December 9th, Air-Vice-Marshal Pulford made one last effort to halt the Japanese air build-up. By that afternoon, it was clear that the enemy was rapidly increasing his fighter strength at Singora. So six Blenheims from Pulford's depleted bomber force set out from Singapore to hit the Singora airfield. They flew without escort, since the fighters assigned to the mission had either been destroyed or were too busy trying to defend their own fields. As a result, three of the six bombers were shot down by Japanese 3rd Air Group fighters, and only a few bombs could be dropped on Singora. A second bombing effort, scheduled for late afternoon from Butterworth, was smashed by a Japanese airstrike before the planes could get off the ground. A single Blenheim, flown by the squadron leader, Flight-Lieutenant A.S.K. Scarf, was already aloft and flew on to Singora alone. Despite heavy anti-aircraft fire and fighter attacks, Scarf managed to drop his bombs on target, and bring the plane back to a crash landing at Alor Star. His crew was unhurt but Scarf died of his wounds that night. His outstanding bravery earned him a posthumous Victoria Cross, the first in the Malayan campaign.

These events convinced Pulford that no more daylight bombing missions could be flown without effective fighter cover. The same morning, in accordance with an earlier Anglo-Dutch agreement, three bomber squadrons and a fighter squadron reached Singapore from the Netherlands Indies. But ironically, the Dutch crews had not been trained for night operations, and Pulford regretfully sent them back to complete their training in the Indies. By now, so powerful was Japanese command of the air, Pulford was forced to withdraw most of his remaining, and fast diminishing, air-force as far south as Singapore Island. If he could no longer support ground operations, perhaps he could at least defend the naval base.

Swift and effective as had been the Japanese air victories, those on the ground were almost as complete. The Kota Bharu landing force, the first to go ashore, approached its target late on the night of December 7th. On board three transports, accompanied by a cruiser, four destroyers, and three other escort vessels, were nearly 6,000 men of the 18th Division. This force — called the Takumi Detachment — was built round Major General Hiroshi Takumi's 23rd Infantry Brigade Headquarters and the 56th Infantry Regiment. A few hours earlier, the escort commander had informed Takumi that weather and beach conditions were suitable for landing.[11] But as the convoy neared the target area, the sea grew dangerously rough. When the ships finally dropped anchor some twenty minutes before midnight, the wind had increased sharply, a heavy swell was running, and the waves were topping six feet. But now there was no turning back.

Meanwhile, on shore the men of Brigadier Berthold Key's reinforced 8th Indian Brigade were thinly spread to defend the thirty miles of beaches and the three airfields in the Kota Bharu area. Numerically they were probably no weaker than the Takumi Detachment, but their difficult mission to hold the airfields and, if possible, prevent an enemy landing, required deployment beyond their means. Making the best of a bad situation, Key concentrated the bulk of his troops round the airfields and placed beach defence forces at the most likely landing points. Mobile patrols and reserves would have to take care of weak or unoccupied points. Fixed positions along the beaches north and east of Kota Bharu included heavy barbed-wire fences with, every 1,000 yards, concrete machine-gun pillboxes surrounded by mines. South of this area, however, only dummy pillboxes and an occasional barbed-wire barricade awaited the enemy.

A few minutes before midnight, the three Japanese transports began lowering landing craft. In the high seas and heavy winds the small boats swung violently in the water, alternately pulling away from the side of a ship and crashing loudly against it. The soldiers, weighed down with equipment, ammunition, and awkward life-jackets, were hard pressed to climb down swinging ropes and nets in the darkness and jump into the heaving landing-craft. Many of the men were tossed into the sea when the rough waves capsized their boats. Then a single 18-pounder gun on the beach opened fire. The Japanese destroyers answered, and the fight for Kota Bharu was under way.

In these extreme conditions, it was a while before the first assault wave could get organised and begin to move shoreward. To the further consternation of the Japanese, the strong current pulled the boats away from the planned landing area. Efforts to correct this drift only brought confusion and scattered the assault wave. Finally a battalion commander decided to make the landing as best he could, and the rest of the craft followed him in. At about 12.45 a.m., the first boats touched down on the beaches north-east of Kota Bharu, just at the point where Key's defences were probably strongest.

Takumi's men concentrated their attack on two pillboxes that dominated the beach. Moving carefully across the sand, they were slowed down by artillery, mines, and the determined small-arms fire of a battalion of Dogras troops. Finally they managed to break through the barbed-wire and get close enough to the pillboxes to overwhelm them. The surviving defenders, according to a Japanese account, 'dispersed deep into the coconut groves like little spiders routed by mosquitos'.[12] It had taken three hours, and some sharp losses, but the Japanese had now gained a solid foothold on the Malayan shore. Troops of the second landing wave — delayed in coming ashore by the rough seas, and then forced to huddle under punishing artillery fire on the open beaches until the first break-through — now fanned out quickly as they moved in.

The third and last wave was further delayed by the arrival of British aircraft. Beginning at about 3 a.m., Hudsons from Kota Bharu airfield made repeated bombing and strafing runs over the Japanese transports and landing craft. They scored hits on all three of the large vessels, setting fire to Takumi's headquarters ship and badly damaging the others, and killed at least fifty soldiers. So fierce was their attack that the naval escort commander wanted to withdraw without landing the remaining troops Takumi refused; and not until nearly dawn, with only part of the third wave ashore and his own ship beached, did he relent. Under strong aerial attack the escorting warships and the remaining transports now beat a hasty retreat to the north.

Ashore there was still heavy fighting. The determined Indian defenders tried several counter-attacks, while the Japanese continued to press inland toward the Kota Bharu airfield. Daylight also brought punishing Japanese air-strikes, both on the airfield and on ground positions. Key threw in more of his reserves, committing practically his entire force, but the enemy* pressure slowly began to tell. As the ebb and flow of battle seeped inland during the late afternoon, it appeared that Japanese troops were about to overrun the Kota Bharu airfield. Before this could be fully checked, someone on the air staff obtained Air-Vice-Marshal Pulford's permission to abandon the field. Buildings and supplies were set aflame and a full evacuation began. By the time Brigadier Key would discover, by means of a personal reconnaissance, that the danger had been greatly over-estimated, it was too late. Aircraft and personnel had already left. But in the haste and confusion of the evacuation, stocks of bombs, torpedoes, and gasoline were left intact for the advancing Japanese.

By now it was about seven in the evening. Despite the growing darkness, Key could see that the Japanese transports had returned. Fearful that his hard-pressed forward troops would be cut off and overwhelmed, he decided to fall back on Kota Bharu, a movement which General Barstow had already authorized if necessary. In pitch blackness and during a heavy downpour, the 8th Brigade troops withdrew from their forward defences, struggled across streams and through swamps, crossed the airfield, and with remarkably few losses made their way back to new positions. They even managed to set fire to the gasoline stores at the airfield, and it was this blazing sight that greeted General Takumi's men when they occupied the field after a brief fight around midnight.

By dawn of the 9th, the Takumi Detachment had in effect achieved its initial objective, the capture of a beachhead and the Kota Bharu airfield. The primary reason for deploying British forces in north-east Malaya had vanished in little more than twenty-four hours.

The events of the next few days were anticlimactic. With all of his force ashore and supplies and equipment being rapidly landed, Takumi pressed ahead. Key, in turn, with his flanks in the air and in constant danger of being cut off, was forced to fall back. Despite the arrival of a battalion of Hyderabad troops from Percival's command reserve, he could do little to reduce the growing threat. The frequent presence of Japanese planes overhead, and the obvious fact that the remaining two airfields in the Kota Bharu area, some twenty miles south of the town, could no longer be utilised by British planes, further impressed on him the futility of trying to hold an untenable forward position. Although he had exacted a relatively heavy toll of casualties from the enemy during the initial fighting, and although the slowly withdrawing Indian troops continued to inflict losses on their attackers, the situation could hardly continue indefinitely. The 8th Brigade was at the end of a long and extremely vulnerable line of communication. Japanese air-strikes could easily cut the single-line railway running south. Nor was there anything to prevent Takumi from sending flanking elements to Key's rear as the fight moved inland. On the 11th, with all three airfields in Japanese hands, General Barstow recommended to Heath that the 8th Brigade should break contact with the enemy and quickly move about 100 miles south to positions covering the first road that gave access across the mountains to western Malaya.

Heath passed this recommendation on to Percival. Concerned about the threat to Key's communications, and even more about growing dangers elsewhere, the Malaya commander, with Brooke-Popham's approval, reluctantly authorised withdrawal. Key then extricated his forces in a difficult and bloody action. Takumi, more concerned with moving down the coastline than with advancing further inland now that he held the airfields, did not follow vigorously. By the 22nd, Key's brigade, weakened by losses in men and equipment but still in good shape, was in position at Kuala Lipis. The Takumi Detachment had suffered heavily – some fifteen per cent of the 56th Infantry had been killed or wounded – but it had gained a significant victory. All of north-eastern Malaya was now in the hands of General Yamashita.

The success of this attack was easily matched by the Twenty-fifth Army's main assault on the Kra Isthmus.[13] The landings at Singora and Patani had been hampered by seas no less violent than those at Kota Bharu. But otherwise they were unopposed, and soldiers of the 5th Division began going ashore within two or three hours of the Kota Bharu assault early on December 8th. Yamashita himself landed at Singora in the pre-dawn hours. Thai constabulary troops offered brief resistance in both towns but this was quickly and easily overcome and by afternoon Japanese forces were advancing down the Singora-Jitra and Patani-Kroh roads. At the same time, planes of the 3rd Air Group swiftly moved into the captured Thai airfields, just in time to drive off a hit-and-run raid by R.A.F. bombers from Alor Star. Further north, the Fifteenth Army was easily succeeding in its invasion of Thailand and the Imperial Guards Division was approaching Bangkok on its long overland march to Malaya.

Meanwhile, thanks to the confusion about *Matador*, it was mid-afternoon before troops of the 11th Indian Division crossed the border on their delaying mission into Thailand. A mechanised column – two reinforced Punjab companies of the 6th Brigade riding Bren-gun carriers – moved up the Jitra-Singora road, a small infantry-engineer detachment in an armoured train crossed the border to the north-west, while Krohcol attempted to seize the Ledge position on the road to Patani.

The column from Jitra drove without difficulty about ten miles into Thailand before stopping at dusk to set up a defensive position. A few hours later, advance Japanese 5th Division elements, an armoured reconnaissance detachment under Lieutenant-Colonel Shizuo Saeki, blundered into these defences. Good shooting by the Indian anti-tank crews knocked out the three leading Japanese tanks, while machine-gunners sprayed the 5th Division infantrymen as they jumped down hastily from their trucks. But Saeki's troops quickly recovered. Soon Japanese riflemen were working their way around the Punjabis' flanks and mortar shells began bursting with increasing accuracy on the main position. In the face of this pressure by an obviously superior force, the British commander gave the order to withdraw. His men managed to extricate themselves from the fight and retreated southwards, destroying three bridges before crossing the border about ninety minutes after midnight. At roughly the same time, the armoured train detachment re-crossed the frontier after an unopposed advance nearly half-way to Singora to blow up a major railway bridge.

The first encounter between British and Japanese forces in Thailand had thus left Yamashita's troops with something of a bloody nose – as well as several important bridges to repair. But the 5th Division had been well rewarded for its efforts. In a bloodstained armoured car on the Singora-Jitra road, Japanese soldiers had discovered a large-scale map of the Jitra area with 11th Division positions clearly pencilled in. It was a far better map than anything the Japanese had and, of course, they were 'extremely happy' to learn the details of the Indian

H.M.S. *Prince of Wales*
in Singapore harbour

Admiral Sir Tom Philips
and Rear Admiral
Palliser *(left)*

H.M. Ships *Prince of Wales* (*upper*) and *Repulse*, after being hit by Japanese torpedoes off Kuantan. A British destroyer is in the foreground

The crew of the *Prince of Wales* abandoning ship as she sinks

defences.[14]

One other bloody action would be fought on the Thai side of the border. Delays in assembly had forced Krohcol to begin its mission with only about half its planned force. Nevertheless, a battalion of Punjab troops set off up the Patani road for the Ledge as soon as the order to advance arrived from General Murray-Lyon. Hardly had it crossed the frontier when it came under heavy small-arms fire from a force of Thai constabulary. The Thais, some 300 strong, fought from behind a series of road-blocks and held their position so well that Krohcol could advance barely three miles before it had to halt for the night. The Thais maintained harrassing fire during the darkness, and it was mid-afternoon of the 9th before the Punjabis could drive off this unexpected opposition and push forward with any speed.

Not until the morning of the 10th, then, could Krohcol get anywhere near the Ledge. And by then it was too late. An advance mechanised force of the Japanese 42nd Infantry Regiment had rushed south from Patani, covering more than twice the distance that Krohcol had, and brought the Indian troops to a halt about three miles short of their objective. Attempts to outflank the Japanese during the afternoon were unsuccessful, and it was soon apparent that the enemy tank/infantry force was more than a match for the unsupported Krohcol infantry. By nightfall, two Punjab companies had been cut off and the rest of the force pushed back nearly ten miles toward the border. Only the destruction of a bridge prevented the Japanese armour from exploiting their advantage.

Krohcol somehow held on during the 11th. One of its lost companies managed to fight its way back; the other had been wiped out. As more and more 42nd Infantry troops reached the battle, Krohcol's position became so clearly precarious that Murray-Lyon authorised a withdrawal. On the 12th, under renewed Japanese pressure, what was left of the force fell back toward the border. The other half of Krohcol had by now arrived and taken up position on the Thai side of the frontier. It was here that the battered Punjabis finally found refuge. The next day the entire force was back in Malaya.

Thus ended the initiative of British forces in the opening phase of the battle for Malaya. The brave but futile efforts of a few small bodies of Indian troops, and the equally courageous and abortive endeavours of Pulford's airmen, were the only manifestations of the bold plan called *Matador*. The unwillingness of British authorities to give Brooke-Popham full power to implement this plan, and the Far East commander's own failure to interpret his limited authority in a more aggressive and imaginative manner, killed whatever chances of success the plan might have had.

Prohibited from committing any unprovoked act of war, and confused by the imprecision of his orders and, apparently, by his own fatigue, Brooke-Popham missed a golden opportunity to slow down or seriously hinder the Japanese invasion. By delaying *Matador* until it died of its own inertia, he allowed Yamashita to establish beachheads at Singora and Patani, to bring forward his vital air support and thus hasten the defeat of British air power, to beat III Corps troops to the important Ledge position, and, indirectly, to gain easy control of Kota Bharu and all of north-eastern Malaya. Worst of all, by his indecision he kept General Murray-Lyon's troops in a state of uncertainty and, as will be seen, left them so off-balance that they would be unable to stage an effective defence of north-western Malaya.

Now it is probably true that *Matador* was at best an extravagent hope, that given British air and ground weaknesses, Brooke-Popham's forces had little chance of holding any gains they might achieve and stood, indeed, a good risk of being destroyed in forward positions. Yet had *Matador* been launched early enough, who can say what might have followed? Japanese plans called for a delay in the Kota Bharu assault, if not in the Singora-Patani landings, in the face of aggressive British action. These postponements, in turn, would have given Air Marshal Pulford additional time to prepare his defences and, in fact, to mount his own attacks. Perhaps the outcome would have been the same. But the cost to the Japanese might well have been higher.

It is not inconceivable, either, that early implementation of *Matador* might have denied the Japanese their most impressive victory of the war. On December 3rd, President Roosevelt had told Ambassador Halifax that the United States would back *Matador* with armed support. Had Brooke-Popham initiated *Matador* on the 6th or even the 7th, those to the east of the International Date Line would have had an additional day or two of warning. Given the American committment, is it unreasonable to assume that in these circumstances the forces at Pearl Harbour would have been more alert?

NOTES

1. The basic sources for this chapter are: Brooke-Popham, *Despatch*, pp. 555-57; Maltby, *Report*, pp. 1363-68; Percival, *Despatch*, pp. 1267-74; Malay Operations Record, pp. 24-27, 38-42; Southwest Area Air Operations, pp. 45-50; Malaya Invasion Naval Operations, pp. 11-24; Kirby, *The Loss of Singapore*, pp. 180-93,

217; Percival, *The War in Malaya*, chap. viii; Gillison, *Royal Australian Air Force*, pp. 199-226, 243-45; Richards and Saunders, *The Fight Avails*, pp. 15-23; Wigmore, *The Japanese Thrust*, chap. viii.

2. Brooke-Popham, *Despatch*, p. 555. But cf. Gillison, *Royal Australian Air Force*, p. 200.

3. Brooke-Popham, *Despatch*, p. 555.

4. Richards and Saunders, *The Flight Avails*, p. 17.

5. Arthur Bryant, *The Turn of the Tide* (Garden City: Doubleday, 1957), p. 225; Major-General Sir John Kennedy, *The Business of War* (New York: Morrow, 1958), p. 183.

6. One squadron-leader's account appears in Okumiya and Horikoshi, *Zero*, pp. 96-98.

7. Morrison, *Malayan Postscript*, p. 47. For other eyewitness accounts, see Glover, *In 70 Days*, chap. v; O.D. Gallagher, *Action in the East* (Garden City: N.Y.: Doubleday, 1942), pp. 84-87; Brown, *Suez to Singapore*, pp. 287-88.

8. Text in Brooke-Popham, *Despatch*, App. M.

9. Percival, *Despatch*, p. 1269.

10. Brooke-Popham does not mention this message in his report, but the request is described in a radio message sent that evening by Adm. Palliser to Adm. Phillips, and is itself quoted in Vice-Adm. Sir Geoffrey Layton, *Despatch; Loss of H.M. Ships Prince of Wales and Repulse*, Dec. 17, 1941, Supplement to the *London Gazette* of February 20th, 1948, p. 1244. For MacArthur's bomber losses, see Craven and Cate (eds.), *The Army Air Forces*, I, 210-14.

11. Malay Operations Record, p. 40. For the action at Kota Bharu, see also Tsuji, *Singapore*, chap. xv; K.D. Bhargava and K.N.V. Sastri, *Campaigns in South-East Asia, 1941-1942*, Official History of the Indian Armed Forces in the Second World War, 1939-1945 (Calcutta?: Combined Inter-Services Historical Section, India & Pakistan, 1960), pp. 121-38; Arthur Swinson, with Major Tokuji Morimoto and Muysuya Nagao, The Conquest of Malaya, *History of the Second World War*, Eds. Captain Sir Basil Liddell Hart and Barrie Pitt (8 vols. London: Purnell & Sons, 1966-1969), II, 797-98; Compton Mackenzie, *Eastern Epic* (London: Chatto & Windus, 1951), Vol. I, pp. 236-40; Hattori, *The Great East Asia War*, II, 26.

12. ATIS, Malaya Campaign, p. 7.

13. Tsuji, *Singapore*, chaps. xiii-xiv; Bhargava and Sastri, *Campaigns in South-East Asia*, pp. 139-58; Mackenzie, *Eastern Epic*, I, 244-53; Hattori, *The Greater East Asia War*, II, 25-26.

14. Tsuji, *Singapore*, p. 91.

5

A Swarm of Ants

The initial successes of General Yamashita, in seizing a foothold for the Twenty-fifth Army, and of General Sugawara, in crippling British airpower, were matched by an even more striking Japanese victory at sea. This triumph was achieved by Admiral Matsunaga's 22nd Air Flotilla at the expense of Admiral Phillips' Eastern Fleet.

Phillips had returned to Singapore from Manila late on December 7th. The news that greeted him, about the approaching Japanese convoys, removed any doubts he might have had; the main reason for bringing *Prince of Wales* and *Repulse* to Singapore – to deter Japanese southward aggression – had vanished. The enemy landing at Kota Bharu a few hours later and the subsequent air raid on Singapore reinforced this conviction. The only question still unanswered was what to do with the small but valuable and potent naval striking force under his command.[1]

Earlier messages from London had suggested that it might be safer for the *Prince of Wales* and *Repulse* to leave Singapore, at least temporarily, and Phillips had agreed with this view. Indeed, he had only delayed acting upon it in order to talk with Admiral Hart. On his return to Singapore, however, he found this Admiralty message: 'On assumption that Japanese expedition in South China Sea on course indicating invasion, report what action would be possible to take with naval or air forces'.[2] This wording hardly indicated that the Eastern Fleet was to shun a fight; on the contrary, it implied offensive action. Phillips now felt the same way, especially since the invasion had become an actuality.

Whatever his earlier and more prudent thoughts, it was now clear to him that he had no choice. The arrival at Singapore of the *Prince of Wales* and the *Repulse* and their accompanying destroyers had been the occasion for a great celebration. In addition to the large official reception party – including many reporters and photographers – that assembled at the naval base, thousands of people from the city and from the little fishing villages up and down the Strait of Johore had gathered near the water to greet the battle fleet that had arrived at last to defend them. The two great warships, serenely powerful as they swept into the harbour, brought to the cheering crowds a sense of relief and satisfaction. 'With what mingled emotions we watched', recalled one observer. 'These strange grey shapes on the skyline, they were symbols of our new-found strength, concrete expressions of the confidence with which we faced any emergency that might arise. . . .'[3] Many a British soldier shared this view. 'Whatever doubts we might have had of our ability to hold Malaya were now set at rest'. These impressive vessels 'were somehow a symbol of absolute security'.[4] Admiral Phillips well understood the effect of his arrival.

Having come so far with his fleet, and having raised such great expectations amidst so much publicity, Phillips could hardly even consider not making an attempt to halt the Japanese. Nor could warships of His Majesty's navy stand aloof when British soldiers and air-forces were engaged in what would surely be a life-and-death struggle. Despite the lack of balance in his force – the absence of an aircraft carrier or of adequate screening or support elements – and the fact that Air-Vice-Marshal Pulford could offer him little cover, it seemed to Phillips, in the words of Admiral Layton, 'inacceptable to retain a powerful naval force at Singapore in a state of inaction.'[5]

Phillips was neither a rash man nor a fool. An able and brilliant officer, clear-headed and careful, he was aware of the dangers awaiting him no less than of the strong call of duty that impelled him to risk them. Despite his small size – which earned him the nickname of 'Tom Thumb' – he was self-assured and not afraid to make hard choices. His decision on December 8th was based on a calm and realistic appraisal of the situation he faced.

Sometime that morning Phillips learned definitely that the Japanese were landing at Singora and Patani. His immediate thought was to make a hit-and-run raid with his powerful striking force on the vulnerable enemy transports and invasion fleet. He had little fear of Japanese warships. From all indications the enemy had half a dozen or more cruisers and a score of destroyers in the area, but only one capital ship, the old battleship *Kongo* (actually a World War I battle-cruiser), and Phillips was confident that his heavier guns and armament, and superior speed, gave him an edge over the Japanese surface force. He felt less easy about the submarines that he was sure the Japanese had deployed to protect their invasion. But by steering a course to the east of the Anamba Islands, some 200 miles north-east of Singapore, he hoped to avoid most of the subs and outrun the rest. This course would also reduce the risk of detection and by-pass whatever minefields the enemy might have laid across the passage between Malaya and the Anambas.

Japanese airpower posed the greatest threat. Admiral Phillips, however, had always been a strong believer in the ability of heavy warships to withstand high-level bombing attacks, especially if their anti-aircraft weapons were numerous and well-manned. He was aware that torpedo planes were a more dangerous anti-ship weapon, but he felt that well-trained gun crews and reasonably strong fighter protection could thwart even the most vigorous torpedo-plane attacks.[6] Indeed, thought Phillips, if his luck held, he might even be able to approach the Japanese anchorages unobserved. In that case, there was small chance that enemy torpedo planes would be in the area, or that Japanese aircraft flying cover there would be carrying armour-piercing bombs. A quick strike and a hasty retreat might allow Phillips' warships to escape before the Japanese could throw together anything in the way of a retaliatory air-strike. Even if surprise were impossible, if Air Marshal Pulford could somehow provide him with fighter cover, Phillips might still execute his attack without taking too much of a beating.

It was of course a very risky proposition. The chance of discovery was high and the danger of a bloody repulse too obvious to ignore. Yet the possible reward was equally great. Destruction of the Japanese invasion force — even if Phillips sacrificed his own fleet to this end — would be a major accomplishment. It would delay the enemy long enough for Malaya to prepare for the next Japanese blow, long enough perhaps even for the successful implementation of *Matador*. It would provide time in which reinforcements could arrive. It might, indeed, be crucial to the successful defence of Singapore. In these circumstances the risk seemed to be worth taking.

The most important question, on which almost everything rested, was whether or not Pulford could provide the desired air support. And it was this point that Phillips stressed on the morning of the 8th in a conference in Brooke-Popham's office. He told the Far East commander that he hoped to sail that evening and take the Japanese by surprise at Singora at daylight of the 10th. To ensure success he needed three things: 1. Air reconnaissance for 100 miles ahead of his fleet as he made his approach, beginning at dawn of the 9th. 2. Air reconnaissance to Singora and beyond it, beginning at first light on the 10th, while he made his final run-in. 3. Fighter cover off Singora at daylight on the 10th, during and after his attack. Brooke-Popham said he would pass. this on to Pulford. Phillips returned to the *Prince of Wales* to discuss the plan with his senior officers.

He talked with them in the cabin of his flagship after lunch. The group included his chief of staff, Admiral Palliser, Captain John Leach of the *Prince of Wales* and Captain William Tennant of the *Repulse*, and a number of others. After describing his plan and the risks involved, Phillips asked for their opinions. There was a short pause. Then Tennant spoke up to support the plan and the others quickly added their agreement. Phillips told them to get ready to sail. He himself would see what decision had been made on air support.

With Palliser, Phillips went to Air Headquarters to see Pulford. The Air Marshal had studied Phillips' earlier request, but was hardly in a position to offer any encouragement. He could promise reconnaissance on the 9th ahead of the fleet. Beyond that he was doubtful. The reconnaissance on the 10th would have to be made by Blenheims based at Kuantan. But the punishing Japanese air-strikes on the 8th had already done great damage to Malayan airfields, and more blows could be expected, so there was no way of telling whether or not Kuantan would be operational on the 10th. Nevertheless, Pulford said that he hoped to be able to give Phillips the reconnaissance that he wanted on that day.

Fighter cover, however, was out of the question. The Brewster Buffaloes were short-range planes. To support the fleet at Singora, they would have to fly from the northern airfields, but these were already either untenable or out of action. Flying from southern fields, they would not be able to remain over Singora longer than a few minutes, and their limited numbers meant that patrols could cover the fleet only intermittently. Pulford would do what he could, but it was impossible to guarantee any really useful fighter protection.

Phillips was clearly disappointed by this answer, so Pulford agreed to think the problem over again in hope of coming up with some more satisfactory solution. Phillips intended to leave Palliser ashore in charge of his headquarters and Pulford promised to give the chief-of-staff a definite answer later. By now it was after 4 p.m. and the fleet would have to sail soon if it was to clear the Anambas by daylight on the 9th. Phillips hurried back once more through the damp heat of the Singapore afternoon to the *Prince of Wales*.

As the ships made their final preparations to depart, a number of the more senior officers were seriously concerned about the fate of their mission. The news of the Japanese attack on Pearl Harbour, coupled with the uncertainty of air protection for their own fleet, seemed to magnify the already evident risks of their venture. Captain Tennant and Captain Leach, while still firm in support of Phillips' plan, confided their apprehensions to each other as they shook hands in solomn farewell. On shore, Admiral Layton was also quite disturbed. He had apparently even tried to talk Phillips out of going. If so, he was the only one to make this attempt. Everyone else seemed possessed by 'a sense of unreality and fatalism'.[7]

The fleet sailed at 5.35 p.m. It left quietly with no fanfare, in marked contrast to the noisy celebration that had greeted its arrival less than a week earlier. Phillips had heard nothing further from Pulford so, just before *Prince of Wales* cast off, he sent the air-vice-marshal a personal note, stressing the importance of fighter protection and asking for an answer as soon as possible. But by now Kota Bharu airfield had been evacuated, the other northern airfields were hardly capable of supporting offensive action, and British air strength had been crippled. If Pulford had once entertained any hope of providing cover, which seems doubtful, it was gone. As the ships passed the Changi signal-station at the eastern end of Johore Strait, Pulford's reply was flashed across the water: 'Regret fighter protection impossible'. Phillips shrugged. 'Well', he said, 'we must get on without it'.[8]

In the wardroom of the *Repulse*, an American war correspondent and a British one were drinking pink gin. A messenger entered and tacked a notice from Captain Tennant on the bulletin board, addressed to the ship's company. 'We are off to look for trouble', it began. 'I expect we shall find it'.[9]

Darkness fell as the ships pushed north-east into the South China Sea, and welcome cloud-cover began to drift across the sky. Moving steadily at the moderate speed of seventeen knots, they were a far cry from the great battle fleet envisioned by Jellicoe two decades earlier. They totalled but six vessels, known collectively as Force Z.

The heart of the force was *Prince of Wales*, a graceful, impressive — indeed majestic — fighting machine. Less than ten months old when she reached Singapore, she embodied some of the latest concepts in battleship design. Approximately one-third of her 35,000 ton displacement consisted of stout armour-plating, including 6-inch steel on her decks and a 16-inch waterline belt, and she boasted extensive and ingenious bulkheading to prevent flooding — all of which helped earn her the nickname. 'H.M.S. *Unsinkable*'. The weight of her armour held her speed to 28½ knots; as fast, nevertheless, as any British battleship in her class, and much faster than the rest.

Her guns and their arrangement probably provided the most novel, as well as questionable, touch about the warship. She carried ten 14-inch guns in two four-gun turrets, fore and aft, and a two-gun turret above the forward main turret. An aft two-gun turret, originally planned, had been ruled out because of the heavy weight of the ship's armour. It was hoped that the high muzzle-velocity and rate of fire of the 14-inchers would make up for their relatively small bore — small, that is, for a battleship — but there was considerable doubt about the efficiency of her newly designed turrets. Indeed, failure of these to operate properly had nearly finished the warship during her first battle. In the fight with the *Bismarck* in May 1941, mechanical difficulties had put several of her big guns out of action within a few minutes. Thus weakened, she was forced to withdraw after destruction of the *Hood*, and had to return to a shipyard for hasty turret modification.

There was nothing questionable about her anti-aircraft armament. Sixteen new 5.25-inch rapid-fire guns could reach at least 30,000 feet into the sky against high-level attacks and could hit low-level targets nearly thirteen miles away. And for dealing with enemy planes closer in, there were eight groups of eight 2-pounder pom-poms, and a mass of 40-mm. and 20-mm. guns and light machine-guns. The number and power of her anti-aircraft guns, and her heavy armour, left few in doubt of the ship's ability to withstand air attacks.

Unhappily for the *Prince of Wales*, however, she had never had a proper shake-down cruise. She had gone off to fight the *Bismarck* before she was really even completed — more than 100 civilian workers still aboard had been forced to sail with her — and then she was pressed into service almost as soon as she was battleworthy again to carry Winston Churchill across the Atlantic. She gained fame, admiration, and the nick-name 'Churchill's Yacht' as a result of this journey, but she lost the opportunity for 'working up'. Nor did she ever regain it. After escorting a vital Malta convoy, she was assigned to Admiral Phillips' Eastern Fleet and sailed for Singapore, still without having had time for training, drills, and gunnery practice. This seriously impaired her efficiency as a fighting unit.

Repulse did not share this weakness. A veteran of World War I, however, she suffered from having been designed for another era. She was a battle-cruiser rather than a battleship, intended not to slug it out toe-to-toe with a heavily-armoured enemy, but to dash swiftly through the sea, striking instantly and then departing, depending on speed and firepower for her protection. Battle-cruisers carried little side armour and almost none of their decks. *Repulse*, despite two attempts to increase her protection, was hardly different from others in her class. Built at a time when no one had any serious worries about air attacks, she lacked thick deck armour. This was a serious deficiency against long-range plunging fire. Against enemy bombers it could be equally disastrous.

Repulse's best advantage lay in her speed, which, despite her age, was still half a knot faster than that of the *Prince of Wales*. Compared with Phillips' flagship she was longer and slimmer and, with far less armour, she displaced no more than 26,500 tons. Only in her main batteries was she heavier: six 15-inch guns in three two-gun turrets, two forward, the other aft. She also carried twelve 4-inch guns and, in a throw-back to her original rôle as a high-speed hit-and-run attacker, eight torpedo tubes. For anti-aircraft defence, she had far lighter and fewer weapons than the *Prince of Wales*. She mounted only half a dozen obsolete 4-inch A.A. guns and a handful of lighter weapons. These inadequate defences and her thin deck armour left *Repulse* highly vulnerable to air attack.

The four other ships in Force Z were destroyers. Two of them, the *Express* and the *Electra*, had come from England with the *Prince of Wales*. They were good ships, built in the mid-thirties, and if they carried slightly lighter weapons than equivalent Japanese or German destroyers, they had nonetheless proved their effectiveness in arduous North Atlantic duty. The two other destroyers that had reached Singapore on December 2nd needed repairs and were both unavailable for Force Z. Phillips therefore substituted *Vampire*, a twenty-year-old Australian destroyer which had been refitting at Singapore, and *Tenedos*, a small, even older destroyer with a limited fuel capacity that restricted her range and endurance.

There was a handful of other destroyers and light cruisers at Singapore; these were either unavailable, or so old and small that Phillips felt he would be better off without them. In any event, he planned to use the accompanying destroyers only until the night of the 9th, when they would return to Singapore. Sustained action at high speeds would quickly exhaust their fuel, a limiting factor of destroyer operations at any distance from base. So the *Prince of Wales* and the *Repulse* would make the final dash into Singora alone, depending on surprise and the weight and range of their heavy batteries to wreak great havoc among the enemy transports and escort vessels.

The success of this attack depended in large part on the availability of fighter cover at Singora. But Phillips had already received Pulford's discouraging reply. And about an hour before midnight on the 8th a message from Admiral Palliser came in with further details. First of all, reconnaissance on the 9th was still available, but it would be undertaken by only a single Catalina. It was still 'hoped' that a dawn reconnaissance could be carried out near Singora on the 10th, but 'fighter protection on Wednesday, 10th, will not, repeat not, be possible'. Palliser added the discomforting news that the Japanese had large bomber forces in southern Indo-China and possibly Thailand, that Kota Bharu airfield had been evacuated and the military position near there did not seem good, and that 'we seem to be losing grip on other northern aerodromes. . . .'[10] The odds against Force Z had lengthened appreciably. Yet Phillips still retained the single advantage of surprise, and until he lost it he would press on.

Force Z rounded the Anamba Islands at dawn on the 9th and headed north. Phillips was now well out into the South China Sea, away from the probable search areas of Japanese planes protecting the invasion. This course took him closer to the Indo-Chinese airfields than might have been prudent, but he hoped it would increase his chances of remaining undetected. He noted with satisfaction that the sky was still dark with low clouds. Short, frequent rain-showers swept the ships, further reducing visibility and hiding them from hostile aircraft or submarines. Phillips signalled a long message to all ships, outlining his intentions and listing tactical instructions. A separate message to the ships' companies of the *Prince of Wales* and the *Repulse* summarized the situation in encouraging tones. It was an 'opportunity . . . to surprise the enemy' before he could 'establish himself'. The two ships might 'have the luck to try our metal' against *Kongo* and smaller warships, and gunners were 'sure to get in some useful practice' with their high-angle anti-aircraft weapons. 'Whatever we meet', concluded Phillips, 'I want to finish quickly . . . So shoot to sink'.[11]

At about 6.20 a.m. someone on the *Vampire*, peering through the rain and misty clouds, got a brief glimpse of a distant aircraft. The plane, if it actually was one, disappeared quickly. Possibly it was Dutch. In any event, the odds against it having seen Force Z were great, and Phillips decided to ignore it. A second plane appeared much closer shortly after noon. 'Action stations' was sounded, but this time the plane was definitely friendly. It was the reconnaissance Catalina promised by Pulford. It swooped low over the *Prince of Wales* and flashed a message that the Japanese were landing troops north of Singora.

The weather continued bad and Phillips pressed ahead, confident that a lucrative target awaited him. But at about two o'clock his luck ran out. Japanese submarine *I-65*, at the end of a patrol line extending eastward from Malaya, spotted Force Z steaming north through the rain. Phillips was unaware of this, but his apprehensions heightened around 5 p.m. when, only an hour or so before dusk, the storm clouds suddenly disappeared, the sky turned blue, and a bright sun illuminated the western horizon. Then, as if to meet a scheduled appointment, a tiny speck appeared in the northern sky. The speck approached and revealed itself as a Japanese naval float-plane. It disappeared and then returned, accompanied by another. The two remained out of range, indeed just barely in sight, watching and reporting on Force Z. The radio officer on the *Repulse* could hear their signals.*

Admiral Phillips knew that he had now lost all chance of surprise. The Japanese amphibious force at Singora could easily scatter during the night and, what was worse, every Japanese surface ship, submarine, and aircraft in the area would be looking for him. He was not afraid of attack, although without fighter cover he might have some difficulty beating off air strikes. But was there any point in risking Force Z for a sortie into an empty anchorage? Clearly there was not. Despite his disappointment, and the disappointment that he knew would be felt by his officers and crews, Phillips had no choice except to turn back. It was frustrating, annoying, and almost embarrassing to be forced to withdraw by a couple of float planes. Yet withdrawal was entirely proper. The junior officers and the men might disagree, as they did, but the support for Phillips' decision was all but unanimous among his captains and other dejected senior officers.

It is not clear just when Phillips made this decision. At 6.30 p.m. he sent *Tenedos* back to Singapore. This was according to plan, since the old destroyer was at the limit of her range. But that afternoon Phillips had given *Tenedos* a message for Admiral Palliser, to be radioed at 8 a.m. on the 10th, when the ship was well away from the main force. This message stated that Phillips was not likely to pass the Anambas until 6.30 a.m. on the morning of the 11th and that all available destroyers should come out to meet him. There was nothing in the message indicating that he had cancelled his attack. And the only message received in Singapore at the time *Tenedos* would have been sending was simply taken to mean that Force Z would return earlier than originally planned.[12]

After despatching *Tenedos* on the evening of the 9th Phillips continued north with the rest of the fleet. At 7 p.m., he altered course to the north-west, towards Singora, and increased his speed to 26 knots, according to his original plan. Not until 8 p.m., when darkness had fallen completely and screened the ships from the shadowing Japanese

* Some sources indicate that there were three planes, but the weight of evidence would seem to indicate three *sightings*, but only two planes.

planes, did Phillips flash word to Captain Tennant on *Repulse* that the raid on Singora had been cancelled, and that they would return to Singapore. Force Z continued north-west for fifteen minutes, to ensure deceiving the Japanese, and then turned south, slowing to 20 knots to conserve the destroyers' fuel.

The wisdom of this decision was confirmed a few hours later by a message from Palliser, who, of course, was unaware of Phillips' change of plan. The message confirmed earlier reports that more Japanese had gone ashore at Kota Bharu, which, said Palliser, should now be as 'fruitful' a target as Singora. But the chief-of-staff also pointed out that heavy concentrations of Japanese bombers in southern Indo-China 'could attack you five hours after sighting, and much depends on whether you have been seen today'. Two aircraft-carriers were also suspected to be near Saigon, the Japanese held Kota Bharu airfield, all British fields in northern Malaya were becoming untenable, and Brooke-Popham had hinted he was considering concentrating all air efforts on defence of the Singapore area.[13]

This news was certainly ominous. But what Phillips could not know nor Palliser tell him was the extent of the Japanese build-up aimed at Force Z. This powerful concentration could not be avoided for much longer.[14]

A week earlier, when the *Prince of Wales* and the *Repulse* reached Singapore, the decision to move additional Japanese naval air strength to Indo-China rather than to increase Admiral Kondo's surface forces was made by no less a personage than Admiral Isoroku Yamamoto, commander in chief of the Japanese Combined Fleet and one of the foremost advocates of naval air-power. It was he who fathered the plan to attack Pearl Harbour and then forced its adoption against the better judgment of most of the naval general staff. And it was he who for years had argued that warships could never be a match for aircraft. Someone once asked him how he expected to sink a battleship except with a battleship. 'With torpedo planes', answered Yamamoto. And then he quoted an old Japanese proverb: 'The fiercest serpent may be overcome by a swarm of ants'.[15] Yamamoto's ants would soon have their chance against Force Z.

In December 1941, Japan's naval pilots were among the best in the world. Years of sustained, vigorous training, enhanced by combat experience in the war with China, had produced a corps of skilled, dedicated veterans. Their weapons were equal in calibre to the men who employed them. The planes were effective fighting machines, especially the newly-developed Zero fighter with its great range, manoeuvrability, and punch. The light torpedo-planes and bombers were also ideally suited to the slashing, aggressive tactics favoured by the Japanese navy. And the powerful, long-range, oxygen-powered torpedoes were not only better than those of the Allies, but could be dropped from a great height and at higher speeds than British and American naval officers believed possible. The Japanese naval air force, then, was formidable and, unhappily for its enemies, underestimated.[16]

Admiral Matsunaga's 22nd Air Flotilla began intensified combat-training in southern Formosa in mid-1941. The exercises concentrated on both land and sea targets, but they took into special account the obvious fact that British and American vessels were likely to be better defended than the Chinese shipping the Japanese were used to attacking. Other Japanese naval air units, preparing to hit the Philippines (including those squadrons later to be shifted to the Malayan operation), were undergoing similar training in Formosa.[17] The result was an extremely high level of combat effectiveness.

On the eve of war, Admiral Matsunaga had established his headquarters at Saigon, and his aircraft at two fields close to the city. By this time, the reinforced 22nd Air Flotilla included the Genzan and Mihoro Air Groups, each with forty-eight twin-engined medium bombers ('Nells'), and the newly attached Kanoya Air Group, with twenty-seven late model twin-engine medium bombers ('Bettys'). All 123 planes could carry either bombs or torpedoes, but none was equipped with radar for night operations. In addition, the 22nd Air Flotilla also included 36 Zero fighters and nine 'Babs' reconnaissance planes.[18]

Ever since the arrival of *Prince of Wales* and *Repulse*, Matsunaga's reconnaissance planes had been making daily flights over Singapore and the waters nearby to pinpoint the location of the two warships. Every pilot well understood that if these great vessels could depart unseen, they might easily catch Japanese invasion forces by surprise and smash them in the space of a very few minutes. Indeed, the whereabouts and movements of the ships 'were of grave concern to all forces engaged in the initial landing operations'.[19] Admiral Ozawa's escort forces and Admiral Kondo's screening units all knew that *Prince of Wales* and *Repulse* were their main concern and primary target. Even before the start of hostilities, on the night of the 6th, a Japanese mine-layer placed nearly 500 mines across the passage between Malaya and the Anamba Islands, while a dozen submarines took position in these waters and near the eastern entrance to Singapore Strait.[20] Everything was aimed at preventing Admiral Phillips from interfering with the landing of the

Twenty-fifth Army. Had Phillips gone to sea on the 7th, Admiral Matsunaga would have cancelled his raid on Singapore that night in favour of finding and sinking *Prince of Wales* and *Repulse.*

On the afternoon of December 8th, a single Babs flew high over Singapore and then returned to Saigon to report that the two British warships were still at anchor. Matsunaga's staff was surprised at this news, but there was general satisfaction that the landing operations were free from the threat of immediate interruption. A reconnaissance flight on the 9th failed to note that Force Z had departed. Instead, the pilot radioed that he could still see the *Prince of Wales* and the *Repulse* at the Singapore base. So Matsunaga called a staff-conference to discuss ways and means of destroying the ships in their berths. So long as they remained afloat, they were a menace to the Japanese beachheads and lines of communication. If they would not leave their base, then the 22nd Air Flotilla would have to attack them where they were.

But even as Admiral Matsunaga was convening his meeting, the submarine *I-65* patrolling at periscope depth about 150 miles north of the Anambas made an important contact. Just before 2 p.m. on the 9th, Commander Harada, the submarine's captain, saw two distant objects under a low-lying rain cloud. As he watched, they grew larger, and soon he could see two great ships heading north, one behind the other. He could not clearly identify the first, although it was obviously a formidable capital ship, but the other he easily recognized as the *Repulse.* Harada tried to manoeuvre for an attack, but a sudden fierce rain-squall all but wiped out visibility. When it had passed, the enemy ships were gone. *I-65* surfaced and flashed a report.

Had Commander Harada's message reached Admiral Matsunaga immediately, the 22nd Air Flotilla might have been able to attack Force Z on the 9th. As it was, someone in the submarine force chain of command was dubious about the report. Just before three, he radioed Harada that air reconnaissance had located the British warships still at Singapore. Was Harada certain of his identification? Harada replied immediately: 'Number one ship is a new type of warship and there is no mistake in the number two ship being the *Repulse*'.[21] Thus assured, Harada's superior passed the initial report on to Saigon. But it was 3.40 p.m. before it reached 22nd Air Flotilla headquarters.

Here too it provoked questions. By now, Matsunaga had decided to launch an immediate attack against the ships he believed to be still sitting in the Singapore naval base. The Nells and Bettys were armed with bombs and were just about to take off when Commander Harada's report finally arrived. On the assumption that the submarine captain had seen some sort of heavy warship, even if not the *Prince of Wales* and the *Repulse*, there was now a serious threat to the landing operations. Matsunaga therefore ordered the bombs to be unloaded and replaced with torpedoes. Even as the ground crews hastened to carry this out, the aerial photographs from the Singapore reconnaissance flight were being developed. The prints showed that the Babs crew had mistaken two large cargo vessels for the *Prince of Wales* and the *Repulse*. The British warships were clearly at sea and heading for the landing areas.

While the 22nd Air Flotilla prepared to attack, a number of other activities were taking place — all focused on the movements of the *Prince of Wales* and the *Repulse*. First of all, a warning was sent to General Yamashita that his beachheads might come under attack that night. Transports were ordered to weigh anchor at sunset and disperse to the north.* At the same time, Admiral Ozawa, with the heavy cruiser *Chokai* and a destroyer, was hastening to intercept Force Z, while an even stronger element of his escort forces — four heavy cruisers and three destroyers under Vice-Admiral Takeo Kurita — was steaming rapidly with the same aim. Two submarine squadrons, with their light cruiser flagships, were also on the move toward the target area. And from his position east of Indo-China, Admiral Kondo was rushing south with the battleships *Kongo* and *Haruna*, two heavy cruisers, and a destroyer screen for a rendezvous with Ozawa's units. In the morning, a co-ordinated attack of the 22nd Air Flotilla and all Japanese surface units would fall upon the *Prince of Wales* and the *Repulse*.

Several of Ozawa's cruisers launched float-planes, for the admiral hoped that these aircraft and the submarines could relocate and maintain contact with Force Z during the night. Part of his hope was realised when a plane from Kurita's flagship and another from one of the light cruisers discovered the British ships in the South China Sea, about 200 miles east of Kota Bharu. Both planes, however, lost Force Z in the growing dusk, nor do their contact reports appear to have reached Admiral Matsunaga. So their success was of little use to the Japanese; all it did was to warn Admiral Phillips, who made the wise decision to give up his raid on Singora.

Had Phillips not changed course when he did, Force Z might have run into a hornet's nest of Japanese cruisers and destroyers. Between 7 and 8.15 p.m., as he made his high-speed dash toward Singora, Phillips was barely out of sight and range of the majority of Ozawa's

* For some reason, only those at Singora did so. (Malay Operations Record, p. 25.)

units – although he had apparently lost the tracking float-planes. And at the moment he turned south, the light cruiser *Yura* was less than fifty miles ahead to the north-east.

No one can say what would have happened if Phillips had met the *Yura*, or if Ozawa or Kurita had joined battle with him. Presumably the heavy guns of the *Repulse* and the *Prince of Wales* would have taken their toll of the lighter Japanese ships. Yet it was getting dark, and a night action is always difficult. Given the relative lack of training of the crew of the *Prince of Wales*, it is not at all certain that British gunnery would have overwhelmed the enemy. The Japanese crews, on the other hand, were well trained, especially in night combat. The five heavy cruisers in the area were fast and strongly armed, and their 8-inch guns, necessarily firing at long range, could drop a punishing, plunging fire onto the thin deck of the *Repulse*. Finally, the Japanese destroyers and both heavy and light cruisers carried the deadly 'Long Lance' torpedoes, with remarkable killing power at speeds and ranges that far exceeded Allied estimates. Later, in the first two years of the war, Japanese warships firing these potent 'fish' in night actions would inflict heavy losses on Allied (mainly American) vessels. Had a naval battle occurred on the night of December 9th, in the South China Sea, the odds would hardly have favoured Force Z. They might, indeed, have been on the other side.

The Japanese plan for a co-ordinated air/sea attack on Force Z in the morning did not deter Admiral Matsunaga from trying to end matters himself on the evening of the 9th. Despite the lengthening shadows of the afternoon, four reconnaissance planes took off at 4.30, to be followed in an hour or so by thirty-three strike aircraft, fifteen carrying torpedoes and the rest armed with bombs. The pilots were faced not only with the rapid approach of darkness, but also by increasingly difficult weather. Flying along the Indo-Chinese coast, they soon encountered heavy, low-lying clouds, and rain, that forced them to break their normal squadron formation and to continue in groups of three. Some of the planes flew above the clouds, hoping for a break in the grey mist through which they might spot Force Z. Others made their difficult way through the storm, while the rest flew beneath the clouds, at less than 1,000 feet, accepting the limited visibility imposed by the rain and their low altitude in the hope that luck would bring them directly over the British ships or across their wake.

But by now several hours had passed since *I-65* had flashed its contact report. Force Z had changed both course and speed. And with darkness closing in, there was less and less chance that Matsunaga's pilots would find their blacked-out targets. Those who could make out anything below them through the rain and gloom saw 'only the dull, weird glitter of the sea'.[22]

To make matters worse, no pilot had any idea where the Japanese warships might be. And in the fast-fading light, the chance of mistaking one of Ozawa's units for a British vessel was a growing and frightening possibility. A Nell from the Mihoro Group dropped a flare over what seemed to be an enemy ship, only to discover that it had illuminated *Chokai*, Admiral Ozawa's flagship. Fortunately for the admiral, the pilot discovered his error and radioed a warning before any of the others could attack.

It was now completely dark. Soon Admiral Matsunaga sent out a recall message, and the weary disappointed flyers headed home. They still faced the difficult and dangerous task of landing on a blacked-out airfield with a full load of armaments. But at least the weather had cleared. A three-quarter moon was due to rise soon and the planes circled the field until the landing strip grew visible in the welcome moonlight. It was close to midnight before all aircraft were down. Ground crews immediately began preparing the planes for the morning's attack. Matsunaga ordered the pilots to get some sleep, but they were too excited to do anything but join in the preparations and make plans. They realised that before they could attack Force Z, they would first have to find it.

Meanwhile, Admiral Phillips and his ships were well on their way south. At their present speed they would pass the Anamba Islands at about dawn and turn for the last leg of their homeward voyage. But unknown to both Phillips and the Japanese, events had taken place that afternoon and evening that would change all this.

Late in the afternoon, a Hudson on a reconnaissance flight off the south-east Malayan coast reported sighting a transport and a group of barges moving toward Kuantan. Alerted by this, at about 7 p.m. troops of the 22nd Indian Brigade thought they detected the approach of small boats toward their beach positions north of Kuantan. Soon others along the shore reported hostile activity, and before long small-arms and artillery fire opened up against what appeared to be a Japanese landing attempt. Word of this reached Percival and Brooke-Popham at about 10 o'clock. Half-an-hour later, Admiral Palliser radioed the information to Phillips that the Japanese were 'reported landing Kuantan'.[23]

Phillips received Palliser's message at about midnight. He at once recognised that a Japanese landing at Kuantan, where an important access road led westward across Malaya, could be extremely dangerous. If the landing was in force, the enemy might well be able to outflank and even cut off a large portion of General Percival's army. At the very least, the Japanese capture of Kuantan would place them less than 200 miles from Singapore; uncomfortably close by land, and within minutes by air. But Kuantan was not too far out of the way for Phillips. By changing course to the south-west and putting on a little speed, he could be off Kuantan by early morning and catch the Japanese in just the same sort of awkward position in which he had hoped to trap them at Singora. He would certainly have the advantage of surprise, since the last Japanese to see him — the float-planes, early in the evening — had observed him heading rapidly toward Singora. The enemy could have no way of knowing that dawn would find Force Z some 200 miles to the south.

There were, of course, risks. Kuantan was not much further from the Japanese air bases in Indo-China than Singora. So if there had been danger of air attack on Force Z at Singora, it was hardly much less at Kuantan. And Phillips knew that the enemy capture of Kota Bharu airfield had provided an even closer base for Japanese planes. Still, the element of surprise would weigh more heavily here than it would have at Singora, and with a little luck he might strike and quickly escape without too much damage. Kuantan was also within range of British fighters based at Singapore. It would not be unreasonable to expect Air-Vice-Marshal Pulford to send support for the Kuantan defenders. And in any event, as Phillips explained to his staff, he assumed that Admiral Palliser, having informed him of the reported landing, would expect Force Z to head straight for Kuantan and would make sure that fighters were there to meet them.

At 12.52 a.m. on the 10th Phillips changed course toward Kuantan and increased his speed to 25 knots. This would bring Force Z to the threatened area at daylight. Phillips did not radio to tell Palliser his intentions lest this should reveal his position to the Japanese, who presumably still thought him to be heading for Singora. He simply assumed that air support would be there. This assumption was to be his undoing.

Actually it would have made little difference if Phillips had broken radio silence, for barely ninety minutes after he turned towards Kuantan a Japanese submarine found him. At a point just west of where Commander Harada had made the original sighting, *I-58* was nearly run down by the fast-moving British warships. Thus far south, the submarine commander had no doubt that they were the enemy. He fired five torpedoes, but in the darkness they all missed their speeding targets. *I-58* promptly surfaced, sent off a contact report to Saigon, and set out in pursuit. In the haste and uncertainty of the sudden night encounter, the submarine commander mistakenly reported Phillips' course as southerly instead of south-westerly, an error he never bothered to correct. For three quarters of an hour *I-58* attempted vainly to keep up with Force Z, but the best speed of the submarine was still too slow, and its quarry finally disappeared just after 3 a.m.

The damage was done, however. Admiral Matsunaga's ground crews hastened their work, while the pilots could hardly contain their impatience for daylight. Admiral Kondo, meanwhile, had completed his rendezvous with Oɀawa's units and was heading south with a sizeable force of warships. On the basis of *I-58*'s report, he concluded that Force Z was heading back to Singapore; he was unaware of any Japanese landing attempt south of Kota Bharu that might attract Phillips' attention. Kondo accordingly ordered the 22nd Air Flotilla and all submarines to attack and destroy Force Z as soon as possible. He himself had no chance of catching the enemy. He cruised south until daylight and then broke off the pursuit.

At Kuantan, meanwhile, firing had ceased at 2 a.m. The Indian defenders could see no one to shoot at, and there was no return fire. At 4 a.m., half a dozen Vildebeestes arrived. They found nothing but three small boats, which they dutifully bombed. Three Hudsons reached the scene a little later and could discover no targets whatsoever. By dawn it was clear that no landing had taken place, and it seems highly unlikely that any was even attempted. A few bullet-ridden boats carrying Japanese equipment turned up a few days later on the beaches to the south as evidence of possible enemy patrol activity. But they might have drifted down from further north and, in any event, Japanese reports fail to mention even a reconnaissance effort so far south.[24]

As dawn was revealing the doubtful nature of the supposed enemy landing at Kuantan, half a world away Winston Churchill was holding a meeting in the Cabinet War Room. It was late in the evening of December 9th in London, and Churchill and the others, mostly Admiralty officers, were discussing the events of the opening days of war in the Far East. The American losses at Pearl Harbour and the Philippines meant that the *Prince of Wales* and the *Repulse* constituted the only major force left between the Japanese and Australia and New Zealand. The two big ships had been sent to Singapore as a deterrent. Obviously they had failed in this mission and were now highly vulnerable. Their best course, it seemed to all those present, was to leave Malayan waters, and vanish out of sight and range of the powerful enemy. Possibly, suggested Churchill, they should cross the Pacific and join the crippled American fleet. But by now it was approaching midnight, so the meeting adjourned, postponing any definite decision until morning. By then there would no longer be a need for any decision.[25]

Bedtime for Churchill was morning in the Far East, and dawn found Force Z rapidly closing on the Malayan coast. If Admiral Phillips had hoped for more bad weather to shield him, he was disappointed. Daylight brought a clear, grey sky which, when the sun rose at 6 o'clock, was soon filled with a brilliant golden glow. Half an hour later, a plane appeared far ahead in the bright eastern sky. Watchers took it to be Japanese, although it seems to have been one of Pulford's Hudsons, making a last search for an enemy landing force.[26] In any event, it was quite distant and soon disappeared. At about 7.30, the *Prince of Wales* catapulted off a reconnaissance plane which found no sign of any Japanese, either aloft or in the sea. Half an hour later Force Z was about ten miles off Kuantan, close enough to spot any invasion force that might be present. But there was still nothing to be seen 'except green in the foreground, and the mountains rising in the back-ground'.[27] As the ships moved along the coast, Phillips sent the destroyer *Express* toward the shore for a closer look. At about 8.45 *Express* was back, flashing a report on her Aldis lamp. 'All's as quiet as a wet Sunday afternoon', it read.[28]

Phillips needed no further proof. A short while later he ordered course to be altered to the east. Then Captain Tennant on the *Repulse* flashed a suggestion. Just after dawn, Force Z had passed at extreme range what seemed to be a small tug towing a few barges or junks. Anxious to get to Kuantan as soon as possible, Phillips had ignored these. But they could well have been landing boats, and Tennant suggested having a look. Phillips agreed and ordered another shift in course. *Repulse* launched a search-plane to keep watch for submarines.

It was after 9.30 by now and Admiral Matsunaga's flyers had been busy for several hours. *I-58*'s mistaken estimate that Force Z was going south would place Phillips some fifty miles beyond the Anambas by dawn, at his reported speed. Since this would put the British warships within four or five hours of Singapore, they would have to be found and attacked as early as possible. At about 5 a.m., as soon as there was enough light to take off by, nine Babs left the Saigon field to begin the search for Force Z. In order not to miss their target, they were to cover a huge sector of ocean, as far south as Singapore and extending well to the east of the Anambas. Each plane carried two small bombs.*

Since it might be several hours before the Babs located Force Z, the bombers and torpedo-planes would have to be airborne when contact was made — otherwise the enemy vessels might reach the relative safety of Singapore before their attackers could hit them. At 6 o'clock the striking force began taking off. First to leave was the Genzan Group: two squadrons of Nells (totalling seventeen planes) armed with torpedoes, and a squadron of nine Nells, each carrying a 500-kilogramme bomb. Then came the Mihoro Group, four squadrons of eight Nells each; one squadron with two 250-kilogramme bombs per plane, two squadrons of one 500-kilogramme bomb per plane, and the final squadron armed with torpedoes. Last off the ground were the twenty-seven Bettys of the Kanoya Group, organised into three torpedo squadrons. Altogether, the three groups totalled eighty-five aircraft: fifty-two torpedo planes and thirty-three bombers.

The striking force flew south along the 105th meridian, which approximately bisected the passage between Malaya and the Anamba Islands, ready to swing off in either direction when the Babs ahead of them reported a contact. They maintained an altitude of between 8,300 and 10,000 feet, with their fuel mixture set at its leanest to stretch their precious gas supply as far as possible. This was particularly critical for the torpedo planes, since the added weight of their armament reduced the amount of fuel they could carry by nearly a third. Unlike previous flights, this one had perfect weather conditions: a clear, bright sky with only a few tufts of white clouds scudding occasionally far beneath the planes. The men were in equally bright spirits, despite the tiring demands of the two previous days and their lack of sleep. If the excitement of the moment was not enough, before departing they had heard inspiring speeches by everyone from Admiral Matsunaga all the way down to their squadron leaders. And then they had taken off to the resounding cheers of the ground crews. Now, as they hastened toward their prey, their emotions were at the highest. Their less spiritual appetites they would satisfy with tasty *ohagi* — rice cakes coated with bean paste — and coffee syrup, a standard air force ration.

For several hours the planes flew south. But there was no sign of Force Z, only the limitless expanse of blue sea.[29] The Genzan Group, in the lead, was now well past the Anambas, and the pilots were becoming increasingly concerned about their fuel. They set their

---

* Sources differ as to the exact number of planes in both the reconnaissance force and the striking force described below. The figures used here seem to have the most support.

mixture controls even lower, to cut consumption to the absolute minimum. This lean fare was inadequate for one of the torpedo-planes, which promptly developed engine trouble and had to break formation and turn back. The others went on. Then at about ten o'clock, off to the left, a small ship appeared, a cargo vessel or perhaps even a destroyer. It was, in fact, the *Tenedos*, on the last leg of her return voyage to Singapore. This was hardly the quarry the Japanese were seeking, but the third Genzan squadron, the bombers, dropped out of the mass formation and swung over the *Tenedos*. The little destroyer promptly changed course and began a twisting evasive action. To the surprise of the watching torpedo-plane pilots, the bombers suddenly dropped their loads. Nine 500-kilogramme bombs hurtled down – and all missed their zig-zagging target. The bombers, having so obviously wasted their effort, could only turn and head for home. The Genzan Group now totalled only sixteen torpedo planes. These continued south. The pilots could make out the lower tip of Malaya, far ahead to the west.

A few minutes later, just as all three groups of the 22nd Air Flotilla were altering course to fly north again, the crews were electrified by a message from one of the Babs reconnaissance pilots, an ensign named Hoashi. At 10.15 a.m. he had sighted Force Z some forty miles east of Kuantan, heading approximately east-north-east.* The striking force immediately turned toward this position.

At about 10 o'clock, Admiral Phillips had heard from the *Tenedos* that enemy aircraft were in sight, and a few minutes later that the destroyer was under attack. Neither of these messages was received in Singapore, but they did alert Phillips to the presence of Japanese bombers only 140 miles away from him. At 10.15, he shifted course to the east, increased speed to 20 knots, and ordered the anti-aircraft gunners to action stations. *Repulse* launched a second reconnaissance plane. In the distance, far out of range, Ensign Hoashi's Babs could be seen from time to time, carefully shadowing Force Z.

A few minutes later, radar on the *Repulse* picked up approaching aircraft to the south. At 11 o'clock eight Japanese bombers came into sight, flying at about 10,000 feet.† Phillips altered course to the south-east and increased speed to 25 knots. Force Z sped forward, the

* His contact report is incorrectly quoted in some sources.
† British sources state that there were nine bombers, but the Japanese number, eight, seems more reliable. Sources disagree as to the numbers of planes and their unit designations in each of the attacks on *Repulse* and *Prince of Wales*. Figures and units given in the following descriptions seem to me the most reasonable.

three destroyers forming the head of an arrow to which the *Prince of Wales* with *Repulse* behind her, formed the shaft. Action stations sounded at 11.07.

Aboard both big ships, and the destroyers as well, the tension was extreme. The force had been at sea for nearly two days now, dashing back and forth through the South China Sea, with missions changed and changed again, without ever having come to grips with the enemy. The first brave anticipation of action at Singora had been replaced by disappointment when the raid was cancelled, then by a bold hope when Phillips shifted toward Kuantan, and then by frustration again when no enemy appeared. The men had sweated and grown weary in the tropical heat below decks, their fatigue increased by the rise and fall of tension, as action appeared imminent or not. Now there was no longer any doubt that they would have their fight. Everywhere you could 'almost feel the electricity'.[30]

The approaching bombers were a squadron of the Mihoro Group armed with 250-kilogramme bombs, which had been the nearest Japanese planes to Force Z when Ensign Hoashi discovered it. They flew high in a tight line abreast, from a point ahead and to starboard of the British ships. At 11.15, the high-angle anti-aircraft guns opened fire, breaking the silence with a chattering deafening roar and spotting the sky around the bombers with angry black puffs. To those in the planes, the shells seemed to 'burst without leaving a bit of free space'.[31] Not a single Nell escaped being hit. On they came, nevertheless, their formation unbroken as they bore down on the *Repulse.* Then, simultaneously, they released their bombs.

From the *Electra* nearby, watchers could see the falling bombs and their impact when they hit:

> It was the most impressive pattern we had ever seen. It horrified us, destroying all misconceptions in its thunder, for in that brief instant *Repulse* had disappeared, had disappeared completely, in a forest of cascading bomb-bursts which, merging together, were replaced in seconds by a giant wall of water. It was a fantastic, near-incredible spectacle. . . .[32]

Moments later they cheered as the *Repulse* dashed clear of the cascading sea with black smoke rising from her deck, yet otherwise apparently no worse for the attack. Most of the bombs had overshot her, but not by much, falling close beyond her port side. One dropped just short of her starboard side. A single bomb had struck amidships, destroying the aeroplane catapult and exploding below on the armoured deck under the Marines' mess. There were some casualties, but no serious damage, and the flames were extinguished in little more than ten minutes. Force Z rushed ahead.

Ideally for the Japanese, the torpedo-planes should have struck while the attention of the British gunners was focused on the high-level bombing attack. But by the time Ensign Hoashi reported seeing Force Z, Admiral Matsunaga's squadrons were scattered over a wide area. They all flew toward the British ships, each group of planes attacking as it arrived on target. The result was a series of unco-ordinated strikes.

At about 11.30 the two torpedo squadrons of the Genzan Group reached the scene. Surprised to find no British fighter planes, they took their time organising attack formations. Finally, after what seemed to watchers aboard Force Z an incredibly long delay, the assault began. Just after 11.40 a squadron of nine planes emerged from a small cloudbank ahead and began its long approach dive on the port side of the *Prince of Wales.* Splitting into groups of three, the Nells seemed to be attacking from several angles. On they came, oblivious it appeared of the heavy wall of fire from every piece of anti-aircraft armament that could be brought into action. As they dropped their torpedoes, Captain Leach turned the *Prince of Wales* toward her attackers, to present a narrow target and, perhaps, pass between the oncoming torpedoes. Most of these did, in fact, go harmlessly by. But one, or more probably two at the same time, struck the giant warship on her port quarter, exactly where she was most vulnerable.

A tremendous explosion shook the stern of the vessel. A huge column of water shot up, and a cloud of black smoke arose. The blow crippled the rudder and jammed the port propeller shafts. Under the pressure of the explosion and the force of its own power, the outer shaft snapped and bent back, slicing a jagged hole in the hull of the ship. Then, free of the drag of the propeller, it raced faster and faster until it clogged and tore apart the machinery that drove it. Tons of water entered the gaping hole, flooding the already shattered engine-room and drowning the jammed machinery.

The great battleship listed thirteen degrees to port, and her speed dropped almost instantly to fifteen knots. She could no longer steer. She had no power for her after 5.25-inch anti-aircraft guns. Much of her internal communication system was out, and radio and radar no longer functioned. Counter-flooding brought the ship up a degree or two from her list, but it was clear that the *Prince of Wales*, in an incredibly brief time, had been crippled. Leach gave the order to hoist two black balls, the international signal for 'not under control'.

The attack on the *Prince of Wales* should have been accompanied by a simultaneous strike at the *Repulse* by the remaining Genzan torpedo squadron. But the squadron-leader hesitated, struck by the fear that the ship beneath him was not the *Repulse* at all, but rather the Japanese battleship *Kongo*. 'The narrow escape of the *Chokai* from our bombers last night was still fresh in my memory', he wrote later,[33] and he carefully checked the warship before finally ordering the attack. Convinced at last that it was indeed the *Repulse*, at about 11.55 he led his seven planes in a steep dive on the port side of the battle-cruiser. Captain Tennant held his course until the attackers appeared to have committed themselves. Then, while his anti-aircraft gunners fired unceasingly, he ordered the wheel to be put over sharply. *Repulse* turned toward her assailant, slewing around at high speed, still spitting fire at the planes, and raced between the tracks of the torpedoes. The underwater missiles flashed by, leaving a white trail as they passed close to the surface. The *Repulse* was unharmed, but the strafing guns of the Nells had stitched her deck and killed several of the crew.

But still the *Repulse* had no respite. Barely had the ship succeeded in 'combing' the Genzan torpedoes than a squadron of eight Mihoro bombers attacked her. They came in the same line-abreast formation that their sister squadron had flown earlier, with the same apparent indifference to the heavy volume of anti-aircraft fire thrown up at them. They dropped their deadly loads with equal co-ordination, but this time just a bit too soon, as the squadron-leader accidentally tripped his bomb release prematurely. The bombs were close, nevertheless; but Tennant manoeuvred his ship skillfully and avoided them all. This was fortunate for the *Repulse*, since these were 500-kilogramme bombs, powerful enough to smash through the thin armour of the battle-cruiser's deck. A hit would have been far more damaging then the earlier blow by a lighter bomb.

Again there was no time for self-congratulation. Out of the east came another Mihoro squadron, this time eight torpedo-planes. As they dropped their missiles, Tennant once more skillfully whipped the *Repulse* around to face them and his gunners hurled a steady barrage of shells and bullets at the charging Nells. Fragments from the bursting projectiles lashed the surface of the sea like hundreds of pebbles hurled by a giant hand. One plane blew up, but the others seemingly impervious came on spraying the decks with machinegun fire. Again Tennant was successful in dodging the torpedoes, and the big ship raced safely between their tracks.

By now it was almost noon, and for a moment there was a lull in the battle. Taking advantage of this interlude, Tennant attempted to signal the *Prince of Wales* but could get no coherent answer by Aldis lamp, and none at all by radio. Fearing that Admiral Phillips had lost the use of his radio, Tennant checked with his own signals staff to find out what intercepts they had of any messages sent by the *Prince of Wales* to Singapore. When he learned that Phillips had not sent any, he understood for the first time why no British planes had arrived to help them. Quickly he sent off an emergency message: 'Enemy aircraft bombing'.[34] This reached Singapore at 12.04 and was rapidly passed to Air Headquarters. Eleven Buffaloes, which had been standing by specifically to provide cover for Force Z if needed, took off a few minutes later. But it would take some time to reach the scene of action, and by then it would be too late.[35]

Even as the Buffaloes were leaving Singapore, the end was approaching off Kuantan. The *Repulse*'s manoeuvres had taken her some distance from the crippled but still moving *Prince of Wales*, so Captain Tennant steamed closer to get a better look at the flagship's damage. At about 12.20, when he was some 800 yards off the *Prince of Wales*' starboard quarter, a flight of nine Bettys appeared low on the horizon, off his own starboard bow. This was a torpedo squadron of the Kanoya Group, which had finally arrived on the scene. The planes approached rapidly and, at a distance of three miles, split into two groups, about half the Bettys turning slightly left toward the *Repulse* and the rest continuing on toward the *Prince of Wales*. Tennant swung his ship to starboard just as the first group released torpedoes nearly a mile and a half away, and he could soon tell that he had again succeeded in placing the *Repulse* between the oncoming tracks. He glanced over at the other planes which seemed to be heading straight for the *Prince of Wales*, now off his port quarter. Just as they came even with the *Repulse*, however, they suddenly swung left, drove straight at her, and dropped their torpedoes at a range of about 2,000 yards.

Whether this 'scissor-like movement' – as one observer put it[36] – was a cleverly-planned manoeuvre, or simply developed by chance when the Bettys attacking the *Prince of Wales* discovered she was already crippled, it proved to be extremely effective. Having committed himself to meeting the first attack head on, Tennant was broadside to the second batch of torpedoes. 'It now became obvious', he wrote the next day, 'that, if these torpedoes were aimed straight, *Repulse* would be most certainly hit'. Any change in course to avoid them 'would have caused me to be hit by the tracks of those torpedoes I was in the process of combing'.[37] With no choice, he grimly watched the torpedoes streaking toward his port beam, and saw that one would obviously find its mark. 'Stand by for torpedo!' the loudspeakers blared.[38] For a minute and a half the deadly missile ran its course. Then it struck amidships. There was a shock and a loud explosion, a fountain of water engulfed the decks, and men everywhere went sprawling. But there seemed to be little damage. Manoeuvring with no difficulty, the *Repulse* raced ahead at 25 knots.

The *Prince of Wales* was not so fortunate. Immediately behind the first Kanoya squadron came a second, nine more torpedo planes loosely grouped. They did not alter their course but drove straight at the flagship's starboard side and dropped their torpedoes. It would have been difficult for all to miss the limping, rudderless target. Three torpedoes crashed home. The first struck well forward, the second exploded almost simultaneously under the stern, jamming the outer starboard shaft in much the same way as the port shafts had been crippled. There was a moment's delay before the third torpedo hit, just under the forward two-gun turret, tearing open the hull. The *Prince of Wales'* speed fell immediately to a mere eight knots. The weight of water running into her starboard side served to balance the earlier list to port. The ship sat almost level now, but, despite the effectiveness of her internal bulkheading, she was beginning to settle noticeably in the stern.

It was approximately 12.25. Barely five minutes had passed since the first Bettys had come over the horizon. Now it was the turn of the third and last Kanoya squadron; the last Japanese squadron, indeed, still armed with torpedoes. This time the Bettys did not attack in a single wave. Splitting instead into three groups, they slashed at the speeding *Repulse* from all sides, like wolves trying to pull down a fleeing deer. Captain Tennant could hardly hope to escape them all, but he did his best, twisting and turning the heavy ship in a skidding dance. His navigating officer relayed each order to the quartermaster in a calm but loud voice, all but drowned by the incredibly heavy roar of the anti-aircraft batteries. The gun crews attempted to fire at the nearest attacker, ignoring those planes that had already dropped their torpedoes, no matter how close they flew or how vulnerable they appeared.

These valiant efforts were not enough. The first torpedo missed, but the second found its mark on the port side near the stern, jamming the rudder. The *Repulse* continued to steam at well over twenty knots, but she was no longer under control. The gunners had a momentary revenge as first one Betty exploded in a ball of fire and then another 'burst into flames and, trailing a long ribbon of smoke, skimmed over the bow of the ship and crashed'.[39] A great roar of approval rose from the crew, more a 'last defiant gesture'[40] than a cry of victory, for already the sloping deck revealed that the *Repulse* was beginning to list. Then in quick succession came three more torpedoes, the first on the port side aft, the second abreast of the port engine-room, and the last on the starboard side well below the waterline. The ship leaned heavily to port and Tennant 'knew now that she could not survive'.[41]

The decision to abandon ship is a hard one for any captain to make. But Tennant felt certain that the *Repulse* had only a few moments left, and he could not delay. Just before 12.30 he ordered everyone on deck, and to prepare to abandon ship. Fortunately for the crew, the loudspeaker system was still functioning well, and almost immediately men began to pour up from below, some carrying wounded. They moved quickly, yet with no sense of panic or confusion, reflecting a disciplined coolness almost incredible in the desperate circumstances. Already the deck was tilted at an alarming angle, the bodies of dead and wounded sliding grotesquely among the empty shell cases. A great ugly cloud of dark smoke rose skyward.

When the list was about thirty degrees to port, Tennant looked down from the bridge and saw a group of two or three hundred men assembled by the starboard rail. Impressed by their order and patience, he shouted words of encouragement. 'I told them', he later recalled, 'how well they had fought the ship and wished them good luck'.[42] Then he ordered everyone off the bridge, and a moment later followed them.

Now men were jumping, sliding, falling over the side of the ship, slithering down the *Repulse*'s slick hull, many slamming cruelly against the projecting bilge keel and snapping their bones. Of those who dived boldly into the oil-coated, debris-filled sea, some miscalculated their distance with dire results. One man leaped from the side only to fall through a gaping hole in the hull and back into the water-filled interior of the ship. Another jumped from high on a mast and smashed into the deck; while yet another dived almost directly down the still-smoking forward funnel. Those fortunate enough to reach the water were quickly covered with a slimy mess of oil and petrol that burned their eyes, clogged their throats and nostrils, and turned many into choking, retching, black-faced caricatures.

By 12.33 the ship was listing seventy degrees. Then she began to slide under, stern first, turning over on herself as she went. From the water, a swimmer could see the bow 'swing straight into the air like a

church steeple', its red underside standing out 'stark and ...
gruesome'.[43] Then the *Repulse* slipped beneath the water, taking many
of the crew down in a sucking, deadly whirlpool. Captain Tennant, still
aboard when his ship sank, went down with her, but somehow managed
to reach the surface. To the jubilant Kanoya pilots, watching from the
sky above, he and his fellow survivors appeared like countless floating
objects on a great yellowish-brown film of oil.[44]

Even before the *Repulse* went down, Admiral Phillips on the *Prince
of Wales* had flashed an order to the *Vampire* and the *Electra* to pick up
survivors. The Japanese planes, with barely enough fuel to return to
base, made no attempt to interfere with the rescue operations — nor,
fortunately, did any sharks. Soon the decks of both destroyers were
crowded with shocked, exhausted, oil-covered men, many of them
wounded, but all still maintaining the discipline of a well-trained crew.
Of the *Repulse*'s complement of over 1,300, nearly 800 were saved, the
majority by the *Electra*. To the *Vampire*, however, went the honour of
rescuing Captain Tennant.[45]

Meanwhile the *Prince of Wales*' radio had apparently regained
power — or, more probably, Phillips was flashing messages to his
destroyers to be relayed on. At 12.40, the War Room at Singapore
picked up this message from the *Prince of Wales* addressed to 'Any
British man-of-war':

EMERGENCY. Have been struck by a torpedo on port side. *Repulse*
hit by 1 torpedo. Send destroyers.*

From its contents, the message had clearly been composed earlier
and was delayed in transmission, either because of the necessity of
passing it on to a destroyer, or because of atmospheric conditions. The
next message received in Singapore, from Phillips, reached the War
Room at 1.04 p.m. and was a more appropriate reflection of conditions
at that time: 'EMERGENCY. Send all available tugs.' Not until 1.10
p.m. did the next message arrive, from the *Electra*: 'MOST
IMMEDIATE. H.M.S. *Prince of Wales* hit by 4 torpedoes. *Repulse* sunk.
Send destroyers.' Seconds later this came from Phillips: 'MOST

---

* This and the following messages are from Log of messages received in Singapore,
quoted in Lieutenant-Colonel P.K. Kemp, *Key to Victory* (Boston: Little, Brown,
1957), p. 205. Admiral Layton's report ignores this, and subsequent messages
similarly addressed, and states categorically: 'the only signal from the
Commander-in-Chief addressed to his base at Singapore' was that sent earlier by
the *Tenedos*; a statement technically correct but curiously misleading. (Layton,
Despatch, p. 1238. I am grateful to Commander Kemp, head of the British Naval
Historical Branch, for providing further information about these messages.

IMMEDIATE. H.M.S. *Prince of Wales* disabled and out of control'.

Even as the waves were closing over the *Repulse*, just after 12.35, the last Japanese squadron, nine Mihoro Nells with 500-kilogramme bombs, was approaching the *Prince of Wales* at about 10,000 feet. The planes came steadily, in the same tight parallel formation employed by the Mihoro squadron that had opened the attack on Force Z less than an hour and a half before. The *Prince of Wales* sat low in the water, limping unsteadily, the seas threatening to flow across her quarter-deck. At 12.41, her remaining 5.25-inch guns and pom-poms opened a scattered, ineffective fire at the high-flying formation. Three minutes later, the Nells released their bombs: another neat, accurate pattern to rival that dropped earlier on the *Repulse*. The bombs straddled the flagship, raising great fountains of water on either side of the stern, showering the deck with lethal steel fragments, and, with a hit on the port side amidships, starting a fire and killing men in the blast and flame. The stoutly armoured deck of the *Prince of Wales* shielded her from any significant damage; but she was doomed in any event. Her speed dropped to six knots, she was listing to port again, and the watching Japanese pilots saw her 'coughing up thick, rolling, black smoke' from her centre and stern.[46]

Neither Admiral Phillips nor Captain Leach was yet ready to admit that *Prince of Wales* was lost. At 12.50, Phillips flashed a message to the *Express*, then running close behind the flagship, telling the destroyer to radio Singapore to 'send all available tugs' to tow him home.* But he also directed the *Express* to come alongside for the wounded. By 1.05 p.m., the plucky destroyer was against the starboard side of the battleship, next to the quarterdeck, taking off casualties. At the same time, Leach ordered up from below everyone who was no longer needed to work the *Prince of Wales*, and these men too began to cross over to the *Express*.

The great battleship settled lower. More and more water flooded in through the gaping holes in her hull and it was apparent that even her stout interior compartments could not save her from the greedy sea. At 1.10, Leach gave the order to abandon ship. Those of the crew not already aboard the *Express* – or trapped helplessly in the *Prince of Wales*'s mutilated internal sections – now leaped or slid into the ocean in much the same way as the men of *Repulse* had made their escape. Lieutenant-Commander F.J. Cartwright, captain of the *Express*, kept his ship alongside the *Prince of Wales* as long as he dared. But as the

* This reached the War Room at 1.11 p.m. A similar request, from the *Electra*, came in six minutes later. (Both quoted in Kemp, *Key to Victory*, pp. 205-206.)

flagship increased her list to port, the starboard bilge keel came up under the *Express* and nearly capsized the little destroyer as she finally pulled away. While she made her escape, the great hull of the *Prince of Wales* turned completely over. Then, at 1.20 p.m., H.M.S. *Unsinkable* went down.

One of the last officers to leave the ship has told of seeing Admiral Phillips and Captain Leach standing on the bridge together at the very end. Neither made a move to leave his station. As the others hastened to safety, Leach waved to them and shouted, 'Good-bye. Thank you. Good luck. God bless you'.[47] And within a few moments Phillips and Leach and their proud ship ended their lives beneath the warm water. But in the twenty minutes from the time the *Express* came alongside until it was too late, most of the men escaped. Out of 1,600 officers and crew, nearly 1,300 survived.

Almost at the instant that the *Prince of Wales* went down, the squadron of Buffaloes arrived from Singapore. It was intensely quiet. The noise and excitement of battle had given way to a calm, almost simple scene as destroyers plucked men from the water. The Buffaloes were too late for anything except to see the departure of Ensign Hoashi, the man who had found Force Z that morning and who had remained to witness its end. His final reports confirmed for Admiral Matsunaga the fact that the *Prince of Wales* and the *Repulse* had actually been sunk, eliminating the need for a second attack. Now, having done his job well, Hoashi wisely fled at the sight of the approaching British fighters.

All that the Buffaloes could do was to provide belated cover for the rescue operations, circling low to watch the human flotsam being pulled from the sea. In a widely-quoted report, the squadron commander expressed his amazed admiration at the stout-hearted behaviour of the men in the water who, for the hour that he remained on the scene, displayed good spirits, waving at him, and 'cheering and joking, as if they were holiday-makers at Brighton'.[48] It has been suggested that what the author of this report mistook for a brave thumbs-up signal was actually the angry fist-shaking of frustrated men who had been under air attack for two hours without any assistance from their own air-force. Or that the survivors were too exhausted and too concerned about getting aboard a destroyer to do more than simply note, with gratitude, that the planes were British and not Japanese fighters, coming to machinegun them in the water. But the awed report of the Buffalo pilot was a stirring tribute to the 'indomitable spirit' of the Royal Navy, a single bright light in an otherwise black and tragic day for Great Britain. It did not lessen the shock of so great a defeat, but it may have made the pain a little more bearable.

It had taken the Japanese 22nd Air Flotilla just about two hours around midday on December 10th to sink the *Prince of Wales* and the *Repulse.* In so short a time, Admiral Matsunaga's fliers had destroyed the heart of the British Eastern Fleet, assured the safety of General Yamashita's lines of communication, and completed the destruction of the last Allied capital ships between San Francisco and the Middle East, thus clearing the south and south-west Pacific sea-lanes for Japanese troop and supply convoys.

The cost to the Japanese of this tremendous victory was insignificant. Three planes were lost, a fourth crash-landed in an Indo-Chinese rice paddy, two more came down safely despite heavy damage, and another two dozen sustained minor damage. Not surprisingly, it was the high-level Mihoro bombers, in their rigid line-abreast formations, that suffered the most hits. Yet, curiously enough, the unarmoured Nells, which lacked self-sealing fuel tanks, survived British fire better than the more modern Bettys of the Kanoya Group, to which two of the three lost planes belonged.

That the British anti-aircraft fire was heavy and persistent is testified to by the Japanese, who repeatedly stress the 'relentless' quality of the 'deadly barrage', the 'rain of fire' in 'a world of death too deadly to describe'.[49] Yet it seems to have lacked that deadly precision so vital to anti-aircraft defence.

In retrospect, however, this ineffectiveness is not too difficult to understand. The first torpedo attack on the *Prince of Wales* knocked out an important segment of her main anti-aircraft batteries, as well as her internal communications system. Centralised control of anti-aircraft fire, as well as much heavy firepower, was thus lost at the very start of the battle. Nor should the lack of gunnery practice by Leach's crew be overlooked. The efficiency and co-ordination so necessary for good shooting had never been achieved, and this lack played its part in the *Prince of Wales*'s inability to defend herself. The *Repulse* had well-trained gun crews, nor did she suffer the type of damage that weakened the *Prince of Wales*'s anti-aircraft defences. But her own anti-aircraft weapons were pitifully inadequate from the beginning. With the most skilled crews to serve them, she still lacked enough punch to beat off her attackers. Finally, it is not clear how many gunners, on both ships, were killed by Japanese machine-gun fire.

Admiral Phillips had been right in depreciating the danger from high-level bombers. Of the twenty-four Nells that actually dropped bombs on Force Z, only two scored hits, and neither of these did more than superficial damage. It was the torpedo-planes — Admiral Yamamoto's swarm of ants — that struck the lethal blows. And it was these assailants that proved the hardest for the British gunners to hit. The fifty-two torpedo planes that reached Force Z attacked from all angles and heights. British reports indicate that the Japanese dropped their torpedoes at a height of 300-400 feet, 'a height noticeably greater than we do'.[50] But it is clear from Japanese sources that this was not always the case and that many drops took place at altitudes of less than 100 feet above the water. In any case, these variations were confusing, and the higher-level drops came as a surprise. Furthermore, the Japanese released their torpedoes at greater distances — usually at least a mile from their target — and at higher speeds — between 150 and 190 miles an hour — than could either British or American torpedo-planes. Whatever training and practice the anti-aircraft gunners had undergone had not prepared them for this, and adjusting to these differences proved difficult. That at most ten torpedoes (about twenty per cent of those dropped) actually hit their targets — a proportion below Japanese standards[51] — is less a tribute to defensive marksmanship than to adroit ship-handling.

A more important consideration than either Japanese tactics or British gunnery is, of course, the basic question of whether the *Prince of Wales* and the *Repulse* should ever have been exposed to enemy attack in such a manner. For this exposure, both Winston Churchill and, to a smaller extent, Admiral Tom Phillips have been criticized. Critics have bitterly attacked the Prime Minister on three fundamental points: 1. His failure to provide strong land-based air defences for Singapore. 2. His despatch of the two warships to the Far East, in these circumstances, without an aircraft-carrier and screening vessels. 3. His failure to withdraw Force Z as soon as it was clear that the outbreak of war had placed it in grave danger. Rashness, stupidity, conceit, and other similar weaknesses have been suggested as the cause of these failures. Admiral Phillips has not been so pilloried, but some critics have censured him for going to sea without air cover, and for a few lesser omissions. Yet in the case of both the Prime Minister and the Eastern Fleet Commander, a more charitable view would seem to be indicated.

There is no doubt that Singapore's air defences were terribly weak, and that responsibility for strengthening them was inevitably that of the Prime Minister. But it must also be recognized that Great Britain was fighting a global war, in which struggle priorities for one theatre inevitably conflicted with the needs of another, and also that for two decades the Far East in particular had suffered from the restraints of Britain's limited peacetime defence budget. In 1941, the danger to the British Isles themselves, the demands of the Middle East theatre, and the importance of keeping the Soviet Union in the war, outweighed the threat from Japan. The Anglo-American decision, made during the spring, to maintain only a defensive position in the Pacific until after the defeat of Germany reinforced these priorities. After a third of a century, that decision still appears correct, no matter how cruelly it denied Singapore and other Allied positions.

The despatch of an unbalanced naval force to Singapore was a combination of strategic and political necessity and bad luck. That a strong naval force was needed — both to deter Japan and as evidence to the Americans of good faith, as well as to meet the Japanese on near-equal terms — seems clear. Yet British naval resources were stretched so thinly in 1941 that there was no chance of matching Japanese seapower that year, and even a sufficient deterrent force was hard to come by. Still, Singapore could not be left naked; and considering what the Americans were already doing for the British in the Atlantic, and in view of continued British pleas for a firm United States stand against the Japanese, not to send even a token force to Singapore would have been out of the question. While Force Z was admittedly less than adequate, the presence of the powerful American Pacific Fleet at Hawaii and of strong air units in the Philippines might influence the Japanese to think twice about tangling with even a weak British fleet.

The absence of an aircraft-carrier from Force Z was simply ill fortune. When the *Indomitable* ran aground, there was no other carrier to replace her. Perhaps this should have ended plans for Force Z. But the continued requirement for a deterrent force meant taking a calculated risk until the *Indomitable* could be repaired. Meanwhile, the *Prince of Wales* and the *Repulse* would have to get along as best they could on their own. Actually, given the scope and timing of Japanese strategy, the presence of the *Indomitable* would not have halted or delayed the opening of hostilities in the Pacific. A carrier at Singapore might have caused a few changes in Japanese plans for Malaya, and would probably have slowed, at least for a while, the enemy advance. But the *Indomitable* could not have preserved the *Prince of Wales* and the *Repulse* indefinitely against Japanese airpower, and the aircraft-carrier itself would surely have succumbed to the 'swarm of ants'.

That Churchill did not withdraw the *Prince of Wales* and the *Repulse* to safety as soon as it was clear that they had failed as a deterrent is perhaps more difficult to defend. One of his strong critics has suggested that the Prime Minister was so relieved that America had finally entered the war and that the United States was now fully and irrevocable committed to the same cause as Great Britain, that he forgot for a moment the exposed position of Force Z. His 'emotions of thanksgiving' erased all other thoughts from his mind until, when he finally considered the danger to Force Z, it was too late.[52] This interpretation is an attractive one. Given the strain under which the Prime Minister had been operating for many months, and the host of new problems and possibilities that now beset him, it is not inconceivable that for two days his mind simply failed to come to grips with the fact that a portion of the proud British fleet was in grave peril. The Board of Admiralty, which had been sufficiently concerned a few days earlier to send two messages suggesting that Force Z should leave Singapore, apparently felt that Phillips had been adequately alerted. At any rate, it sent no further warnings.

Churchill's decisions undoubtedly led to the loss of the *Prince of Wales* and the *Repulse*. Certainly they were coloured by an underestimation of Japan's immediate capabilities and an outdated, almost sentimental, confidence in 'the traditional values of sea power': the influence of the capital ship and the majesty of its heavy armament[53] — misjudgments in which he was hardly alone. Still, except possibly for his final error of omission, the Prime Minister's actions were not unreasonable when viewed against the perspective of world-wide political and strategic considerations. When judging a leader responsible for the fate of a great nation this is the only perspective to take, no matter how cruel or bitter the defeat that cries out for explanation.

As for Admiral Phillips, it is wrong to criticise his decision to seek out the enemy when he did. Aphorisms about the need for air cover come easy in the cold light of hindsight, but on December 8th, 1941, Phillips had no choice but the one he made. He did his best to secure fighter protection for his ships, and when this proved to be unavailable he relied on bad weather and surprise to balance this weakness. His decision to turn back after he knew Force Z had been discovered, late on the afternoon of the 9th, is clear evidence that he was unwilling to risk impossible odds. What is less clear is why Phillips did not immediately radio his change of plan to Singapore. The Japanese obviously knew where he was at that moment, and despatching a radio message before he changed course would not have given anything else away. Yet there was always the possibility that the enemy aircraft had not seen him, or had not correctly estimated his position, or that enemy reports were not getting through to their base. Because of this Phillips may have been unwilling to break radio silence.

An even more crucial question concerns the reported landing at Kuantan. Critics have challenged Phillips' decision not to inform Admiral Palliser that he was heading for Kuantan. Perhaps Phillips, in assuming that Palliser would understand this anyway, and provide him with air cover, was expecting too much of his chief-of-staff. Or perhaps he felt that this was yet another risk he must take in order not to break radio silence and draw the Japanese down on him at a time when surprise was still the essential.

In this connection, Admiral Palliser has not escaped criticism. He has been rebuked for failing to inform Phillips that the report from Kuantan was unconfirmed and in fact false. But his message to Phillips simply referred to a 'reported landing'; there was heavy firing at Kuantan for several hours thereafter; and not until dawn was it clear that there had been no landing – by which time Force Z had nearly reached Kuantan.

It is difficult to see how Palliser could have known that Phillips was going to Kuantan. In the first place, he had no clear idea where Force Z was, and in the absence of any message from Phillips could only assume it was still heading for Singora, or possibly for Kota Bharu. British aircraft reconnoitering Kuantan as late as half an hour after daylight saw no sign of Force Z. Nor did the message subsequently relayed by the *Tenedos* in any way contradict the assumption that Phillips was still far to the north. It did, indeed, strengthen it, since if Force Z would not pass the Anambas until 6.30 a.m. on the 11th, it could hardly have been close enough to Kuantan to reach that point twenty-four hours earlier. Not until 11.30 a.m. on the 10th, when the *Prince of Wales*'s reconnaissance plane landed at Penang, did Singapore learn that Phillips was off Kuantan.[54] Why no planes were sent to cover him at this time is unclear, but by then, in any event, they could not have reached Force Z in time to save it.

Where Admiral Phillips appears most vulnerable to criticism is in his failure to notify Singapore as soon as he discovered Ensign Hoashi's Babs shadowing him at mid-morning of the 10th, or at the latest when the first Mihoro bombers appeared at 11 a.m. Initially, he may have hoped that somehow the Japanese reconnaissance plane had not fixed his position accurately, or that its report might be delayed in transmission. At any rate, Phillips had no way of knowing that enemy bombers and torpedo-planes were already in the area looking for him. Despite the attack on the *Tenedos*, he probably assumed that additional

Japanese air units would have to be despatched from their home bases, and that it would take them several hours to reach him. On this assumption, maintaining radio silence for a while longer might be a reasonably calculated risk.

Once the first bombers attacked, the need for keeping silent would seem to have vanished. Yet if the relative ineffectiveness of this attack reinforced Phillips' lack of concern about high-level bombers, he may still have been unwilling to reveal his whereabout in any way to searching torpedo-planes. If this was so, it was a fatal mistake, a final, irrevocable error; for when the Genzan torpedos struck home half an hour later they destroyed his ability to send messages to Singapore. By now it mattered little; only if he had radioed Singapore no later than 11 a.m. – fifteen minutes before the initial bombing attack on the *Repulse* – could fighters have reached Force Z in time to do any good.

In retrospect, it appears that Phillips placed too much stress on the need for radio silence, a concern not unusual in the fleet. As a well-qualified observer has commented, 'it was one that had for some time been a fetish in the British Navy'.[55] In this case, it proved the undoing of Force Z, for even a single squadron of Buffalo fighters could probably have interfered seriously with the unescorted Japanese bombers and torpedo planes. The respite, to be sure, might have been a brief one, lasting only until Admiral Matsunaga could send his own fighters to the scene. Yet the cost to the Japanese would certainly have been higher.

Force Z, it seems clear, was doomed from the moment it reached Singapore. Unless the ships had retreated back across the Indian Ocean, or some-how made their way to American or Australian waters as soon as war began, it is highly improbable that the Japanese navy would have rested until it had hunted them down and destroyed them. A similar fate would have awaited Phillips' ships if he had elected to remain at anchor in Johore Strait. And once he ventured north, there was no longer any escape. He would have been lost if he had reached Singora – a bold sacrifice to the hope of destroying the Japanese amphibious forces. He would have been lost if he had never gone to Kuantan – for surely Japanese submarines and aircraft would have found him again in any event. But if, by some means, he had managed to return safely to Singapore with his ships, he would then have been faced with the 'excruciating decision' of 'what to do next'.[56]

In this sense perhaps it was even well that Force Z went down as it did fighting valiantly to the end, and that its gallant commander died with it, spared the increasingly difficult decisions and the bitterness that might well have followed.

A day or so later, a single Betty of the Kanoya Group flew over the scene of the battle. Where the ocean had been torn by the thunder of bombs and the spray of shell fragments, its surface stained with dirty black oil and the bodies of dying men, all was now serene. On the 'blue waves glistening below, as though nothing had ever taken place there before . . . the members of the crew threw a large floral wreath'.[57]

NOTES – Chapter 5

1. The basic source for British naval activities: Layton, *Despatch: Loss of H.M. Ships Prince of Wales and Repulse*. Additional or corroborative material Brooke-Popham, *Despatch*, pp. 557-58, and Maltby, *Report*, pp. 1368-69. See also Roskill, *The Defensive*, chap. xxvi and App. D; Grenfell, *Main Fleet to Singapore*, pp. 95-136; Hough, *Death of the Battleship*, pp. 70-83, 115-96; Bernard Ash, *Someone Had Blundered* (Garden City: Doubleday, 1961). Useful eye-witness accounts are: Brown, *Suez to Singapore*, pp. 293-336; Gallagher, *Action in the East*, chaps. iii-iv; Lieutenant Commander T.J. Cain, as told to A.V. Sellwood, *H.M.S. Electra* (London: Frederick Muller Limited, 1959), pp. 163-77.

2. Quoted in Hough, *Death of the Battleship*, p. 134.

3. Morrison, *Malayan Postscript*, p. 16.

4. F. Spencer-Chapman, *The Jungle is Neutral* (London: Chatto & Windus, 1949), p. 17.

5. Layton, *Despatch*, p. 1237.

6. Hough, *Death of the Battleship*, pp. 116-17, 125; Grenfell, *Main Fleet to Singapore*, p. 124. See also the comment on this point by Marshal of the Royal Air Force Sir John Slessor in *Royal United Service Institution Journal*, CXI (November 1966), p. 346.

7. Hough, *Death of the Battleship*, pp. 137-38; Jahn Toland, *But Not in Shame* (New York: Random House, 1961), p. 60.

8. Grenfell, *Main Fleet to Singapore*, p. 114.

9. For the entire notice, Gallagher, *Action in the East*, pp. 40-42. Part also in Brown, *Suez to Singapore*, p. 298.

10. Chief of Staff, Eastern Fleet, to C-in-C, Eastern Fleet, 2253GH/8, in Layton, *Despatch*, p. 1244.

11. C-in-C, Eastern Fleet, to *Prince of Wales, Repulse*, in *ibid.*, p. 1244.

12. Brooke-Popham, *Despatch*, p. 557. There is some confusion in secondary sources about the content of this message and I have accepted the summary of the message in Layton, *Despatch*, p. 1238.

13. Chief of Staff, Eastern Fleet, to C-in-C, Eastern Fleet, 2145GH/9, in Layton, *Despatch*, p. 1244.

14. Basic sources for Japanese operations described in this chapter are: Malaya Invasion Naval Operations, pp. 12-16, 21-29; Okumiya and Horikoshi, *Zero*, chap. ix; Interrogation of Captain Kameo Sonokawa, in United States Strategic Bombing Survey (Pacific) (hereafter USSBS), *Interrogations of Japanese Officials* (2 vols.; Washington: U.S. Government Printing Office, 1946), II, 333-36; ATIS, Enemy Publications, No. 6, Hawaii-Malaya Naval Operations, May 27th, 1943, pp. 12-21; Ito, *The Japanese Navy*, pp. 44-49; Tsuji, *Singapore*, chap. xvi.

15. Willard Price, America's Enemy No. 2: Yamamoto, *Harpers Magazine*, CLXXXIV (April 1942), p. 458; Robert E. Ward, The Inside Story of the Pearl Harbour Plan, *United States Naval Institute Proceedings*, LXXVII (December 1951), pp. 1272-78.

16. Saburo Sakai, with Martin Caidin and Fred Saito, *Samurai* (New York: Ballantine, 1957), chaps. iii-vii; Hough, *Death of the Battleship*, pp. 65-68; USSBS, *Japanese Air Power* (Washington: U.S. Government Printing Office, 1946), pp. 4, 34-35; Roberta Wohlstetter, *Pearl Harbour: Warning and Decision* (Stanford: Stanford Univ. Press, 1962), pp. 337-38, 369-70. For Japanese torpedoes, see also Samuel Eliot Morison, *The Rising Sun in the Pacific, 1931-April 1942* (Boston: Little, Brown, 1951), p. 23; Donald Macintyre, *Battle for the Pacific* (New York: Norton, 1966), pp. 227-28 and *passim*.

17. Interrogation of Captain Bunzo Shibata, in USSBS, *Interrogations*, II, 37.

18. See also interrogations of Captains Chihaya Takahashi and Bunzo Shibata, in *ibid.*, pp. 74, 379. Sources differ slightly on the number of planes in Admiral Matsunaga's command. The figures used here seem to have the most support.

19. Malaya Invasion Naval Operations, p. 21.

20. For submarine operations, see also Mochitsura Hashimoto, *Sunk; The Story of the Japanese Submarine Fleet, 1941-1945* (New York: Holt, 1954), pp. 38-40.

21. ATIS, Hawaii-Malaya Naval Operations, p. 13.

22. ATIS, Hawaii-Malaya Naval Operations, p. 15. Grenfell, *Main Fleet to Singapore*, pp. 116-17, suggests that an erroneous estimate by *I-65* of the position of Force Z may have led the pilots astray; he apparently bases this on a statement by Captain Sonokawa. But the position given in Commander Harada's report was actually quite accurate. It is quoted in Hattori, *The Great East Asia War*, II, 27, and paraphrased in Malaya Invasion Naval Operations, pp. 21-22.

23. Chief of Staff, Eastern Fleet, to C-in-C, Eastern Fleet, 1505Z/9, in Layton, *Despatch*, p. 1244; Kirby, *The Loss of Singapore*, p. 193; Bhargava and Sastri, *Campaigns in South-East Asia*, p. 225.

24. Maltby, *Report*, p. 1368; Bhargava and Sastri, *Campaigns in South-East Asia*, p. 225; Kirby, *The Loss of Singapore*, p. 193.

25. Churchill, *The Grand Alliance*, pp. 615-16.

26. Maltby, *Report*, p. 1368.

27. Brown, *Suez to Singapore*, p. 313.

28. Quoted in Cain, *H.M.. Electra*, p. 170.

29. ATIS, Hawaii-Malaya Naval Operations, p. 15.

30. Brown, *Suez to Singapore*, p. 314.

31. ATIS, Hawaii-Malaya Naval Operations, p. 16.

32. Cain, *H.M.S. Electra*, p. 171.

33. Okumiya and Horikoshi, *Zero*, p. 112.

34. Capt. Tennant's report, in Layton, *Despatch*, p. 1241.

35. Maltby, *Report*, p. 1368.

36. Cain, *H.M.S. Electra*, p. 172.

37. Capt. Tennant's report, in Layton, *Despatch*, p. 1241.

38. Brown, *Suez to Singapore*, p. 321.

39. ATIS, Hawaii-Malaya Naval Operations, p. 16. For the Japanese squadron leader's story, see Toland, *But Not in Shame*, pp. 70-75.

40. Gallagher, *Action in the East*, p. 69.

41. Capt. Tennant's report, in Layton, *Despatch*, p. 1242.

42. *Ibid.*

43. Brown, *Suez to Singapore*, p. 328.

44. ATIS, Hawaii-Malaya Naval Operations, p. 17.

45. For the *Vampire*, see G. Herman Gill, *Royal Australian Navy, 1939-1942* (Australia in the War of 1939-1945, Series 2, *Navy*, Vol. I) (Canberra: Australian War Memorial, 1957), pp. 481-82.

46. ATIS, Hawaii-Malaya Naval Operations, p. 17.

47. Quoted in Brown, *Suez to Singapore*, p. 336.

48. Flt.-Lt. T.A. Vigors to C-in-C, Far Eastern Fleet, December 11th, 1941, in Layton, *Despatch*, p. 1243.

49. Ito, *The Japanese Navy*, p. 47; Okumiya and Horikoshi, *Zero*, p. 117; ATIS, Hawaii-Malaya Naval Operations, pp. 16, 19.

50. Layton, *Despatch*, pp. 1239, 1241. But cf. Sonokawa, in USSBS, *Interrogations*, II, 333, 335; Okumiya and Horikoshi, *Zero*, pp. 106, 113-14.

51. Hough, *Death of the Battleship*, pp. 67-68.

52. Ash, *Someone Had Blundered*, pp. 198-99; Churchill, *The Grand Alliance*, pp. 606-608.

53. Hough, *Death of the Battleship*, p. 109.

54. Kirby, *The Loss of Singapore*, p. 198.

55. Grenfell, *Main Fleet to Singapore*, p. 127.

56. *Ibid.*, p. 131.

57. ATIS, Hawaii-Malaya Naval Operations, p. 17; Toland, *But Not in Shame*, p. 78.

6
Destruction of the 11th Division

Singapore greeted the sinking of the *Prince of Wales* and the *Repulse* with shocked disbelief and, in the words of one witness, a 'chill sense of calamity'.[1] At Raffles Hotel, the famous ornate, sprawling symbol of imperial luxury overlooking the water, couples dancing on the vast covered veranda 'suddenly felt terribly guilty — caught out drinking', somebody recalled later,[2] and the party came to an abrupt halt. By the next morning, however, people seemed to have regained their composure. It became a matter of pride for the British population not to let the grim reality of war interfere with either business or pleasure. Freedom from Japanese air raids for the next three weeks, and the knowledge that the battle-field was 400 miles away, helped to nurture a sense of security. People went to dances or the movies, dined out, or drank, recalled one writer, 'at an even faster rate';[3] they played golf or tennis, and seemed to refuse to admit that there was any real danger. It would be some time before they realised how surely the loss of the two great ships presaged further disaster. Now, on Malaya's third day of war, only a very few people began to consider the frightening possibility that Singapore itself might fall. In the month that followed events further north would turn that possibility into a grim probability.[4]

A few hours before dawn of December 10th, forward elements of Lieutenant-General Takuro Matsui's 5th Division, pushing down the Singora-Jitra road, crossed the border into Malaya. Their objective was the Perak River, a twisting waterway that rose some forty miles south-east of Kroh and ran generally south, roughly parallel to the west coast, until it curved out to the Strait of Malacca about a third of the way down the peninsula. To reach the line of the Perak River. Matsui would have to crush the British defences he knew were at Jitra, some seventeen miles below the border. A determined energetic commander, he did not hesitate. Already most of his division's 9th Brigade was well forward on the Singora-Jitra road. Further east his 42nd Infantry

Regiment would later attack down the Patani-Kroh road, over-land due south to the upper Perak, and move down the river to cut off British forces between the Perak and the sea. But the 42nd Infantry was still back in Thailand, engaged with Krohcol, so Matsui's immediate objective was the 11th Indian Division at Jitra.

For the British, the defences at Jitra left much to be desired. Not until two days earlier, with the cancellation of *Operation Matador*, had General Murray-Lyon known whether his mission was to be offensive or defensive. Until then, the 11th Division had been forced to plan, train, and deploy for either possibility and with some justification had concentrated on preparing to attack. So little had been done to make ready fixed defences. When Murray-Lyon's troops rushed back to the Jitra position on the 8th, they not only found it incomplete but, to their dismay, also discovered that two days of steady rain had made a water-soaked mess of everything. Under the twin pressures of haste and a continuing downpour, they had to put in barbed-wire and mines, lay telephone cables, manhandle supplies along slippery paths, and re-clear fields of fire that the fast-growing vegetation had already reclaimed. In the steady rain, supplies were flooded, demolitions soaked, and field cables smothered in mud. The drenched unhappy troops did what they could, but the arduous work was a strain on their energies and their subsequent readiness for combat.

Nor did Murray-Lyon help his men by the dispositions in which he chose to place them. There were two main approaches to Jitra, the Singora road and another road coming down from the north-west. The Japanese were already known to be on the former and, advancing with tanks and other vehicles, could be expected to hold to the roads. Instead of concentrating his defences in depth along these avenues, however, Murray-Lyon tried to cover every possible approach across more than a dozen miles from Jitra to the sea. The 15th Brigade, on the right, was responsible for about a quarter of this distance, defending Jitra itself and a line of jungle, swamps, flooded rice fields, and rubber estates. The 6th Brigade, to the left, was stretched thinly along the rest of the line, most of which consisted of deep swamp, with a single battalion extended some five-and-a-half miles inland from the coast. Few elements along this line had actual physical contact with any other unit, and outpost detachments, placed well forward, were completely out of touch. Several batteries of artillery provided support, and the 28th Brigade – III Corps reserve, released to Murray-Lyon when *Matador* was called off – was in reserve below Jitra.

This wide dispersal, the fact that the ground to be defended was broken by countless streams, bogs, and paddy-fields, and the effect of the heavy rain on communications, all combined to frustrate mobility and mutual support within the division. Few units were capable of assisting any other. Some could barely keep in touch over the signal net.

In these circumstances, the condition of the troops took on an even graver note. While each brigade contained a battalion of English soldiers, the rest of the defenders were Indian troops, poorly trained, unused to the sight and sound of modern weapons, and led by officers themselves inexperienced and without practice in leading their units in the field. The men were dispirited by the shift from offensive to defensive, tired by the rapid changes in their deployment, and nearly worn out from working in the mud and rain. Given more realistic defensive positions, they might have overcome these difficulties. Along the Jitra line as it was, their chances of doing so were slim.

First contact came early on the 10th. Colonel Saeki's armoured reconnaissance detachment, still leading the 5th Division's advance, met forward elements of Brigadier K.A. Garrett's 15th Brigade astride the Singora road just south of the border and forced them back. Saeki kept up the pressure during the day, and by evening was opposed by a battalion of Punjabi troops concentrated about a dozen miles north of Jitra. The Punjabis had blown up small bridges and causeways as they fell back, but it was clear that demolition alone could not stop the Japanese. To gain time for more work on the Jitra defences, General Murray-Lyon ordered Garrett to hold the Japanese north of the town until the 12th. To help him in this task, he gave him, from the reserve 28th Brigade, a Gurkha battalion which Garrett promptly put into position astride the road at Asun, mid-way between Jitra and the advance Punjabi unit.

Meanwhile, Major General Saburo Kawamura, commander of the Japanese 9th Infantry Brigade and in overall charge of the attack on Jitra, was becoming increasingly concerned about the delays caused by British demolitions. He attached additional tanks and engineers to Saeki's force, and ordered him to drive forward as rapidly as he could, capturing bridges and other critical points before their defenders had time to blow them up.

Saeki attacked on the morning of the 11th, and by early afternoon the weary, rain-soaked Punjabis were once more retreating through the heavy downpour. The Japanese, slowed by demolitions and British artillery fire, their vision restricted by the curtain of rain, followed grimly. The Punjabis had broken contact, but just after 4.30, two miles above Asun, Saeki's advance unit regained it with a vengeance. A column of medium tanks and motorised infantry struck the retreating Punjabis, crushed their initial defences, and drove through the entire battalion, scattering it. Anti-tank guns which might have halted the attack were still limbered up for the withdrawal to Asun. A particularly heavy rain-storm, 'the devil's own deluge', according to one British officer,[5] had driven the gunners to cover just before the tanks appeared, and they had no time to unlimber their pieces. Saeki's tanks smashed ahead, over-running guns, vehicles, and whatever infantry tried to stop them.

Barely half an hour had passed and now, in the growing twilight, the Japanese tanks were approaching the bridge before Asun, held by the Gurkha battalion. The rain-soaked demolition charges proved useless, but the Gurkhas managed to knock out the lead tanks with gunfire. This blocked the road and temporarily halted the Japanese armour. Saeki's infantry, however, poured round the tanks to outflank the Gurkhas, opening the way for a renewed advance by the entire Japanese column. This force quickly overwhelmed the battered defenders, and by evening had reached the main position at Jitra. The Punjabi and Gurkha battalions were both destroyed, all equipment lost, and the survivors scattered in the swamps and sodden jungle. Many were taken prisoner. The Indian troops, reported General Matsui, 'have no fighting spirit . . . they are glad to surrender [and] relieved to be out of the war'.[6] Barely 200 of the defenders managed to find their way back to friendly lines the next day.

To the west, meanwhile, forward elements of the 6th Brigade, while not under pressure, were falling back to avoid being outflanked and to join in the Jitra defence. The premature demolition of a bridge by an inexperienced and understandably nervous young officer forced the withdrawing troops to leave most of their vehicles, anti-tank guns, and artillery behind. This loss clearly increased Murray-Lyon's difficulties at Jitra. By now the 11th Division commander had discovered that Brigadier Garrett was among those cut off during the action above Asun. Murray-Lyon ordered Brigadier W. St. J. Carpendale, commanding the 28th Brigade, to take over the 15th Brigade, and gave him a second Gurkha battalion from the 28th to help him to hold Jitra. Since the remaining battalion of the 28th was protecting the airfields at Alor Star and Sungei Patani, Murray-Lyon had now committed his entire divisional reserve.

As if sensing the British disarray, Colonel Saeki pushed ahead. Patrols probed the Jitra defences after dark on December 11th, and at about 8.30 a column of tanks, their headlights blazing boldly, attacked the centre of Carpendale's position. The Japanese were delayed only slightly by demolitions – many explosives were too watersoaked to go off – but ran into sharp opposition from a battalion of English troops, the 1st Leicestershires. This halted the tanks and forced the accompanying infantry off to the east. They soon penetrated a swampy area between the Leicesters and a Jat battalion defending the British right. Here they made some headway, but still found the going quite difficult.

With the fighting heavy and confused in the continuing rain, exaggerated reports of enemy progress led Carpendale to believe that the situation was much worse than it was. In his concern he did not check with Murray-Lyon, but called immediately on Brigadier William Lay, commanding the 6th Brigade, for reinforcements. During the course of the night, Lay sent Carpendale a battalion and a half of Punjabi troops, amounting to his entire brigade reserve. These Carpendale committed, practically as soon as each company arrived, to meet renewed and heavier Japanese blows.

Saeki, by now, had also put in his reserves and was using his entire force. Under heavy shelling, the Japanese engineers attempted to remove British demolition charges, while tanks and infantry probed forward on the road, and riflemen waded waist-deep through the swamp in an effort to outflank the defenders. Try as he might, however, the disappointed Saeki could not split the British line. The battlefield at dawn was a morass of mud, splintered and fallen rubber trees, and crippled tanks and smashed vehicles. The Japanese had solidified and somewhat increased their penetration of Carpendale's line, but could go no further. Carpendale had managed to halt the enemy, yet lacked the power to eject him.

Murray-Lyon reviewed the situation early on the 12th. Carpendale appeared to be holding, but his forces were nearing exhaustion. Furthermore, the unauthorised shift of troops from Lay's brigade left no other units available to meet renewed or additional Japanese pressure. To add to Murray-Lyon's difficulties, Krohcol, off to the east on the Patani-Kroh road, was under heavy pressure and withdrawing toward Kroh. Once the Japanese reached that point, they would be able to turn west and cut in behind him. Since the 11th Division's instructions to halt the Japanese did not include a defence in position to the death, Murray-Lyon telephoned III Corps headquarters and asked permission to withdraw to a previously chosen position at Gurun, some thirty miles to the south.

General Heath was then on his way to Singapore to talk to Percival about the critical situation at Kota Bharu, unhappily for Murray-Lyon whose request was passed directly to the Malaya commander. The worried Percival, still hoping to deny the north-western airfields to the Japanese, aware that few preparations had been made at Gurun, and concerned about the 'demoralizing effect' of 'such an early and long withdrawal' on both troops and the civilian population, refused permission.[7] He directed Murray-Lyon to hold the Jitra position.

In this decision, General Percival had been supported by the Far East War Council, a body newly created to provide political guidance for Brooke-Popham and to relieve him of non-military responsibilities. The War Council was headed by Alfred Duff-Cooper, Resident Minister for Far Eastern Affairs and, in effect, Churchill's personal representative. It included the Governor of the Straits Settlement and the Malayan High Commissioner, Sir Shenton Thomas, and the various top military commanders. In practice, it proved something of a fencing ground for Duff-Cooper on the one hand and Thomas and the military on the other. It had little or no effect on the military aspects of the campaign, although it was doubtless a useful co-ordinating body on civil problems. In this instance, its endorsement of the decision to stand at Jitra was probably aimed at preventing a complete breakdown of civilian morale, already none too high after the loss of the *Prince of Wales* and the *Repulse* and the other disasters of the previous days. Percival might perhaps have done better to avoid consulting the War Council on this purely tactical matter, and to follow the recommendation of his commander on the ground. The decision to stand at Jitra merely compounded Murray-Lyon's problems and increased the certainty of subsequent defeat.[8]

During the morning of December 12th, the fighting at Jitra was confused, bloody, and indecisive. The 15th Brigade, reinforced by elements from the 6th and a newly arrived artillery regiment, continued to bear the brunt of the action in the flooded swamp. A counter-attack by Punjabi troops was aborted when they accidentally came under fire from the Jat* battalion, and Japanese penetration remained a dangerous threat. Saeki's men, however, were receiving increasingly heavy artillery fire, which caused their commander great concern. Towards noon the 2nd Battalion, 41st Infantry, reached the scene and, just about 12 o'clock, attacked the Jats. Despite punishing British shellfire, the Japanese troops were not to be denied. In two hours of fierce combat, they over-ran and practically wiped out the Jat forward left

---

* People of N.W.-India and (now) Pakistan.

company. Towards the end of the action, the commander of the exposed Jat company telephoned to say that he was almost out of ammunition and that many weapons were becoming clogged with mud. 'The men cannot fire, Sir,' he told the battalion commander.

'I can't give you permission to withdraw,' was the reply.

'O.K. Sir. We will fight it out with grenades and bayonets. The men are splendid. I reckon we have got about five minutes left.'

'Gook luck to you.'[9]

The Japanese had now driven a deep wedge between the Jats and the Leicesters. Part of the attacking force swung against the exposed right flank of the Leicesters while the rest engaged other 15th Brigade troops further south.

By mid-afternoon, the Japanese advance appeared to be halted. Nevertheless, a large and dangerous gap had been torn in the Jitra line, enemy pressure continued, and confusion and doubt were growing among the defenders. Attempts to close the gap and, when these failed, attempts to form a new line below it, brought more casualties and increased disorder. False reports of a Japanese armoured attack did nothing to improve matters, and by late afternoon the situation in the 15th Brigade sector was close to desperate.

Furthermore, General Kawamura, disturbed by Colonel Saeki's earlier difficulties, had ordered a full-scale attack by the entire 41st Infantry, supported by the 11th Infantry. Both of these regiments had finally reached the battlefield, but the events of the afternoon made their help unnecessary. Murray-Lyon, seeing that the continuing deterioration of the Jitra position could expose his division to a tank attack that could only destroy it, knew that he must withdraw. Continued bad news from Krohcol reinforced this conclusion. At 7.30, he again asked for permission to pull back.

This time he received it. Heath was now at Singapore and, after talking with Percival, sent word to Murray-Lyon that he could evacuate Jitra. The 11th Division was still charged with defending northern Kedah, but Murray-Lyon was relieved of responsibility for Krohcol, a distracting concern during this hectic period. Also, reinforcements would be sent as soon as possible.

Withdrawal from Jitra began after midnight, just in time to escape General Kawamura's attack. Heavy rain, the exhausted state of the troops, breakdowns in communication, and continued Japanese pressure, made a bad situation worse. Confused, disorganised, and generally miserable, most of the 11th Division were able to break contact by about 4.30 a.m. on December 13th. Several companies were late getting out, and these and some of the other units staggered south in almost complete disarray. Many men never rejoined the division. A great deal of equipment, especially artillery, was lost.

The British defeat at Jitra was a costly one, all the more so because the Japanese had accomplished it with so small a force. An aggressive assault had proved too much for Murray-Lyon's extended defences and inexperienced troops. Saeki's command — a reconnaissance detachment supported by artillery, engineers, and light and medium tanks; the whole force numbering roughly 600 men — had done most of the damage, with a single battalion of infantry joining in at the end. Together they reduced the 15th Brigade from about 2,400 men to 600, inflicted serious losses on the 6th Brigade, and destroyed the equivalent of a battalion of the 28th. They captured great quantities of weapons, vehicles, and communications equipment, together with more than 1,000 prisoners. The 11th Division, exhausted and badly shaken, with no ready replacements for men or equipment, would be hard-pressed to continue as an effective fighting force. The cost to the Japanese was twenty-seven killed and eighty-three wounded.

The tattered elements of the 11th Division passed rapidly south through Alor Star on December 13th, leaving the airfield there, and a large stock of bombs and aviation fuel, to the on-coming Japanese. Demolition of installations, begun on the 10th, had been halted because the sight of huge fires and smoke, and the sound of explosions, had proved bad for the morale of the troops at Jitra — who, after all, were supposed to be defending the airfield. When they arrived, the Japanese were delighted to find that destruction was far from complete.

The Japanese victory also brought with it the first success in Major Fujiwara's programme to subvert Indian troops in Malaya. The Indian prisoners, including most of the Punjabi battalion that Colonel Saeki's force had smashed above Jitra, were turned over to Fujiwara and a Sikh, Pritam Singh, an exiled Indian nationalist. Fujiwara and Pritam Singh established their headquarters at Alor Star, where they immediately set about working on the anguish and fears of the captured Indians. Addressing a large assembly of the prisoners, Pritam Singh spoke glowingly of the aims of the Indian Independence League, while Fujiwara expressed the Japanese hope to liberate the oppressed peoples of eastern Asia and asked the Indians for their assistance.

One of the captured Punjabi officers was Captain Mohan Singh, who even before the war had been active among disgruntled Indians who resented real or imagined racial prejudice within the British forces. Now, he proved more than willing to co-operate with the Japanese. Fujiwara placed him in charge of all the Indian prisoners, ordering him to organise them into a force that could assist Twenty-fifth Army units in maintaining order in the rear and, as additional Indian troops were captured, help with their indoctrination. When General Yamashita established his command-post at Alor Star on December 16th, both Pritam Singh and Mohan Singh were granted an audience. They seem to have been greatly impressed by the general's sincere sympathy with Indian nationalist aims. By the end of the month, indeed, Yamashita had accepted Mohan Singh's proposal to form an Indian National Army, consisting primarily of Indian troops captured in Malaya, which would co-operate with Japanese forces and eventually help to liberate India from British rule.[10]

Meanwhile, on December 13th General Murray-Lyon was seeking a way to halt the Japanese advance. The Kedah River line, just below Alor Star, offered an obstacle behind which he hoped to rest his troops briefly and reorganise them. But he was afforded little opportunity. Even as he stood watching his engineers preparing to blow up the road bridge, three Japanese motor-cyclists appeared as if from nowhere and charged across the span in a daring effort to cut the wires to the explosive charges. The riders, part of an advance detachment from the 11th Infantry, were quickly shot down and the charges exploded, but shortly afterwards more Japanese troops arrived and opened fire across the river. During the afternoon a small force of the attackers managed to reach the south bank of the Kedah. A Gurkha counter-attack threw them back; but Murray-Lyon realised that his weary troops could hardly stand up to renewed pressure. Under cover of darkness, with heavy rain contributing to the confused disorganisation, the 11th Division began withdrawing again. Most of the units reached the Gurun area, nearly twenty miles further south, by dawn of December 14th.

Gurun, in the words of General Percival, was 'one of the strongest natural positions in North Malaya'.[11] A narrow north-south pass between a steep, rocky height on the west and heavy jungle on the east, it seemed an ideal place to halt the Japanese drive. Unfortunately for the 11th Division, nothing had been done to supplement the natural defences. An attempt to develop the position with civilian labour a few days earlier had never really got under way, and Murray-Lyon's muddied and exhausted soldiers had little time to remedy the situation. Japanese patrols reached the area around noon of the 14th. About two hours later, three Japanese tanks and a dozen truck-loads of infantry attacked the 6th Brigade, on the left of the position, and began to push it back. Brigadier Lay organised and personally led a counter-attack to regain most of the lost ground. But the Japanese still held an important crossroads and had continued to build up their forces, now in strength a battalion or more of the 41st Infantry.

That evening, General Heath, having visited Murray-Lyon, telephoned Percival and recommended withdrawing the 11th Division all the way back to the Perak River, with perhaps a brief pause along the Muda, the first river line below Gurun. This would give the division more time to concentrate and reorganise than would be possible during a phased series of shorter withdrawals. Percival agreed to a withdrawal only as far as the Muda, pending other developments.

Heavy Japanese mortar-fire, beginning at about 10 p.m. preceded a second attack on the 6th Brigade a few hours after midnight. Fighting was severe. The British gunfire, noted one Japanese soldier in his diary, sounded 'like the cracking of beans', and a 'hailstorm of bullets' flew over his head.[12] Nevertheless, the 41st Infantry troops quickly overwhelmed two of the defending battalions, penetrating as far as brigade headquarters. Brigadier Lay was not there, but everyone else was killed, and only prompt action by 28th Brigade units prevented a complete Japanese breakthrough. Murray-Lyon now realised that withdrawal was necessary to save his division from destruction. His troops fell back during the day, Gurkha and English soldiers fighting a gallant rearguard action. By morning of December 16th, the division was safely south of the Muda. But again, casualties and losses of equipment had been heavy.

The halt at the Muda had been dictated by the need to protect nearby Penang Island, in an attempt either to hold it or, if necessary, to cover its evacuation. Penang was important for its port facilities, its supply installations, and as the terminous of overseas cables. Its garrison had been reduced by the despatch of a battalion to Krohcol, and there was no longer any possibility that additional troops could be sent to the island.

Penang had in fact been under aerial attack since the 11th, when nearly sixty 3rd Air Group bombers and fighters, inflicted heavy casualties and great damage. General Sugawara's planes had since returned in somewhat smaller numbers daily. On the night of the 13th, the Penang authorities evacuated hospital patients and all European women and children to the mainland. This move shocked and surprised both the local inhabitants and those who were forced to leave. The latter especially felt that they were deserting the native people who depended on them, and they were deeply shamed. They had no choice, however, and launches manned by survivors of the *Prince of Wales* and the *Repulse* – the local crews had deserted – ferried them to the mainland under cover of darkness.

The next day Percival raised the question of Penang with the War Council. Removing the garrison would be another blow to morale, but the group decided that unless the Japanese could be stopped on the mainland, there was no point in trying to hold Penang. Percival passed this decision on to Heath, who found himself with little option. Unburied bodies, and the breakdown of sanitary facilities on the island, raised the strong possibility of an outbreak of cholera or typhoid. Nor did there remain any chance of holding Penang or of using it to delay the Japanese advance. Towards noon on December 15th, Heath ordered that the garrison should leave by daylight of the 17th.

The successful evacuation of Penang left a bad taste in everyone's mouth. It appeared that the Malayans had been discriminated against and, worse still, that the British were doing nothing to make good their pledge to defend the local inhabitants. These matters were probably beyond anyone's control. Defence, in the circumstances, would have been pointless, and there was clearly no possibility of evacuating everyone on the island. Many natives did actually leave, and more could have gone; but those who remained in their homes were probably better off than if they had joined the lines of refugees streaming south on the mainland. Nevertheless, Penang's evacuation and the way it was conducted caused a serious shock throughout Malaya, reinforcing forbodings of defeat that had begun with the loss of the *Prince of Wales* and the *Repulse.*

Equally distressing was the inability of the garrison to do a thorough job of demolition. When Japanese troops occupied Penang on the night of the 19th, they found most supplies and installations destroyed. But the powerful Penang radio station was practically intact, and was soon broadcasting Japanese propaganda all over South-east Asia. The hastily withdrawn garrison also failed to destroy two dozen motorboats and many large junks and barges, deserted by their crews in Penang's harbour. These craft would soon be put to use by the Japanese with devastating effect.[13]

There was now little reason to hold the Muda River line, which was in danger of being outflanked by the Japanese advance down the Patani-Kroh road. Heath visited Murray-Lyon on the morning of the 16th. The 11th Division was clearly exhausted and in no shape for any sort of combat. The corps commander ordered a withdrawal to the Krian River. There, where the swampy ground and river line provided a good natural tank-obstacle, Murray-Lyon's battered troops might at last have a chance to rest and refit.

Others were not afforded this opportunity. The threat from the Patani-Kroh road had been growing steadily since late on December 13th, when Krohcol — now reduced to about a battalion and a half of Punjabi troops — had fallen back across the border to positions west of Kroh. The pursuing Japanese force, Colonal Tadao Ando's reinforced 42nd Infantry Regiment, did not follow immediately, but it clearly represented a danger to the 11th Division's flank. From Kroh, two roads led to the west coast. The first ran generally west to Sungei Patani and was now blocked by Krohcol. The other, little more than a narrow trail, followed the west bank of the Perak River to join the west coast trunk road further south near Kuala Kangsar. Krohcol's withdrawal through Kroh had left this second avenue wide open to the 42nd Infantry. It was, in fact, to be the main axis of advance for Colonel Ando's force.

While the British were unaware of this Japanese plan, they did not leave Ando unopposed. On the night of the 12th, following the disaster at Jitra, Percival had placed at the disposal of III Corps his command reserve, Brigadier A.C.M. Paris's 12th Indian Brigade (less a battalion of Hyderabads at Kota Bharu), and had ordered it to Ipoh. Heath sent the brigade north to protect Murray-Lyon's right flank. By midday of the 16th, when the 11th Division withdrew from the Muda River, Paris's brigade was facing not only the 42nd Infantry but, in fact, practically the whole of the Japanese 5th Division. A Punjabi battalion was guarding the partially-demolished Muda bridge at Batu Pekaka on the Kroh-Sungei Patani road. One company of the 2nd Battalion of the Argyll and Sutherland Highlanders was at Grik, about twenty-five miles south of Kroh on the Perak River road. The remainder of the Highlanders were in position west of Kroh. Krohcol itself had withdrawn and rejoined the 11th Division.[14]

The Punjabi battalion was the first to meet the enemy. During the afternoon, Japanese troops of the 11th Infantry succeeded in crossing at Batu Pekaka. The Punjabis threw them back, however, and finished blowing up the bridge. On orders from Brigadier Paris, meanwhile, the Argyll battalion withdrew (unhindered) through Batu Pekaka and turned south, along an inland road, to the town of Titi Karangan. Early on the 17th, Paris pulled back the Punjabi battalion. Closely followed by the 11th Infantry, the Punjabis passed through the Argylls' position and continued south. The Highlanders were soon under heavy attack. Some of the first Japanese troops appeared to be wearing Malay dress, which surprised and disconcerted the defenders. The Argylls held, nevertheless, but after about an hour it became clear to their tough commander, Lieutenant-Colonel Ian MacArthur Stewart, that if he wished to hold his position only a counter-attack could save his battalion from encirclement. Just as he was ordering this assault, however, he received authority from Paris to withdraw. Since the attack would have been a costly and dangerous one, Stewart cancelled it and began to fall back. Breaking contact, his men soon caught up with the rest of the 12th Brigade, and the entire force continued south. By dawn of December 18th, they had joined the 11th Division below the Krian River.

The brigade had no time to rest. The Argyll company at Grik had been under attack by the 42nd Infantry since late on the 16th. Heavy rain and the poor condition of the road from Kroh had forced Colonel Ando to leave his tanks behind, but he had little difficulty in driving back the outnumbered Highlanders. In view of this increasing threat to the 11th Division's flank, General Heath withdrew Paris's brigade to Kuala Kangsar and, during the night of the 18th, sent the Argyll battalion up the Kroh road to try to halt Colonel Ando's advance.

The struggle for Malaya had now been under way for ten days, and General Percival was beginning to appreciate just how difficult a task he faced. The Japanese clearly had naval and aerial supremacy and, Percival believed, they had put three divisions of troops into Malaya and were capable of reinforcing them at will. Actually, his estimate of Japanese troop strength was quite high, since General Yamashita at this time had less than a division on the west coast and little more than a regiment in the east. By aggressive tactics, executed against weary, dispirited, and inexperienced opponents, the Japanese gave the appearance of much greater strength than they actually possessed. 'You shoot down five hundred Japanese', complained General Heath, 'and before you can turn around there are five hundred more in their place'.[15] Japanese tactics relied primarily on bold frontal attacks by tank/infantry columns, supported by flanking or infiltrating units that caused havoc and dismay in the defenders' rear, and frequently cut off and destroyed British units trying to escape. In north-west Malaya the road and river net favoured the attackers from the north, and Yamashita's troops took every advantage of this circumstance to keep their enemy off balance.

Often, in executing flanking movements, Japanese forces would have no fixed objective or route of advance, but would merely set out for the rear of a position and attack where terrain or the lack of adequate defences made assault seem most profitable. Individual Japanese soldiers would lie in wait in the jungle for hours in the hope of springing an ambush. Occasionally, Japanese riflemen would tie themselves into trees to shoot at unsuspecting targets, although this method was used less frequently than the British claimed. Indeed, when questioned about this after the war, the Japanese insisted that this was a British practice that they had sometimes emulated.* Actually, the defenders rarely saw the Japanese until it was too late.[16] In the thick, dark, suffocating jungle, as General Barstow explained, 'these Indians are fighting blind. They feel as if they have a hood over their eyes'.[17]

At times small groups of Japanese, lightly and often informally clad in the tropical heat, seemed to be wearing Malay dress and purposely disguising themselves as natives. This may have been true in some instances, but more often than not it was the lack of uniformity in either the colour or form of their clothing, their predilection for all sorts of headgear – from steel helmets and khaki caps to slouch hats taken from prisoners or the dead – and the general similarity, in British eyes, of all Asians, that made the Japanese appear like natives to the bewildered westerners. Japanese troops were even reported to be led by German officers – highly improbable, and not confirmed by Japanese sources.

While the British soldiers tended to endow the Japanese with unusual if not extraordinary capabilities – a habit not unusual among troops who are losing – General Yamashita was not completely satisfied with his men. On occasion, he railed at subordinate commanders for not carrying out his orders with sufficient speed or aggressiveness. Nor did his troops themselves, for all their enthusiasm, always reflect a high state of training. Yet whatever their faults, which might have spelled disaster on the defensive, they seemed to matter little in the swift Japanese advance. If the troops were too noisy in the jungle, they frightened the uneasy foe before them. If they lost their way, they nevertheless managed to come in somehow on the enemy flank where they were least expected. If they failed to maintain contact one day,

---

* Throughout the Pacific war, there were frequent reports of Japanese riflemen in trees, but this was more often imagined than real. The Japanese often used trees as observation posts, and on occasion did fire from trees. But the field of fire from a tree is limited and usually obscured by foliage. The noise of a rifle-shot in the jungle is difficult to localise, the bullets clipping branches may sound like the discharge of a weapon in a tree to a nervous soldier. Finally, Japanese field manuals did not prescribe such tactics, although Japanese believed that the Allies employed them. Allied manuals did not encourage the practice either. Clearly, there was a great deal of imagination involved on both sides when it came to sighting snipers in trees.

they applied unrelenting pressure the next. And if they sometimes took foolish risks, they also proved the value of bold tactics. Most important of all, they kept moving, and thus rarely allowed the defenders the chance to catch their breath.

Yamashita's troops displayed great mobility in moving on foot through the jungle and swamps, while using trucks, motor-cycles, and bicycles to advance rapidly along the road, and small boats to move across and up and down waterways. They were adept at utilising local means of transport, rounding up bicycles and boats in almost every village and town. Their forward troops travelled lightly, carrying only small-arms, light mortars, and grenades, and a limited quantity of rations, leaving the heavier supplies and equipment to come along behind them in trucks. They used artillery when they had it handy, but depended more on rapid, tank-led thrusts than on formal infantry attacks prefaced by long artillery preparations. So far, Japanese air strength had been directed primarily against British airfields, but the defending units had felt the sting of air attack, and the fear of parachute assaults weighed heavily on their minds. Japanese air units moved forward quickly to each newly captured airfield, enabling combat planes to spend more time over their targets and less in flying back and forth to their bases.

The Malayan campaign, in short, was an excellent example of the proper employment of well-trained, aggressive, and highly mobile troops, led with bold imagination and ably supported.

Against these devastating tactics, Percival had no tanks and little airpower. His troops were ill-trained and equipped for this sort of combat, and were constantly being overwhelmed in detail. To defend a huge area, he had the equivalent of one full division in north-west Malaya, battered and exhausted from continuous defeat, and a two-brigade division in the north-east. The 8th Australian Division (two brigades) was in Johore, still uncommitted, and of course there were garrison troops on Singapore Island. But he felt he could not move these troops north from Johore or Singapore, for this would leave his rear vulnerable to seaborne assault. And commitment of only a part of the 8th Division would not only be undesirable tactically, but also would be unpopular with the Australians, who had strong feelings against piecemeal employment of the division. He could not expect much help from the depleted British air units at Singapore. The bulk of these were now assigned to the defence of the Singapore base; to protect it and the southern Johore coast against seaborne invasion, to secure the port and airfields for the arrival of outside aid, and to give convoy protection when help actually came. Percival would have to fight with what he had in northern Malaya, until reinforcements arrived.

These reinforcements were already on the way, although it would be a while before they could reach Malaya. A week earlier, hard on the loss of the *Prince of Wales* and the *Repulse*, the British Chiefs of Staff had considered what they might send to Singapore. Allowing for the demands of other theatres, there was not much available. There was still, for example, nothing in the way of a fleet for Admiral Layton — who had resumed command in the Far East after Admiral Phillips's death. The aircraft-carrier *Indomitable*, originally planned for Force Z, would reach Cape Town on New Year's Day, and five old battleships would soon be in the Indian Ocean, but no modern and balanced fleet could reach the area before spring at the earliest. Clearly, British naval power could not be brought to bear in time to affect the outcome in Malaya.

Ground reinforcements were another matter. The British 18th Division and its supporting units, then on their way to the Middle East, were diverted to India, and another division scheduled to leave India for the Middle East was held in India. The hope that these forces would not be needed in Malaya and could be used to defend India was quickly destroyed by General Yamashita's swift successes. On December 16th, Air-Chief-Marshal Brooke-Popham asked for a brigade and other troops from India, and warned that he would need further reinforcements as well. The Chiefs-of-Staff immediately arranged to send him the 45th Brigade from India as well as the 53rd Brigade, 18th Division, then still on the high seas. Other reinforcements were also soon put under orders for Malaya, but it would be weeks, perhaps months, before any of these units could arrive and get into action.

Air reinforcements held promise of the earliest arrival. Eight Hudsons were soon on their way from Australia and eighteen Blenheim bombers from Egypt. The Japanese cut the air route to Singapore in mid-December, however, when Fifteenth Army troops occupied the airfield at Victoria Point in southern Burma. Bomber reinforcements could continue to fly into Singapore, but the badly-needed, but shorter-range, fighters could no longer get within flying distance of their goal. Thus, fifty-one Hurricanes diverted to Malaya had to be sent in crates by sea, put together on arrival, and tested before they could be of any use. These and other aircraft were nevertheless soon under way to Singapore. Unfortunately, because of the distances involved, many had difficulties en route and failed to arrive. Others were very slow in coming in. The delay in fighter reinforcements was particularly hard on the Singapore defenders.

The problem of reinforcements — particularly of fighter planes — in effect dictated Percival's strategy. 'I held the view', he wrote later, 'that the first step towards recovery of any sort was to regain control of the air and that this could only be done by bringing in more fighters. I was prepared to make almost any sacrifice to get these fighters in safely. . . .'[18] His general plan, endorsed by the Chiefs of Staff and again by an Allied conference at Singapore on December 18th, was to hold the Japanese as far north in Malaya as possible to prevent their seizing areas, particularly airfields such as those at Kuala Lumpur and Kuantan, from which they could cut off the arrival of reinforcements. In so doing, however, he had to bear in mind the necessity of preserving suitable forces for the ultimate defence of Singapore itself, another reason why neither he nor Brooke-Popham was willing to draw on the Australians in Johore nor the troops on Singapore Island for operations in the north.

Percival's objective, on which he, Brooke-Popham, and the Chiefs of Staff agreed, was the defence of the Singapore naval base.[19] This had always been the objective: to hold the naval base for the arrival of the fleet. Much has been made of Winston Churchill's references to the Singapore 'fortress', and of the difference between defending the 'fortress' — i.e., the island — and protecting the naval base on its north shore.[20] The fortress could presumably be held even if all the mainland were lost, whereas protection of the naval base — the use of which by the fleet could be denied by an enemy in southern Johore — implied the defence of Johore as well. While Churchill and many others had an exaggerated notion of the strength of the 'fortress', there would seem to be little doubt that all involved realised that the key to holding the 'fortress', the naval base, and, indeed, southern Johore, was Singapore Island, through which reinforcements would have to flow.

But to bring in these reinforcements required a delaying action in northern Malaya that might lead to the commitment and destruction, before help could arrive, of those very forces necessary for whatever ultimate defence might be contrived. Everything depended on reinforcements, particularly in aircraft, and Percival was ready to stake all to ensure their arrival. He was, perforce, playing an all-or-nothing game. Without reinforcements, neither the naval base nor the fortress could be held, yet the strategy necessary to gain time for the arrival of reinforcements was such that, if it failed, it automatically doomed Singapore. This was the tragic irony of the defence of Malaya — and

Percival's bitter dilemma.

Percival's strategy, then, was to hold the Japanese as far north as possible, while limiting his own losses as best he could. On December 17th, General Heath told him he was worried about the Japanese flanking movement down the Kroh-Grik road and asked permission to withdraw all of III Corps behind the Perak River line. The Perak, running parallel to the Japanese line of advance for most of its course, would be difficult to defend. But there seemed little choice. After a personal reconnaissance on the 17th and 18th, Percival told Heath to delay as long as he could west of the Perak, authorised him to withdraw across it when necessary, and instructed him to prepare further delaying positions below the river. For the latter, Heath would have to depend primarily on his own resources, for in order to ensure the safe arrival of reinforcements Percival assigned priority of the available labour supply to the maintenance of airstrips in southern Johore and on Singapore Island. The 11th Division would be reorganised, combining the depleted 6th and 15th Brigades into a single unit called the 6/15th Brigade. All Murray-Lyon's brigade commanders had been wounded, so Lieutenant-Colonel H.D. Moorhead, who had commanded Krohcol, would command the 6/15th, and Lieutenant-Colonel W.R. Selby would take over the 28th Brigade. Paris's 12th Brigade would be incorporated as the third brigade of the division. Seaborne raiding units would be formed to prevent any Japanese advance by water along the west coast and to raid enemy communications inland. In north-eastern Malaya, meanwhile, the 9th Division would continue to hold their ground, denying Kuantan airfield to the Japanese and protecting the 11th Division against attack from that quarter.

The delaying of the Japanese west of the Perak fell to the 28th Brigade, at the Krian River on the trunk road, and the Argyll battalion of the 12th Brigade, now well below Grik. The 6/15th Brigade was reforming at Ipoh, to the south, having already crossed the Perak. The Japanese, meanwhile, maintained pressure along both the trunk road and the Grik road in the hope of breaking through on one of these avenues to capture the important Perak River bridges intact. This was no easy task. The 28th Brigade troops held out for two days; but finally, to avoid being outflanked, they withdrew down the trunk road. At the same time, the Argyll battalion, supported by other 12th Brigade forces, fought a grim delaying action. Colonel Ando's troops attempted to get behind Paris's units by moving down the river and through the low-lying swamps. The defenders managed to avoid these traps, and set their own ambushes for the aggressive Japanese. Soon however it became a question of whether the 42nd Infantry advance along the Grik road would cut off 28th Brigade troops on the trunk road, or whether the main force of the 5th Division on the trunk road would cut off the 12th Brigade before it could get south. The two brigades took turns to withdraw, covering each other's flank, and by early on December 23rd both units had crossed the Perak in the Kuala Kangsar area. To the dismay of the Japanese, they also succeeded in doing a thorough job of destroying all the bridges.

But the retreat had taken its toll. With little or no chance to sleep, the defenders were weakening rapidly. 'It can't go on like this', wrote one officer. 'The troops are absolutely dead-beat. The only rest they're getting is that of an uneasy coma as they squat in crowded lorries which jerk their way through the night. . . . They're bound to crack soon'.[21]

A slight pause in operations gave the defenders a brief time to rest and complete the reorganization of the 11th Division. Percival now felt that an officer more experienced in jungle warfare was needed to command the division, so he relieved Murray-Lyon and replaced him with Paris. Stewart of the Argylls took over the 12th Brigade. Another command change occurred in Singapore. Several weeks before the start of the war, the Chiefs of Staff had obtained approval from Churchill to replace Brooke-Popham with a younger officer with more recent field experience. Brooke-Popham's successor was delayed in leaving London however, and not until late December did Lieutenant-General Sir Henry Pownall reach Singapore and assume the Far East command. By then, the command had been somewhat reduced. In mid-December, London had shifted responsibility for Burma to the commander in India. Hong Kong, Brooke-Popham's other charge, surrendered two days before Pownall arrived.

On the Japanese side, meanwhile, more of General Yamashita's forces were reaching Malaya. Despite damaging attacks by Dutch submarines, additional tank units and service and support troops had landed at Singora and Patani. Lieutenant-General Takuma Nishimura's Imperial Guards Division was moving overland from Thailand. More and more 3rd Air Group units were also moving south, into position to provide close support for the ground troops. Yamashita planned to continue to drive forward as quickly as possible in western Malaya with the 5th Division. When the Guards Division reached the battlefield, the two divisions would leap-frog each other, in order to maintain continuous pressure from a fresh unit against the obviously weakened British. The Twenty-fifth Army commander hoped that the rapidity and force of his advance would keep the defenders off balance and prevent them from mounting any organised resistance. If necessary, part or all, of the Guards Division would be thrown in with the 5th against difficult objectives. In the east, at the same time, Yamashita planned to capture Kuantan airfield, to provide a base for close air support for operations in southern Malaya.

Although the Japanese had expected to have to fight to cross the Perak, the north-south direction of the river and the shape of the local road-net removed this necessity. The British defenders had easy access to the river at only two points, the main trunk road crossing near Kuala Kangsar and a secondary crossing some twenty miles south at Blanja. Laterial movement east of the Perak between these points was extremely difficult. The Japanese, on the other hand, could move at will west of the river up and down the Kuala Kangsar-Blanja road, and could attempt a crossing wherever they pleased with little fear of immediate opposition. So, to avoid being outflanked in a hopeless attempt to defend the riverline General Heath decided not to make the effort. He ordered the 11th Division to fall back east of the Perak prepared to make a major stand at Kampar on the trunk road about thirty miles south-south-east of Kuala Kangsar. North of Kampar was a broad, open area, with good observation points and fields of fire, dominated by a high rock- and jungle-covered hill which blocked the main route of advance. Jungle to the east and swamps to the west made the position all but impossible to outflank, except by troops in boats moving down the coast or through the lower reaches of the Perak. The reorganised 6/15th Brigade took up a position at Kampar, while the 12th Brigade fought delaying actions on the trunk road to the north around Ipoh, and the 28th Brigade did the same to the east of Blanja. These dispositions were generally complete by Christmas Day.

While this was taking place, General Yamashita, anticipating a disputed crossing of the Perak, had concentrated the 5th Division around Blanja, and the 4th Guards Regiment, which had just arrived, at Kuala Kangsar. Engineers brought forward bridging-equipment and boats in preparation for the assault. Simultaneously, the 3rd Air Group began heavy attacks on the Kuala Lumpur airfield, forcing Air-Vice-Marshal Pulford to withdraw to Singapore fighter planes brought forward to support III Corps. Other Japanese aircraft bombed and strafed the main Perak crossings, and 11th Division troops and vehicles east of the river.

General Sugaware could even spare a few planes to drop propaganda leaflets on Singapore and elsewhere in Malaya. These were in several languages – English, Malayan, Chinese, Hindustani, Urdu, and some others, none very idiomatic – aimed at civilians and soldiers of all nationalities. Some were boldly illustrated in bright colours; they were crudely drawn but the meaning was unmistakeable. One type of leaflet sought to turn the local population against the British, calling for war on the 'White Devils', and picturing a fat European planter exploiting his Tamil workers or drinking whiskey with his foot on a Malay's neck. Another propaganda message urged British troops to stop risking their lives for the upper classes, while still others warned of reprisals for alleged mistreatment of Japanese civilians. Explicit pictures showed what sort of ugly treatment the European women in Singapore could expect from the Japanese. Australian soldiers, at the same time, found pictures of enticing young ladies imploring them to come home to their waiting arms.

Pamphlets dropped to Indian troops showed how their British officers hid in safety while the Indians braved the dangers of the front. Other messages, prepared by Major Fujiawara and Captain Mohan Singh, called on Indian units to surrender. Fujiwara also sent a few well-indoctrinated Indian prisoners back to the British lines to tell their compatriots how nicely they had been treated and how strong the Japanese were.[22]

Late on the afternoon of Christmas Day, from his command-post barely twenty miles from the front Yamashita gave the order to advance. 'The enemy in the northern area of Malaya has been annihilated', he announced. The remnants of the 'defeated force' were fleeing beyond the Perak River, destroying roads and bridges as they fled. The Twenty-fifth Army would 'quickly pursue the enemy by crossing the Perak River to occupy Kuala Lumpur'.[23]

Shortly after 8 a.m. on the morning of the 26th, the 4th Guards Regiment crossed the river near Kuala Kangsar. To the astonishment of all, there was no opposition. The men traversed the broad river – without their vehicles – in small boats, some of which had been brought overland all the way from Singora. Close behind came engineers to repair the bridges and open the way for the advance of tanks and other vehicles. The Guards regiment did not wait, but reformed and began to move along the trunk road toward Ipoh. That afternoon it made contact with the 12th Brigade about ten miles north of the town. A fierce struggle ensued, all but halting Japanese progress. But 12th Brigade casualties were severe. The Hyderabad battalion, back from north-eastern Malaya, lost nearly a company in a daring attempt to outflank the aggressive Japanese Guards force.

By late afternoon of the 27th, General Paris was seriously concerned about the brigade. The troops were exhausted, especially since the growing activity of General Sugawara's air units prevented them from getting much rest. 'Officers and men moved like automata', recalled one observer, 'and often could not grasp the simplest order'.[24] The defenders might be able to hold their ground above Ipoh, but only at the cost of heavy casualties which would destroy their further effectiveness. They were now also faced with a new threat. Colonel Kanichi Okabe's 41st Infantry had begun crossing the Perak at Blanja early on the evening of the 26th. Unopposed except by patrols, it was moving east and would soon encounter the main body of the 28th Brigade. Paris had hoped to retain the 28th undamaged for the defence of Kampar, but withdrawing it now would expose the 12th Brigade to encirclement. Late on December 27th he ordered both brigades to pull back after dark. The 28th would move in on the right of the 6/15th at Kampar, while the 12th had the difficult task of delaying the enemy advance along the trunk road. That evening Ipoh was abandoned to the Japanese. The Japanese 4th Guards Regiment entered the city 'in high spirits over their success so early in the war'.[25]

While the Guards enjoyed their moment of triumph, the 41st Infantry was pressing ahead from its bridgehead at Blanja. On the morning of December 28th, it reached the trunk road and turned south. Brigadier Stewart had planned an elaborate ambush for the Japanese, but Colonel Okabe's troops attacked the 12th Brigade positions before the trap was ready. Early in the afternoon, they began infiltrating the Hyderabad battalion. Soon a full-scale battle developed. The Hyderabads retreated gradually, while the Argylls, on their left, successfully fought off a flanking attempt. The fighting continued during the night and in the morning the Japanese attacked again, this time supported by dive-bombers and punishing artillery fire. As the defenders fell back slowly, General Paris authorised them to withdraw across the Kampar River that evening. In mid-afternoon, however, Okabe launched a combined frontal and flanking attack, and then sent eight tanks and a column of truck-borne infantry straight down the trunk road. This proved too much for the defenders. Some armoured cars and trucks from the Argyll battalion managed to delay the tanks, at great cost to the Highlanders, and a skillfully handled antitank gun also did some damage, but the Japanese were no longer to be denied. The 12th Brigade crossed the Kampar shortly after 6 p.m. on the 29th, passed through the defences there, and continued south to go into reserve and, they hoped, to get some rest. Confused orders and damp explosives nearly resulted in the Kampar bridge remaining intact.

Australian troops, in training, moving along a jungle path in single file, December 1941

Admiral Sir Geoffrey Layton

Major General H. G. Bennett

Finally, however, after several discouraging attempts, one end of the span was dropped into the river.

Further west, meanwhile, the British were experiencing a rare, if minor, triumph. Percival's decision of December 18th to form a seaborne raiding unit to disrupt Japanese communications had been in part the result of a suggestion by Major Angus Rose, an officer of the Argylls on duty at Malaya Command headquarters. Two days after Christmas, a small raiding party called Roseforce – a platoon of Australians with Rose going along as observer – sailed up the west coast to a point south-west of Kuala Kangsar, landed, and made its way inland. After stumbling around in the swamps and jungle, avoiding Japanese patrols, the raiders eventually managed to set a somewhat haphazard ambush. They succeeded in shooting up a small Japanese truck convoy, apparently killing some senior officers in the process, and made good their escape by sea. The members of Roseforce were the first Australian infantrymen to go into action against the Japanese in World War II.

Another British officer, Lieutenant-Colonel Spencer Chapman, and a sergeant, who passed through Japanese lines at the same time intending to rendezvous with Roseforce and guide it to suitable targets, were unable to find the Australians. But both Roseforce and Chapman returned with much useful information about activities in the enemy rear. Their exploits also revealed the vulnerability of the long Japanese lines of communication; a weakness that the British, unhappily for the defence of Singapore, were never able to exploit.*

Back at the Kampar position, things remained relatively quiet until New Year's Day, 1942. Patrols from the 41st Infantry probed 28th Brigade defences north-east of Kampar on December 30th, and stronger elements of Colonel Okabe's regiment brushed up against 6/15th Brigade positions west of Kampar on the 31st. Heavy British artillery-fire discouraged any direct frontal attack down the trunk road, but in the face of growing pressure the defenders pulled back some of their outpost units. Okabe's men were thus able to cross the Kampar River, despite punishing British shellfire.

By now, General Matsui, the aggressive 5th Division commander, was becoming concerned over the slow progress of his troops. To assist Okabe, he had sent most of the 42nd Infantry through the swamps west

---

* Rose was only an observer with the force that bore his name since British officers did not normally command Australian troops, a point on which the Australians tended to be sensitive. Angus Rose, *Who Dies Fighting* (London: Johnathan Cape, 1944), chaps. iv-v; Chapman, *The Jungle is Neutral,* chap. iii.

of the trunk road in an attempt to outflank the Kampar defenders. But Colonel Ando's men were making little progress. Chest-deep in the marshy jungle, covered with leeches, and exhausted by their struggle in the tropical heat, the troops advanced little more than a mile a day. On New Year's Eve, as they ate their cold rice and shivered in the damp night air, they were still too far away to participate in the battle. Matsui, nevertheless, urged Okabe to press on.

At 6.30 a.m. on January 1st, Japanese artillery began a heavy bombardment of the main Kampar defences. Half an hour later, the 41st Infantry attacked down the trunk road toward the 6/15th Brigade. The assault struck the British Battalion — a combination of the survivors of the East Surrey and Leicester battalions of the 6th and 15th Brigades — and fighting raged all day along a series of ridge lines. Okabe's men suffered relatively heavy casualties but managed, by nightfall, to gain a foothold at one end of the British position.

By now a stronger Japanese threat was developing. In his orders on Christmas Day, General Yamashita had directed Matsui to send a large detachment by water down the west coast to cut off the British withdrawal route. On the 26th Colonel Tsunahiko Watanabe took about a battalion and a half of his 11th Infantry Regiment, with artillery and engineer support, and began moving south along a coastal road toward Lumut, a small harbour west of Kampar. It was probably part of this movement that Roseforce ambushed, but otherwise Watanabe experienced no difficulty. By the 30th he had assembled his force at Lumut, with about sixty small steamers, barges, motor-boats, and other craft, of which many had been carried overland from Singora and about a score captured at Penang.

That night, the flotilla sailed.* Air reconnaissance from Singapore spotted it the next day, as did 11th Division patrols operating near the coast. These patrols made another sighting on New Year's Day, and a request was flashed to Singapore for air or naval action against the Japanese flotilla. Naval forces were unavailable — even the boats assembled for Roseforce had since been put out of action by the Japanese 3rd Air Group — and most of the slim British air resources were required for the protection of the first reinforcement convoy, then approaching Singapore. Nevertheless, a few planes managed to fly up that day and strafe some of Watanabe's boats, wounding a number of his men.[26]

* British accounts state that Watanabe sailed from further north, but Japanese sources indicate that he left from Lumut. His boats obviously sailed down the coast to that point, which may account for the confusion.

Watanabe's objective was the coastal town of Kuala Selangor, well to the south. But fearing further air attack he landed on the evening of January 1st a few miles below the mouth of the Perak, and sent a pessimistic message to General Matsui recommending that the amphibious manoeuvre should be called off. Matsui was still worried about the unexpectedly strong resistance at Kampar. He asked Yamashita for permission to postpone Watanabe's original mission, and to use his force now to outflank the Kampar position. Opinion at Twenty-fifth Army headquarters was divided — some staff officers even recommended that Watanabe should be relieved — but Yamashita decided to approve Matsui's request. New orders went out to Watanabe, who quickly advanced inland, driving back 11th Division patrols south-west of Telok Anson.

It was now General Paris's turn to be worried. Despite the success of the British Battalion at Kampar, Watanabe's landing posed a strong threat to the 11th Division line of communication. Paris had shifted some elements to the south-west on first receiving word of the Japanese amphibious move. Now he sent Stewart's 12th Brigade to hold the approaches from Telok Anson to the trunk road. He also asked Heath's permission to withdraw from Kampar if this became necessary. General Percival was visiting III Corps headquarters at the time and he agreed to allow Paris to use his discretion, so long as Heath felt this would not interfere with plans to delay the Japanese in central Malaya.

The next morning, January 2nd, Colonel Okabe's men attacked again at Kampar. If anything, the fight was heavier than on New Year's Day. Two gallant counter-attacks in the afternoon succeeded in wiping out Japanese gains, but the defenders were suffering heavy casualties. Although the 41st Infantry was also taking losses, it was clear that the Japanese attacks would be increasingly hard to repulse. But again the primary threat was amphibious. From Ipoh, the 3rd Battalion of the 4th Guards Regiment had sailed down the Perak River in captured boats and just after dawn on the 2nd the Japanese troops began landing at Telok Anson. British patrols engaged them and then fell back on the 12th Brigade, east of the town. The Guards battalion, joined during the day by Colonel Watanabe's force, advanced along the road and in boats up the many streams that flowed through the muddy tide-lands around Telok Anson. By nightfall, the defenders had been forced east, nearly halfway to the trunk road, the only line of retreat for the Kampar defenders.

Paris no longer had any choice. On the night of the 2nd, he ordered the 11th Division to disengage and withdraw south to the next major delaying position. His forces executed the difficult manoeuvre without too much trouble, covering each other in turn as they fell back during the night and on the next day, January 3rd. He was hampered only by heavy Japanese air attacks. Unopposed in the air, General Sugawara's flyers bombed and strafed at will, crippling vehicles and inflicting many casualties. The morning of January 4th nevertheless found Paris's troops nearing the Slim River, well to the south.

By now, the Japanese 42nd Infantry had finally made its way out of the swamps west of Kampar – too late to interfere with the 11th Division's retreat, but just in time to relieve the 41st Infantry in the drive down the trunk road. Supporting Colonel Ando's advance were elements of the 1st Tank Regiment, strong engineer units, and the reassuring presence of the 3rd Air Group. Additional assistance would be provided by a battalion of the 11th Infantry and most of the 4th Guards Regiment, advancing by sea and along a coastal trail to Kuala Selangor.

From Kuala Selangor several narrow roads and streams ran east and south-east, giving access to the main British lines of communication. Since this seemed a likely place for a landing, a small British detachment, with artillery, was stationed there, and on January 2nd and 3rd they drove off attempts to land by the 3rd Battalion of the 11th Infantry Regiment. General Heath detached a battalion from the 6/15th Brigade to help cover the area. On the 4th, however, about a battalion of Guards troops, which had apparently come south along the coastal trial, met the British north of Kuala Selangor and pushed them rapidly back. By the next day, the Japanese had driven inland to a point barely eleven miles from the trunk road, some seventy miles below the main 11th Division position. Heath at once sent the rest of the 6/15th to meet this threat, placing Brigadier Moorhead in charge of all coastal defences in the area. Moorhead counter-attacked, drove the Guards battalion back, destroyed a number of bridges, and succeeded in stabilising the situation by the 6th. The threat to the 11th Division's line of communication was halted for the time being, but General Paris now had only two brigades left with which to face the 5th Division attack.

To meet this blow, Paris deployed his forces across the main avenues leading to the Slim River crossings. 'I loathe this talk of position and holding lines', he had noted a week earlier. 'In this country there is one and only one tactical feature that matters – the roads. I am sure the answer is to hold the roads in real depth'.[27] The dispositions he now ordered reflected this view.

Above Trolak, several miles north of the Slim River, was Stewart's 12th Brigade, deployed in depth astride the trunk road and the railway line, which at this point were only a few hundred yards apart. The Hyderabad battalion, now only three companies strong, was out-posted forward. A battalion of Punjabis held the main position. The Argyll battalion was echeloned in the rear, extending well into the jungle on both sides. A reserve Punjabi battalion was below Trolak, ready to move forward if necessary. The three Gurkha battalions of the 28th Brigade were further south, but not yet in position, since General Paris had ordered the brigade to get some more rest before deploying along the north bank of the Slim.

The division had had nearly two days in which to prepare its defences, but the men were exhausted, many lethargic from lack of sleep and others demoralised from continual defeat. Japanese planes, almost constantly bombing and strafing during the day, restricted work to the hours of darkness, and prevented sleep at other times. Lieutenant-Colonel C.C. Deakin, commanding the Punjabis in the main position, found his men dispirited and 'thoroughly depressed', apparently unwilling to do anything 'but sit in slit trenches'.[28] Stewart's brigade, nevertheless, had managed to erect wire and a few tank obstacles, to put in some mines, and to make a start at digging in. Bridges across streams to the rear had been prepared for demolition. But there were few anti-tank guns available and, in the thick jungle, most of the artillery had been moved back to the 28th Brigade area. Nor, of course, could the defenders count on any air support.

Meanwhile, the Japanese 42nd Infantry Regiment was approaching on the trunk road. The men rode on bicycles, peddling cheerfully along, their arms and equipment slung across their backs or tied to their bikes, looking for all the world like some large and somewhat disorganised group of sportsmen with nothing on their mind but shooting.[29] At almost every one of the many streams that crossed the road, the bridge had been blown up. This failed to stop the riders, who simply lifted their bicycles to their shoulders and waded through the shallow water, but the bridge and road demolitions seriously delayed tanks, artillery, and other equipment. The engineers worked feverishly to make repairs, doing such a good job that by noon of the 6th the heavy vehicles had caught up and were in position to support Colonel Ando's attack.

Before then, on the afternoon of the 5th, one or two companies of Japanese infantry tried to push on down the railway tracks unsupported. Heavy fire from the Hyderabads, at close range, drove them back with considerable losses, so Colonel Ando decided to await the

arrival of his tanks. He spent most of January 6th feeling out the flanks
of the Hyderabad position and preparing to attack. Refugee reports
reaching the 11th Division late that afternoon warned the defenders
that the Japanese were massing tanks.

The night of the 6th was lit by brilliant moonlight. Shortly after
midnight, the Hyderabads opened fire on Japanese infantry advancing
down both the trunk road and the railway tracks. At about 3.30 a.m.
on the 7th, right on schedule, Ando's supporting mortars and artillery
began firing, and the infantry pressure increased. Japanese troops
quickly overran the forward tank obstacles and the anti-tank gunners.
Then a column of tanks and truck-borne infantry swept down the road,
firing heavily, and broke through the first Hyderabad company. Other
Japanese troops advanced down the railway, while still more tanks
came in on the defenders' flanks along an overgrown and abandoned
loop road. The Hyderabad battalion was completely cut up and
dispersed. Some of the men managed to escape, but many more were
killed or taken prisoner.

Barely half an hour had passed. So far only the 3rd Battalion of the
42nd Infantry, and a few platoons of tanks, had engaged the 12th
Brigade. Colonel Ando had sent his other two battalions on flanking
sweeps through the jungle on either side of the main advance, and
neither of these had yet made contact. But it seemed that the 3rd
Battalion and the tanks would be sufficient.

The tank column continued forward until at about 4.30 a.m.; when
it reached the Punjabi battalion, the leading tank struck a mine and
halted. As the others stopped behind it, a heavy struggle at close range
began. 'The din,' recalled Colonel Deakin, 'defies description. The
tanks . . . were nose to tail — their engines racing, their crews yelling,
their machine-guns spitting tracer, and their mortars and cannon firing
all out'.[30] The Punjabis tried to knock out the tanks with Molotov
cocktails and anti-tank weapons, but the Japanese infantry swept
around their flanks and subjected them to punishing fire. Then the
tanks discovered another unused loop road, moved round on this, and
drove in again on the flank. The forward Punjabi units were overrun
and sliced to pieces, and many of the men retreated south through the
jungle in an attempt to escape. Not until the Japanese reached the last
Punjabi defences, held by the reserve company and battalion headquarters, was their attack halted. Here again mines stopped the tanks,
and for about an hour the defenders held, taking heavy casualties. Then
the Japanese tanks discovered still a third loop road. The Punjabi's
commander, with less than three dozen men left, decided that he could

do no more. With his small force he fell back through the jungle, losing most of his men to infiltrating Japanese or the difficult terrain. Of the entire battalion, less than seventy survived the encounter, and many of these were killed or captured before they could reach safety.

By about 6.30 a.m. the attack had reached the Argylls. A breakdown in communications had prevented accurate word of the Japanese success from getting back, so when the leading tanks struck the first Highland roadblock, the defenders were taken off-balance. The Japanese armour swept through the block and ploughed forward. A second block, backed by a few armoured cars, offered only a little more resistance, and the tanks crashed through. At Trolak, the charges on a bridge failed to go off – the Japanese claim their tank commander cut the wires with his sword – and the tanks continued on. By now, sometime after 7.30, the entire Argyll area was a confused mass of small fights. Japanese infantry and tanks swept through, firing in all directions, encountering islands of resistance which they either overran or flowed round. Some of the Hyderabad and Punjabi troops reached the area from their forward positions, and they too joined the battle or were once more overwhelmed by the Japanese. Casualties were heavy. A company of Argylls, attempting to block a minor road to the west, was practically annihilated by one of Colonel Ando's flanking battalions. Like the other 12th Brigade units, the Argyll battalion was smashed and scattered; less than 100 men managed to make good their escape. Many others, exhausted, sick or wounded, and hungry, staggered through the jungle until they eventually succumbed to the elements or to Japanese patrols.

Even as the Highland battalion was meeting its end, the Japanese tanks, pushing forward swiftly, ran headlong into the reserve Punjabi battalion as its companies moved forward in a column on the trunk road. The encounter took place beside a cemetery about a mile or so below Trolak. The tanks by now had outrun their infantry support, but again surprise served the Japanese well. Making good use of their mobility and firing-power, they overran the few anti-tank guns, killed or wounded most of the Punjabis, and scattered what was left of the batalion.

With the 12th Brigade virtually destroyed, it was now the turn of the 28th Brigade. The breakdown in communications had denied General Paris word of the unexpected Japanese breakthrough until 6.30 a.m. He immediately ordered the 28th to occupy its positions along the Slim River without delay. But Brigadier Selby's men were still on the move when the Japanese attack reached them.

The trunk road and railway from the north part company at the Slim River, the railway continuing straight ahead across the river while the road turns east and runs for five miles along the north bank of the river before it turns south again and crosses over. Selby planned to place one of his Gurkha battalions at the railway bridge, one on the trunk road immediately to the east, and the third on the road midway between this point and the highway bridge. Only the railway bridge was occupied when, at 8 a.m., the leading tanks pushed past the second Gurkha battalion, just getting on to the trunk road. The battalion had no way of halting the tanks, so simply continued to move into position, anticipating that Japanese infantry would be immediately behind the armour.

Selby's third battalion was still marching east in close column formation when the Japanese tanks overtook it. The tanks ploughed through the surprised and terrified Gurkhas, scattering them into the jungle and river to escape the punishing fire of the Japanese weapons. With nothing to stop them now. the tanks continued on toward the road bridge. They halted momentarily to shoot up two batteries of British artillery and an ambulance unit, parked and waiting beside the road, and then swept on to reach the bridge at about 8.40; barely five hours and seventeen miles after they had started their dash through the 11th Division.

At the Slim River bridge, an anti-aircraft battery, deployed there to protect the span against aerial attack, now found itself face to face with an unexpected enemy. The gunners depressed their barrels and opened fire, but the light shells bounced off the tanks like so many tennis balls. The Japanese quickly overran the battery and charged across the bridge before anyone could blow it up.

Leaving one or two tanks to guard the bridge, the Japanese pushed on. As they continued south, they encountered small parties of British rear echelon troops, and shot up and dispersed each group as they reached it. Finally, two miles below the bridge, at about 9.30, they met their match: a regiment of field artillery, moving forward to support the 28th Brigade. The Japanese overran part of the surprised artillery column; but then a howitzer detachment got its 4.5-inch piece into action. At a range of only thirty yards, it knocked out the leading tank and impressed upon the others the wisdom of withdrawal. The Japanese fell back to the bridge where, without infantry support, they were content to remain, guarding their valuable prize.

While this was taking place, the rest of the 28th Brigade was still in position in the area above the railway bridge, which Brigadier Selby hoped to hold until dark. Colonel Ando's infantry, apparently engaged in mopping up the 12th Brigade, did not make contact with Selby's troops until mid-afternoon when, under pressure, the Gurkha battalions began to withdraw across the railway bridge. Most of the men got over the river during the night, although some who attempted to swim were carried downstream by the swift current. Selby and the survivors made their way across country to a point on the trunk road well to the south, where the British hoped to make their next stand.

The Slim River battle was a disaster for III Corps and a brilliant victory for the Japanese 5th Division. Most of the damage was done by one company of medium tanks, supported by a battalion or so of infantry and a force of hardworking engineers. Without taking away any credit from the aggressive Japanese tactics, it is difficult to overlook the failure of the defenders to make better use of anti-tank defences, the breakdown in their communications, and their apparent inability to absorb the lessons of earlier encounters with enemy tank/infantry teams. Yet it is also a fact that the 11th Division was mentally and physically exhausted by a month of uninterrupted combat, by constant batterings and withdrawals, by repeated aerial attacks, and by a fatiguing and enervating tropical climate whose effects were increased by all the other circumstances. If the troops of the 11th Division broke at the Slim, it is to their credit that they lasted till then.

The division was now almost completely destroyed as a combat formation. The 12th Brigade, assigned to replace the brigade lost earlier, was now reduced to about three companies. The 28th Brigade was only slightly better off. The two together totalled less than 1,200 men. The 6/15th Brigade, depleted and reduced, had not been engaged at the Slim River. But it was already involved in fighting off Yamashita's amphibious forces, and it too was taking losses it could ill afford. The Japanese had captured great quantities of weapons, vehicles, and other equipment, and more than a thousand prisoners. They could hardly be blamed for boasting, as they did, of annihilating an entire division.

Major Fujiwara played an important role in rounding up the prisoners, almost all of whom were Indians. Immediately after the battle, Indian troops captured earlier and organised by Mohan Singh appeared in the area. They wore white armbands marked with the letter — for Fujiwara *Kikan* (Organisation). Calling on their compatriots to surrender, they passed out white flags and armbands to those who did. As first, Major Fujiwara sent the new prisoners back to Ipoh in captured British trucks, but as more and more scattered Indian troops surrendered in the next few days the facilities at Ipoh quickly became overcrowded. Larger assembly areas would be available at Kuala Lumpur to the south. Although the British still held Kuala Lumpur, Fujiwara apparently anticipated its early capture. He ordered the Indian prisoners to be organised into groups of thirty to fifty men. These groups, without guards, but carrying a white flag with a large F and a safe conduct pass, were to make their way south to Kuala Lumpur. During the next few days, Japanese troops moving forward toward the front were astonished to encounter these strange units. After the fall of Kuala Lumpur, Mohan Singh began assembling all Indians captured so far — by now at least 3,500 — in camps there, and organising his Indian National Army. Fujiwara provided small-arms for two companies of Indian troops, and these units began training for future employment.[31]

On the battlefield, meanwhile, Japanese successes continued. The sacrifice of the 11th Division had been made in an attempt to hold the Japanese in northern Malaya, so that they could neither interfere with the arrival of reinforcements at Singapore nor capture the island before these reinforcements could land. And a primary reason for Percival's decision to fight in northern Malaya was to keep the airfields, especially those at Kuala Lumpur and Kuantan, out of General Sugawara's hands. Capture of these airfields would give the 3rd Air Group excellent bases from which to dominate the skies over Singapore. Despite the destruction of the 11th Division, Kuala Lumpur was still in British hands. The same could not be said of Kuantan.

By mid-December, the Takumi Detachment — a force built around the 56th Infantry Regiment, 18th Division, which had landed at Kota Bharu — had pushed the 8th Brigade, 9th Indian Division, all the way back to Kuala Lipis in central Malaya. Despite the heavy losses he had sustained, General Takumi had also begun moving south along the coast, through swamps and jungles and across extremely rugged terrain. Within a few days of Christmas he was approaching Kuantan. General Yamashita had originally assigned the capture of Kuantan to the 55th Infantry Regiment, 18th Division (less one battalion), which he planned to land there in late December. The advance of the Takumi Detachment, however, led him to reconsider. An amphibious assault on Kuantan would still be in danger of air attack from Singapore, not to mention a warm reception on the beaches. Since Takumi was already approaching Kuantan overland, Yamashita decided to let him take the town. He ordered the 55th Infantry to land at Kota Bharu and follow Takumi south.[32]

The defence of Kuantan was the responsibility of the 22nd Brigade,

9th Division. The brigade's mission, however, was not really clear. As the 11th Division retreated in western Malaya, General Heath had kept in mind the idea that the 9th Division should attack across the Malayan peninsula against the Japanese flank, using roads running west from Kuantan and Kuala Lipis. Accordingly, he told General Barstow commanding the 9th Division, that while it was important to hold Kuantan at least until the arrival of the first reinforcement convoy at Singapore in early January, he should not risk the destruction of the 22nd Brigade before it could participate in the contemplated flanking attack. There appears to have been some misunderstanding between Percival and Heath on this point, for Percival clearly wanted to keep the Japanese out of Kuantan airfield until January 10th, while Heath was more concerned with preserving the 22nd Brigade for an attack to the west.

Since Barstow received his orders from Heath, the 22nd Brigade dispositions reflected Heath's priorities. As the approach of the Takumi Detachment made the Japanese intentions clear, Barstow ordered Brigadier Gordon Painter, commanding the 22nd, to fall back from the shore-line to ensure his ability to withdraw his force intact. Before Painter could obey, however, General Takumi attacked, on the morning of December 30th. Supported by the 3rd Air Group, the Japanese quickly occupied Kuantan and turned inland toward the airfield. Painter, under orders to hold out as long as possible without jeopardising his force, resisted strongly but had to fall back, not without losses.

Fighting continued for the next few days, the 22nd Brigade giving ground grudgingly and continuing to take casualties. It was becoming clear that Painter could not hold on to the airfield without serious risk of losing most of his brigade. However, the evacuation of Kampar settled the issue. If the 9th Division was not to be trapped in central Malaya by Japanese forces blocking the few roads out of the area, Barstow's men would have to move out now. On January 3rd, orders reached Painter to evacuate Kuantan. His men carried out demolitions, and that night the brigade withdrew. A final Japanese attack succeeded in destroying nearly two companies of the rearguard, but the remainder of the force escaped to the west.

By the 8th of January, then, one month after the start of the war, all of northern Malaya was in Japanese hands. A line drawn from Kuantan in the east, straight across the peninsula, would cross the Slim River. Except for a small area in central Malaya, everything north of this line belonged to General Yamashita. The sacrifice of the 11th Division had delayed the enemy long enough for the first reinforcement convoy, carrying the 45th Indian Infantry Brigade, to reach Singapore two days after New Year's Day. More reinforcements were on the way, but they would have to arrive soon if Singapore was to be saved. The Japanese, too, were building up their strength. With the advantage they held already, to keep them from overrunning all of Malaya would be even more difficult than the abortive effort to hold the north had been. The 11th Division, at any rate, could no longer be expected to help.

NOTES – Chapter 6

1. Morrison, *Malayan Postscript*, pp. 59-60.

2. Noel Barber, *A Sinister Twilight: The Fall of Singapore 1942* (Boston: Houghton Mifflin, 1968), p. 48. Also *ibid.*, pp. 40-58 *passim*; Kenneth Attiwell, *Fortress: The Story of the Siege and Fall of Singapore* (New York: Doubleday, 1960), p. 59; Brown, *Suez to Singapore*, pp. 343-78 *passim*.

3. Glover, *In 70 Days*, pp. 125, 134.

4. Basic sources for this chapter as follows: (1) British operations: Percival, *Despatch*, pp. 1270-83, 1287-93; Kirby, *The Loss of Singapore*, pp. 203-19, 229-62, 269-81; Bhargava and Sastri, *Campaigns in South-East Asia*, pp. 140-233; Percival, *The War in Malaya*, pp. 121-64, 187-206; Mackenzie, *Eastern Epic*, I, 245-63, 268-81, 320-30; Brooke-Popham, *Despatch*, pp. 558-64; Wigmore, *The Japanese Thrust*, pp. 146-52, 157-69, 181-97; Maltby, *Report*, pp. 1369-74. (2) Japanese operations: Malay Operations Record, pp. 27-38, 42-65; Tsuji, *Singapore*, pp. 111-76; ATIS, Malaya Campaign, pp. 18-34, 41; Hattori, *The Greater East Asia War*, II, 55-60; Southwest Area Air Operations, pp. 52-73; Malaya Invasion Naval Operations, pp. 30-42.

5. Mackenzie, *Eastern Epic*, I, 247.

6. Swinson, *Four Samurai*, p. 104.

7. Percival, *The War in Malaya*, p. 133.

8. For the War Council, see also Duff Cooper, *Old Men Forget* (New York: Dutton, 1954), pp. 301-305; Churchill, *The Grand Alliance*, pp. 426, 611-12; Barber, *A Sinister Twilight*, pp. 43-46 and *passim*.

9. Bhargava and Sastri, *Campaigns in South-East Asia*, p. 163. See Major J.H.H. Coombes, *Banpong Express* (Darlington: Wm. Dresser, [1948]), pp. 19-20.

10. Japan Defence Agency, *Mare Shinko Sakusen*, pp. 329-34, 455; Khan, *I.N.A. & Its NETAJI*, pp. 14-15; Mahmood Khan Durrani, *The Sixth Column* (London: Cassell, 1955), pp. 2-4.

11. Percival, *The War in Malaya*, p. 132.

12. Diary of Superior Private Yamashita, 3rd Battalion, 41st Infantry, in ATIS, Current Translations, No. 45, June 1, 1943, p. 27. See also diary of another 41st Infantry soldier, in ATIS, Current Translation, No. 54, June 14, 1943, p. 29.

13. For Penang, see also Maxwell, *Civil Defence of Malaya*, pp. 105-109; Glover, *In 70 Days*, pp. 108-17; David George Kin, *Rage in Singapore* (New York: Wisdom House, 1942), pp. 237-39.

14. The account of the Argyll's in this chapter is also based on Brigadier I. MacA. Stewart, *History of the Argyll & Sutherland Highlanders 2nd Battalion: Malayan Campaign, 1941-1942* (London: Thomas Nelson, 1947), pp. 10-86.

15. Brown, *Suez to Singapore*, p. 376. For Japanese tactics and equipment in Malaya, also *ibid.*, pp. 374-76; Brooke-Popham, *Despatch*, pp. 564-65; Morrison, *Malayan Postscript*, pp. 78-83; Chapman, *The Jungle is Neutral*, pp. 27-29; Swinson, *Four Samurai*, p. 107.

16. See Japanese post-war interrogations in U.S. 'Far East Command, General Headquarters, Military History Section, Japanese Research Division, Special Studies (5 vols.; 1951-1960), I, Tab 12. See also John Miller, jr., *Guadalcanal: The First Offensive* (United States Army in World War II: The War in the Pacific) (Washington: Historical Division, Department of the Army, 1949), p. 318.

17. Morrison, *Malayan Postscript*, p. 103.

18. Percival, *The War in Malaya*, p. 153.

19. On this point, see also Gwyer and Butler, *Grand Strategy*, III, 412-14.

20. See, for example, Attiwell, *Fortress*, pp. 52-56.

21. Mackenzie, *Eastern Epic*, I, 262.

22. Maxwell, *Civil Defence of Malaya*, pp. 81-83; Morrison, *Malayan Postscript*, pp. 96-97; Japan Defence Agency, *Mare Shinko Sakusen*, p. 455.

23. Malay Operations Record, pp. 49-50.

24. Kirby, *The Loss of Singapore*, p. 243.

25. Tsuji, *Singapore*, p. 146.

26. Gillison, *Royal Australian Air Force*, pp. 323-24.

27. Bhargava and Sastri, *Campaigns in South-East Asia*, p. 194.

28. Kirby, *The Loss of Singapore*, pp. 275-76.

29. For an eye-witness account of a Japanese bicycle movement, see Chapman, *The Jungle is Neutral*, pp. 27-28.

30. Mackenzie, *Eastern Epic*, I, 324.

31. Japan Defence Agency, *Mare Shinko Sakusen*, pp. 455-58; Khan, *I.N.A. & Its NETAJI*, pp. 15-17; Durrani, *The Sixth Column*, p. 27.

32. See also Replies to Questions Concerning Operations Plans of the Japanese Forces for the Malaya Invasion, in Far East Command, *Special Studies*, I, Tab 8.

7

Decisive Struggle for Johore

The swift Japanese victories in December 1941 – not only in Malaya but throughout the Far East – and the growing disarray of Allied defensive forces, emphasised the critical need for some overall direction of the Allied effort in that theatre of war. On January 3rd, 1942, the Pacific Allies established ABDACOM (American-British-Dutch-Australian Command), a unified headquarters to control and co-ordinate operations in the general area of Burma, Malaya, the Netherlands Indies, and the Philippines. General Sir Archibald Wavell, Commander-in-Chief India, who had previously led British armies in Africa and Greece, now became the commander of ABDA. Fifty-seven years old, a distinguished soldier, linguist, and writer, he had a trim figure, sandy hair and moustache, and the rugged face of an outdoor man. Blind in one eye and naturally taciturn, he seemed shy and unimpressive. But those who knew him well held him in the highest esteem. Wavell's appointment eliminated the need for a British Commander-in-Chief Far East, and General Pownall assumed the post of ABDACOM chief of staff. Unlike either Pownall or Brooke-Popham before him, Wavell commanded naval as well as ground and air forces. Unified command in the ABDA area thus brought with it, for the first time, unified command in Malaya.[1]

On January 7th, the day of the crushing British defeat at the Slim River, Wavell flew into Singapore en route for his new headquarters on Java. After conferring with Percival, he went north on the 8th to visit the forward area and talk to local commanders, and then returned to give Percival general instructions for the defence of southern Malaya. Percival had been developing his own scheme of operations during the preceding week, and the two plans differed significantly only in the forces designated to implement their component missions. Basically the strategy called for holding the Japanese in northern Johore until sufficient reinforcements could arrive – at the end of January or in mid-February – to initiate a counter-offensive against the Twenty-fifth Army.

In view of what had happened to the 11th Division, it would be all but impossible to stop the Japanese north of Johore. Between the Slim River and Johore, the Malayan road system was a well-developed complex that would permit General Yamashita to make good use of his tanks and other mobile forces to outflank the defenders, while the exposed west coast was wide open to Japanese landings aimed at cutting the British line of retreat. According to Wavell's plan, after a temporary delaying action north of Kuala Lumpur the remnants of the 11th Division would retreat along the trunk road nearly 100 miles to northern Johore. The 9th Division, in central Malaya, would also withdraw to Johore. Strong defences would then be established along a general line from Mersing, on the east coast, through Segamat, to Muar, barely 120 miles from Singapore itself.

Percival had planned to hold the western half of this line with Heath's III Corps, consisting of the 9th and 11th Divisions plus the newly arrived 45th Indian Brigade, while defending eastern Johore with the two brigades of the Australian 8th Division, already concentrated in that area. Wavell, however, felt that Heath's troops were in no shape to do much fighting without first taking time out to rest and refit. He therefore ordered Major-General Bennett's 8th Division (less one brigade defending Mersing) to move to north-west Johore and prepare for 'a decisive battle'[2] along the general line of Segamat-Muar, with the 9th Division and the 45th Brigade coming under Bennett's command to help support this line. The remainder of III Corps, meanwhile, would defend the southern Johore coastline, rest, reorganise, and build a general reserve as additional reinforcements arrived. Bennett's other brigade would rejoin the 8th Division as soon as it could be relieved by troops from Singapore Island, probably in about a week's time when the 53rd Brigade of the British 18th Division reached Malaya. The arrival of the rest of the 18th Division later in the month would provide additional strength for holding the Japanese until mid-February when a two-division Australian corps was scheduled to arrive and, it was hoped, could spearhead a counter-offensive.

There were several disadvantages to this plan. It allowed the Japanese to advance dangerously close to Singapore, weakened the defences of eastern Johore, and temporarily split the 8th Division, depriving General Bennett of a fresh and well-trained brigade. It also placed the burden of controlling four brigades on an 8th Division staff that had not previously worked with three of these units, had no first-hand experience with Japanese tactics, and knew little of the terrain over which the units would be fighting.

Japanese soldiers advance into Penang

Japanese forces enter burning Kuala Lumpur

Japanese soldiers cautiously approach Johore Bahru

One of Singapore's coast defence guns, part of the 'Fixed Defence'

While the withdrawal from central Malaya and the weakening of eastern Johore were unavoidable, a more satisfactory defensive organisation might perhaps have been adopted. A better scheme, as suggested by the British official history of the campaign,[3] would have been to entrust the defence of north-west Johore to III Corps, as Percival had planned. Since Heath's troops had admittedly taken quite a beating certain changes would clearly have been necessary. An immediate shift of beach defence units from Singapore to Mersing, while involving some risk, would have allowed Bennett's entire division to be shifted west. The 8th and 9th Divisions and the 45th Brigade could then have constituted Heath's main defensive force, with the 11th Division and, when it arrived, 53rd Brigade, forming his reserve. The experienced III Corps staff would have had little difficulty in controlling these units, and the result would have been a much stronger, better-co-ordinated force opposing the Japanese advance.

Why Wavell did not adopt such dispositions is not entirely clear. The weakened state of Heath's troops did not preclude the further utilisation of III Corps headquarters staff, and the 9th Division was far from incapacitated. Wavell's judgment may perhaps have been affected by the views of General Bennett, an aggressive and outspoken officer with little patience for tactical conservatism. For some time now Bennett had been critical of what he considered a lack of determination and fighting spirit on the part of Heath. He was particularly disturbed in early January, and had made his views known to Percival, the Australian government, and presumably Wavell as well, when the ABDA commander visited him on the 8th. Bennett had furthermore told Percival that he was not anxious to place Australian forces under Heath, and had urged instead that III Corps be disbanded and all its forces put under his own command for the defence of Johore.[4] Whether these arguments convinced Wavell, or whether he simply believed the III Corps command echelon to be as exhausted as the troops, is not evident. But it is clear that Wavell was impressed with Bennett and with the Australian's manifest self-confidence. He had, furthermore, considerable disdain for the Japanese army and a firm belief that it posed no problem for properly led British forces.[5] This being so, Bennett's aggressive spirit may have seemed to be just what was needed to stop Yamashita. In any event, Wavell did not adopt what now appears to have been the most logical organization and command structure for the defense of Johore.

Wavell left Singapore for Java on January 10th, and on that day Percival issued his final orders. Bennett's command, to be known as

Westforce — consisting of the 8th Australian Division (less a brigade), the 9th Indian Division, and the 45th Indian Brigade — would hold the area between Muar and Batu Anam, a town some eight miles north-west of Segamat. The 22nd Australian Brigade at Mersing would come under III Corps, which was responsible for defending southern and eastern Johore. The 11th Indian Division would be rested and reorganised in Johore, while the 12th Brigade would be released from the division and moved to Singapore Island to be re-formed and re-equipped. To give the 11th Division an Indian Army commander who might better restore its confidence in itself, Percival now placed it under Key (formerly 8th Brigade, 9th Division). Paris, who would not otherwise have been relieved, would return to take over the 12th Brigade, and Stewart revert to the command of the Argyll and Sutherland Highlanders. In a further troop shift, two battalions from Singapore would come to the mainland; the 2nd Loyals to reinforce the 9th Division, and a battalion of Dogras troops to join III Corps on the east coast. On these dispositions, whatever their weaknesses, rested the fate of Johore and, indeed, Singapore.

Visiting Malaya again on the 13th, Wavell felt confident that Bennett and the Australians 'would handle the enemy roughly'. But he cabled the British Chiefs of Staff that the fight for Singapore would be 'a close run thing'.[6]

By now, all of Malaya north of Johore had been abandoned to General Yamashita. The 11th Division's withdrawal had been difficult and costly, but not the complete disaster it might have been had the Japanese chosen to press their advantage to the full. General Matsui had decided to rest most of his 5th Division, assigning only the 11th Infantry Regiment to pursue the battered enemy, while the 4th Guards Regiment was still the only unit of General Nishimura's division available in the combat area. These two regiments nevertheless applied continuous pressure, the 11th Infantry advancing down the trunk road and the 4th Guards along the coast by land and by amphibious movement. In several sharp engagements, Indian troops of the rearguard managed to thwart repeated Japanese efforts to break through. Losses among the defenders were heavy — the equivalent of about a battalion — but once the division had passed through Kuala Lumpur in the pre-dawn hours of the 11th, it was able to break contact and continue south unmolested except by sporadic Japanese air attacks. The withdrawal of the 9th Division, at the same time, was unhindered.

Both divisions profited from the failure of the Japanese to exploit their overwhelming aerial superiority. General Sugawara had turned his attention to the Singapore airfields, for British air units based there had become active again. Intensifying his attacks on Singapore, the 3rd Air Group commander apparently paid little attention to the tactical situation further north. Japanese air attacks on the retreating Indian columns were far lighter than they might have been. Nor do they seem to have been too well planned and co-ordinated. Their effectiveness was limited, and inadequate to hamper the III Corps escape. By dawn of January 14th, all of General Heath's units had passed through the forward Westforce positions.

The abandonment of Kuala Lumpur, capital of the Federated Malay States and the second city of Malaya, was nevertheless another serious blow to British prestige and an even greater boost to Japanese morale. Soldiers of the 11th Infantry Regiment entered the city unopposed on the evening of January 11th. They quickly dispersed great mobs of looters who, in the absence of civil authority, had roamed through the streets for hours, breaking into stores and houses and stealing at will.[7] To their delight, the Japanese discovered that much of military value remained. Retreating Indian troops had managed to demolish all the bridges in the area, but Kuala Lumpur had been a major III Corps base and not all the vast stores of supplies and equipment there could be destroyed or removed. An equally important prize, of course, was the Kuala Lumpur airfield, damaged but still usable.

With Kuala Lumpur in his hands, General Yamashita was ready to begin his final drive down the Malay peninsula. His strength for this drive was significantly greater than that he had so far been able to throw against the British, since more and more Twenty-fifth Army ground forces were now reaching the forward area. General Matsui's 5th Division was now up to full strength: four infantry regiments organised into two brigades. The 5th Guards Regiment and other supporting units of Nishimura's Imperial Guards Division had also arrived from Thailand. Nishimura himself was arrogant, tempermental, and often difficult to deal with; but the forces he commanded would add greatly to the weight of Yamashita's attack. And additional Twenty-fifth Army support and logistical units had landed at Singora and were coming south to support the general advance.

In eastern Malaya, too, Lieutenant-General Renya Mutaguchi's 18th Division was in the process of building up. Already the Takumi Detachment — the 23rd Infantry Brigade Headuarters and the 56th Infantry Regiment — had taken Kuantan, while Colonel Hiroshi Koba's 55th Infantry Regiment (less a battalion) was moving overland from Kota Bharu to join Takumi. Division headquarters, the 114th Infantry

Regiment, the other battalion of the 55th Infantry, and additional units were on transports in Camranh Bay, ready to make an assault landing at Endau, above Mersing in eastern Malaya. This landing, planned by Southern Army, was intended to cut the British route of retreat in eastern Malaya. In combination with a simultaneous naval seizure of the Anamba Islands to the east, it would provide advance air-force and naval bases to support the final drive on Singapore.

To General Mutaguchi's disappointment, however, the assault landing did not take place. Increased British air activity in early January — attacks on Singora and on Japanese-held Malayan airfields — which had already forced General Sugawara to turn his attention to Singapore Island, now caused a delay in the Endau operation. Endau was too close to the Singapore fields to be attacked in the face of British air power. Nearly 130 naval bombers and fighters of the 22nd Air Flotilla, and almost as many from the 3rd Air Group, were assigned the sole mission of knocking out the Singapore-based air-force units. On January 12th and 13th, large formations of these planes attacked Singapore. Less than sixty British and Dutch fighters were available to meet them, and while their pilots fought bravely, could do little to halt the Japanese. Anti-aircraft weapons were also frustrated by the Japanese tactics of flying at heights of over 20,000 feet. This was above the effective range of the 3-inch and smaller weapons that constituted the bulk of Singapore's anti-aircraft defences. Only the 3.7-inch anti-aircraft guns could reach the bombers, but there were only forty of these, widely scattered about the island.

Fortunately for the defenders, poor Japanese bombing and heavy weather combined to blunt the edge of these raids. The attackers did little significant damage and, to the dismay of Japanese commanders, were unable to prevent continued British air operations over Malaya and the nearby waters of the South China Sea. The mistaken report by a naval reconnaissance pilot that he had seen a battleship at Singapore proved equally upsetting. In view of these factors — and since by now General Yamashita had driven British ground forces all the way to Johore anyway — the Endau operation was postponed and eventually cancelled. General Mutaguchi remained afloat at Camranh Bay, fretting and fuming over his inability to join the drive on Singapore. A bold, aggressive commander, whose enthusiasm for combat was matched only by his love of wine and women, he made no effort to hide his anger and frustration.[8]

Mutaguchi would eventually reach Malaya; but General Yamashita could not wait for him. Under pressure from Southern Army to capture

Singapore quickly, and aware of the heavy British losses, the Twenty-fifth Army commander decided to press ahead. He estimated correctly that General Percival would make a final stand in northern Johore, and he appreciated the necessity of attacking before the defenders could complete their preparations. His plan was simple and effective. The 5th Division, his largest combat element, would continue to drive down the trunk road towards Singapore. The Imperial Guards Division (less one regiment still in Thailand), advancing on General Matsui's right, would maintain its attack through the western coastal area, threatening the flank of British forces opposing Matsui, and itself pressing on toward Singapore. The 55th Infantry, 18th Division, would relieve the Takumi Detachment at Kuantan and continue south overland to take Endau and Mersing, allowing the Takumi Detachment to move west and back up the main Japanese offensive.

Before beginning this advance, Yamashita decided to allow the 5th Division a few more days' rest. Matsui's troops, after over a month of combat and pursuit, were weary. While they paused, an armoured task-force under direct Army control struck down the trunk road to the town of Gemas, where the long railway line from Kota Bharu through central Malaya met the western railway and the trunk road and where, as it happened, General Bennett's Australians had established their main defensive positions.

The Westforce dispositions were designed to cover the approaches to north-west Johore. There were two possible Japanese axes of advance. The first was along the trunk road which, at Tampin, some sixty miles south of Kuala Lumpur, turned inland to describe a great arc through Gemas, Batu Anam, Segamat, Yong Peng, and Ayer Hitam, before resuming a direct course toward Singapore. From Tampin also a branch left the trunk road and ran along the coast through Malacca and Muar to Batu Pahat, where it split, one branch leading inland to Ayer Hitam and the other continuing on down the coast parallel to the trunk road. A number of smaller roads lay between these primary avenues, the two most important ones linking Muar and Yong Peng, on the trunk road, and Batu Pahat with the Muar-Yong Peng road. This great network of roads obviously offered the attacking Japanese several options and, by the same token, made the task of the defenders all the more difficult.

The key to north-west Johore was the forty-mile-wide corridor between Muar and the trunk road. The Muar River traversed this area; but it was a long, meandering, stream, with many U-turns and reverses, its banks thickly overgrown with vegetation that limited visibility, so that an attempt to defend the river line would have required far more troops than were available in Westforce. The aggressive Bennett therefore decided to use the river where he could, but to place strong forces in front of it near Batu Anam, where he expected the main Japanese attack. His best troops — fresh and reasonably well-trained — were Brigadier D.S. Maxwell's 27th Australian Brigade, and these he put astride the trunk road at Gemas, with forward positions extending several miles west along and beside the road. Behind the Australians was Barstow's 9th Indian Division: the 8th Brigade was at Batu Anam, and the 22nd Brigade behind the 8th and to its left, at Segamat and covering lesser roads approaching that town from the west. Defence of the coastal area around Muar was the responsibility of the newly-arrived 45th Indian Brigade, which was mostly deployed along the lower reaches of the Muar River.

General Bennett believed firmly in a bold and active defence. The use of mobile striking forces and early counter-attacks to punish an incautious enemy appealed to him. He was particularly impressed by the value of ambushes, especially in rough, overgrown country like Malaya, and for some time had felt that the trunk road west of Gamas was an ideal spot to spring such a surprise. He had discussed this with Brigadier Maxwell as early as December 30th, and the Australian 30th Battalion* had been reconnoitering the terrain there and rehearsing for an ambush ever since.

Now the trap was about to be sprung. The 30th Battalion, Maxwell's forward unit, was in position about four miles west of Gemas. Three miles further west, a wooden bridge carried the trunk road across a small river. The terrain on the far side of the bridge was open, but east of the river it was thickly overgrown with jungle, providing ample concealment along both sides of the road. It seemed an ideal place for an ambush (although General Percival felt it was too far forward of the main defensive positions) and Bennett ordered it to be set. The bridge was wired for demolition, and a company of the 30th concealed itself nearby in the jungle along the road to the east, while the rest of the battalion took up supporting positions. At the same time, a battery of field artillery made ready to fire on the road west of the bridge, where the Japanese were expected to bunch up once the span was blown. These dispositions were completed early on January 14th. 'Now', wrote

* The correct designation of this unit is 2/30th, the figure 2 indicating that this was the second time that the 30th Battalion had been constituted a unit of the Australian Imperial Force (the name given to Australian overseas volunteers). Since all six Australian battalions in Malaya — the 2/26th, 2/29th, and 2/30th of the 27th Brigade, and the 2/18th, 2/19th, and 2/20th of the 22nd Brigade — were so designated, the 2 will be dropped, in this account, for the sake of simplicity.

Bennett in his diary, 'the moment has arrived for which the A.I.F. [Australian Imperial Force] in Malaya has been waiting. Will we stop the Japanese? How will the men fight? The immediate question is, "Will the . . . ambush succeed?" '[9]

By now, General Yamashita's advance armoured task-force was rapidly approaching Gemas. The Mukoda Detachment, as it was designated,* consisted of Colonel Munehiko Mukoda's 1st Tank Regiment, the 3rd Battalion, 41st Infantry, and small engineer, artillery, and other support elements. It had pushed rapidly south from Kuala Lumpur, its advance speeded by the British decision to leave bridges intact in order to give the impression of a hasty, wild retreat and thus fool an overconfident enemy into blundering into the ambush. The Japanese infantry, mounted on bicycles, led the way. 'Without giving the pedals a rest', one machine-gunner wrote in his diary, 'we are advancing to Singapore'.[10]

At about four o'clock on the afternoon of the 14th, a column of these cyclists, as many as half a dozen riders abreast, chatting and completely at ease, approached the ambush bridge. The Australians let them cross. Within half an hour, roughly two companies had passed over the river, more cyclists were bunched on the bridge, and still more could be seen on the road to the west. Then the ambush commander gave the word to blow the bridge and open fire. The blast tore the wooden span to pieces, throwing men, bicycles, and planking in all directions. At the same time, the cyclists east of the river were caught in a murderous crossfire from which there seemed to be no escape. Completely surprised, few had any chance to use their weapons, still tied to their bikes. Of those Japanese who survived the initial blow, one later wrote a graphic description:

They attacked us with trench mortars, hand grenades, automatic rifles, and [Bren] guns. We waited only for the chance to escape this danger. Leading Private Kawaguchi was hit by a grenade on the left hand and fainted. The enemy, realising that we were unable to use our weapons, attacked with pistols. Our lives now depended only on swords. When the enemy came within [twelve feet] of our position, Sergeant Miyamoto fought them with a sword only in vain. Then I saw the last of the old soldier Dannoue. Having found an opportunity to get away, I called Kawaguchi but there was no reply. I left the road and entered the dense jungle. . . .[11]

---

* In some British sources this name appears as Mukaide.

This soldier was fortunate. Many of his compatriots lay dead or dying in the dust of the road or the shallow water beneath the crumpled bridge. Even luckier were those still on the far side of the river, on whom Australian artillery was set to fire. Infiltrating Japanese had found and cut the field wire leading back to the artillery position and the gunners, hearing the battle but unable to fire without direction or knowledge of the situation, did not put their weapons into action. Nevertheless, a great many Japanese had been killed or wounded, and very few Australians.

The action has lasted perhaps twenty minutes. Now, having done all the damage they could, the ambush company began to withdraw. This was not so easy, for many of the Japanese further down the road, who had escaped the initial crossfire, had now re-grouped. Some of these tried to make a bayonet charge, but were a poor match for the big Australians. Others established a roadblock further east, forcing the withdrawing Australians to execute a wide detour through the jungle. By night, most of the latter were back in the main 30th Battalion position, satisfied with their victory. They were unaware, however, that the absence of supporting artillery fire had allowed additional Japanese infantry to begin crossing the river in small boats and that Colonel Mukoda's energetic engineers had almost finished restoring the demolished bridge.

By dawn on the 15th, Mukoda had enough tanks and infantry across the river to test the 30th Battalion defences. His initial attacks were piece-meal, however, and the Australians threw them back, knocking out several tanks in the process. But as more Japanese reached the battle, Mukoda increased his pressure, while 3rd Air Group planes attacked 30th Battalion headquarters as well as the town of Gemas. The Australians fought well, delivering several punishing counter-attacks, but by mid-afternoon there were too many Japanese to deal with. The battalion fell back through Gemas that night, breaking contact with the enemy before it continued on into the main 27th Brigade positions in front of Batu Anam.

At Twenty-fifth Army headquarters, meanwhile, General Yamashita ordered the 5th Division to resume the attack and released the Mukoda Detachment to General Matsui. Matsui, in turn, attached Mukoda to General Kawamura's 9th Brigade (11th and 41st Infantry Regiments), directing Kawamura to press the assault along the trunk road. Kawamura spent the 16th getting ready — a British air attack on 5th Division truck convoys west of Gemas that day may have delayed his build-up — but on the 17th he attacked the 27th Brigade and forced it back. General Matsui, at the same time, ordered Major-General Eikichi Sugiura's 21st Brigade (21st and 42nd Infantry Regiments) to advance over secondary roads south-west of the trunk road, by-passing Batu Anam and attacking toward Segamat. This two-pronged assault would probably have been too much for the Westforce units defending Segamat. But, as had happened so often before in the Malayan campaign, events taking place elsewhere prevented any real test.

The Imperial Guards Division had reached Malacca on January 14th and continued its southward advance toward the Muar River with both available regiments. Colonel Kentaro Kunishi's 4th Guards moved down the coastal road, sending its 1st Battalion by water in a long sweep toward Batu Pahat in the British rear. On Kunishi's left, Colonel Takeo Iwaguro's 5th Guards proceded along another road several miles inland. Since the mouth of the Muar was wide, and 3rd Air Group reports indicated that the defenders had moved all local boats to the south shore, General Nishimura decided to make his crossing upstream under cover of darkness. While Kunishi's regiment kept the defenders busy in the coastal area, the 5th Guards would make a night assault on the riverline further inland and, once across, move down the south bank to attack the town of Muar from the east. Overhead, meanwhile, 3rd Air Group planes had once again returned to the support of ground operations.

Westforce defences, if they were to meet Nishimuras threat, suffered from several deficiencies. First of all, the Muar area was the responsibility of Brigadier H.C. Duncan's 45th Indian Brigade, an inexperienced unit new in Malaya, inadequately trained, and, in the opinion of many senior Indian Army officers, unfit for combat.* Secondly, while General Bennett was aware of this, he apparently did not expect a strong Japanese attack down the coast; he concentrated on the defence, not only of the main avenue of advance through Muar, but also of practically every route the Japanese might take through the coastal area. And finally, holding firmly to the principle of an active defence, he ordered the brigade into positions more suitable for attack than for the protection of the Westforce flank, which was its primary mission.

The 45th Brigade front was about twenty-five miles long as the crow flies — but much longer in fact, because of the twists and turns in the River Muar; not to mention the brigade's exposed seaward flank along

* This point much later was reiterated by Brigadier Sir John Smyth, former commander of the 17th Indian Division, from which the brigade was taken. (*Times Literary Supplement* (London), August 8th, 1968, p. 857.)

the coast. On Bennett's orders, Duncan placed a battalion of Jats on the brigade's right, to cover the upstream crossings of the Muar, and a battalion of Rajputana Rifles on the left, protecting the lower river, with two companies from each battalion north of the river to conduct a forward defence. Duncan's reserve, a battalion of Garhwal Rifles, was some ten miles south of the river at Bakri, with a company pushed forward toward Muar and a detachment on the coast. An Australian field battery provided artillery support for the entire brigade.[12] These dispositions – and the tactics that Bennett ordered to be adopted: 'no fixed defensive position but plenty of mobile fighting patrols'[13] – would have been difficult even for the most experienced troops. For the raw, unblooded men of the 45th Brigade, they were impossible.

The Rajputana battalion in the Muar area was the first to meet the Japanese. On the morning of the 15th, the 4th and 5th Guards Regiments attacked the two Rajputana companies north of the Muar, quickly overwhelmed them, and drove forward to the river before word of their presence could even reach battalion headquarters. Colonel Kunishi's men opened fire on Muar, and despite the skillful work of an Australian 25-pounder crew some 4th Guards troops managed to launch boats and sail round the town to landing points further south.

Upstream, meanwhile, the 5th Guards Regiment was busy collecting small boats from the nearby rice-fields. That night, a few men slipped across the river in these, and returned with some larger boats that had been tied up on the south shore. After midnight, the regiment began crossing and brushing aside an Indian patrol advanced west on the morning of the 16th against the Rajputana right flank. Iwaguro's men surprised and routed a defending company, struck the forward company of the reserve Garwhal Rifles, and cut the Muar-Bakri road. Counter-attacks failed to drive the Japanese out, and the Garwhalis, after suffering heavy casualties including their commander, fell back on Bakri. At Muar, 4th Guards' attempts to cross the river were defeated by Australian gunners firing over open sights. But the 5th Guards troops, attacking from the east, overwhelmed the remaining Rajputanas and occupied Muar. The British commander and his second-in-command were both killed leading an abortive counter-attack, and that night all that was left of the Rajputana battalion – two officers and 120 men – retreated to Bakri. The Jat battalion, which had experienced only a brief brush with 5th Guards elements, had also begun to withdraw from the river area.

By the evening of January 16th, General Nishimura's advance across the Muar had in effect crumpled the Westforce left flank and opened

the way for the Guards Division either to make a wide swing through
Yong Peng against Bennett's rear or to drive ahead against limited
opposition down the coast toward Singapore. Although not fully aware
of the extent of the 45th Brigade's defeat, Bennett knew enough about
it to take action. He ordered his reserve, the Australian 29th Battalion,
27th Brigade, to Muar to restore the situation.

General Percival at this time was at 11th Division headquarters,
where he received a report of the Guards' landing near Batu Pahat. He
was becoming increasingly concerned about Bennett's ability to control
the widespread defences of north-west Johore. He therefore decided to
extend the III Corps responsibility well forward to cover a line from
Batu Pahat to Yong Peng, thus relieving Bennett of the need to worry
about his communications. To assist General Heath, Percival gave him
the British 53rd Brigade — which had just arrived — and ordered the
brigade forward into the area newly-assigned to III Corps. Heath in turn
attached the brigade to the 11th Division, and General Key assigned
one battalion to relieve 11th Division troops near Batu Pahat and
another to hold a vital defile at Bukit Pelandok, on the Muar-Yong Peng
road just east of its junction with the road to Batu Pahat.

Percival, Bennett, and Key discussed these dispositions at Westforce
rear headquarters after lunch on the 17th. Bennett was unhappy about
III Corps taking over responsibility for his communications, since he
felt: 'I should keep a close personal eye on this threat to my rear'.[14]
But he apparently did not press the point too much, for he was more
disturbed over Percival's failure to use the 53rd Brigade to relieve his
own 22nd Australian Brigade on the east coast, freeing the latter to join
Westforce. Percival's decision, indeed, had been contrary to General
Wavell's orders for the two units, but the Malaya Commander felt that
he had no time to follow the original plan. Nevertheless, since Percival
and Bennett agreed that the Muar-Segamat area should be held, Percival
authorised the transfer of the 19th Battalion, 22nd Australian Brigade,
to the 45th Brigade. The remaining battalion of the 53rd Brigade would
replace the 19th on the east coast.

While these discussions and movements were taking place, an
attempt by the Australian 29th Battalion to re-take Muar had failed
before it could begin. General Nishimura had ordered his regiments to
keep driving forward, the 5th Guards Regiment, on the division's left,
to Yong Peng, and the 4th Guards to Batu Pahat, where Colonel
Kunishi's 1st Battalion had already landed. On the evening of the 17th,
the Garhwali battalion of the 45th Brigade, moving west from Bakri to
the coastal road to participate in the counter-attack, ran headlong into

a 4th Guards ambush. The Japanese inflicted heavy losses on the surprised Indian troops, quickly reducing the battalion to about 400 men and a single officer. Dispersed and confused, the remaining Garkwalis staggered back to Bakri. Meanwhile, the Australian battalion which had taken up positions in front of Bakri on the Muar road, was also under light attack from an advance patrol of the 5th Guards. In these circumstances Brigadier Duncan, the brigade commander, called off the proposed counter-attack.

During the night of January 17th-18th, Colonel Iwaguro's advance troops, the 3rd Battalion of the 5th Guards Regiment, maintained pressure on the 29th Battalion. Just before dawn, a Japanese light tank company reached the scene, and on the orders of its commander attacked straight down the road without infantry support. This proved to be less than wise. Australian anti-tank gunners were ready and coolly opened fire. There were eight tanks in the attack; a few penetrated the battalion position, but all were quickly knocked out. 'One by one they were smashed, set on fire, and rendered useless and uninhabitable', recalled an Aussie officer. The sound from the tanks 'resembled an Empire Day celebration as the ammunition within them burnt, and cracked with sharp bursts, and hissed, with every now and again a louder explosion as larger ammunition ignited'.[15] Australian riflemen took care of the surviving crew members, including the brave but imprudent tank commander. When Iwaguro's infantrymen attempted to follow up this tank assault with one of their own, they too were halted.

Brigadier Duncan now realised that he would have to concentrate his forces before he could mount any sort of an attack. He ordered the Jat battalion of his brigade, still well forward toward the River Muar, to fall back on Bakri, and the Australian 19th Battalion, which had just arrived, to help to form a perimeter round the town with the remnants of the Rajputana and Garhwal battalions. The 29th Battalion still held its forward position on the Bakri-Muar road. During the day, infiltrating Japanese managed to establish a roadblock between the 29th Battalion and Bakri, but the Australians, with great difficulty, cleared this out by evening. Duncan still hoped to resume the attack the next day when the Jats reached Bakri.

Others were less optimistic. By the evening of the 18th, General Bennett had become quite concerned about the main Westforce position at Batu Anam. The Japanese 5th Division was exerting increasing pressure on these defences, while the advance of the Imperial Guards through Muar raised a growing threat to the Westforce flank. Bennett therefore telephoned Percival and asked permission to withdraw to Segamat, behind the broad Segamat River, as a preliminary to a possible further withdrawal. Percival's intelligence staff had only just then informed him of the strength of the Japanese force attacking north-west Johore, and of the fact that the Imperial Guards Division — considered by the British to be a crack unit — had joined the assault. This danger, plus the growing activity of the 4th Guards troops that had landed near Batu Pahat, convinced the Malaya commander that the whole Westforce area was in peril. The 46th Brigade might easily be cut off, the line of communication to Batu Anam was vulnerable, and there was a distinct threat to III Corps units at Batu Pahat. Percival authorised Bennett to withdraw and, despite the Australian commander's earlier objections, transferred control of the Muar front to General Heath, in order to allow Bennett to concentrate on the trunk road and at the same time to ensure better co-ordination of operations in the Muar-Yong Peng-Batu Pahat area.

Bennett's withdrawal to Segamat was completed by the morning of the 19th. At the same time, the 5th Guards Regiment resumed its attack on the 29th Battalion in front of Bakri, while the 2nd Battalion, 4th Guards, attacked the southern edge of the 19th Battalion's perimeter at Bakri itself. A desperate defence managed to beat off the Japanese, but some of the 5th Guards troops drove all the way round the town and cut the Yong Peng road. To make matters worse, at about 10 a.m. 3rd Air Group planes attacking Bakri scored a direct hit on 45th Brigade headquarters, knocking out communications, killing or wounding almost all the staff officers, and badly stunning Brigadier Duncan and his second in command. In these circumstances Lieutenant-Colonel C.G. Wright-Anderson of the 29th Battalion temporarily assumed brigade command.

A few hours later, General Percival called a conference at Yong Peng of all the major British commanders in north-west Johore. After a lengthy discussion — and apparently some hard words between the volatile Bennett and the less excitable Heath — Percival issued these orders: the 53rd Brigade (including its battalion in eastern Johore, which would be returned) would concentrate at the Bukit Pelandok defile. The 45th Brigade would fall back through Bukit Pelandok to a position west of Yong Peng. The Australian 27th Brigade and the 9th Indian Division, at Segamat, would continue their withdrawal to about twenty miles beyond Segamat.

Communication difficulties prevented this decision from reaching the 45th Brigade until about 8 o'clock that evening. By that time, Colonel Anderson had already concluded that he would have to pull out of Bakri. During the day, the Jat battalion had fought its way into the Bakri perimeter, but at heavy cost, losing its commander and nearly half its men to a 5th Guards ambush. The Australian 29th Battalion, which had remained west of Bakri to cover the Jat movement, had itself been under renewed assault during the afternoon. A counter-attack relieved this pressure, but the victory was only temporary. When the 2nd Battalion, 4th Guards, made another attempt to breach the southern edge of the Bakri perimeter, Anderson ordered the 29th Battalion to fall back into the village. By now, however, 5th Guards troops were in force between the battalion and Bakri. The two Australian companies closest to the perimeter were able to fight their way in by nightfall, but the rest of the 29th was cut off, scattered, and ultimately destroyed. It was now clear to Anderson that further defence of Bakri could only bring disaster to his remaining troops.

Early the next morning, January 20th, the battered and exhausted Bakri defenders began their retreat along the Yong Peng road. The column stretched for more than a mile, Australians a vanguard and rearguard, Indians on both flanks, and artillery, armoured cars, and ambulances on the road in the middle. At about 8 a.m. the advance troops struck a 5th Guards roadblock. The Japanese block − felled trees covered by machine-gun fire − resisted several efforts to break it, while Colonel Iwaguro's men rained mortar and artillery shells onto the packed 45th Brigade column. Not until after 10 o'clock was Anderson, himself leading the final bayonet charge, able to clear the enemy barrier and open the way. By this time Japanese forces had driven through Bakri, and supported by light tanks were attacking the rear of the 45th Brigade column. Counter-attacks succeeded in easing the pressure, but casualties were heavy and Brigadier Duncan, by now partially recovered from his former injury, was killed leading one assault.

Somehow the column moved ahead, encountering successive roadblocks, the last of which Anderson only succeeded in overcoming with a mass attack using every available support weapon. In the final assault, infantrymen directed mortar fire on to targets only a few yards before them. Gun crews pushed their 25-pounders into close range of enemy obstacles and fired directly over the sights, while armoured cars drove within a few feet of machine-gun positions to knock them out. The troops attacked in the face of heavy automatic-weapons fire, using bayonets and axes. With the axes, recalled one Australian, 'some chopped the tree trunks [forming the barriers], others chopped the Japanese who lay behind them'.[16]

By nightfall, Anderson's men had cleared the last of the Japanese blocks, killing many of the enemy – including the Japanese battalion commander – but suffering heavily themselves. The trucks and ambulances were full of wounded. Japanese artillery fire and air attacks had done as much damage to the centre of the column as ground fighting and road blocks had done to the front and rear guards. Care of the dead and wounded had become a major problem.

It was close on midnight when the column reached the shelter of some large rubber estates about ten miles east of Bakri. Here Anderson received a report that a small but important bridge at Parit Sulong, two or three miles further east, was in Japanese hands – ominous news, which he soon confirmed. Somehow the enemy had once more managed to cut the route of escape. The weary, crippled 45th Brigade faced still another battle.

The Japanese at Parit Sulong – and, unknown to Anderson, at other points further east of the Yong Peng road – were troops of the 4th Guards Regiment. How Colonel Kunishi's men came to be there is a story of Japanese foresight and of British troops' confusion and inexperience. Early on the 19th, General Nishimura concluded that with a little effort he could probably block the 45th Brigade's route of retreat. The 5th Guards Regiment and the 2nd Battalion, 4th Guards, were heavily engaged at Bakri. But the 3rd Battalion of the 4th Guards Regiment was moving down the coast road toward Batu Pahat, and the 1st Battalion was already ashore in that area. Nishimura therefore ordered Kunishi to occupy Batu Pahat and send a force inland to seize that portion of the Bakri-Yong Peng road that lay between Parit Sulong and Bukit Pelandok. Kunishi apparently decided to head immediately for Parit Sulong and Bukit Pelandok with his 3rd Battalion, by-passing Batu Pahat for later occupation by the rest of his regiment.

The Parit Sulong-Bukit Pelandok area was held at this time by the 6th Battalion of the Norfolk Regiment, of Brigadier C.L.B. Duke's 53rd Brigade, with reinforcements on the way but still a few hours distant. The brigade had landed less than a week earlier – without its vehicles and guns, due on a later convoy – after nearly three months on troopships so crowded that the men had been practically unable to exercise. Unlike the 45th Brigade, the 53rd was reasonably well-trained, though for desert rather than jungle warfare since it had originally been scheduled for the Middle East; none of its troops had any combat experience. The men had spent the time since arrival unpacking, sorting equipment, exchanging winter uniforms for tropical clothing, and moving forward. The unpracticed troops, ill at ease in the strange jungle and distressed by the tropical heat, were not ready for an early fight.

The 6th Battalion had been in position little more than a day when, at about 1.30 on the afternoon of January 19th, Colonel Kunishi's advance troops surprised one of their companies which was holding Bukit Pelandok and seized the village and nearby hillside, thus capturing that portion of the Bakri-Yong Peng road. An attempt to drive off the Japanese that night by a newly-arrived company of the 2nd Battalion, the Loyals, was frustrated when the troops became confused in the darkness and thick jungle. A second effort, by a Punjabi battalion newly attached to the 53rd Brigade from the 11th Division, was even more disastrous. In the pre-dawn gloom of the 20th, the Punjabis were fired upon by the Norfolks, who were also attempting to join in the attack, and the two battalions both came under heavy and punishing fire from the Japanese. Kunishi's men then swept forward and cleared the area, inflicting severe casualties on both the Indian and British units. General Key, commanding the 11th Division, ordered another attack, but Brigadier Duke succeeded in gaining a delay on the grounds that his men were in no condition to make an immediate assault. By 8 o'clock that night, General Percival, increasingly concerned over the threat to the Westforce flank and line of communication, ordered Bennett to continue his withdrawal by another fifteen miles along the trunk road and main railway line, sending a brigade as quickly as possible to hold the important road junction at Yong Peng.

While all this had been taking place, two Norfolk Regiment platoons at Parit Sulong had been without rations since the 18th, and had been out of touch with their battalion since the 19th. On the morning of the 20th, fearing they had been cut off the inexperienced troops left their vital position and set out across country for Batu Bahat. By mid-afternoon, a detachment of the 4th Guards had occupied the town and its key bridge without so much as firing a shot. The Japanese thus sealed the western end of the important Bukit Pelandok defile and, with it, the fate of Colonel Anderson's trapped 45th Brigade.

There was one more abortive effort to break the Japanese grip. Early on the 21st, in order best to co-ordinate the movements and communications of the withdrawing Westforce and 45th Brigade, Percival placed all troops in the Muar-Yong Peng area back under General Bennett's command. Key had already directed Duke's 53rd Brigade to recapture Bukit Pelandok as quickly as possible, and the aggressive Bennett strongly reiterated this command at least twice. Despite these orders the attack never got under way.

Brigadier Duke's command consisted of three scattered battalions —

the battered Norfolks and Punjabis and the 2nd Battalion of the Loyals, now in full strength but tired after a hasty move – and a limited amount of artillery. Communications were poor and there were difficulties in organising reconnaissance and artillery support. But the main problems seem to have been lack of experience and training in the brigade staff, and a degree of caution in the brigadier himself that is difficult to understand in view of the urgency of the situation. The counter-attack and preparations for it were delayed and postponed; and not until the morning of the 22nd did Duke begin his artillery registration. This took so long that Japanese aircraft had plenty of time to arrive on the scene and heavily bomb and machine-gun the troops preparing to attack. With surprise obviously gone, Duke now concluded that he could not recapture the defile or, at any rate, hold it long enough to do the 45th Brigade any good. He cancelled the attack and took up defensive positions.

In retrospect, the ill-prepared and tired 53rd Brigade could probably not have prevailed. The Japanese forces building up before it were strong; the terrain favoured them, and they had air support. Yet a quick, determined assault on the 20th, when Key first ordered it, or even early on the 21st, while Colonel Kunishi had only about a battalion in the defile, might have gained the upper hand for just long enough for Anderson's desperate force to escape. As it was, the situation was now hopeless.

Early on the 21st, the vanguard of the trapped 45th Brigade had made an unsuccessful effort to take Parit Sulong. The necessity to protect his flanks and rear prevented Anderson from committing a large force to this attack, and the 4th Guards troops had little difficulty beating it off. At about the same time, the pursuing 5th Guards Regiment, with tank support, was attempting to roll up the brigade rear. A section of 25-pounders did yeoman work in blunting this assault, but Colonel Iwaguro's men returned again and again to the attack. By now, Anderson's column had been compressed to a section of the road about three-quarters of a mile long, and Japanese artillery and aircraft were exacting a heavy toll from the trapped Australians and Indians. Radio contact with Westforce was intermittant, but a message from Bennett in the morning that an attack was under way to relieve the brigade proved a healthy spur.

All day the fight continued, the desperate defenders being forced into a smaller and smaller area west of the bridge. A major attempt to break out at about noon succeeded in pushing through Parit Sulong and reaching the bridge. But it was halted there by 4th Guards troops and by the need to meet increasing pressure from the rear.

Anderson's men were now nearing exhaustion. They had eaten little for two days and were extremely low on ammunition and medical supplies. The number of casualties, especially the badly-wounded who could not be attended to, was becoming alarming. Anderson asked Bennett for a morning air drop of food and morphine, and for an air attack on the approaches to the other side of the brigde. Then he made one last effort to help his seriously wounded.

Placing the most nearly hopeless cases in two ambulances, he sent them forward to the bridge under a flag of truce. The medical officer in charge asked the Japanese to be allowed to pass through to British lines, only to be refused and told that the wounded men would be cared for if Anderson surrendered. Furthermore, insisted the Japanese commander, he would hold the ambulance on the bridge, blocking the way, until his demand was met. Anderson, still under the impression that relief was coming, refused. But Japanese machine-guns, trained on the ambulances, prevented them from withdrawing. There they remained until after dark, when an officer in one ambulance and the driver of the other, both badly wounded, released the brakes, and the two vehicles rolled backwards down the sloping ramp of the bridge. Then they quickly started their engines and, despite enemy fire, raced back to safety.

Early the next morning, January 22nd, two planes from Singapore dropped food and medicine to the 45th Brigade, and released a few bombs on to the Japanese across the bridge. The 5th Guards attacks from the rear continued and Anderson, fearing that his mounting casualties would soon prevent him from taking any offensive action, made another effort to capture the bridge. When this failed, he was convinced that he could do nothing further and his force would be completely destroyed by the time a relief unit reached him. At 9 a.m., he ordered all heavy weapons, vechicles, and equipment to be destroyed, and directed every man capable of travelling on foot to make his way eastward through the swamps and jungle to Yong Peng. Volunteers remained behind with the badly wounded, some 110 Australians and 35 Indians.

Even as this was taking place, General Bennett sent a message to Anderson informing him that the relief attack had been cancelled and authorising him to take precisely those actions which the brigade commander had already decided upon. 'Sorry unable help after your heroic effort', he concluded. 'Good luck'.[17] Anderson apparently did not receive this message, but he and most of his men managed to slip out of the perimeter and escape. Eventually, about 500 Australians and 400 Indians were able to reach safety, including Anderson himself who later received the Victoria Cross for his bold leadership. But the 45th Brigade — which, with its attached units, had numbered 4,000 men — was no more. It had inflicted heavy, but hardly equal losses on the enemy, and had held up General Nishimura's main advance for several days.

The unfortunate wounded who were left behind paid a bitter price for this repulse. The Guards troops, perhaps to revenge their own losses, treated their prisoners savagely. They beat and kicked the helpless men without mercy, crowded them tightly into a tiny building, denied them food and water in the tropical heat, and laughed at their agony. Then, at dusk, they tied the captives together, dragged them to a stream, and shot or beheaded all but a few who managed to escape by playing dead and later crawling away. It was a cruel end for brave soldiers who deserved a better fate.*

Some 600 Indian prisoners captured elsewhere during the Muar-Bakri battles were assembled at Muar. There Captain Mohan Singh's men set about housing, feeding, and providing medical care for their newly-arrived compatriots — as a prelude to inducing them to join the Indian National Army.[18]

While the 45th Brigade was making its abortive effort to escape from Bakri, General Wavell visited Singapore again on January 20th. He quickly saw that his hope of delaying the Japanese in northern Johore would not be realised and that in all probability Percival's troops would be forced back to Singapore Island. He nevertheless ordered Percival to try to hold out on the mainland until additional reinforcements could land, at the same time preparing for the final defence of Singapore Island. Percival decided to make his initial fight north of a line from Jemaluang (in eastern Malaya, south of Mersing), through Kluang (on the central rail line) and Ayer Hitam, to Batu Pahat. He organised his units into three main forces under III Corps, each with its own line of communication to Singapore. In the east was Eastforce, under Brigadier H.B. Taylor, consisting of his 22nd Australian Brigade (less the 19th Battalion) and other units. It would hold the Jemaluang area and cover the road south through Kota Tinggi to Singapore. General Bennett's Westforce, responsible for the Yong Peng-Kluang-Ayer Hitam area,

---

* A post-war war-crimes tribunal sentenced Nishimura to death for this massacre. For an analysis of another, better-known example of Japanese maltreatment of prisoners, and an attempt at an explanation of such deeds, see Stanley L. Falk, *Bataan: The March of Death* (New York: Norton, 1962), especially pp. 221-36.

would continue to protect the railway line and the main road. Key's 11th Division, to which the 53rd Brigade would revert, would defend the Batu Pahat area and the coastal road to Singapore.

The Jemaluang-Batu Pahat line was only about sixty miles north of Johore Strait, and covered the last lateral road across Malaya to remain in British hands. By dawn on the 24th, the bruised, tired defenders were back in position protecting this line. Their movement had been easier than might have been anticipated, owing primarily to the absence of large Japanese units in eastern Malaya and to the failure of General Matsui's 5th Division to press Westforce as closely and heavily as it might have done.

The east coast withdrawal to Mersing had been harrassed only from the air, and not until January 22nd did the first 55th Infantry patrols make contact with Taylor's outposts. Australian defences easily beat off a probing attack that day, and Colonel Koba's troops made no further effort to advance. Further west, meanwhile, the 5th Division was slow to follow up General Bennett's withdrawal. After occupying Batu Anam on the 19th, General Kawamura's 9th Brigade was relieved by Sugiura's 21st Brigade, with the fresh 21st Infantry in the vanguard, which now took over the pursuit. Bridge destruction, ambushes, and other vigorous defensive measures, however, kept Sugiura from following too closely. Indian troops fell back along the railway line, while the Australians used the main road, holding at Yong Peng long enough to cover the passage of the 53rd Brigade from the Bukit Pelandok area. The latter unit barely managed to fight off a heavy, tank-supported attack by the 5th Guards before escaping with heavy casualties on the night of January 23rd. Morning of the 24th found the Indian 9th Division at Kluang and the Australian 27th Brigade at Ayer Hitam, both out of contact with the Japanese. For the first time since the Japanese crossing of the Muar, General Bennett's troops were not in danger of being cut off from the west. 'Now', recalled Percival, 'we breathed again'.[19]

The situation at Batu Pahat was less reassuring for the British. After his victory over the 45th Brigade, General Nishimura decided on an all-out effort to close another trap around the defenders of Batu Pahat, the 11th Division's 6/15th Brigade, now commanded by Brigadier B.S. Challen and consisting mainly of the British Battalion and a Cambridge battalion of the 53rd Brigade. The 1st Battalion, 4th Guards, was already threatening to cut the coastal road below Batu Pahat. Late on the 21st, while the Guards Reconnaissance Regiment engaged Challen's attention with a frontal attack, the rest of the Guards Division began a sweep around the inland flank of the town in an effort to seal off the entire area. General Heath, hoping to make Batu Pahat into another Tobruk — a strongpoint threatening the enemy line of communications from the rear — had earlier strongly denied Challen's request for permission to withdraw to a less exposed position further east.

On the 22nd, the Japanese cut the Batu Pahat-Ayer Hitam road and, except for one brief lapse, resisted all efforts by British forces to regain it. Challen's communications with the 11th Division went out on the 23rd, but the steady build-up of Imperial Guard forces north-east of Batu Pahat, and the increasing threat to the coastal road, convinced him that an immediate withdrawal was necessary ·to save his brigade. He regained radio communication only after he had begun his move. In accordance with Heath's earlier order, General Key immediately told Challen to get back to Batu Pahat, a decision that Heath and Percival quickly confirmed, despite the obvious risk. Happily for Challen, only a few Japanese had entered the town and the 6/15th pushed them out and reoccupied its former positions that night. The western end of the Malayan defence line was thus restored, but it was under growing and ominous pressure.

Except in the 45th Brigade area, the withdrawal from northern Johore had not been unduly hampered by Japanese air attacks. Nor did the 3rd Air Group make any vigorous attempt to block the movement of reinforcements from Singapore to the Johore front, or the lateral shifting of units behind that front. General Sugawara's main effort was now aimed at completing the destruction of British airpower and preventing its revival. Since Air-Vice-Marshal Pulford had been forced to withdraw all his planes to Singapore Island, the island and its four airfields became Sugawara's prime target. Japanese bombers and fighters struck at Singapore with increasing severity and regularity, flying too high for the island's puny anti-aircraft defences, taking their toll of whatever defenders rose to meet them, and inflicting heavy damage on ground installations, the naval base, and the city and dock areas, as well as on the airfields and any British planes caught unprotected on the crowded fields. To ease this last problem, some of the British bomber squadrons were transferred to Sumatra. At the same time Dutch fighter units which had been participating in the battle were withdrawn to help protect the Netherlands Indies, reducing even further the available air defence of Singapore. Civilian casualties were far from light, and the effect, and impunity, of the Japanese air-raids were serious blows to morale. The city, it was clear to more than one resident, 'was going to be a very uncomfortable place to live in the weeks to come'.[20]

The small British air-force was sorely taxed to cover Singapore while at the same time endeavoring to provide something better than token support to Percival's hard-pressed troops. Their resources were even further stretched as the result of an ABDACOM air directive that stressed the necessity of protecting incoming reinforcement convoys, but also called for major efforts against Japanese seaborne expeditions aimed at eastern Malaya or objectives south of Singapore, and for simultaneous attempts to slow General Yamashita's advance by attacking his base at Singora. 'To carry out efficiently all these tasks', in the words of a senior air-force officer, 'was beyond the strength of the Air Forces available'.[21] Nevertheless, they tried their best, even mounting a number of small, scattered raids on Japanese airfields and truck convoys. They were assisted by American B-17's from Java which, staging through Sumatra, struck Malayan air bases a few light blows. All of these attacks probably did little to affect the Japanese advance, but they forced Sugawara to withhold some aircraft for defensive purposes.

British morale received a boost with the arrival on January 13th of the second reinforcement convoy. This carried, with the 53rd Brigade, fifty-one crated Hurricane fighter-planes — the most modern aircraft to reach Singapore — and two dozen pilots. The planes were quickly put together and made ready for action. On the 20th, they joined the fight, shooting down eight of twenty-seven unescorted Japanese bombers that attacked Singapore that day. The appearance of the Hurricanes brought considerable elation to both civilians and troops in the field, but this emotion was short-lived. The next day the Japanese bombers returned with an escort of fighters, and these proved more than a match for the slower, less agile, and usually outnumbered Hurricanes. They achieved good results against heavy odds; but within a week less than half were operational and it was clear that 'too much had been expected of this handful of Hurricanes'.[22]

While air battles took a severe toll of British planes and pilots during these weeks, Japanese preoccupation with Singapore not only made life somewhat less difficult than it might have been for the troops in Johore, but also permitted the arrival of additional reinforcements. During January, five convoys reached Singapore, bringing troops, supplies, and equipment; Japanese command of the air could almost certainly have intercepted them had the effort been made. These convoys had to make their approach through narrow waters, with limited air and naval escort, and, because of the need for speed, they risked hazardous daylight runs instead of making their final dash under cover of night. Yet the Japanese made no real attempt to intercept them. The primary reason for this was the decision to concentrate on achieving and maintaining 'absolute air supremacy'[23] over Singapore and Malaya. But there were other, contributing factors.

General Sugawara had no aircraft capable of long-range over-water reconnaissance and, without early warning of approaching convoys, was apparently unable to switch his striking forces from targets on Singapore Island in time to hit the vulnerable transports. The naval 22nd Air Flotilla, based in southern Indo-China, lacked the range to maintain constant reconnaissance over the Strait of Malacca or waters further south. The staging forward to Malayan airfields was hampered by planning problems, and the fact that Sugawara enjoyed a higher priority for the use of these fields. Admiral Matsunaga also seems to have been more concerned to support naval and amphibious operations in the South China Sea, a preoccupation that also distracted Japanese warships and submarines from any attempt to seal off Singapore. Notwithstanding all of this, it would still appear that the Japanese had sufficient air superiority to dominate Malaya and attack the convoys as well. Better co-ordination of air activities – and better army-navy cooperation in these matters – might well have thwarted most of the British efforts at reinforcement.

Thanks to lack of Japanese interference, troops to the equivalent of nearly two divisions reached General Percival during January, sailing unscathed into Singapore harbour under a small but proud escort of reconnaissance and fighter planes. The first convoy, on January 3rd, brought the Indian 45th Brigade, and the second, ten days later, the 53rd Brigade and other troops, together with the Hurricanes. On the 22nd, the Indian 44th Brigade and 7,000 individual Indian replacements arrived. Two days later, an Australian machine-gun battalion and 1,900 replacements came in. And on the 29th, almost all the rest of the British 18th Division and an Indian light tank squadron disembarked.

Unhappily for Percival, the quality of most of these troops was such that the Japanese lost little by their failure to intercept the reinforcement convoys. The unsatisfactory condition of the 45th Brigade and the weaknesses of the 53rd have already been discussed and demonstrated. The 44th Brigade was no better off than the 45th, its sister unit from a newly-formed Indian division, while the replacements that accompanied the 44th were ill-prepared and included very few non-commissioned officers. The Australian machine-gun battalion was well-trained, but the 1,900 individual replacements were mainly raw recruits, many of them inducted less than a week before they sailed. The main body of the 18th Division, while hardly green, suffered from the same deficiencies as the 53rd Brigade. And the light tank squadron consisted of worn, obsolescent vehicles, several of which needed immediate overhaul, manned by half-trained crews.

The despatch of poorly-trained Indians, on the grounds that no others were available, and of raw Australian troops, appears to have been pure administrative bungling;[24] it did little to enhance the strength of Malaya Command. That it doomed these unfortunates to death or captivity without commensurate gains demonstrates tragically the ill-prepared and shocked state of Allied Far Eastern defence at the outbreak of the war.

This particular tragedy, nevertheless, might have been averted at least in part. On January 21st, Winston Churchill, increasingly concerned over the swift Japanese advance and the evident probability that Singapore would fall, raised a basic question with the British Chiefs-of-Staff; which was more important, he asked, Singapore or Burma? If Singapore was doomed, would it not be better to divert the reinforcements to the sorely-pressed Burma front, to hold the Burma Road and the supply-line to China, rather than to sacrifice additional lives in futile defence of Singapore? 'We may', he warned, 'by muddling things and hesitating to take an ugly decision, lose both Singapore and the Burma Road'.[25] Unhappily for the doomed reinforcements, neither the Chiefs-of-Staff nor the Defence Committee could reach a decision, nor could Churchill himself — all, perhaps, refusing to concede the inevitability of a swift collapse at Singapore; and a strong message from the Australian Prime Minister, Curtin, protesting at what he feared would be 'an inexcusable betrayal' of Australian defence interests, did nothing to help them. In the end, no action was taken. 'There is no doubt', wrote Churchill later, 'what a purely military decision should have been'.[26] But the political necessity of defending Singapore for as long as possible, the effect of a reduced British effort while the Americans were still holding out in the Philippines, and the inexorable march of events, ruled out the option of diverting the reinforcements to Burma.

Even as Churchill and his advisers hesitated, the Japanese were applying the last crushing blows in Johore. On January 24th, General Nishimura resumed his efforts to envelop and crush the 6/15th Brigade at Batu Pahat. Brigadier Challen had by now been reinforced by the 5th Norfolks, the third battalion of the 53rd Brigade, shifted only a few days earlier from its former position in eastern Malaya. But the defenders were still hard pressed, and Challen again reported that he was in great danger of being cut off and his forces destroyed. Once more he received orders to hold Batu Pahat; but General Key at the same time was vigorously pressing Heath for permission to withdraw the 6/15th. Most of the senior commanders had by now been informed in secrecy of a provisional plan developed by Percival to withdraw in stages from Johore on to Singapore Island. Both Challen and Key urged that whether or not this plan was now to be implemented further defence of Batu Pahat would be suicidal.

By noon of the 25th, the situation was nearly desperate. The Guards Reconnaissance Regiment was attacking Batu Pahat in force, the 4th Guards had swung well round the town, and the latter's 1st Battalion had finally managed to establish a block on the coastal road a dozen miles below Batu Pahat. The 53rd Brigade (now consisting of the battered 6th Norfolks, a half-strength Punjabi battalion, and a few other troops) had attempted to drive forward along the coastal road, had fought off an ambush, and had then run up against the 4th Guards roadblock below Batu Pahat.

On the Westforce front, meanwhile, Matsui's 5th Division was driving forward with both brigades. A counter-attack by the Indian 22nd Brigade before Kluang on the railway-line stung the Japanese 9th Brigade, while the Australians and Loyals at Ayer Hitam, despite enemy air-attacks, had succeeded in halting the Japanese 21st Brigade on the trunk road. The action above Kluang had climaxed in a roaring bayonet charge by a Sikh unit. 'Yelling at the top of their voices, their fighting blood thoroughly aroused, the Sikhs fell upon the Japanese. . . . The war-cries of the Sikhs and the squeals of the Japanese caused veritable pandemonium. . . .'[27] This was not the first time the defenders had used bayonets to good advantage in Malaya; although they were seldom employed in World War II. British, Australian, and even Indian troops had had bayonet assaults emphasised in training, so that the smaller Japanese, who prided themselves as bayonet fighters, often got the worst of these encounters. A month earlier, indeed, British troops reported that the enemy 'did not relish bayonet fighting', and by the end of the campaign the Japanese themselves admitted a growing concern over bayonet casualties.[28] 'I can well imagine', wrote one British correspondent about the action near Kluang, 'that nothing is more calculated to put fear into a Japanese than the spectacle of an enormous bearded and turbaned Sikh descending upon him with his bayonet, yelling like mad'.[29]

Early on the afternoon of January 25th, General Percival decided to seek 'a full discussion with my subordinate commanders ... before definitely authorising a withdrawal from any part of the front'.[30] At 3.15, he met Heath, and Key, at Bennett's rear headquarters. Bennett, as usual, was full of fight. He believed that Westforce could hold if any way could be found of protecting his western flank. But the situation on the west coast, where no reserves remained to oppose a breakthrough or a new landing, could not be ignored. Percival therefore ordered the 6/15th Brigade to evacuate Batu Pahat and withdraw along the coastal road to the position held by the 53rd Brigade. Westforce would have to conform, falling back about a dozen miles on both the trunk road and railway line. In eastern Malaya, also, Brigadier Taylor would pull back those units still north of Jemaluang. These positions would be held at least until the night of the 27th. Subsequent withdrawals would be made to selected positions 'which would in turn be held for a minimum fixed period and longer if possible'.[31]

Percival, at this time, had still made no decision about pulling back to Singapore. But apparently, because of the discussions of this possibility, and because he allowed Heath to issue a map bearing withdrawal phase lines on it, the three subordinate commanders left the conference with the impression that Johore would definitely be evacuated, with the last troops reaching Singapore Island on the night of January 31st. This confusion did not immediately affect operations, but it may have contributed to later difficulties. Above all, it indicates the state of mind of weary commanders, under great pressure, on whom the events of the previous seven weeks could only have had the effect of a heavy and debilitating shock.

The decision to evacuate Batu Pahat came a day too late; perhaps several days. Once General Nishimura's troops had seized Bukit Pelandok in force, they had no need to take Batu Pahat in order to threaten Bennett's western flank. Instead of trying to hold Batu Pahat, a British defence in the swamps and rubber estates between Ayer Hitam and the coast below Batu Pahat might have protected Bennett more effectively; and being less exposed it would have decreased the chance that the 6/15th Brigade might suffer the fate of the 45th. Now, Brigadier Challen's men faced just that danger.'

Challen began to withdraw on the night of the 25th, his rear covered by fire from a British gunboat. The next morning, the brigade ran into the 4th Guards roadblock. Colonel Kunishi's troops now held this in force and the 6/15th, in three separate attacks, failed to make any progress. To rescue Challen, General Key ordered the 53rd Brigade to break through; the second time that Brigadier Duke was faced with the difficult task of relieving a cut-off unit. He made a much greater effort now, but again was unsuccessful. A column of armoured cars, artillery, and infantry in trucks pushed forward rapidly, only to be stopped, badly mauled, and broken up by Kunishi's roadblock. Duke was unable to help, for advance elements of the 5th Guards Regiment, making a wide sweep around Batu Pahat on the inland flank of the 4th Guards, now reached the coastal area below the roadblock. Most of the 53rd Brigade became heavily engaged with Colonel Iwaguro's men.

A single bren-gun-carrier from Duke's mechanised column broke through to the 6/15th Brigade. On learning of the situation along the road, Challen concluded that he could no longer hope to escape with his guns and vehicles. He destroyed all of these, left the seriously wounded with medical personnel, and ordered everyone else to get off the road and make their way on foot to the rear of the 53rd Brigade positions down the coast.

About 1,200 men, moving inland of the road, managed to straggle back unmolested, reaching the 53rd Brigade nearly exhausted on the next afternoon, January 27th. The rest of the 6/15th troops, attempting to escape between the road and the sea, found their passage blocked by an unfordable river, on the night of the 26th. Challen was captured while trying to find a crossing, but his second-in-command sent an officer by boat down the coast to the 11th Division with word of what had occurred. Gun-boats and small craft from Singapore, working carefully in uncharted waters and coastal swamps, were able to evacuate the men during the next four nights. Almost the entire brigade thus escaped the fate of the 45th Brigade. All guns, vehicles, and heavy equipment had been lost, but this time the wounded who had been left behind were not maltreated.

In eastern Malaya, meanwhile, in conformance with Percival's order, Brigadier Taylor began withdrawing his forward units toward Jemaluang on the evening of January 25th. Ten miles north of that town the 18th Battalion, 22nd Brigade, prepared an ambush. At midnight on the 26th, the leading battalion of the Japanese 55th Infantry Regiment blundered into the Australian trap. Colonel Koba's troops had made a difficult four-day detour through the swamps and jungles in a needless flanking movement to capture Mersing — which was now theirs for the taking since Taylor had evacuated the town. Exhausted by their efforts, the Japanese were surprised and sharply punished by skillfully-placed mortar and artillery fire. Around noon of the 27th, Taylor withdrew his forces according to plan, falling back through Jemaluang the next morning.

Koba, badly mauled, made no effort to regain contact with the enemy. His repulse, indeed, led General Yamashita to send a strong relief force — Colonel Saeki's 5th Reconnaissance Regiment with attached infantry, artillery, and engineers — dashing east along the Kluang-Jemaluang road. Saeki occupied the Kahang airfield early on the 28th, and that evening linked up with the 55th Infantry at Jemaluang.

On Twenty-fifth Army orders, Koba now set out for Kluang, where the Takumi Detachment was already assembling and where the rest of the 18th Division would soon arrive. General Mutaguchi with his headquarters, the 114th Infantry, and other divisional units had finally sailed from Camranh Bay on January 20th and landed two days later at Singora. From here the force moved south by road to Kluang where, on February 1st, General Mutaguchi resumed control of all his units in Malaya.* Since the 18th Division had few vehicles and for want of adequate shipping had left its horses behind in Canton, Twenty-fifth Army staff officers had called on the Guards Division and the 5th Division to provide motor transport for the move from Singora. Neither Nishimura nor Matsui was happy about this diversion of trucks and drivers, which may indeed have slowed their own operations.

In the meantime, while Eastforce had been giving Colonel Koba a bloody nose at Jemaluang, the Japanese had gained a minor air and sea victory at Endau. On January 24th Zero fighters, possibly from the light carrier *Ryujo*, shot down two Australian Hudsons making reconnaissance flights along the east coast. The next night a Catalina reported Japanese ships moving south in this area, and early on the 26th Hudson pilots discovered a convoy approaching Endau. The Japanese ships were part of a combined operation to seize the Anambas and at the same time to land airfield and signals troops at Endau with supplies, fuel, and bombs for use at the Kluang and Kahang airfields.

Japanese jamming successfully interfered with radio communication, and not until the Hudsons escaped the enemy fighters and returned to Singapore could they report their sighting. By then, it was clear that the Japanese convoy was close to shore and an attack would have to be made soon to do any good. Of the limited number of aircraft available, however, most had just returned from other missions and had not yet re-fuelled and re-armed. The majority of them were the obsolete Vildebeestes, whose crews had been well trained in torpedo attack techniques but which now, since the Japanese ships were in shallow water, would have to be loaded with bombs instead of torpedoes.

---

* Not all of the 18th Division was present. The 35th Brigade Headquarters and 124th Infantry were elsewhere and did not participate in the campaign.

It was early afternoon before the attack could be launched, and only two more waves could take off before nightfall. These succeeded in doing some slight damage to transports and a cruiser, and in shooting up troops in landing craft and on the beach. But shore-based 3rd Air Group fighters took a heavy toll of the attackers, destroying about half the Vildebeestes and a number of fighters, and damaging many more. Japanese losses were relatively light, and still fewer aircraft now remained to defend Singapore.[32]

While this action was taking place, two old destroyers, the *Vampire* and the *Thanet*, left Singapore in a brave effort to stop the Japanese convoy. Approaching Endau in the pre-dawn hours of the 27th, they encountered a Japanese screening force of destroyers and smaller vessels. The out-classed British warships launched their torpedoes — they each carried but three — and missed, succeeding only in drawing a heavy return fire. Japanese shells, mostly from the destroyer *Shirayuki*, struck the *Thanet* in the engine room. When *Vampire* tried to cover the mortally-wounded ship with a smoke screen, she herself came under attack from the Japanese destroyers. *Thanet* went down in about twenty minutes, but somehow the *Vampire* managed to escape completely unscathed and get back to Singapore. The Japanese at Endau were bothered no more.[33]

On the afternoon of January 26th, meanwhile, General Heath had issued a withdrawal timetable conforming to the phase lines shown on the map he had passed out on the 25th. This timetable was in accordance with the understanding already held by those at the previous day's meeting: the last troops were to cross the causeway from Johore Bahru to Singapore Island on the night of January 31st. Percival, however, had not made his final decision, although he was clearly on the verge of doing so. That evening, he sent Wavell news of the loss of Batu Pahat and of the landing at Endau, which he mistakenly believed had been made by fresh Japanese combat troops. The situation, he said, was 'becoming grave'. With his reduced strength, he was having difficulty in standing up to the combined enemy ground and air attacks. His men were 'fighting all the way' but might be forced back to Singapore Island 'within a week'.[34]

General Bennett was by now under the impression that Percival had already approved an evacuation in accordance with Heath's map and schedule; perhaps the growing pressure of Matsui's 5th Division against Westforce units encouraged Bennett in this belief. At any rate, shortly after midnight on January 26th-27th, Bennett issued definite orders for a step-by-step Westforce withdrawal to Singapore Island.[35] To maintain secrecy, only five copies of this order were reproduced for distribution within Westforce. None of these went to Percival, who apparently was not even informed, despite the fact that Westforce began pulling back during the morning to its first phase line. Bennett did visit Heath, however, to ask for a detailed order of march across the causeway.

Percival, meanwhile, had his eyes on the west coast, where the dispersal of the 6/15th Brigade, and the pressure on the 53rd, threatened to open the coastal road to a swift Japanese advance down that avenue all the way to Johore Bahru. The situation, he cabled Wavell that evening, had become 'very critical'. The Japanese, unless they could be halted in the west, might well swing down and behind British troops in Johore and prevent their escape to Singapore. And if all Percival's remaining forces did not get back to the island, defences there would be 'a bit thin'.[36] His fear was far from groundless, for General Yamashita was already pressing the Imperial Guards Division to hasten its advance from Batu Pahat with just that objective in mind.

Wavell replied to Percival at once, authorising him to use his judgment about when to withdraw. The primary object, he said, was to gain time and punish the enemy. But the evacuation of Johore should not be delayed for so long that losses and disorganisation would occur that might jeopardize Singapore's defence, which Percival would have to maintain 'for many months'.[37]

Early the next morning, January 28th, Percival met Heath and Bennett at III Corps headquarters. It was now no longer a question of whether or not to withdraw, but of how soon. Clearly, attempts to delay the Japanese any longer in southern Johore would endanger the entire British force. Percival advanced Heath's earlier withdrawal schedule by one day, ordering the final evacuation to take place on the night of the 30th. He reported this decision to Wavell, who promptly approved it.

The withdrawal plan called for all forces to fall back through a four-mile-deep perimeter covering the causeway, a broad 1,100-yard-long concrete and stone structure which provided the only access to Singapore Island from Johore. This perimeter would be defended by Brigadier Taylor's 22nd Brigade, from Eastforce, reinforced by a battalion of Gordon Highlanders recently attached to Westforce from the Singapore garrison, and supported by field artillery in nearby positions on the island itself. The Australians and Gordons would delay the Japanese until all III Corps troops in Johore had withdrawn through the perimeter – probably about daylight on the 31st – and then would themselves fall back through an inner perimeter line manned by the 2nd

Argyll and Sutherland Highlanders. The Argylls, whose strength had been built up again to about 250, would fight, if necessary, to the death. They would be the last to leave the mainland, and would carry the heavy responsibility of blowing up the causeway. It was a fitting assignment for a unit whose forerunners had earned the title, 'The Thin Red Line', for their magnificent stand against a Russian cavalry charge at Balaclava nearly a century earlier. To prevent Japanese bombers from destroying the causeway before the withdrawal was completed, the vital link was heavily protected by anti-aircraft guns and searchlights. If the Japanese should succeed in breaching the causeway, the Royal Navy would have to ferry Percival's troops across Johore Strait by whatever means were available.[38]

Once Percival had made his decision, there was little time to lose. Eastforce continued to withdraw south from Jemaluang, Taylor's brigade occupying its perimeter positions on the 30th, while the rest of the troops passed on over the causeway. In the west the 11th Division fell back along the coast, destroying bridges as it went to slow down pursuit by the Guards Division. The 53rd Brigade reached Singapore Island on the night of the 29th, while the 28th Brigade vigorously defended Pontian Kechil, where the coastal road turns east to join the trunk road a few miles outside Johore Bharu. The 5th Guards Regiment attempted in vain to capture Pontian Kechil on the 29th, and Japanese patrols moved inland in an unsuccessful effort to cut the road behind the 28th Brigade. That night, the brigade withdrew about ten miles to the east where, except for continuous Japanese patrol action, there was little enemy contact during the 30th The withdrawal was resumed after dusk, the last Gurkha troops passing across the inner perimeter and clearing the causeway shortly after midnight.

The evacuation of Westforce was neither as simple nor as successful. Bennett's troops, falling back along the main road and the railway line under continuous pressure from most of the 5th Division and the 3rd Air Group, had a most difficult manoeuvre to execute, requiring careful timing and co-ordination. On the road, the reinforced Australian 27th Brigade fought off heavy attacks by the 21st Brigade. General Sugiura's men, supported by low-flying and unopposed bombers and fighters, made repeated efforts to crush the Australians. On January 28th, a violent battle in a rubber estate in which a Japanese battalion attempted a flanking movement culminated in the afternoon in a punishing bayonet assault by the Australians. The Japanese, recoiling from this counter-blow, used smoke to cover their retreat, raising fears for a while that the yellow fumes were some sort of poison gas. Without gas-masks, the Australians were temporarily choked and blinded, and were thus unable to follow up their initial attack. The 27th Brigade withdrew to its next position that night and held it through January 29th against steady attacks. Again a bayonet charge threw back Sugiura's men, and the Australians broke contact after dark and fell back once more. The 21st Brigade, having taken many casualties, did not attack on the 30th. During the night, the Australians continued on unmolested across the causeway.

The withdrawal down the railway line by the Indian 9th Division encountered even greater difficulties. General Barstow planned to leap-frog his two brigades in successive moves, one holding while the other passed through to occupy the next position, until the entire force had crossed Johore Strait. The manoeuvre was complicated by the fact that the road parallel to the railway ended abruptly at Layang Layang, more than thirty miles from Johore Bahru, so that the division's artillery and vehicles, if they were to reach the causeway, would have to move west via a secondary road and then travel south along the trunk road ahead of the 27th Brigade. The main body of Barstow's division, covering the railway, would have to walk the rest of the way out, carrying everything including any wounded, and relying on mortars to do the work of artillery. This force would also be without its radios, since the heavy sets were truck-mounted, and would have to use the railway telegraph line for communications. With General Kawamura's 9th Brigade already pressing strongly against the Indian troops, this was clearly the most vulnerable part of the entire III Corps evacuation.

On January 27th, Brigadier Painter's 22nd Indian Brigade took up positions a few miles above Layang Layang, covering the escape-route of the divisional artillery and vehicles. Around noon, Brigadier Lay's 8th Brigade broke contact with the Japanese further north and fell back through the 22nd. An hour or so later, the guns and vehicles moved west to the trunk road and made their escape along that route, shielded by the hard-fighting Australians. A Japanese reconnaissance pilot, spotting this movement, reported, 'the enemy automobiles are fleeing south, rubbing each other like potatoes being washed'.[39]

Kawamura's troops reached the 22nd Brigade at about 4.30 p.m. and pushed forward to the outskirts of Layang Layang, where Painter managed to halt them. Under the withdrawal plan, he would have to hold the Japanese for another twenty-four hours at this point in order to cover the Australians' right flank. Now, however, events conspired to defeat him. About midnight, someone prematurely blew the railway bridge across a stream a few miles to the rear. This not only meant that rations could no longer come forward by rail, but it also cut the railway telegraph line and, in the absence of radio sets, meant that Painter was out of communication with Lay and Barstow. He was unaware, therefore, that the 8th Brigade had withdrawn further south than originally planned or that the railway bridge had been blown.

During the night, the Japanese discovered a number of small roads in the rubber estates east of the 22nd Brigade, and began to move along these round Painter's right flank. By dawn of the 28th, Painter realised that enemy troops had swung around him and were, in fact, astride the railway to his rear. Despite his previous orders, he decided to withdraw down the western side of the tracks in an effort to regain contact with Lay's brigade.

By now General Barstow concerned at the loss of communication with Painter had come forward to the 8th Brigade. He was shocked to learn that Lay had withdrawn further than he should have, that the railway bridge had been destroyed, and that nothing had been done to repair the telegraph line. He immediately ordered Lay to send forward his leading battalion, and then, with more courage perhaps than wisdom, he set out with two staff officers to find the 22nd Brigade. Advancing along the railway track beyond the bridge – which was still passable on foot – the three encountered a Japanese patrol and Barstow was killed. By this time, Kawamura had moved at least a battalion of troops between the two Indian brigades, and when Lay's leading battalion, after considerable delay, finally tried to advance, the unit came under heavy fire from a Japanese-held ridge. The Indians attacked but, without artillery support, could make no progress. Brigadier Lay did not try again to break through to the 22nd Brigade, while the latter, in turn, was taking increasing casualties as it attempted to make its way down the railway.

That evening General Bennett, unaware that Painter had been cut off, directed the 9th Division to pull back further south in order to conform with a withdrawal by the Australian 27th Brigade. Neither divisional headquarters nor the 8th Brigade, to whom the order was passed, raised any question about the fate of the 22nd Brigade. Lay began pulling back at once.

Early the next morning January 29th, 9th Division headquarters ordered the 8th Brigade to move north again, if possible, in an effort to rescue the 22nd. Despite the lack of Japanese pressure, Brigadier Lay appears to have made no attempt to advance. A few hours later, in order to meet the new schedule for evacuating Johore the next night, the division ordered Lay to resume his withdrawal that evening. Reconnaissance on the 30th, by ground patrols and a few aircraft, failed to locate Painter's force, and the 8th Brigade now made ready to co-ordinate its final moves out of Johore.

That morning General Wavell flew in again and talked with Percival, Heath and Bennett, at Bennett's headquarters. He approved the final withdrawal plan and also directed that most of the fighter-aircraft on Singapore's airfields – three of which would now be exposed to Japanese artillery fire, while the fourth was badly cratered by bombs – should move to Sumatra; where, indeed, the surviving bombers had already taken refuge. The one remaining fighter-squadron offered scant protection to the troops on the ground, but it would have been impossible to maintain any greater force in such an exposed position.

The final movement of III Corps troops to the causeway began in mid-afternoon, unhampered by the Japanese either on the ground or in the air. Although Wavell and the others had agreed that morning that the withdrawal could not be delayed on the slim chance that the 22nd Brigade might still escape, General Heath refused to give up hope. He ordered Westforce to hold its final position for as long as it could – specifically, at least an additional two hours – provided it could still cross the causeway before dawn on the 31st. This change at the last moment threatened the carefully-worked-out co-ordination scheme, and indeed increased the danger that other Westforce troops might be cut off. To make matters worse, Bennett was not available to either Heath or his own staff; he spent most of the day visiting subordinate headquarters and then, at 5 p.m., left for Singapore Island. In the end, no delay proved possible. It was simply too late to make changes. At about 7 o'clock in the evening of January 30th, with General Kawamura's troops again becoming active against the 8th Brigade, the final movement began. Unmolested by air attacks or even artillery fire, the mass of troops and equipment from Westforce, Eastforce, and the 11th Division converged on Johore Bahru and passed across the causeway perimeter.

Despite General Heath's good intentions a delay of a few hours, or even of several days, could not have helped the 22nd Brigade. On the afternoon of January 28th, Brigadier Painter had concluded that, without artillery support nor any hope of co-ordinating an attack with other friendly units, he had small chance of fighting his way out at a reasonable cost. Unwilling to take heavy casualties that could not be evacuated, he decided to leave the area of the railway and risk a trek through the jungle. His troops set out on a wide sweep to the west and south, hoping to remain hidden in the thick vegetation and somehow link up with the 8th Brigade.

But the odds were too great. Exhausted, encumbered by their wounded, and without food, the unfortunate Indian troops hacked their way through the endless jungle, lurching and floundering through steaming swamps — occasionally exchanging fire with Japanese patrols, but avoiding them when they could — until they could go no further. On February 1st, after four days of wandering and suffering, Painter finally surrendered to a force of Kawamura's troops that blocked his way. With him were 350 men. Many others, who had been separated from the brigade, were also captured, or died in the cruel jungle. Less than 100 survivors managed to reach Johore Strait and get across to Singapore Island.

The last of the III Corps troops (a battalion of the 11th Division) had meanwhile gone over the causeway at about 5.30 a.m. on January 31st. All night long, recalled one observer, a full moon 'so bright that lights were unnecessary' had illuminated the area.[40] But still no Japanese planes appeared to challenge the crossing. None, indeed, had made any effort to bomb the causeway in the nearly two months since the start of the campaign. The broad span had remained untouched; a vital link between the mainland and Singapore Island, especially in the last days of January when the traffic coming and going reached a peak. At the height of the evacuation, the mass of men and vehicles jammed together around and on the causeway presented a target that would have satisfied even the greediest of bombardiers. Despite the lure and vulnerability of this target, however, there is no evidence that General Yamashita ever requested the 3rd Air Group to attack it during the fighting (when the Twenty-fifth Army commander was most anxious to cut off large British forces on the mainland) nor even in the last, most critical days of the withdrawal. Sugawara himself displayed little initiative. Not until the final days of the month did he even assign a reconnaissance unit to keep an eye on the causeway, and there is no indication that he ordered a single attack. 'The thing that puzzled us', recalled an 11th Division truck driver, 'was why the Japs weren't bombing hell out of it'.[41] The 3rd Air Group made a few ineffectual high-level raids on the inner perimeter, but did not dive-bomb the causeway nor targets within the perimeter.

Throughout the fighting in Malaya, Sugawara's planes had done a good job of protecting convoys and anchorages, of destroying aircraft and ground installations, and of providing close support for Yamashita's troops. But the 3rd Air Group had either made no major effort to cut

British lines of communication, or had failed to control and co-ordinate its attacks in any effective manner. Trucks, trains, artillery, and even tactical units, seemed to be able to move up and down the long peninsula without too much difficulty, despite sporadic air attacks, even as reinforcements continued to reach Singapore. Had General Sugawara used his overwhelming air superiority to prevent the free movement of supplies and troops, Percival's army would doubtless have fared even worse than it actually did. And the Japanese failure to knock out, or seriously damage, the Johore causeway (or even to attack it) and thus cut off or destroy large British forces looms as a major and inexplicable error.*

On the ground, the Japanese also displayed a reluctance or inability to maintain contact with III Corps troops during the final stages of their withdrawal. The diversion of trucks to General Mutaguchi at this time (see p. 188) may possibly have affected front-line operations. But more credit must go to the effective job of bridge and road demolition carried out by the retiring British forces. In the last week of fighting on the mainland, Japanese engineers (on the 5th Division front alone) working under great difficulties in swamps and jungle, had been forced to reconstruct nearly a score of bridges of various sizes, in the area below Ayer Hitam and Kluang. The delays involved clearly slowed down Yamashita's pursuit of the foe. And the absence of Japanese tanks from the fighting after the 23rd, while possibly due to fuel shortage, may also be credited to the demolitions.

In the pre-dawn hours of January 31st, then, no Japanese appeared to test the causeway perimeter defences. Brigadier Taylor's troops, thus unmolested, withdrew from their positions and crossed the long causeway just before 7 a.m. The only two remaining Argyll pipers – Stewart and Maclean by name – played them over. Then came the Gordon Highlanders, while the shrill notes of *Cock o' the North*, their regimental march, rose sharp and clear in the air, all but covering the muffled sound of tramping feet. Now it was broad daylight. Still the enemy had failed to make an appearance. Two Buffalo fighter-planes were overhead, unchallenged. The last boats withdrew from the Johore shore and only the Argylls, the 'Thin Red Line', were left on the

---

* A month earlier, a similar Japanese failure to attack a vital bridge in the Philippines enabled part of General MacArthur's forces to escape to Bataan. (Louis Morton, *The Fall of the Philippines, United States Army in World War II: The War in the Pacific* (Washington: Office of the Chief of Military History, 1953), pp. 208-209.

mainland. General Heath signalled them to go. The men formed up in extended order, the two pipers at the head of the column, and, to the strains of *A Hundred Pipers* and *Hielan' Laddie* and finally *Blue Bonnets over the Border*, the Highlanders marched out of Johore in the hot morning sun. The last to go were Colonel Stewart, their commander, and Drummer Hardy, his batman.

For several days, army engineers assisted by naval technicians had been inserting demolition and depth charges under the 70-foot-wide causeway and its lock system, its steel drawbridge and heavy railway tracks. To destroy a large enough portion of this great span was a challenge, but now the sappers signalled that they were ready. At 8.15 a.m., they blew the charges. The drawbridge and the centre of the causeway disappeared with a roar in a cloud of smoke. Watchers standing on the Singapore shore could see the water of Johore Strait running freely through a seventy-foot gap. Ironically enough, however, the Strait at this point was barely four feet deep at low tide; easily fordable by determined men.[42]

Yet on the morning of January 31st, Japanese determination might have been questioned. Not until nearly six hours later did the first Twenty-fifth Army troops, the vanguard of the 5th Division, enter Johore Bahru. Yamashita's men had come a long way and accomplished much in a relatively short period. In fifty-five days, they had advanced the 400-mile length of the Malay Peninsula, a triumph as much for the engineers, who had repaired or rebuilt some 250 bridges, as for the combat troops, who had displayed mobility, fire-power, and flexibility. At a cost of less than 2,000 killed and 3,000 wounded, they had destroyed the equivalent of at least two British divisions, seriously crippled many more units, and captured great quantities of supplies, vehicles, and equipment. In the air, Japanese army and naval pilots had practically swept British planes from the skies, while the sinking of the *Prince of Wales* and the *Repulse* had shocked the entire Allied world. Yet despite these magnificent victories, the Japanese in Malaya had faltered at the last moment. By their failure to cut the British line of retreat or to prevent reinforcements from reaching Singapore, and their unwillingness or inability to press closely against their retreating foe, they had allowed the greater part of Percival's army to escape their grasp. This army now stood on Singapore Island. Battered, exhausted, its morale badly shaken, it might not stand for long. But for Yamashita, it still remained a force to be reckoned with.

NOTES – Chapter 7

1. The ABDACOM Directive is reproduced as App. A to General Sir Archibald Wavell, *Despatch by the Supreme Commander of the ABDA Area to the Combined Chiefs of Staff on the Operations in the South-West Pacific* [Aug. 1942] (London: His Majesty's Stationery Office, 1948). Basic sources for this chapter are as follows: (1) British operations: Percival, *Despatch*, pp. 1291-1306; Wavell, *Despatch*, pp. 1-11; Kirby, *The Loss of Singapore*, pp. 263-68, 282-89, 301-46; Wigmore, *The Japanese Thrust*, pp. 198-283; Bennett, *Why Singapore Fell*, pp. 88-163; Bhargava and Sastri, *Campaigns in South-East Asia*, pp. 233-300; Percival, *The War in Malaya*, pp. 207-49; Mackenzie, *Eastern Epic*, I, 331-75; Maltby, *Report*, pp. 1374-82. (2) Japanese operations: Malay Operations Record, pp. 60-80; ATIS, Malaya Campaign, pp. 33-71; Tsuji, *Singapore*, pp. 176-215; Southwest Area Air Operations, pp. 72-95; Malaya Invasion Naval Operations, pp. 38-58; Hattori, *The Greater East Asia War*, II, 59-62.

2. Wavell, *Despatch*, p. 2.

3. Kirby, *The Loss of Singapore*, pp. 342-43.

4. Bennett, *Why Singapore Fell*, p. 94. For Bennett's views, see especially *ibid.*, pp. 22-23, 95-97; Wigmore, *The Japanese Thrust*, p. 199 and *passim*.

5. Brigadier Sir John Smyth, *Before the Dawn* (London: Cassell, 1957), pp. 110, 120; Brigadier C.N. Barclay, *On Their Shoulders* (London: Faber and Faber, 1954), pp. 63, 137.

6. Wavell, *Despatch*, p. 5.

7. Morrison, *Malayan Postscript*, pp. 110-17 and Kin, *Rage in Singapore*, pp. 272-74 are eyewitness accounts of the evacuation of Kuala Lumpur and the subsequent looting.

8. See also, Replies to Questions Concerning Operations Plans of the Japanese Forces for the Malaya Invasion, in Far East Command, Special Studies, I, Tab. 8; Gillison, *Royal Australian Air Force*, pp. 325-32. Mutaguchi's state of mind is described in Tsuji, *Singapore*, pp. 207-208; Swinson, *Four Samurai*, pp. 116-17.

9. Bennett, *Why Singapore Fell*, p. 111.

10. Diary of Pvt. Yamashita, in ATIS, Current Translations, No. 45, p. 28.

11. *Ibid.* See also the diary of another 41st Infantry soldier, in ATIS, Current Translations, No. 54, p. 29.

12. Russell Braddon, *The Naked Island* (Garden City: Doubleday, 1953), pp. 67-90, is an account, by a survivor, of the battery's operations while it was attached to the 45th Brigade.

13. Bennett, *Why Singapore Fell*, p. 106.

14. *Ibid.*, p. 128.

15. Wigmore, *The Japanese Thrust*, p. 227.

16. Braddon, *Naked Island*, p. 77. For the following action, see also Takeo Iwaguro, *Seiki no Shingun: Shingaporu no Sokogeki* ("March of the Century: The Assault on Singapore") (Tokyo: Shio Shobo, 1956), pp. 123-38, 135-38. I am grateful to Mr. Louis Allen for calling this to my attention and providing a translation.

17. Bennett, *Why Singapore Fell*, p. 142.

18. Japan Defence Agency, *Mare Shinko Sakusen*, pp. 460-61.

19. Percival, *The War in Malaya*, p. 233.

20. Glover, *In 70 Days*, p. 158.

21. Maltby, *Report*, p. 1377. For air operations, see also Gillison, *Royal Australian Air Force*, pp. 336-46; Richards and Saunders, *The Flight Avails*, pp. 34-37; Craven and Cate (eds.), *The Army Air Forces*, I, 379, 383.

22. Maltby, *Report*, p. 1379.

23. Southwest Area Air Operations, p. 87. See also Reasons for Failure of Japanese to Halt Reinforcements of Singapore by Sea, in Far East Command, Special Studies, II, Tab. 5.

24. Wigmore, *The Japanese Thrust*, pp. 258, n. 4; 290, n. 5. For the light tanks, see also Mackenzie, *Eastern Epic*, I, 382.

25. Prime Minister to General Ismay, Jan. 21st, 1942, in Winston S. Churchill, *The Second World War*, Vol. IV, *The Hinge of Fate* (Boston: Houghton Mifflin, 1950), p. 56. This discussion is based on *ibid.*, pp. 55-59; Wigmore, *The Japanese Thrust*, pp. 285-87; Gwyer and Butler, *Grand Strategy*, III, 416-18; Bryant, *The Turn of the Tide*, pp. 236, 248.

26. Churchill, *The Hinge of Fate*, p. 59.

27. Morrison, *Malayan Postscript*, p. 158.

28. Brown, *Suez to Singapore*, p. 376; Wigmore, *The Japanese Thrust*, p. 70, n. 8.

29. Morrison, *Malayan Postscript*, p. 159.

30. Percival, *The War in Malaya*, p. 241.

31. Minutes of Conference Held at Headquarters, Westforce, 1515 Hours, January 25th, 1942, App. G to Percival, *Despatch*.

32. See also Gillison, *Royal Australian Air Force*, pp. 343-46.

33. Gill, *Royal Australian Navy*, pp. 559-60.

34. Kirby, *The Loss of Singapore*, p. 339.

35. Westforce Operation Instruction No. 4, January 27th, 1942, App. 24 to *ibid.*

36. *Ibid.*, p. 339.

37. Bhargava and Sastri, *Campaigns in South-East Asia*, p. 287.

38. The plan was largely the work of Colonel Stewart of the Argylls. Stewart, *History of the Argyll and Sutherland Highlanders*, pp. 90-91, 95-97; Rose, *Who Dies Fighting*, p. 110; Lt. J.O.C. Hayes, R.N., The Withdrawal to Singapore Island, *The Army Quarterly*, XLV (November 1942), pp. 107-10. Hayes was the naval liaison officer with Stewart. An abbreviated version of his account appears as App. III to Stewart's book.

39. ATIS, Malaya Campaign, p. 63.

40. Rose, *Who Dies Fighting*, p. 115.

41. Attiwell, *Fortress*, p. 108.

42. Stewart, *History of the Argyll and Sutherland Highlanders*, pp. 97-99; Hayes, *The Withdrawal to Singapore Island*, pp. 110-13; Rose, *Who Dies Fighting*, pp. 112-17.

8
The Fort That Never Was

The Japanese occupation of Johore doomed the island of Singapore. General Yamashita now held all the Malayan peninsula, while other Japanese forces had already occupied strategic points in Borneo, invaded Burma, and were preparing to isolate Singapore even further by seizing additional areas in Burma and the Indies. Clearly it was only a matter of time before Singapore, too, would be crushed. For the defenders of that tiny cidadel, there was no longer any point in holding the naval base for the eventual arrival of the battle fleet, since Japanese guns across Johore Strait rendered the great base valueless to British warships. It was now simply a question of denying the enemy the use of Singapore; of defending the island for as long as possible, to keep Admiral Kondo's warships out of the base, to tie down Yamashita's divisions in Malaya, and to block Japanese access to the Indian Ocean via the Singapore and Malacca Straits.

How long could Singapore be held? For years the British had cultivated its image of impregnability. Most of the world thought of it as a powerful fortress. Yet the island was by no means a fortress. It was, rather, in the words of General Percival, simply 'a large defended and inhabited area'.[1] Frequent references to Singapore as a fortress, in official and public statements and documents, had strengthened the myth of its impregnability. Many, including most British people, who might have known better, were fooled by this myth. But the Japanese, at whom the carefully elaborated legend of impregnability was aimed, were not misled.

The Singapore Fortress, as it was officially called, consisted of the island itself, a few small adjacent islets, and a point on the southern tip of the mainland overlooking the estuary of the Johore River and the eastern entrance to Johore Strait. The strait itself is 5,000 yards wide at this point, but most of it is not so broad, especially the stretch west of the causeway where it narrows in some places to barely 600 yards. Singapore Island — twenty-seven miles from east to west at its widest, and no more than thirteen miles from north to south — consists of somewhat rolling terrain with only two large hills, in the west-central part of the island, and a short ridge-line overlooking the ocean west of the city of Singapore. Except for the south-east coast, most of the shoreline consists of mangrove swamps linked by small rivers and streams, flooded in great part at high tide. The island, in 1942, was mostly covered with jungle, rubber plantations, and tiny farms, but several good roads provided ready access to almost any area.

In addition to its relative lack of natural defences — Johore Strait was little more than a shallow moat, difficult to defend along its western arm — Singapore was vulnerable for two reasons. Its defences were aimed at withstanding an assault from the sea (for which, incidentally, they were quite adequate). And very few people, until it was too late, really believed that the island would have to be defended against attack by land.

Singapore's primary defences, sited to protect the naval base against amphibious attack, were the so-called Fixed Defences, on which the legend of impregnability had grown. These included the five famous 15-inch naval rifles, six powerful 9.2-inch guns, and eighteen 6-inch guns, as well as a small assortment of lighter, short-range pieces.[2] The guns were organised in two fire-commands of approximately equal strength: Changi, guarding the eastern approach to the naval base, and Faber, protecting the western arm of Johore Strait and Keppel Harbour, the commercial port, just south of Singapore city.

Changi Fire-Command

Johore Battery	3 15-inch	Singapore Island, eastern tip
Tekong Besar Battery	3 9.2-inch	Tekong Besar Island, east of Singapore Island
Sphinx Battery	2 6-inch	Tekong Besar
Changi Battery	2 6-inch	Singapore Island, eastern tip
Beting Kusah Battery	2 6-inch	Singapore Island, eastern tip
Pengerang Battery	2 6-inch	Tip of mainland, east of Singapore Island

Faber Fire-Command

Buona Vista Battery	2 15-inch	Singapore Island, west of the city
Connaught Battery	3 9.2-inch	Blakang Mati, Keppel Harbour
Serapong Spur Battery	2 6-inch	Blakang Mati
Siloso Battery	2 6-inch	Blakang Mati
Silingsing Battery	2 6-inch	Brani Island, Keppel Harbour

| Labrador Battery | 2 6-inch | Singapore Island, Keppel Harbour |
| Pasir Laba Battery | 2 6-inch | Singapore Island, west coast |

Almost on a par with Singapore's pre-war myth of impregnability has been the post-war legend that the Fixed Defence guns pointed 'the wrong way' and could fire only seaward. As a matter of fact, all the 15-inch guns had 360 degree traverse,[3] and the three 9.2-inch guns of Connaught Battery and the two 6-inch guns of Pasir Laba Battery also had arcs of fire covering the northern approaches to the island. The other guns did not — but this was due as much to their location in shielded positions and their lack of range as to their limited traverse. Nevertheless, the 6-inch batteries at Serapong, Labrador, and Changi could fire on targets on Singapore Island itself if necessary.

The problem was not which way the guns faced, but rather what kind of ammunition they had. Since they have been expected to fire primarily at naval vessels, their basic ammunition was armour-piercing; lethal against warships, but almost entirely ineffective against troop concentrations, hostile artillery, and other land targets, since the heavy shells would bury themselves deeply in the soft ground before detonating. It took high explosive shells to knock out most ground targets, and there were only a limited number of these available for the larger weapons. The 15-inch guns had none at all, while the 9.2-inch guns had only about thirty rounds of high explosive apiece.

Had more suitable ammunition been available, there were still other vital handicaps. The foremost of these was lack of observation. The jungle, and the general topography of Johore, hid the Japanese from the view of Singapore Island, aerial observation was out of the question in face of the Japanese command of the air, and while it would have been possible to place a few ground observers on the mainland, they had no means of communicating what they saw in time to do any good. Artillery fire without observation is shooting in the dark: the gunners have no idea where their target is located or whether their shells are even landing near the enemy. There are methods of finding some targets without either ground or aerial observation, but the Malayan terrain would have made these difficult to employ, even if the British had been equipped and trained to use them. And the problem of assessing and ensuring accuracy still remained.

The guns of the Fixed Defences, also, unlike howitzers or other high-angle weapons, fired their rounds on a relatively flat trajectory. This, again, is ideal for shooting over open water at unshielded targets, but it is of little use in counter-battery fire or in attacking an enemy who is at all dug in, protected, or in defilade — especially if the gunners are coast artillerymen, as they were at Singapore, unaccustomed to shooting at land targets, and firing armour-piercing ammunition.

In the latter part of January, Winston Churchill had suggested that a higher, more suitable trajectory could be obtained by firing the Fixed Defence guns with reduced charges, and that somehow high explosive ammunition might be brought into Singapore and thus put to good use.[4] But no high explosive rounds reached Singapore — despite Percival's request for this type of ammunition — and the plan for firing with reduced charges offered no sure answer to the trajectory problem. For one thing, while reducing the charge would have raised the trajectory somewhat, it is not clear that the difference would have been significant. But even more important is the fact that without good observation of where their rounds were falling, or previously developed firing tables to guide them, the Singapore gunners could have practically no way of judging the effect of a given reduction in the firing charge. In these circumstances, shooting with reduced charges would be a tricky business. Removing only a small amount of powder might have done practically nothing to raise the trajectory, while weakening the charge too much could have caused the round to fall dangerously short. There is no indication whether or not Churchill's suggestion was tried, but it seems doubtful. Few artillerymen, at any rate, would recommend it without observation or prior experience.

Despite all these difficulties the Singapore defenders did all they could to make ready the Fixed Defence guns for use against Yamashita's expected assault — without, however, lessening their usefulness against a seaborne attack, which always remained a possibility. The gunners worked out a counter-bombardment plan, cleared fields-of-fire, and improvised arrangements for the limited observation of targets on the mainland. More than 150 anti-aircraft guns were available after the withdrawal from Johore. These were now deployed to protect the Fixed Defence guns — which had no overhead protection against air attack — as well as Keppel Harbour, the airfields, and other vital points. But the loss of observation posts on the mainland, which had previously warned of approaching Japanese planes, greatly reduced the effectiveness of the anti-aircraft guns. And most of these weapons lacked the range to hit high-level enemy bombers.

Next in importance to the Fixed Defences, in the protection of Singapore Island, were the beach defences. These, like everything else at Singapore, had been designed to beat off attacks from the sea. They extended along the southern beaches from the eastern tip of the island for some twenty miles to a point well to the west of the city. They included concrete machine-gun pillboxes every 600 yards, a number of 18-pounder field guns, timber anti-boat and anti-tank obstacles, searchlights, and barbed wire. There were also land mines, but in the humid Malayan climate corrosion was constant, and there was no way of knowing how long a minefield would remain 'live' — nor was it safe to attempt to remove the corroded mines and find out.

Behind the beach defences, two so-called 'switch lines' had been selected to cover the centre of Singapore Island against a successful enemy landing on either the east or west coast. The western position, called the Jurong Line, lay across the three-mile neck of land between the source of the Kranji River, which flowed north into Johore Strait, and of the Jurong River, which ran south to the sea. The position in the east, the Serangoon Line, covered Kallang airfield and ran north to the Serangoon River. Although the ground along the two switch lines had been examined before the war, and defences planned, no digging or construction had been done. After December 8th, work began on an anti-tank ditch along the Jurong Line and a few positions were built and fields-of-fire cleared. Hardly enough was accomplished to make these efforts worth while.

The incomplete state of the switch lines only reflected the inadequacy of Singapore's defences against anything but a seaborne attack. Indeed, the lack of defensive positions on the northern and western coasts of the island made it highly vulnerable to any assault across the narrow western arm of Johore Strait. The reasons for this go back to the original mission of the Singapore defenders, which was not to hold Singapore Island, as such, but to protect the naval base. As General Dobbie had pointed out over four years earlier, protection of the naval base meant preventing an enemy from placing observed artillery fire on it from Johore, or bombing it from nearby bases. But Dobbie's programme to build extensive defensive positions in Johore had foundered on the rocks of economy measures and financial restrictions, and little had actually been accomplished to erect defences to keep the Japanese out of southern Malaya. It is of course true that any defences would have been of limited value without strong air power to protect them, and that air reinforcements were unavailable. Yet the idea of protecting the naval base on the Malayan mainland, rather than on Singapore Island, persisted, and nothing was done to secure the Johore side of the island against attack. No one had apparently considered that in the event Singapore might have to be defended less to hold the naval base for a British fleet than to deny it to Japanese warships.

Not until nearly two weeks after the Japanese invasion of Malaya — with General Yamashita's forces on the Perak River — did it occur to anyone that something must be done about Singapore Island's northern defences. On December 23rd, as part of a broad directive outlining his policy to hold the Japanese on the mainland as far north as possible to cover the arrival of reinforcements, General Percival ordered Major-General Keith Simmons, commanding the Singapore Fortress, to 'arrange for reconnaissance of the north shore of Singapore Island to select positions for the defence of possible landing places'.[5] Only a few officers could be spared for this work, but Percival was apparently satisfied. 'It was intended', he wrote after the war, 'to start the actual construction of the defences about the beginning of January'.[6]

If this is so, it is difficult to understand a conversation that Brigadier Ivan Simson, Chief Engineer of Malaya Command, says he had with Percival late on the evening of December 26th. No witnesses were present and Percival does not mention the meeting in his post-war publications. According to Simson, he strongly urged Percival to allow him to begin erecting defensive positions to cover Johore Strait; but, says Simson, Percival refused on the grounds that such defences would be bad for morale.[7] If Percival actually intended to begin construction in early January, then what Simson recalls makes no sense. If, on the other hand, Percival's recollection of his intentions is in error, then several possibilities arise.

Perhaps he did not, even now, believe that the Japanese would reach Johore Strait. Perhaps he felt that if they did, they would certainly be strong enough to take Singapore Island, no matter what defences were built. The events of the previous two weeks had already been a serious blow to both military and civilian morale, and Percival's reluctance to do anything else to destroy it is readily understandable. Perhaps he felt that at the moment the reconnaissance he ordered would be enough, that there would be ample time to erect defences later — it hardly seemed possible that the Japanese could reach Johore Strait in another five weeks — and that there was no point in further ruining morale by apparently conceding all of the mainland to the enemy so early in the campaign.

Whatever the reasons, no actual construction work was begun. On January 7th, when General Wavell paid his first visit to Singapore, the new ABDA commander was shocked to discover that 'no defences had been made or even planned in detail on the north side of Singapore Island, although it was obvious by now that we might be driven back into the Island and have to defend it'.[8] Wavell immediately ordered

Percival to see that defences were built. But except for increased site reconnaissance along the north coast, nothing seems to have been done.

A large part of the problem lay in lack of labour. Until the eve of war in the Far East, British labour policy in Malaya sought to avoid any interruption in the production of rubber and tin to support the struggle against Germany and Italy. This policy constantly thwarted attempts by Percival and his predecessors to recruit or conscript local labour or even to organise a labour mobilisation scheme. Percival, was further hampered by the unrealistically low rate of pay that London authorised for civil labour. When the Japanese attacked, despite his continued efforts there was no approved plan for conscripting civil labour, or even controlling it, in time of war. To make matters worse, Percival's appeals notwithstanding, Malaya Command contained only three military labour companies.

Once war began, the situation grew steadily worse. In the face of Japanese air raids, it became increasingly difficult to maintain any sort of civil labour force at critical points. Up and down Malaya, labourers refused to work as soon as the bombing grew at all intense. At Gurun and elsewhere in the north, workers who had been assembled to build defence positions dispersed almost immediately. Air raids on Penang scattered labourers there. In Singapore itself as early as December 20th work-crews disappeared, sometimes for a whole day, whenever air raid alarms sounded – despite the fact that the island was not actually attacked for three weeks after the initial raid on the 8th. By January, when air raids occurred almost daily, so few men were willing to remain in the heavily-bombed dock area that troops had to be assigned to unload the vital reinforcement convoys. Since Percival had given airfield reconstruction and maintenance a high priority, most of the labour available was used in an effort to keep the airfields operational. Even here, however, air-force officers had great difficulty organising and maintaining working parties, and badly-needed combat replacement troops had to be diverted to these efforts.

By early January the situation on Singapore Island was practically hopeless. The few troops and military labour units available were involved primarily in repairing bomb-damage to the airfields and other installations. There was practically no civilian labour to be had. And not until towards the end of the month did military and civil authorities agree on a compulsory labour scheme and a realistic rate of pay. By then it was too late – by at least six months.

This situation was clearly not appreciated by the Prime Minister; Winston Churchill. On January 19th, he read a report from Wavell that came as an ugly shock. 'Little or nothing' had been done to build defences on the north side of Singapore, and the fortress's guns, because of their flat trajectory, would be of small help in protecting the island.[9] Churchill was stunned. He had seen Singapore as a mighty fortress, on a par with Verdun, capable of withstanding a long seige; a great citadel to which the Japanese would have to drag masses of heavy artillery and ammunition, through the Malay jungles, before they could even begin to think of attacking it. He had not even considered that there might be no permanent defences to protect Singapore's landward side, and none of his military advisers had mentioned the possibility. Wavell himself had been unaware of the situation before his visit to the island.

Yet the British Chiefs of Staff were apparently not surprised. Singapore Island 'had never been considered defensible against close attack', according to Major General Sir John Kennedy, then Director of Military Operations. 'The channel was narrow, mangrove swamps impeded the fire of the defences; and the aerodromes, water supply and other vital installations were within artillery range from the mainland'. The Chiefs believed that any last ditch defence would have to take place in Johore rather than on Singapore.[10]

Churchill, however, was unconvinced that Singapore Island could not be defended. He fired off a broadside of instructions to the Chiefs-of-Staff and to Wavell, ordering a major effort to construct defences, using the 'entire male population' under 'the most rigorous compulsion'. Landing-points should be mined and obstructed, barbed wire and booby traps placed in the swamps, field artillery and searchlights positioned to destroy Japanese amphibious efforts, and attempts made to improve the capability of the fortress's guns. Every inch of the island, especially the city of Singapore, was to be 'defended to the death' with no thought of surrender — or at least not 'until after protracted fighting among the ruins' of the city.[11]

Churchill's directions while basically sound contained nothing that his military commanders did not already know. But his order to defend Singapore 'to the death' raised ominous questions about the fate of nearly a million helpless civilians in the city. It was one thing to conscript civilians to dig trenches, but quite another to expose them to the mercy of a ruthless and savage foe. Fortunately for the inhabitants of Singapore, the Prime Minister's orders in this respect would be disregarded.

Wavell, meanwhile, was concerned about the fighting in Johore. He cautioned Churchill that Singapore could probably not hold out if

Johore fell, and he urged Percival to make his stand on the mainland. Everything possible should be done to prepare Singapore's defences, he told Percival, but this should be carried out in complete secrecy. The battle was to be 'fought out in Johore' until reinforcements arrived, and the troops on the mainland 'must not be allowed to look over [their] shoulders'.[1 2]

As if building defences in secret while fighting a decisive action in Johore were not enough of a problem for Percival, he now received orders from the Chiefs-of-Staff to prepare to destroy everything of military value on Singapore, if the island should fall, in order to keep it out of Japanese hands. Percival replied that he would try his best, but that he could not 'fight and destroy simultaneously with 100 per cent efficiency', and he would have to concentrate on fighting until all hope was gone. Also, he already had a serious morale problem, and obvious preparations to destroy things might bring a complete collapse of civilian will.[1 3]

On January 23rd, Percival issued secret orders to his major commanders outlining defence plans for Singapore. The island's north and west shores, he said, were 'too intersected with creeks and mangroves for any recognized form of beach defence'. Defence, then, would be based on 'small defended localities', supported by mobile reserves, covering approaches inland along rivers, creeks, roads, and trails. Apart from whatever might be necessary to organise covering positions and to clear fields of fire, he ordered no defensive work except the digging of slit trenches for the protection and concealment of reserve forces.[1 4]

General Simmons, the Fortress commander, was charged with working out the details of Percival's plan. In accordance with earlier orders, he had already taken some steps to make ready the island's defences, and he now continued with a greater sense of urgency. By the time Johore was evacuated, a week later, a good deal had apparently been accomplished. Sites for the 'defended localities', reserve assembly areas, artillery observation posts and gun positions, and formation headquarters were reconnoitered and selected. Communications were arranged, machine-gun and anti-tank positions built, and oil obstacles and depth charges set in some of the creeks offering likely avenues of approach to the Japanese. How extensive these preparations were is not clear, but the troops coming back to Singapore – who, like everyone else except the Japanese, had been fooled by the myth of the island's impregnability – were considerably shaken by the lack of visible fortifications.

They were equally disturbed to discover that the great Singapore naval base, for which presumably the whole campaign had been fought, had been evacuated. In accordance with instructions from the Admiralty to evacuate as many skilled naval and dockyard personnel as possible, the local naval command had abandoned the base on January 28th, moving the naval staff and all European civilians to Singapore, from which port most of them sailed for Ceylon on the 31st. The evacuation was clearly justifiable in the circumstances, but it hardly went down well with soldiers who thought they were defending the naval base and who knew that there was no escape if they failed.

Percival issued his final orders for the defence of Singapore on January 28th. Three days later the withdrawal from Johore was completed, and the troops began occupying their allotted positions on the island. On February 5th the last reinforcement convoy arrived, carrying the final units of the British 18th Division and a few Indian troops. Unlike previous convoys, this one was attacked. As the four ships neared the harbour, they were struck by Japanese bombers. One vessel suffered heavy damage and had to be abandoned in flames. Most of the troops were rescued, but almost all the weapons and equipment, including the guns of an anti-tank regiment, were lost.

There were now between 90,000 and 100,000 men in the Singapore defence area, of whom some 75,000 to 80,000 were fighting troops.* In normal circumstances, these might have constituted a powerful force, including as they did thirty-eight rifle battalions. But these numbers were misleading. Of the seventeen Indian battalions only one was up to strength, a dozen consisted primarily of recruits, and the other four, still reorganising, were not yet ready for action. The thirteen British battalions included six, from the 18th Division, that had only arrived on January 29th, while the rest were all under strength because of heavy casualties. Two of the six Australian battalions

* After the withdrawal from Johore on January 31st Percival, according to his later recollection, had 'in the neighbourhood of 85,000 troops', of whom some 70,000 were armed and equipped for combat.[15]

The convoy that arrived on February 5th may have carried as many as 5,000 troops, which would raise the total to about 90,000. At this time, however, the British War Office estimated that there were at least 100,000 troops on Singapore Island.[16]

The Japanese also claimed to have captured about 100,000 prisoners, (of whom 50,000 were white) on the island, when Percival surrendered.[17] A source based on Indian records indirectly confirms part of this by stating that 45,000 Indians were captured on Singapore. (Mackenzie, *Eastern Epic*, I, 403.) If this figure is correct, there were certainly enough British, Australian, and local troops on the island to bring the total close to 100,000. For a further discussion of strength figures, see below, Chapter 10, footnote 12.

contained a high percentage of untrained replacements, and the other four also included many raw troops. The two Malay battalions, part of the Fortress troops, were unblooded, and one of these had been raised only in December. Most supporting units were under strength or had newly arrived, while volunteer organisations, constituting the remainder of Percival's force, were inexperienced, poorly trained, and of no significant value. Many units, especially those who had fought on the mainland, had taken heavy losses in weapons and equipment. The men were tired. There were several thousand wounded in hospital. Morale, in general, was low.

An obvious major weakness was the lack of air support. About a dozen fighters at Singapore, and a limited back-up from Sumatra, offered little in the way of air-power. At the end of January, forty-eight Hurricane fighters reached ABDACOM, flying in from the aircraft carrier *Indomitable*. Some of these flew in to Singapore, and thanks to them Air-Vice-Marshal Pulford was able to maintain a daily average strength of ten fighters on the island. During the first week in February, Japanese artillery fire forced the evacuation of all but Kallang airfield, just east of Singapore city, and even that could be maintained only with great difficulty in the face of Japanese bombing.[18]

The supply situation was relatively good. There was food enough for three months and ample medical supplies; and water, coming from three reservoirs in the centre of the island, was more than sufficient if carefully used. There were more vehicles than could be utilised, and no problem about fuel. Ammunition was also plentiful, although there were shortages of field artillery and anti-aircraft shells, two important categories. Of more concern than any scarcities was the location of supply-dumps and depôts. Sited to support defences from seaward attack, and widely dispersed for protection against air attacks, most of them were in the centre of the island and some, including important ammunition magazines, were in the northern area, vulnerable to early capture by an assault from Johore. Japanese shelling and the shortage of labour thwarted attempts to move ammunition supplies to less exposed areas. This would have made a difference during the fighting on the island.

Troops in forward areas held a ten-day reserve of ammunition and other supplies; in the face of Japanese air attacks it would be questionable how much re-supplying could be carried out once the battle was joined. Even now, enemy air activity limited supply movements to the hours of darkness and, with civilian labour at a premium, the weary troops did most of the work of transferring stocks.

Those not engaged on this job turned to building up their defensive positions – on February 4th, all civilians within a mile of the north coast were moved out of this area – but the great number of swamps along the coast, and the island's high water table, made it impossible to do much digging near the beaches. Slit trenches quickly filled with brackish water, and it was difficult to keep equipment and ammunition dry. So the usual defensive position took the form of breastworks covered by double-apron barbed wire and anti-tank mines. The majority of these were prepared for all-round defence, with supporting positions close by. Constant air attacks, soon joined by artillery fire, restricted most of this work to the night, which meant that few of the troops were getting any decent amount of sleep.

Percival expected Yamashita to attack as soon as possible, to free troops and planes for other operations, and he thought the blow would fall any time after the first week in February. He judged correctly that Yamashita had three divisions for the assault, but he over-estimated Japanese strength by assuming that there were more divisions on call for early commitment in Malaya and Indo-China. The primary assault, he felt, would come from the mainland, but there was a good chance of a seaborne attack from the Anambas or via the Strait of Malacca. Nor did he rule out an airborne effort to seize the Singapore airfields, or the simultaneous application of several of these operations. The island had seventy miles of coastline, and Percival considered all of it to be vulnerable.

In this situation, he had two alternatives. The first was to try to prevent Yamashita from landing or, failing that, to counter-attack and expel or destroy the Japanese forces. This course was difficult, since neither the size and strength of his army nor the broken, swampy nature of the shoreline allowed any strong coastal defence. The second alternative was to put only light screening forces near the beaches, keeping his main strength in reserve for a general battle further inland. This course would mean the early loss of many supply depots, would leave him little depth to fight outside the city of Singapore, and would allow Yamashita to attack through jungle terrain favourable to Japanese tactics. There was also the important consideration that in the face of a successful Japanese landing troop and civilian morale might collapse. The choice was not an easy one. Weighing all factors, Percival decided to take the first alternative. Despite the obvious difficulties, he would try to keep the Japanese off the island altogether, using the tactics he had outlined in his order of January 23rd.

Given the nature of the terrain, which would preclude close control of the troops by Percival himself, he divided the island into three combat zones covering the coastline – the Northern, Western, and Southern Areas – with a Reserve Area in the middle. Each Area commander would control the battle in his zone, with Percival retaining command of the Reserve Area, and prepared to support whichever of his subordinates was under pressure.

There had been some difference of opinion between Percival and Wavell over which troops to assign to which Areas. When Wavell visited Singapore on the 20th, he had told Percival to place his freshest and strongest troops, the British 18th Division, in that part of the island most likely to be attacked. Wavell thought this would be the north-west coast, in front of the main Japanese axis of advance down the peninsula. The Australian 8th Division, he said, should hold the next most dangerous position, the north-eastern part of the island. The Indian troops should be held in reserve, as much as possible, for reinforcement and counter-attack. However Percival, perhaps recalling the pre-war fear of a Japanese landing in eastern Johore for a direct attack on Singapore, believed that the main enemy assault would come down the Johore River, against the north-east coast of Singapore Island. He proposed to place the 18th Division here and the 8th Division in the west. Wavell allowed himself to be persuaded, since Percival was the commander on the scene and had been studying the problem for some time.[19]

Percival's specific dispositions reflected the conclusions he had reached about the most probable danger area. Of his three combat sectors, he obviously viewed the Northern as the key. This extended from near the north-east tip of the island west almost to the causeway. Defending it was Heath's III Corps, consisting of Major-General Merton Beckwith-Smith's 18th Division and Key's 11th Division, which had absorbed the remnants of the 9th Division. It also included considerable artillery: five field artillery regiments and three separate batteries plus one mountain and two anti-tank regiments. Furthermore, during the first week in February, Percival ordered Brigadier Simson to move large stocks of engineer defence equipment from the north-west to the north-east part of the island.[20]

The Western Area was held by Bennett's Australians, with the raw 44th Indian Brigade attached, and three field artillery regiments and an equal number of anti-tank batteries in support. Bennett was responsible for defending almost all of western Singapore Island, from a point just east of the causeway all round the western arm of Johore Strait to the mouth of the Jurong River on the south coast. His force was weaker than Beckwith-Smith's in both infantry and artillery, and the terrain he held was more difficult to defend.

The Southern Area, from Changi, on the north-east, to the Jurong River, was the responsibility of General Simmons' Fortress troops. Simmons had very little field or anti-tank artillery, but his sector included all the Fixed Defence guns except the 6-inch battery at Pasir Laba, in Bennett's zone. Percival retained only the 12th Indian Infantry Brigade, now only two under strength battalions, in his Command Reserve. Weak garrisons were also placed on some of the outlying islands. And finally, a small Chinese volunteer unit known as Dalforce — lightly-armed, partially-trained irregulars under Lieutenant-Colonel John Dalley, a Singapore police officer — was assigned to help patrol the difficult mangrove swamp areas of the northern and western coasts.

In view of these dispositions, Percival's post-war statements are somewhat confusing. In his official report on the campaign, he wrote that he expected the Japanese attack 'to develop from the west'.[21] He repeated this point later, in his book, adding that he had 'specially selected' the Australian division for the Western Area because it was the freshest of his experienced units.[22] If, in fact, he expected the attack to come from the west, then he was under orders from Wavell to place the 18th Division there. Assigning Beckwith-Smith's division, along with most of the artillery, to the Northern Area indicates his belief that this was the critical sector, regardless of what he wrote later.

Percival's difficulties were compounded by the large number of civilians on Singapore Island, over whom he had practically no control. Governor Sir Shenton Thomas declared martial law on December 20th, delegating certain powers to Malaya Command. But Thomas retained almost all of his civil authority, Percival had nothing to do with civil administration, and questions of co-ordination were settled at the Far East War Council, chaired by Alfred Duff-Cooper, the Resident Minister for Far Eastern Affairs. When General Wavell's appointment as the ABDA commander ended the need for a Resident Minister, Duff-Cooper left in mid-January and Thomas replaced him as head of the War Council. The governor, while uninspiring, was a competent administrator and ran Singapore well enough to earn Percival's confidence.

After the withdrawal from Johore, the question arose of Percival's assuming complete control of Singapore Island. That he had no authority to do so, however, was clear. Thomas was the King's representative, responsible only to the Colonial Office, and the civil

government was still maintaining law and order without difficulty. Percival could have done nothing without London's approval and it is not clear that he would have been justified or wise in seeking it. General Bennett suggested that a Military Advisor to the Governor be appointed, to be 'the strong man behind the throne ... who would force the civil administration out of its peace-time groove'.[23] Percival — with perhaps more humour than he is generally given credit for — asked Bennett if he wanted the job. Bennett said he would rather be Military Governor, in fact if not in name, and there the matter rested. Someone else suggested that Percival should at least take over part of the civil government. Again, he saw little point in this, concluding that the resultant confusion would outweigh any possible gain. Even more important, however, was the fact that both he and his staff had their hands full directing military operations. Trying to run part of the civil government, or all of it as Military Governor, while also fighting a difficult battle would have been foolish and pointless — and at this stage of the campaign would not have helped matters.

The difficulty of trying to wear both a military and a civil hat was illustrated by problems encountered by Brigadier Simson, Percival's engineer officer, who also became Director-General of Civil Defence for Singapore at the end of December. Civil defence arrangements in Malaya at the outbreak of the war were still fairly rudimentary. The air raid, medical, and fire auxiliary organisations were barely established, there were dangerous gaps in the observer system, and shelters were scarce or non-existent. At Singapore itself, the confusion apparent at the time of the first air raid was symptomatic of these defects; the relative lack of air raid shelters was the most obvious. The surface of the island was barely above water, so that digging enough large shelters would have been impossible, Even trenches quickly filled with water, and were more suitable for breeding malarial mosquitoes than for protection; while the presence of Chinese graveyards on the few tiny hills inhibited excavation there. Nor was there much room for above-ground shelters in the congested city, especially in the crowded, highly-inflammable Chinese sections, and plans to build them elsewhere on the island were not carried out on a large scale, perhaps because it was clear that few people would be able to get to the shelters in time to do any good. A major shelter-construction programme, moreover, would have required heavy equipment and large amounts of cement, sand, hard timber, reinforcing steel, and skilled labour, all of which were in demand by the military authorities. Once hostilities began, the shortage of materials and labour became even more acute. Some shelters were erected, a few slit trenches were dug, and a good deal of work was done to sandbag and otherwise reinforce public and private buildings.

The absence of air raids after December 8th undoubtedly contributed to complacency. Ten days later Duff-Cooper wrote to Churchill that he was very concerned about the lack of urgency in civil defence preparations. At the end of the month, at the suggestion of Duff-Cooper, the War Council agreed that Brigadier Simson should take over from the civil authorities the complete control of civil defence at Singapore. Unhappily for Simson, his authority was vague, limited and somewhat diluted. He certainly did not enjoy the full powers that Duff-Cooper had envisaged when he made his recommendation, nor did he have sufficient authority to force government offices and civilian agencies to carry out his orders. Duff-Cooper's original idea had been a good one, but his choice of Simson was unwise. Percival's engineer officer had all he could do to carry out his military duties, and the civil defence job meant less time to prepare Singapore's military defences. Simson himself protested against the appointment, both on the foregoing grounds and because he felt that it was now too late to accomplish much in civil defence. He was overruled, however, and despite his fears he managed in the short time left to tighten up the system significantly and to expedite somewhat the building of air raid shelters.[24]

Simson's appointment came just as Japanese bombers were returning to Singapore..From New Year's Day onwards the island, and indeed the city itself, came under almost daily attack. Both the 3rd Air Group and the 22nd Air Flotilla were concentrating more and more on the helpless, exposed target. The planes usually came boldly by daylight, sometimes in small groups but usually in formations of twenty-seven, fifty-four, and even eighty-one aircraft. The bombers flew alone — winging high to escape the short-range anti-aircraft guns — or with fighter escorts. Often these fighters flew low to strafe airfields, gun positions, the harbour and dock areas, and other objectives. The weight of these attacks increased in the second half of the month. Two and sometimes three raids occurred daily: precise formations of twenty-seven and fifty-four bombers, escorted by aggressive fighters, flying in an almost leisurely way, it seemed, in relative safety four miles above the ground. They apparently tried to concentrate on military targets — but not always with success.[25]

Despite the good work of Brigadier Simson in organising and directing civil defence forces, the accuracy of Japanese bombing and the intensity of the attacks took an increasing toll of installations, buildings, and, of course, human lives. No one will ever know how many died in these raids, but throughout the city, and especially in the crowded Asiatic sections, casualties were heavy. Hundreds were probably killed each day, while the number of wounded, sick, and homeless rose steadily. In many residential areas the destruction of sewers and household sanitation systems, the cutting of the water supply, and the clogging of drains, introduced the danger of epidemic disease. The authorities offered free typhoid injections, but could do little or nothing about the foul stench that arose from the blocked or broken sewers. Even worse was the sight and smell of dead bodies, putrefying in the heat before they could be claimed and buried by relatives, or if no one came for them interred in mass graves.

Civil defence workers, especially Chinese volunteers, laboured frantically to clear the streets, maintain deliveries of food and milk, extinguish fires, remove inflammable or explosive stores from bombed areas, and shift tons of rubble to rescue trapped citizens or to uncover corpses. In some areas, they were able to maintain a semblance of normality. The streets in the business centre of Singapore retained their peacetime cleanliness, and many stores, banks, cinemas, and other concerns continued to open and close at their normal hours, offering goods and services calmly and efficiently. Elsewhere, grass was neatly cut, dances and parties took place, schools remained in session, children frolicked in their normal play areas, and everyone, indeed, seemed intent on carrying on as usual.

The shops appeared to have almost a holiday air. Great throngs of British and other European women, evacuated from their homes on the mainland, wandered up and down the streets, often with small children, window-shopping and discussing the purchases they were unable to make because they had brought so little money with them. Their husbands, and even some of the women, had gone to work driving trucks and ambulances, fighting fires, or helping the police. But the better shops still offered their enticing stocks of fancy clothes and other luxury items as if nothing had changed.

Still, there was no hiding the growing destruction. The docks were a shambles, large areas of the city were reduced to rubble or smouldering ashes, warehouses were empty shells, and little by little the essential services of Singapore were being damaged or crippled. As labour disappeared and it became more and more difficult to recruit work-gangs, repairs were slower or could not be made at all. More streets became blocked, and ambulances and other vehicles were forced to crawl slowly through them or make wide detours to avoid the blasted areas. At the overcrowded hospitals and first aid posts, doctors, nurses, and volunteers worked twelve-hour shifts to help the increasing number of wounded and sick. Even the trucks carrying bodies to the burial pits were often so heavily loaded that it was impossible to conceal their gruesome cargoes.

In spite of all this, civilian morale remained surprisingly high. This seems to have stemmed from an implicit faith in the British Empire and the strength of Singapore, an unwillingness to accept the obvious fact of defeat after defeat or the clear evidence of Japanese military strength, and the steady tenor of official statements which stated that Singapore would undoubtedly be held. These optimistic statements had a marked effect on morale. 'Perhaps the most extraordinary feature of the situation', comments one authoritative account, 'was the complete confidence of the European community in the Government announcements of the impregnability of the island'.[26]

There were many, of course, who refused to believe the official words. Newspaper correspondents, some with military experience and others equally alert, regarded the public announcements as fatuous if not evil attempts to mislead the people and deny them the facts they should have had. Many post-war accounts, especially by men who were there, are extremely outspoken on the subject. Yet an alternative course would not necessarily have improved matters. There was clearly undue secrecy about events well known to the Japanese; but a steady died of pessimistic announcements and coldly realistic assessments of the odds might well have depressed civil and military morale so quickly that Singapore would have fallen even more swiftly than it actually did. Indeed, it was to counter rumours that the Japanese could not be opposed much longer, or that Singapore would not be defended, that many over-hopeful if not clearly misleading statements were issued.

Many critics seem to feel that more honest official announcements would have spurred on both soldiers and civilians to greater efforts, helped to improve defences, and stiffened the chances of throwing back the Japanese. Perhaps so. But it is not clear that anyone would have done more had he been told that all his efforts were practically in vain. If life went on as usual in many quarters for longer than it should have done, there was at the same time no panic, no breakdown of law and order, no riots or looting, no wild rush to escape, and no interference with military efforts to defend the island — all of which might have taken place had civilian morale crumbled beneath the weight of impending defeat. Undoubtedly defeat would have come as less of a shock to those prepared for it; but there is no guarantee that preparing them would have delayed that defeat – or that it would not, in fact, have hastened it.

The optimistic official statements clearly had a bad effect in one important way. They persuaded many European women that there was no need to hurry their departure from Singapore or (in many instances) to leave it at all. Indeed, the entire official evacuation policy left much to be desired; from the beginning, it was disorganised and mishandled. The withdrawal of civilians southwards down the mainland before the Japanese advance was generally a local decision or a case of individual initiative, and refugees streamed toward Singapore with no central direction, co-ordination, or assistance. Once they reached the safety of the island, the men were all registered and put to work – many, of course, had already joined their volunteer units or civil defence organisations – but the women were left alone for the most part. Many women were short of money, had only the clothes on their back or a single suitcase, were caring for small children, and sometimes they even had difficulty finding a place to live in. They roamed the streets of Singapore, seeking friends, or their husbands, or simply something to do, and were generally at a loss. But since there was no official policy to evacuate these unfortunates, very few felt the necessity to leave.

In mid-December, London had instructed the Governor to evacuate as many *bouches inutiles* as he could from Singapore; but perhaps because of the shortage of shipping, or for other reasons not entirely clear, he apparently decided to leave evacuation on a strictly voluntary basis.[27] Even those who wished to leave were given little guidance. In the absence of any central clearing agency, they had to arrange for their own passage, were required to meet peacetime passport and visa requirements, and were usually unaware that if they had no money, which was often the case, the government would pay their passage.

The result of this combination of optimism and red tape was that at first few civilians were anxious to go. Others insisted on waiting for a passage direct to England, and passed up the opportunity to escape via India or Australia. During December and January several ships left with room for many more passengers. Not until the end of January did the civil authorities at Singapore do anything to co-ordinate and speed up the evacuation, although even then it remained a strictly voluntary matter. The last two days of the month saw the beginning of a major exodus which continued, on the few ships available, until the final surrender. Now almost everyone wanted to go; although some, engaged in important voluntary work, refused to leave their posts. These brave individuals, and those who still had faith in Singapore's impregnability, or who could find no passage on the crowded ships, remained behind to face an uncertain fate.

For the hundreds of thousands of Asian civilians, especially the Chinese and Malayans, there was little choice. Some Indian women left for India; but those whose homes were in Malaya had little desire to leave — and, indeed, nowhere to go.

The presence of almost a million civilians on Singapore Island — helpless, disorganised, unarmed, of all ages and conditions — presented General Percival with a major problem. His defence, perforce, was aimed as much at protecting these people as it was at securing more strictly military objectives. He could not expose Singapore's naked multitudes to the unchecked fury of Japanese forceful occupation, yet he could do little to shield them unless he held the island. Nor could he allow full knowledge of their plight to plunge Singapore's inhabitants into panic and disorder.

It was with this in mind that, at the beginning of February, Percival issued a public announcement designed to reassure and encourage the people of Singapore, while at the same time cautiously warning them of the trials ahead. The battle of Malaya, he said, was over, and the battle of Singapore had begun. The defenders had sought to gain time in order to allow the concentration of Allied forces in the Far East. Now, he continued, 'we stand beleaguered in our island fortress'. The task now was 'to hold this fortress until help can come — as assuredly it will come'. Everyone would have to do his part to destroy any enemy who tried to enter the fortress and to eliminate the enemy already 'within our gates'. There could be no more 'loose talk and rumour-mongering'. Everyone's duty was clear, and 'with firm resolve and fixed determination' the defenders would 'win through'.[28]

NOTES — Chapter 8

1. Percival, *Despatch*, p. 1308. General sources for this chapter are: *Ibid.*, pp. 1307-15; Percival, *The War in Malaya*, pp. 76-90, 183-85, 250-65; Maltby, *Report*, pp. 1376, 1379-82, 1388, 1405-06; Maxwell, *Civil Defence of Malaya*, pp. 29-33, 56-59, 73-81, 91-127; Kirby, *The Loss of Singapore*, pp. 160-62, 325-26, 259-69; Bennett, *Why Singapore Fell*, pp. 165-72, 221-22; Barber, *A Sinister Twilight*, pp. 55-162 *passim*. Much useful material on civilian life at Singapore also appears scattered throughout the following eye-witness accounts: Morrison, *Malayan Postscript*; Glover, *In 70 Days*; Attiwell, *Fortress*; Brown, *Suez to Singapore*; Giles Playfair, *Singapore Goes Off the Air* (New York: Books, Inc., 1943); George Weller, *Singapore Is Silent* (New York: Harcourt, Brace, 1943).

2. For Singapore's guns, see also Maurice-Jones, *History of Coast Artillery*, pp. 215-18, 264-71; U.S. Army Forces, Far East, Japanese Monograph Series: No. 68, Report on Installations and Captured Weapons, Java and Singapore, 1942, *passim.*

3. On this point, see also General Wavell to Prime Minister, January 16th, 1942; in Churchill, *The Hinge of Fate*, p. 48.

4. *Ibid.*, p. 51.

5. Headquarters, Malaya Command, Order No. 28, December 23rd, 1941, App. C to Percival, *Despatch.*

6. Percival, *The War in Malaya*, pp. 254-55.

7. Barber, *A Sinister Twilight*, pp. 65-67.

8. Wavell, *Despatch*, pp. 3-4.

9. Wavell to Prime Minister, January 16th, 1942, in Churchill, *The Hinge of Fate*, p. 48. Churchill did not see this until the 19th because he had been in Washington. For the Prime Minister's reactions, and additional messages from Wavell, see *ibid.*, pp. 47-57; Kirby, *The Loss of Singapore*, pp. 316-19.

10. Kennedy, *The Business of War*, p. 196.

11. Prime Minister to General Ismay, January 19th, 1942, and to Wavell, January 20th, 1942, in Churchill, *The Hinge of Fate*, pp. 51, 53.

12. Wavell to Percival, January 21st, 1942, in Kirby, *The Loss of Singapore*, p. 316; Wavell, *Despatch*, p. 10.

13. Percival, *The War in Malaya*, p. 260; Percival, *Despatch*, p. 1306; Kirby, *The Loss of Singapore*, p. 318.

14. Percival, *Despatch*, p. 1309.

15. Percival, *Despatch*, p. 1311; Percival, *The War in Malaya*, pp. 261-62; Kirby, *The Loss of Singapore*, p. 362.

16. Prime Minister to Wavell, February 10th, 1942, in Churchill, *The Hinge of Fate*, p. 100; Charles Eade (ed.), *Winston Churchill's Secret Session Speeches* (New York: Simon and Schuster, 1946), p. 63.

17. Malay Operations Record, p. 101; Tsuji, *Singapore*, p. 270; Hayashi, *Kogun: The Japanese Army in the Pacific War*, p. 36.

18. Arthur G. Donahue, *Last Flight from Singapore* (New York: Macmillan, 1943), pp. 20-41; a personal account by a Hurricane pilot.

19. Kirby, *The Loss of Singapore*, pp. 318-19, 404; Wavell, *Despatch*, p. 12.

20. Barber, *A Sinister Twilight*, pp. 132-33.

21. Percival, *Despatch*, p. 1312.

22. Percival, *The War in Malaya*, pp. 261-62.

23. Bennett, *Why Singapore Fell*, p. 168; Wigmore, *The Japanese Thrust*, p. 303; Percival, *The War in Malaya*, pp. 258-59.

24. Kirby, *The Loss of Singapore*, pp. 158-59, 233-35, 295; Percival, *The War in Malaya*, pp. 180-82; Barber, *A Sinister Twilight*; Duff Cooper, *Old Men Forget*, pp. 302-303; Wigmore, *The Japanese Thrust*, pp. 287-88.

25. See also Southwest Area Air Operations, pp. 73-93; Reasons for Failure of Japanese to Halt Reinforcement of Singapore by Sea, in Far East Command, Special Studies, II, Tab. 5.

26. Maxwell, *Civil Defence of Malaya*, p. 62.

27. Churchill, *The Hinge of Fate*, p. 53; Duff Cooper, *Old Men Forget*, pp. 303-304.

28. Percival, *Despatch*, App. H.

9

'All Ranks Have Done Their Best'

While the British were hastening their defensive preparations, General Yamashita was also making ready. Planning for the assault on Singapore had begun after the capture of Kuala Lumpur in mid-January under the direction of General Suzuki, the Twenty-fifth Army Chief-of-Staff. Yamashita issued outline instructions to his commanders on the morning of the 31st and detailed orders four days later. X-Day, as the Japanese called it, was originally set for February 7th, but to allow additional time for preparation Yamashita postponed the attack until the 8th.

The rapid British withdrawal down the Malay peninsula had persuaded some Twenty-fifth Army planners that Percival would either surrender Singapore quickly or try to evacuate as many of his troops as possible without attempting any all-out defence of the island. Others, however, believed that the British would fight stubbornly, perhaps to the last man. Suzuki himself held the latter view, although he felt that Percival would not expose Singapore's huge civilian population to the dangers of a last-ditch defence. In any event, his plans called for the entire strength of the Twenty-fifth Army to be thrown against Singapore in a massive effort to crush it as quickly as possible.

The Japanese estimated that Percival's forces had been reduced to about two divisions, with a total effective combat strength of some 30,000 men. They were aware that Singapore's permanent defences faced seawards, but also knew that some of the big guns could fire on Johore and that work had been done to strengthen the island's northern coastline. They realised, however, that the Johore Strait defences amounted to little more than ordinary field positions, and were only a thin shell, easily crushed with field artillery. They felt that the British would soon be forced back, to make a last stand in the general area of the Jurong line.[1]

Japanese pre-war planning had foreshadowed the seizing of

Singapore Island by means of an assault on the north-west coast. Not only was Johore Strait narrowest here, but the nearby mainland had roads fully capable of supporting the assembly of troops, supplies, and equipment. Through this area, also, flowed many rivers and streams that offered excellent concealment for the large force of landing craft that would undertake the operation. Suzuki's planners at first considered a simultaneous three-division attack along a broad front stretching from east of the naval base, all the way along Johore Strait, to the western side of the island. But intelligence reports of the strong defences in Percival's Northern Area (east of the causeway) and a more realistic appraisal of Japanese strength, quickly persuaded the Twenty-fifth Army staff to drop this idea and go back to the pre-war concept of a concentrated attack against the north-west coast.

The main assault would be launched with two divisions abreast on a narrow front of less than five miles at the north-west corner of the island. General Mutaguchi's 18th Division, on the right, would use two regiments and a battalion in the attack, with its remaining regiment (less a battalion) in reserve. To its left, General Matsui's stronger 5th Division would throw three regiments into the assault and hold its fourth in reserve. Matsui also commanded the 1st Tank Regiment for this operation. Attacking at night, the two divisions were expected to land without difficulty, seize Tengah airfield by morning, and then push rapidly toward Bukit Timah, the highest point on the island, north-west of Singapore city.

The Imperial Guards Division — two infantry regiments plus a newly-arrived battalion of its remaining regiment and the attached 14th Tank Regiment — had a task of a different nature. Nishimura's troops would pretend to mount an attack on the north-east coast. On the night before the main assault, they would land a small force on Ubin Island, in the eastern mouth of Johore Strait. The rest of the division would move west and, the night after the main attack, would cross Johore Strait west of the causeway. Then, with a regiment plus two battalions in the assault and a regiment (less a batalion) in reserve, the Guards Division would strike south-east through the high ground of Bukit Mandai and drive on to cut off the eastern third of the island and prevent a British withdrawal into that area. General Nishimura had contested the use of his division in a supporting role, arguing that his men had earned the honour of leading the main assault. As the weakest division in the Twenty-fifth Army, however, his had clearly been given the proper assignment.

Despite Nishimura's displeasure, the planned assault by the 5th and

18th divisions included ample strength to overwhelm British defences. The Japanese were concentrating sixteen infantry battalions, backed by five more in reserve, and about fifty light and medium tanks, against a narrow front held by a single Australian brigade of three under strength battalions.

The thinness of these defences was due in part to the relatively long coastline included in General Bennett's Western Area. In an apparent effort to strengthen the Northern Area by excluding a major danger zone from General Heath's responsibility, Percival's defence plan had placed the line between the two Areas just east of the causeway instead of on a more natural boundary, the Kranji River, little more than two miles to the west. Bennett s sector was thus divided – by the Kranji and, on the west coast, the Berih Rivers – into three unequal parts. The overall defence plan had also allocated frontages within Areas down to the brigade level. Difficulties of communication and control, and the importance of the causeway-Kranji River sector, had ruled out the idea of placing any of Bennett's three brigades astride a river, and had necessitated putting an entire brigade in this small zone. Thus, Maxwell's 27th Brigade held the narrow frontage from the causeway to the Kranji, Taylor's 22nd Brigade an eight-mile sector from the Kranji to the Berih, and Brigadier G.C. Ballentine's raw 44th Indian Brigade the ten miles of coast from the Berih to the Jurong; the largest area, but the one least likely to be attacked.

While it is clear that the causeway-Kranji front required strong defences, a better solution might have been to incorporate it in the Northern Area and assign a strong brigade to it. Putting it in the Western Area greatly increased Bennett's problems and meant that a single brigade had to defend the entire Kranji-Berih sector. The length of coastline thus assigned to the 22nd Brigade forced Brigadier Taylor to place all three of his battalions in the line, with no reserve except a company from each battalion held in the rear of its position. Also, the front was so long, that it could hardly be occupied continuously. There were broad gaps between company positions, protected only by covering fire and swamps. In these vulnerable dispositions, Taylor's right battalion would face the entire 5th Division assault, while the other two would share the attack of the 18th Division. Understandably, neither Percival nor Bennett felt easy about the situation. The latter confessed in his diary that he was beginning to worry about the extreme weakness of Taylor's zone.[2]

The Japanese, meanwhile, continued their preparations in great secrecy. To mount the assault, they assembled some 300 craft in the rivers and streams flowing into the north-west arm of Johore Strait. Two-thirds of these were collapsible motor-boats, capable of carrying a dozen fully equipped soldiers or a partially disassembled field artillery piece. There were also sixty motor-driven pontoons which could be used for bridging or as twenty-man landing craft. Seven heavy pontoons were available to transport trucks and tanks. And thirty small landing craft, or motorised barges, could each carry three dozen troops. Most of these craft had reached southern Malaya by truck. The motorised barges came by train and then by sea down the west coast. Near Johore Strait, the Japanese moved all craft by hand in order to conceal their preparations. Because of the short time available, and since most of the assault troops were trained and experienced in amphibious and river-crossing operations, only limited rehearsals took place. Engineers, however, worked with landing craft for three days on the Muar River to ensure their familiarity with the boats.[3]

No less important than the assembling of landing craft were the steps taken to make ready the Japanese artillery. Army and divisional artillery to be used in the attack, including some captured weapons, totalled 168 pieces of all sizes. For these General Suzuki insisted on stocking an unusually large amount of ammunition: 1,000 rounds per field artillery piece and 500 rounds for each of the heavy guns. Divisional artillery moved into commanding positions for direct support of the assault units, while Army artillery took up positions on top of the highest ground in southern Johore, a hilly area north-east of Johore Bahru, to fire on the Singapore airfields and on British artillery positions and lines of communication. Two days before the main attack, Army artillery units would begin to move west to add supporting fire to the 5th and 18th divisional artilleries. To prevent the British from draining oil from the big Singapore fuel tanks into Johore Strait and then setting it on fire, the Japanese artillery were to try to destroy the oil tanks well before the start of the assault. One additional task for the 18th Division artillery, on the right of the main assault force, was to defend against any British vessels attempting to enter the western mouth of Johore Strait to disrupt the Japanese crossing. An observation balloon and 3rd Air Group reconnaissance planes could be expected to handle artillery spotting without difficulty.

Air support for the Singapore operation was solely the responsibility of General Sugawara, since the efforts of naval aircraft were now concentrated on blocking the escape of British shipping from Singapore and on supporting the forthcoming invasion of Sumatra.[4] These last missions were also assigned, to a limited degree, to the 3rd Air Group, which was still responsible, for the defence of airfields and landing areas in Malaya and southern Thailand. Sugawara, nevertheless, was able to allot eighty heavy and light bombers, forty fighters, and fourteen reconnaissance planes to the Singapore attack – a force more than adequate for the task, in view of the almost complete lack of British air opposition.

All the while, the great job of mounting the attack continued. Japanese truck and railway units laboured feverishly to bring forward the large stocks of ammunition and fuel required for the battle, while the engineers continued their back-breaking task of repairing roads and bridges and keeping the supply lines open. Other engineers carefully reconnoitered Johore Strait, checking tides, currents, and depths. A small officer-patrol even slipped across to Singapore Island to look at beach defences and obstacles.

To ensure secrecy during these preparations, the Japanese cleared all inhabitants out of a twelve-mile strip along Johore Strait. The 5th and 18th Divisions assembled well back from the coast, hidden by thick jungle from any prying eyes on Singapore Island. Not until the night of February 6th would they move forward to their assault zones. Landing craft also remained concealed far upstream. The Guards division, meanwhile, made every effort to feign preparations for an attack on the north-east coast of Singapore. Nishimura's men built camps near the Johore shore across from the naval base, placed artillery fire on the north-east of Singapore Island, and each evening drove columns of empty trucks eastwards, their headlights shining, to simulate heavy troop movements in that direction. These efforts may perhaps have been the reason for Percival's continued preoccupation with his north-eastern defences.

Japanese artillery units opened fire on Singapore Island almost as soon as they reached southern Johore. For several days, however, this amounted to little more than a nuisance. The gunners registered their pieces, plotted British positions, and developed target range tables. On February 4th, they began shooting in earnest, delivering an increasing weight of fire on to the island in the days that followed. The primary bombardment fell on the three northern airfields, quickly forcing their evacuation, and on installations, oil tanks, road junctions, and artillery positions. One long-range gun even lobbed shells for more than a dozen miles, into the heart of Singapore city. Heavy air attacks continued, while reconnaissance flights swooped in boldly at a low level. Japanese bombers and strafing fighters pounded the airfields, dock areas, supply dumps, and residential sections of the city. They also attacked the

15-inch guns of Johore Battery, at the eastern tip of the island, but did
little damage.

Work parties attempting to prepare defences were under continuous
fire. It was 'very much a case of cat and mouse', wrote one artilleryman
about a typical attack:

> A shell whined; everyone ducked: crump, crump – 300 yards away;
> we picked up ourselves and our tools; the roar of 27 aircraft caused
> us to look up – they were coming our way; another dive for cover
> and then – boom, boom, boom, ba-boom! the ground shook: some
> poor devils half a mile away had got that; back they came wheeling
> around, as we gathered ourselves together again and a sudden burr!
> rat-tat-tat-tat, warned us to go to ground again, machine guns this
> time – and so it went on.[5]

The British responded feebly to this combined artillery and air
bombardment. To avoid giving away the location of fixed positions,
counter-battery fire was undertaken mainly by roving field artillery
sections. And because of the shortage of field artillery ammunition,
these sections were restricted to twenty rounds per gun each day, on
the assumption that Singapore might have to hold out for three
months. Other restrictions limited firing that might harm civilians or
impede the escape to Singapore of any men from the lost 22nd Indian
Brigade who managed to reach Johore Strait. The Australians were
particularly incensed at not being allowed to fire at the tower of the
Johore Bahru administration building, which the Japanese were using as
an observation post. They finally received permission on the 5th, and
badly damaged the building. But they were impotent to touch the
observation balloon that floated mockingly over the city, in clear view
of almost everyone on the beleaguered island. Nor could the defenders
do much to halt the continued Japanese air strikes. Anti-aircraft guns
were prime targets for these attacks, and their fire decreased each day.
The few remaining fighter planes also made valiant efforts, but they
could not stand up to the weight of General Sugawara's attacks.

Japanese artillery fire on the north-eastern sector of Singapore Island
increased noticeably after the 5th, but the nightly British patrols that
crossed Johore Strait east of the causeway could find no troop
concentrations in this area. Further west, meanwhile, Bennett's
Australians could hear the sound of chopping, hammering, and other
activities coming from the mainland. These signs, and other indications,
led Percival's intelligence staff to conclude on the 6th that Yamashita
was just about ready to attack the north-west corner of the island. That
night, two patrols from Taylor's brigade slipped across to Johore.
Returning on the night of the 7th, they reported seeing no landing

craft — they had actually not gone far enough upstream to discover the boats — but they described large troop concentrations and heavy vehicle movements. At about the same time, other Australian troops fired on and sank a boat carrying about thirty Japanese trying to cross Johore Strait west of the causeway. Clearly something was up, but no one knew exactly what.

Shortly after midnight of February 7th-8th, a 400-man detachment of the Guards Division landed unopposed on Ubin Island. British patrols and forward observers withdrew immediately and the Japanese proceeded to emplace light artillery on the island. In view of the lack of opposition, they wondered if their feint had failed in its purpose. In the morning, the entire Guards artillery force opened fire on the north-east coast of Singapore Island to maintain the appearance that an attack was pending. By now, however, British attention was focused further west. The seizure of Ubin Island denied the Singapore defenders an important observation post, but it did not achieve its primary objective of drawing British troops to the north-east. Actually, in view of Percival's dispositions, the Japanese ruse was hardly necessary.[6]

Early on February 8th, Sugawara's planes began bombing and strafing the north-west coastal area of Singapore. They went for 22nd Brigade defences, seeking to knock out guns and searchlights. A few hours later, Japanese artillery joined in, the bombardment becoming very heavy in the early afternoon and dropping a punishing fire on Australian forward defences, communications, and headquarters. Despite the intensity of the fire, neither General Bennett nor General Percival believed an immediate assault was in the offing. Both apparently interpreted the shelling as only the beginning of a softening-up bombardment that might last for several days. Percival issued no instructions to fire on the probable Japanese troop concentration areas. Nor did he feel it necessary to order the shelling of Japanese guns, since he had not intended his earlier restrictions on the artillery to affect counter-battery fire under these conditions. Bennett did order fire to be returned, and Western Area artillery gave a good account of itself. But it was pitifully weak when compared with the Japanese.[7]

By afternoon, large parts of Singapore Island were covered by a haze of black and grey smoke. The Japanese artillerymen, unable to observe targets or see the impact of the shells, were reduced to firing completely by previous registration and target plotting. Sunset brought a brief pause. Then the bombardment was resumed, even more heavily than before. The weight of explosives crashing down on the Australians was beyond the experience of any of the defenders. Officers who had served in World War I had never seen such sustained, concentrated shelling. Casualties, strangely enough, were not heavy, thanks to the shallow two-man slit trenches, (by now often half-filled with water) that most of the Australians had dug. But communications suffered heavily. Telephone wires were cut repeatedly and in many places, beyond the ability of linemen to repair. By late evening, Brigadier Taylor's battalions were completely out of touch with their forward companies.

At about 9.30 p.m., the first assault troops of the Japanese 5th and 18th Divisions boarded landing craft and began moving downstream toward Johore Strait. Japanese artillery fire increased, and soon mortars joined the covering bombardment. The roar of the guns and the explosion of bursting shells drowned the sound of the boat-engines as the landing craft began to cross the strait. On the opposite shore, although the intensity of the bombardment almost certainly indicated a coming assault, searchlights remained dark. To avoid their premature destruction, they would only be illuminated on specific instructions from unit commanders; and the destruction of telephone lines now prevented delivery of the necessary orders. By 10.30, the Australians could make out the approaching landing craft. They immediately opened fire with machine-guns and other infantry weapons and, despite the darkness, scored heavily. One boat caught fire, and then several others, the light of the flames illuminating a broad sector of the water. Calls for artillery fire, however, were frustrated by the severed telephone lines, and signal flares apparently could not be seen by the gunners. Instructions to the artillery therefore had to be relayed from batalion headquarters over the crippled communications net. Radio sets, which might have helped, had been called in for maintenance when the 22nd Brigade reached Singapore, and had been returned only on the morning of the 8th; they had not reached forward positions when the Japanese struck. Nevertheless, the Australian artillery did go into action, and artillery in the 44th Brigade area to the south, including the 6-inch pieces at Pasir Laba, also joined in.[8] But poor visibility and delayed communications gave the guns only a limited and entirely inadequate effect.

The first waves of Japanese suffered heavy casualties, but a few managed to get ashore. Subsequent waves were more successful, and troops landed in increasing numbers up and down the coast. Mortar and machine-gun fire from barges moored close inshore suppressed defensive fire, and Japanese infantrymen, many with compasses strapped to their wrists, pressed into and around the forward Australian positions. Hand-to-hand fighting took place in some areas. Elsewhere, as Australian troops exhausted their ammunition or fell back to escape being trapped, the Japanese swept forward freely. From his command post in the sultan's palace at Johore Bahru, General Yamashita could see the coloured signal-flares announcing the successful landing of both divisions.

By midnight, Japanese troops were ashore in force, infiltrating through the thin Australian defences, creating panic and chaos among the many raw replacements in the 22nd Brigade, and scattering even the more experienced troops, who were worn down by the incessant bombardment and the strain of uncertain and difficult night combat. The 18th Division attack, on the Japanese right, struck at the juncture of two Australian battalions, drove a wedge between them, and advanced rapidly. The heavier 5th Division assault, concentrated almost entirely against a single battalion, overwhelmed the defenders by sheer weight of numbers and fire-power. At about 1 a.m. on February 9th all three Australian battalions began to fall back, attempting frantically to organise defences further inland. In the darkness and confusion, many men and groups of men became separated from their units, missed assembly areas, and stumbled rearward far beyond designated battalion positions.

Some of the troops, panic-stricken, were almost running as they fled from the shock and terror of defeat. Most of them had dropped their packs and weapons and in many cases were wearing only shorts. One witness saw 'a file of men walking, staggering, dragging along . . . some were bootless, some shirtless, and a few had not even trousers. . . . They were covered with mud from head to foot, scratched and bleeding, exhausted, beaten'.[9]

By now, General Bennett had ordered the reserve unit of the 27th Brigade — the 29th Battalion, consisting largely of untrained recruits — to move to Tengah airfield, and had put them under Taylor's orders. A few hours later he also sent Taylor the so-called Special Reserve Battalion, a provisional unit organised earlier from service troops and a few infantry replacements. Percival, meanwhile, had alerted his command reserve, the 12th Brigade, but uncertain whether the Japanese assault was Yamashita's main attack or merely a diversionary blow he held back from committing his force.

Meanwhile, the Japanese continued to press ahead. By dawn of the 9th, both General Matsui and General Mutaguchi had all their infantry ashore. The aggressive Mutaguchi had been slightly wounded during the early part of the assault and the regiment on his left, the 114th

Infantry, had missed its way in the dark after landing and blundered into Matsui's area. But this had not affected the general advance. Just after daylight, 5th Division troops cut off, split up, and scattered Brigadier Taylor's right hand battalion as it attempted to pull further inland. The Australian centre battalion beat off a Japanese attack on the town of Ama Keng, only to be forced back finally by a strong enveloping movement. Taylor's left hand battalion, which included a large number of recruits, found itself encircled by 18th Division units. Only scattered elements were able to cut their way out. By about 10 a.m., the remnants of the 22nd Brigade, all semblance of combat organisation shattered, had managed to reach Tengah airfield.

At Tengah, the Australians joined the newly-arrived 29th and Special Reserve Battalions and a battalion of Indian airfield defence troops. By now, Percival had ordered the under strength 12th Brigade — a weak batalion of Hyderabads and the 2nd Argylls — to join Bennett, but it had not yet reached the forward area.[10] Bennett nevertheless ordered Taylor to counter-attack and re-establish a line on Ama Keng. As Taylor soon discovered, this was impossible against the overwhelming Japanese strength opposing him. Before he could organise and mount his attack, elements of the 5th Division began working round his flanks, and it was all he could do to hold his troops in place during the morning. Communication with Bennett was now impossible, so Taylor had no idea of the latter's plans or of the situation anywhere else. In view of the mounting pressure on his front and the necessity of preserving troops to defend the Jurong Line, he concluded that he would have to fall back from Tengah. He began withdrawing at about 1.30 p.m., hoping to establish a good defensive position on and in front of the Jurong Line. With the newly-arrived 12th Brigade, his own reinforced 22nd Brigade, and the 44th Indian Brigade — which he felt would have to be withdrawn from its position to the south — Taylor reasoned that a strong defence of the Jurong Line might now be possible.

Bennett, meanwhile, was getting only scattered information, and apparently had no idea whatsoever of the strength of the Japanese forces opposing him. He was still thinking in terms of attack, so was shocked to learn of Taylor's actions and was unwilling to sanction an early withdrawal to the Jurong Line of both the 22nd and 44th Brigades. Yet in view of what had already taken place there was little he could do about the Australian troops, who were clearly unable to attack westward again.

The Japanese had not followed up Taylor's retreat closely. Perhaps because of their heavy initial casualties, perhaps because they needed to reorganise and re-supply, they now hesitated. The pause in their attack provided the weary Australians with a welcome opportunity to consolidate their forces and lick their wounds.

During this lull, General Percival arrived at Bennett's headquarters to discuss the situation. The first matter to be settled was the disposition of the 44th Brigade, still holding its extended positions along the south-west coast. Brigadier Ballentine's men had not come under attack except from artillery and aircraft, and a few 18th Division troops who landed too far south. Early that morning, dive-bombers had knocked out the two 6-inch guns at Pasir Laba, but otherwise little damage had been sustained. On the other hand, the Japanese advance clearly threatened Ballentine's flank and his line of withdrawal. Percival and Bennett considered using the 44th to make an attack on the Japanese right flank. But the rawness of Ballentine's Punjabi troops and their scattered positions seemed to make this impracticable.

Percival therefore decided to withdraw the 44th Brigade to occupy the southern portion of the Jurong Line, with the 12th and 22nd Brigades being responsible for the remainder. Bennett's other brigade, the 27th, defending the Kranji-causeway sector, had not been attacked, so it would continue to hold in place. A few hours earlier, Percival had directed General Heath to alert the Northern Area reserve unit, the 6/15th Brigade. Now he placed the 6/15th under Bennett's command and ordered it to the Bukit Timah area, to guard the food, fuel, ammunition, and supply dumps east of the town against a possible Japanese breakthrough.

During the evening, the 44th Brigade withdrew to the Jurong Line with little enemy interference. Tengah airfield was firmly in Japanese hands. Its capture by the 5th Division came roughly eight hours later than Yamashita had planned, but Generals Matsui and Mutaguchi were now ready to resume their advance.

The Jurong position offered the opportunity to halt this drive. But Percival, understandably worried about a possible Japanese break-through, was preparing a plan for the final defence of south-central Singapore. Ruling out a withdrawal to the eastern end of the island, he decided that if necessary he would concentrate on holding a huge perimeter, with the city of Singapore as its hub. Within this area would be the main supply depôts and hospitals, two of the three reservoirs, Kallang airfield, and Bukit Timah and other high ground. Percival issued his plan an hour after midnight in the form of a 'Secret and Personal' instruction to his senior commanders and staff, to be used if and when necessary to fight 'the final battle for Singapore'.[11]

Percival had cause for concern. Air-Vice-Marshal Pulford's tiny group of Hurricanes, after a final bold effort to drive off Japanese bombers, were now forced to withdraw to Sumatra. Bomb-cratered Kallang airfield, with but a single landing strip in precarious operation, would henceforth be used only as a staging or emergency base. The almost completely unopposed Japanese air units could be expected to attack with even greater ferocity. And, as the loss of the Pasir Laba guns clearly showed, none of the Fixed Defence weapons could be expected to remain in action if Japanese dive bombers concentrated on them. Even more ominous, though the information was not yet available to Percival, was the fact that Yamashita now had the bulk of two divisions on the island and was sending over supplies, vehicles, and reinforcements as fast as boats could carry them. These reinforcements included at least one medium tank company of the 1st Tank Regiment with more to follow, to bolster the 5th Division's drive.

By now, too, an equally dangerous threat had developed to the north — although Percival was not yet aware of it. Having easily captured Ubin Island, General Nishimura's Imperial Guards Division moved west through Johore Bahru on the night of February 8th and prepared to board landing craft concealed upstream from Johore Strait. Beginning at daylight on the 9th, Japanese artillery and aircraft struck heavily at the area between the Kranji River and the causeway, held by Brigadier Maxwell's 27th Australian Brigade. This unit had been weakened by the loss of its reserve battalion to Taylor's brigade early that morning, by the need to guard its exposed left flank along the Kranji River against a possible attack by the Japanese 5th Division, and by the fact that Maxwell had just had to replace both remaining battalion commanders. The new commanders were faced with the conflicting tasks of holding their positions on the coast while also preparing to withdraw, if necessary, to tie in with the northern end of the Jurong Line. Also, the Japanese bombardment had severed most of the forward telephone wires and smashed important beach defences.

At about 8.30 in the evening, Japanese artillery fire ceased and boats carrying a battalion of the 4th Guards Regiment swung down into Johore Strait and began to move across towards their intended landing beaches just east of the mouth of the Kranji. Most of the Australian searchlights had apparently been knocked out, but a few flashed on, although communication difficulties, and other problems frustrated calls for artillery fire. Thus the Japanese had little initial opposition, although in the darkness, and with an incoming tide, many of the boats drifted off course and ended up in swamps or moved inland along two large coastal streams.

Shortly after 9 p.m., when only a part of the Guards battalion had landed, Australian machine-guns and mortars, with some field artillery, opened up on the attackers. The heavy defensive fire proved very effective. Mortars sank a number of landing craft, while many Japanese troops, stranded in the swamps by the rising tide, were caught in a deadly crossfire. But more and more Japanese were coming ashore. Fighting was at close quarters and often hand-to-hand, with many casualties on both sides. By midnight, the Guards troops had forced Maxwell's left hand battalion well back from the coast. The right hand battalion, its flank now threatened, received permission from Maxwell to withdraw as well since there was no reserve available to redress the balance.

The withdrawal was to be delayed long enough to cover the destruction of a number of large oil tanks in the battalion area. This took more time than expected, for a shell destroyed the demolitions truck and the officer responsible had no recourse other than to open the valves and let the oil run out into Johore Strait. He then went back for more explosives, returned, and set them off. The flowing oil immediately became a sea of flame. It streamed into Johore Strait and, caught by the incoming tide, floated back into the swamps and streams, catching Japanese landing craft and troops in its blazing fury. When word of this reached General Nishimura, he immediately assumed that the flaming oil was part of a large-scale British effort to cover all of Johore Strait with fire. He rushed to Yamashita's headquarters and asked permission to call off his attack and land the remainder of the Guards Division on the 5th Division beachhead the next morning.

Yamashita was disturbed but unruffled. He sent three staff officers across to Singapore Island to find out exactly what had occurred. By the time they reached the front, most of the flames had died down and the Australian battalion that had remained to cover the demolitions had been withdrawn. There was no longer any reason to hold back, and at about 4.30 a.m. on the 10th Nishimura was able to resume the landing of his division.[12] The 27th Brigade was now nearly two miles back from the coast, on the top and on the western slopes of the Bukit Mandai hill mass. The Singapore side of the causeway was in Japanese hands and the western flank of Heath's Northern Area open to attack by the Imperial Guards.

With the Twenty-fifth Army well established on Singapore Island, Yamashita's next objective was the high ground from Bukit Mandai south to Bukit Timah. The key was the village of Bukit Timah and the 581-foot hill that towered over it, commanding the north-west approaches to the city of Singapore. The village was an important road junction, linking the north and west shores with the city. From the causeway, the Woodlands Road ran south through Mandai Village (west of Bukit Mandai) and Bukit Panjang Village to Bukit Timah, and thence, as Reformatory Road, south to the sea at Pasir Panjang. From the west, the Choa Chu Kang Road connected Tengah airfield with Bukit Panjang Village. South of this road, the Jurong Road ran from Pasir Laba to Bukit Timah. And from Bukit Timah itself the Bukit Timah Road led straight to Singapore.

Once the Bukit Panjang-Bukit Timah area was in his hands, Yamashita believed, the British would have to surrender. From his newly-established command post at Tengah, then, on the morning of the 10th, he ordered the 5th and 18th Divisions to attack eastwards along the Choa Chu Kang and Jurong Roads. Since little if any of the Japanese artillery had yet crossed Johore Strait, the assault would be made at night, relying on surprise to make up for the lack of artillery support. 'The forces', read the order, 'will attempt a night attack with bayonets on the 10th to secure Bukit Timah heights by dawn of the 11th, *Kigensetsu*'.[13] (*Kigensetsu* was traditionally the anniversary of the coronation of the legendary Emperor Jimmu, the first to ascend the Japanese throne, and a great holiday in Japan. Victory on the 11th would thus be doubly welcome.) To further ensure success, the Imperial Guards Division would continue with its original mission of seizing Bukit Mandai and pressing on to the south-east. But long before the evening of the 10th brought the beginning of Yamashita's attack, British confusion, inexperience, and — undoubtedly — fatigue would open the way for the Japanese advance.

In the pre-dawn hours of February 10th, the forces holding the Jurong Line were, from north to south: the 12th Brigade, the Special Reserve Battalion, the 6/15th Brigade, and — below the Jurong Road and extended down the east bank of the Jurong River — the 44th Brigade. The 6/15th, General Bennett's only reserve, should not have been there, but Bennett had committed it on the basis of erroneous reports that the 44th Brigade had been cut off. Taylor's 22nd Brigade, holding a covering position astride the Choa Chu Kang Road a mile west of the 12th Brigade, began withdrawing according to schedule at daybreak. In the process, the Australian rear guard caught a large group of Japanese 5th Division troops in an ambush, machine-gunned them thoroughly, and thus discouraged further pursuit. Taylor put most of his tired and battered force in reserve several hundred yards behind the Jurong Line, but placed the 29th Battalion in an unoccupied part of the line between the Special Reserve Battalion and the 12th Brigade. One company of the 29th became separated from the rest of the battalion and wound up on the left instead of the right of the Special Reserve Battalion.

At about 9 a.m. Taylor received a Western Area order based on Percival's secret preparatory instructions for a final perimeter. Although the Western Area order clearly indicated the tentative nature of the withdrawal directive and stated that only reconnaissance of the perimeter position was to be undertaken at this time, the nearly-exhausted Taylor misunderstood it to call for immediate occupation of the perimeter. He therefore told all his units, except the 29th and Special Reserve Battalions, to withdraw to the allotted 22nd Brigade sector of the perimeter, on Reformatory Road about a mile south of Bukit Timah. Taylor himself stopped off at Bennett's headquarters at Bukit Timah to report. Bennett was angered by Taylor's action, but did not countermand the brigadier's orders. The Jurong Line was thus without a reserve.

The position had already been weakened when Brigadier Paris, the 12th Brigade commander, shifted his largely-untrained Hyderabad battalion from its original place on the left of the Argyll battalion to a position in depth behind the Highlanders. The 12th Brigade front was thus narrower than planned, and when the 29th Battalion, itself missing a company, moved in on the left of the Argylls there remained a half-mile gap between the 29th and the Special Reserve Battalion to the south. Shortly thereafter, a few Japanese 5th Division troops began probing the left flank of the 29th and, at about 8 a.m. on the 10th, with mortar, machine-gun, and air cover, a stronger force started to move round the Highlanders' right flank. 'It was almost impossible', recalled one Argyll officer, 'to recognize a target on account of a ground haze which . . . made lines and shapes indistinguishable. Occasionally one got a glimpse of movement between the trees, but nothing one could guarantee to hit'.[14] Without artillery support, and in danger of encirclement, Paris withdrew his brigade, including the 29th Battalion, to a position on higher ground less than a mile to the rear. The right flank of the Special Reserve Battalion was now open, and the gap between it and the 12th Brigade had grown to about a mile.

By this time, Brigadier Paris was worried about another gap. His patrols had been unable to find Maxwell's 27th Brigade in the Mandai hill area to the north-east, but they had spotted some of General

Nishimura's Guards on the northern portion of the Woodlands Road. Paris was out of touch with Bennett's headquarters, and he feared an enemy advance down the open Woodlands Road behind him all the way to Bukit Timah. He therefore ordered a further withdrawal to covering positions around Bukit Panjang Village, at the junction of the Choa Chu Kang Road and Woodlands Road. The move, completed by early afternoon, protected the northern approach to Bukit Timah, but it completely uncovered the right flank and rear of those forces still holding the southern half of the Jurong Line.

These units were extremely tired from their retreat during the past day, and this may account in part for what followed. During the morning of the 10th, 3rd Air Group planes bombed and machine-gunned the entire Jurong position. At about 1 o'clock in the afternoon, Mutaguchi's 18th Division began heavy small-arms fire against the right hand battalion of the 44th Brigade, on the Jurong Road and immediately south of it. Some of the raw Punjabi troops broke and began moving back. This caused confusion in the other battalions and, before anything could be done, the retreat got out of control. Most of the brigade streamed south, cross-country toward Pasir Panjang, many units believing they had been ordered back to Percival's perimeter.[15] At about 5 p.m., Brigadier Ballentine managed to halt and re-form his troops on the beach at Pasir Penjang. He was now well within the Southern Area. General Keith Simmons, also perhaps misinterpreting Percival's preparatory instructions, ordered Ballentine to move up Reformatory Road toward the position occupied earlier by Taylor's 22nd Brigade.

The withdrawal of the 44th Brigade exposed the left flank of the 6/15th Brigade, immediately north of the Jurong Road. To avoid being cut off, and possibly influenced by the Western Area order about the final perimeter, the 6/15th retired along the road during the afternoon to a point more than half way to Bukit Timah. The next unit up, the company of the 29th Battalion, was now dangerously exposed. Out of touch with headquarters, it too withdrew all the way back to the 22nd Brigade area.

The Special Reserve Battalion was now the only unit left on the Jurong Line. With both flanks open and ample evidence of strong Japanese units to its north and south, the battalion fell back across country and joined the 6/15th Brigade on the Jurong Road west of Bukit Timah. All these withdrawals had bared the right flank of the 1st Malaya Brigade, on the coast at the western end of the Southern Area, and it, in turn, pulled back to Pasir Panjang.

By the evening of February 10th, without really having made any effort, General Yamashita was in full possession of the Jurong Line. The British evacuation of this line, the best defensive position west of Singapore city, had been the result of misunderstanding, weariness, and the lack of any attempt by Bennett to control or co-ordinate the operation. Bennett's failure can probably be blamed in large measure on inadequacies and breakdowns in communications. But it is not clear that he did anything to try to remedy this deficiency; as a result, both he and General Percival, who depended on Bennett for information of developments in Western Area, were forced to operate in the dark.

Percival himself had contributed to the confusion by issuing his preparatory instructions for the final perimeter when he did. While it was necessary to inform his major subordinate commanders of his plans so that they would know in which direction to withdraw if they had to, Percival might have done better to forbid revealing his order to lower echelons. The 'Secret and Personal' classification on the order was apparently outweighed by its contents, which implied at least some dissemination of the information it contained to units in the field.

Perhaps even more critical was Percival's overestimation of the forces available to General Yamashita. This, combined with his preoccupation with defending the north-east coast, led him to spread his troops too thinly and to locate and continue to maintain his strongest concentration in the wrong part of the island. These errors apparently prevented him from reacting as fast and as strongly to the Japanese landings as he might have. Had Percival committed his reserve to the support of the weak 22nd Brigade as soon as the Japanese landed, he might have stopped or at least slowed the initial enemy advance. Failing this, once the Japanese had made their second major landing, he might well have pulled large forces out of the Northern Area and used them to form a strong mobile reserve. This reserve, in turn, could have reinforced the Jurong Line and/or counter-attacked to recapture the Kranji-causeway sector, retention of which was necessary to support the flank of the Jurong Line. That none of this took place cannot be blamed entirely on faulty intelligence appreciation or the poor state of communications. The situation clearly called for calculated risks. But by now Percival, worn down by over two months of continuous pressure and successive defeats, may no longer have been capable of making the bold decisions necessary to prolong the fight.

The C-in-C Malaya was not a forceful man. Although his earlier combat record was excellent, he rarely gave the impression of vigour or aggressiveness. He seemed to lack conviction, and when he did show firmness it appeared to others that he was simply being negative or stubborn. Perhaps in the final weeks the strain and worry of defeat had somehow magnified these traits, deadening his capacity for sudden change or major decision. As early as the end of January, some of those around him had detected what they took to be indecisiveness. On Singapore Island, this seemed to grow worse. One staff officer noted later that during the last week of battle he had become used 'to seeing Gen. Percival's painful inability to give a decision, and on three occasions to make any reply whatever, when points of operational importance were referred to him. . . .'[16] If these assessments were correct, they may in part explain Percival's sad inability to grasp the requirements of a rapidly changing situation.

General Wavell, meanwhile, was once again on Singapore Island, having flown in early on the morning of the 10th. He and Percival immediately went to Bennett's headquarters, where they found the Australian commander somewhat in the dark about the tactical situation and 'not quite as confident as he had been' about his ability to halt the Japanese.[17] After a bomb nearly fell on all three generals, Wavell and Percival drove to the Northern Area to find out for themselves what had happened in the causeway area. They discovered that the withdrawal of Maxwell's 27th Brigade had exposed the III Corps western flank and that Key's 11th Division, holding that flank, had been unable to re-occupy more than a small portion of the lost ground. In addition, the counter-attacking Indian troops had suffered heavy casualties for General Nishimura had by now been able to ferry most of his Guards over to Singapore Island. British artillery fire had so far prevented Japanese engineers from repairing the causeway, but the causeway itself provided defilade against fire from the east, and Nishimura's men came over easily in their boats.

To strengthen the III Corps flank, Percival put the 27th Brigade under Key's command. He told Maxwell to reoccupy Mandai Village (a move that Key had also been urging on the brigadier) in order to block the Woodlands Road approach to Bukit Timah. And finally, to provide additional protection for Bukit Timah, Percival ordered General Heath to send a three-battalion force toward it, as a new Western Area reserve under Bennett's command. Percival might better have committed most of the British 18th Division to this mission, but he was still concerned about defending the north-eastern shore against the additional divisions he thought Yamashita had in reserve. Heath, in turn, had little choice. Unable to shift an entire brigade from its coastal position without great

The causeway bridge across the Johore Strait linking Singapore island
(*in the background*) with the mainland

One of the many rubber plantations razed to the ground by the British
forces before they retreated to Singapore

Bren-gun carriers in a Malayan jungle swamp: an indication of the conditions under which the campaign was fought

Dramatic pictures of Singapore's waterfront in flames

difficulty, he drew a battalion apiece from two of the British brigades, added the division reconnaissance battalion and other elements, and organised them as Tomforce, under Lieutenant-Colonel L.C. Thomas.

Back at Bennett's headquarters, in the early afternoon, Wavell and Percival were able to get a somewhat clearer picture of events further west. Wavell immediately ordered Percival to 'counter-attack with all troops possible'[18] to recapture the Jurong Line. Percival told Bennett to launch the counter blow, but did nothing to increase the units available, beyond the earlier assignment of Tomforce.

Wavell left Singapore at about midnight, 'without much confidence in any prolonged resistance'.[19] He had just received a dramatic message from the Prime Minister. Bristling with Churchillian eloquence, it urged a fight 'to the bitter end at all costs'. There could be 'no thought of saving the troops or sparing the population'. All commanders and senior officers were expected to 'die with their troops'. The honour of the British Empire and the army was at stake.[20] In the circumstances, Wavell had no choice but to order Percival to fight to the end with no thought of surrender, an order that Percival dutifully passed on to the forces on Singapore Island. More realistically perhaps, Wavell ordered the last British airmen, with whatever aircraft they could still fly, to withdraw to the Netherlands Indies. Percival, having learned that the Japanese had captured the Kranji ammunition magazine practically intact, with large stocks that had been put aside for the final defence of the island, ordered the reserve fuel depot east of Bukit Timah to be set on fire lest it, too, fall to the enemy. Flames and smoke covered the area for two or three days, further accentuating the grim state of the weary, battered, and disorganised defenders.

While Bennett was organising his counter-attack, efforts to regain Mandai Village came to naught. Poor communications, delayed orders, confusion about commands, and the impact of the premature release of Percival's perimeter plan, all combined to frustrate efforts in the causeway area. At nightfall on the 10th, despite some further gains by the 11th Division, General Nishimura's beachhead was practically intact and Mandai Village remained in Japanese hands. Nishimura had done little in the way of attempting to advance, however, to the intense annoyance of Yamashita and his staff.

All attention now was focused further south, for the news of the planned counter-attack had somehow spread. 'A big drive was being organised', one Gurkha unit of the 11th Division noted jubilantly in its War Diary, 'to drive all the enemy back into the sea'.[21] Bennett's plan, based perforce on incomplete and inaccurate information, called for a three-stage assault beginning late on the 10th to re-occupy the Jurong Line by 6 p.m. on the 11th. The assault, to be made by the 12th, 6/15th, and 22nd Brigades – now reduced to less than 4,000 men all told – with limited artillery support and inadequate communications, was a difficult undertaking. Fresh troops in greater numbers might have increased the chance of success, especially in view of the absence of Japanese artillery. But the forces available to Bennett, as Taylor pointed out in a vain protest, were clearly insufficient. By now, six Japanese infantry regiments – probably totalling at least 15,000 men – had reached the area of the Jurong Line. Most of the 1st Tank Regiment had joined the 5th Division on the Choa Chu Kang Road. And Yamashita's *Kigensetsu* attack was about to begin.

The Japanese struck first. Just after dusk, advance elements of the 5th Division attacked the 12th Brigade at Bukit Panjang Village. They smashed and scattered the Hyderabad battalion in front of the village, and were then halted by the 29th Battalion in Bukit Panjang itself. But the Australians lacked anti-tank guns – Brigadier Paris had not deployed them here, in the belief that the Japanese could not yet have landed tanks – so when a column of medium tanks joined the attack there was no stopping this Japanese armour. Most of the tanks broke through and headed south on the Woodlands Road. Increasing infantry pressure forced the 29th Battalion into the hills to the east. The Australians later moved south and were reunited with their missing company south-east of Bukit Timah.

Now only the Argyll battalion and some Royal Marines from *Prince of Wales* and *Repulse* remained, a small force pitifully inadequate to stand up to the powerful enemy. Hastily improvised roadblocks of vehicles and antitank mines just south of Bukit Panjang Village provided only a moment's delay. The Japanese force, including practically the entire 1st Tank Regiment, smashed through the blocks, destroyed a single bold armoured car that sought to challenge it, and by around 11 p.m. was pushing south toward Bukit Timah. Colonel Stewart's battalion and 12th Brigade headquarters had no choice but to move east to higher ground. But 5th Division infantrymen struck them again, forcing a further retirement south of the Bukit Timah Road.

Meanwhile, around midnight, the Japanese tank/infantry force reached the road junction at Bukit Timah. Here it halted, presumably because it had reached its objective. Had it driven ahead, it might have pentrated all the way to downtown Singapore, for there was nothing in front of it but a single road block below Bukit Timah, put up when Paris sent back a warning of the enemy break-through. The block was covered by anti-tank guns and artillery, but unprotected by infantry, and an immediate, co-ordinated Japanese attack could probably have overrun it in the darkness. It was 2.30 a.m. on the 11th before Bennett learned of the break-through at Bukit Panjang Village. He ordered Tomforce to send a battalion forward. But the presence of Japanese troops and tanks in Bukit Timah ruled out any immediate advance to Bukit Panjang, and the Tomforce battalion took positions in support of the roadblock below Bukit Timah.

General Matsui's capture of Bukit Timah cut off those Western Area units on the Jurong Road that were preparing to carry out Bennett's counter-attack. Unaware of the threat to their rear, these units were moving to their jumping-off points when, at about 3 a.m. on the 11th, Mutaguchi's 18th Division struck east along the Jurong Road. The Japanese push overwhelmed part of the 22nd Brigade and, although it was halted by the 6/15th Brigade and the Special Reserve Battalion, forced cancellation of the projected counter-attack. Mutaguchi renewed the assault at 7.30 a.m. His troops, recalled one Australian, 'pushed up to our line firing around and dodging behind trees, crawling along drains and using every fold in the ground. Many had cut a bush and used this to push in front of themselves as they crawled forward, while others smeared mud and clay over their faces and clothing'.[22] This attack was also stopped, after bloody hand-to-hand fighting, permitting the defenders to disengage. Since withdrawal down the Jurong Road was now clearly impossible, they fell back across country towards Reformatory Road.

The area between Jurong Road and Reformatory Road was now a hunting-ground for strong 5th Division patrols, sweeping south and south-west from Bukit Timah. The Japanese shot up Australian forces attempting to hold the area, as well as the columns of exhausted troops retreating before General Mutaguchi's attack. Matsui's men also came close enough to the Buona Vista 15-inch battery to force its crews to destroy the big guns lest they fall to the enemy. In the confused fighting, the Japanese inflicted heavy casualties and scattered the shaken defenders even further. By the early afternoon of the 11th, the survivors had reached the 22nd Brigade positions at Reformatory Road, while the Japanese in turn had fallen back to consolidate. Meanwhile, an attempt by Tomforce to re-take Bukit Timah late in the morning had failed in the face of determined opposition by both Japanese divisions, supported by dive-bombers, heavy mortar fire, and artillery, which was at last beginning to reach the battle area.

The capture of Bukit Timah and the sight of 'the Rising Sun

fluttering above the summit'[23] now led General Yamashita to call on Percival to surrender. In anticipation of this moment, Lieutenant-Colonel Ichiji Sugita, Yamashita's intelligence officer, who spoke English, had drafted an elaborate message. Early on the morning of the 11th, a single Japanese reconnaissance plane flew low over the city of Singapore and dropped twenty-nine copies, in English and Japanese, addressed to 'the High Command of the British Army, Singapore'.[24] Each copy was rolled in a wooden tube eighteen inches long, with red and white marking streamers. In polite and considerate tones, the message complimented the British forces for their brave and gallant stand, but pointed out the hopelessness of their position and the great and growing danger to the civilians in the beleagered city. It urged Percival to capitulate or face an all-out Japanese drive into Singapore. Percival, under orders to fight to the end and in any case with no means of replying, ignored Yamashita's message.

He had, moreover, other things to do. General Matsui's troops on the high ground south-east of Bukit Panjang Village were practically unopposed if they chose to drive toward Singapore through the west side of the reservoir area. Percival quickly formed a provisional infantry unit of replacement troops and positioned it just west of MacRitchie Reservoir. He moved a Southern Area battalion at Changi, the 2nd Gordons, westwards to come under Bennett's command. And he made General Heath responsible for most of the newly-threatened area. Heath in turn directed General Beckwith-Smith to form another composite brigade-sized unit to operate directly under III Corps control. This unit, called Massy Force after its commander, Brigadier T.H. Massy-Beresford, began moving toward MacRitchie Reservoir.

The wisdom of these steps, however limited they may now appear, was quickly demonstrated by events further north, where command and control arrangements were still in a state of confusion. Brigadier Maxwell had received an order — from whom is still not clear — removing his 27th Brigade from 11th Division control, and directing it to recapture Bukit Panjang Village, presumably in support of the Tomforce effort that morning to regain Bukit Timah. Inadequate communications, plus aggressive action by the Imperial Guards Division, delayed, distracted, and confounded Maxwell's undertaking. As a result, instead of attacking Bukit Panjang Village the brigade became split and retired to the south-east. One battalion ended up well below the Bukit Timah Road, the other north of Pierce Reservoir. Most of the Bukit Mandai hill area was now in General Nishimura's hands, and the western flank of III Corps was even more vulnerable than before.

To avoid envelopment from the west, General Heath ordered the 11th Division to swing back from the coast and block any advance by the Imperial Guards along the north side of the reservoir area. This meant abandoning the naval base, and final demolitions took place during the afternoon. By 6 p.m. on the 11th, Key's division held a line facing west, running from the coast just east of the naval base down along Thomson Road to Pierce Reservoir. What was left of the 18th Division, which had lost most of its infantry to Tomforce and Massy Force, still remained on the coast.

Further south, meanwhile, the various units covering the north-west approaches to Singapore city had attempted no further offensive action in the face of the obviously strong Japanese force before them. Field artillery fired constantly and effectively, while the infantry reorganised and formed a long curving line. Tomforce was withdrawn from Bennett's command and absorbed by Massy Force. By evening, the combined forces occupied the area from MacRitchie Reservoir to the Bukit Timah Road. Immediately south of the road were the Gordons and on their left a reorganized and strengthened 22nd Brigade. On the left of the Australians, along the west side of Reformatory Road, was the 44th Brigade and extending the line to the coast at Pasir Panjang was the 1st Malaya Brigade, somewhat reinforced. It was 'a line of gaps', as one officer put it, 'gaps between [and] within formations of dispersed and in many cases isolated detachments in an area ill-suited to a defensive battle'.[25]

The Japanese brought very little pressure to bear on this line as they waited for artillery and much-needed supplies to catch up with their forward elements. The 5th Division concentrated its 21st Brigade in Bukit Timah, while its 9th Brigade occupied the hill area to the north-east. The 18th Division also had troops in Bukit Timah. Then in mid-afternoon General Mataguchi launched an attack against the 22nd Brigade to the south. Closely supported by low-flying aircraft, elements of the 56th and 114th Infantry Regiments tried in vain to crack the Australian position, only to be driven back with sharp losses.

There was no other Japanese ground action, but much of General Sugawara's air effort was directed at the big Singapore Fixed Defence guns, whose fire was proving troublesome. The 15-inch guns of Johore Battery and the 9.2-inch guns on Blakang Mati had been shelling Tengah airfield and Johore Bharu and, since its capture, Bukit Timah. Lacking observation, they were of course, firing blindly; and with only armour-piercing rounds for the 15-inch guns, and very few high explosive shells for the others, it was not clear to the gunners whether they were doing any damage at all. Nevertheless, and despite the necessity of frequently taking cover themselves in their slit trenches, they did manage to keep Japanese heads down. Yamashita's operations officer, Colonel Tsuji, was forced to dive into a ditch beside the Choa Chu Kang Road when the heavy projectiles began falling east of Tengah. The shells, he reported, 'tore holes in the ground fifteen or sixteen metres in diameter and four or five metres deep'. Their blast 'shocked our eardrums' and 'jarred our spines'.[26]

But by now the British situation was quite critical. Percival's earlier reluctance to denude his north-eastern defences had prevented him from launching a major counter-offensive. Now he could only hope to concentrate on defence. Yet the loss of the food, fuel, and supply dumps at Bukit Timah meant that he had only about a two-week food supply left and that he was dangerously low on fuel. And his weakening grasp on the reservoir area raised grave questions about Singapore's water-supply.

The situation grew worse on the 12th. Just after dawn, Imperial Guards forces began infiltrating the 11th Division in the Nee Soon area north of Pierce Reservoir. A Punjabi battalion, consisting of raw replacements for the most part, started to crumble; General Key counter-attacked with a reserve Gurkha battalion. Further south, Japanese tanks attacked down Bukit Timah Road against the left wing of Massy Force. They were stopped by anti-tank guns after a short penetration, but at about 9 a.m. General Matsui tried again with almost three whole infantry regiments. Kawamura's 9th Infantry Brigade (less a battalion) made the main effort, on the division's left, striking across the hills toward MacRitchie Reservoir. By noon, despite many casualties, the Japanese began to make way. Massy-Beresford ordered a withdrawal to the line of Adam and Farrer Roads, which meet on Bukit Timah Road nearly three miles south-east of Bukit Timah. Japanese planes bombed and strafed the retiring Massy Force* almost continuously, but the British troops, covered by fire from field artillery and the 15-inch Johore guns, made it successfully back to their new line by late afternoon.[27]

General Percival, meanwhile, had come forward during the morning to view the situation for himself. He soon concluded that General Matsui was in an excellent position to break through on the Bukit Timah Road and drive all the way into Singapore. Percival then visited

---

* Massy Force included the Indian light tanks that had arrived on January 29th, but it is not clear how or if they participated in the action.

Heath, and the two agreed that with the city so vulnerable there was no point in maintaining forces in the northern and eastern part of the island. Clearly, the time had come to fall back into the Singapore perimeter — although the speed of the Japanese advance had already reduced the size of the area that it was practicable to try to hold. Percival therefore ordered a perimeter to be established that night. Starting from just east of Kallang airfield, it would run inland to include the Woodleigh water pumping station, thence west to MacRitchie Reservoir and along its south shore to Adam Road, down Adam and Farrer Roads, and so on to the coast immediately west of Buona Vista village.

In accordance with Percival's instructions, Heath began pulling back the 11th Division and what was left of the 18th at noon on February 12th. A few hours later, the 4th Guards Regiment, together with the light tanks of the 14th Tank Regiment, attacked toward the Nee Soon road junction. Indian troops, supported by anti-tank guns and artillery, threw the assault back, and the withdrawal then continued. General Simmons' units at the eastern end of the island also pulled back that evening, destroying the Fixed Defence batteries of the Changi Fire Command as they withdrew. General Bennett's troops had considerably more trouble, as the 56th and 114th Infantry Regiments of Mutaguchi's division, now with artillery as well as air support, continued to attack the 22nd Brigade. Fighting was heavy and at close quarters, the Australians continuing to demonstrate their proficiency with the bayonet while the Gordons valiantly guarded the flank of the position. But the pressure was too great and Bennett's forces had no choice but to fall back on the perimeter line that evening. The 44th Brigade on the left conformed. The 1st Malaya Brigade, holding the coast, did likewise, but maintained positions as far forward as Pasir Panjang.

By now, Singapore resembled something out of Dante's *Inferno*. Parts of the city were burning fiercely, the flames leaping skyward unchecked in the absence of adequate water-pressure to fight them. Great dark clouds of smoke covered the sky, and from them the ever-present Japanese planes, completely unopposed, darted low to dive-bomb and machine-gun, spreading destruction at will. The streets were blocked by craters, fallen telegraph poles, wrecked and burning vehicles, and by long lines of slowly-moving military convoys. They were littered with rubbish and unburied bodies, and covered with great tangled piles of electric cables and telegraph and telephone lines. Demolitions under way in factories and other installations added to the flames, noise, and smoke.

Few civilians ventured into this nightmare except to jam the docks and the shoreline, seeking some last means of transport away from the doomed city. But many soldiers wandered through the streets, stragglers and deserters, armed and in greater numbers than the military police could handle, looking for loot or a means of escape. Some forced their way aboard ships leaving for the Netherlands Indies while others stole small boats to strike out on their own. Most of these men were probably recent arrivals, poorly-trained replacements; but the break-down in their discipline was symptomatic of the general disintegration in both military and civilian morale throughout the small area of the island still in British hands. Even for those who got safely to sea, there was no longer any guarantee of escape. The Japanese planes, as if to make up for their failure to prevent reinforcements from arriving earlier, now seemed determined to stop anyone from leaving. They bombed and strafed the wharves and dock areas and any ship that ventured from the harbour. One convoy of two merchant ships and four small warships, carrying mainly critical military personnel, came under particularly heavy attack. The ships escaped without much damage, but others were not so lucky.

Nor were those who remained behind. The loss of the depôts had drastically reduced food supplies — military food reserves would suffice for only a week more — while constant air attacks had smashed many water mains, reducing pressure and allowing the precious liquid to flow away through the breaks. Fuel was also very low now; although the main roads were so jammed with vehicles that it was hard to move along them anyway. Communications were rapidly falling apart. Few people had any clear idea of what was going on — a difficulty shared by most troops and their commanders — and rumours spread rapidly across the beleagered city. Whatever Singapore had once been, she was now clearly dying. 'Except as a fortress and battlefield', in the words of the Australian Government Representative, 'Singapore has ceased to function'.[28]

But still the battle continued. By mid-day on February 13th — Friday the 13th — the last of Percival's forces had completed their withdrawal to the perimeter. On his own initiative General Bennett had ordered the Australian units, including the attached 2nd Gordons, to take up an all-around defensive position in his sector of the main perimeter. All Australian troops on the island, except those in hospital, were now with Bennett. The Australian sector was manned on all sides, to meet any Japanese force that might break through elsewhere and attempt to take it from the rear. There was sufficient food and water within the area for at least several days, and Bennett had decided 'to make our final stand on the position occupied'.[29]

The Japanese 5th and 18th Divisions continued to apply pressure on the north-west and west, while elements of the Guards Division had pursued the British 53rd Brigade down Thomson Road and had reached the perimeter at Thomson Village. Yamashita was now in the position to place artillery fire anywhere in the city of Singapore. And while the engineers were still having trouble repairing the causeway, a great deal of divisional artillery had been ferried across Johore Strait and was making itself felt.

This was particularly true in General Mutaguchi's area. Having been unable to break through Australian defences on the 12th, Mutaguchi had turned his attention to the 44th Brigade, on the Australian left, and in particular to Brigadier G.G.R. Williams' 1st Malaya Brigade, still extended forward along the coast on Pasir Panjang Ridge and astride Raja Road immediately to the north. Williams' command now consisted of nearly two battalions of British troops and two Malayan battalions, in relatively good defensive positions. After a heavy artillery preparation, enhanced by mortar fire and air-strikes, Colonel Yoshio Nasu's 56th Infantry attacked Pasir Panjang Ridge during the morning of the 13th. The 1st Malaya fought stubbornly throughout most of the day, supported by fire from the remaining 9.2-inch and 6-inch guns of Faber Fire Command. The big guns drew heavy counter-battery fire and air attacks, and finally, in mid-afternoon, a particularly violent artillery concentration knocked out the two 6-inch pieces of Labrador Battery, the nearest Fixed Defence guns to the fighting.[30] Within another hour or so, the 56th Infantry had wrested the western end of Pasir Panjang Ridge from its defenders.

Colonel Nasu could now place enfilading fire on 1st Malaya troops covering Raja Road, so Williams was forced to pull his entire brigade back to the eastern end of the ridge after dark. Colonel Hisashi Kohisa's 114th Infantry advanced down Raja Road and to avoid being outflanked the 44th Brigade also fell back to conform with Williams' troops. The Australian position, to the right of the 44th Brigade, was now an exposed salient, but since Bennett's troops were prepared to defend it on all sides, there was no need for an Australian withdrawal.

At 2 o'clock that afternoon Percival held a conference with his senior commanders and staff officers at Fort Canning, his bombproof command post a few blocks from the Singapore waterfront. Percival told them that he hoped to stage a counter-attack to relieve the deteriorating situation. Since there were no longer any reserves left, this would have to be launched by the troops already in the line. All the senior commanders pointed out that the men were completely exhausted after continuous day and night and operations, that morale in many units was at breaking point, and that a counter-attack would have little hope of success. Generals Heath and Bennett suggested that it was time to surrender, to spare the civilians in Singapore further punishment from air and artillery bombardment and to protect them against the possible slaughter that might occur in case of a sudden Japanese breakthrough. The others supported this view, especially General Key, who emphasized the necessity of giving up while the Japanese troops could still be controlled by their commanders. A second Japanese demand for surrender, dropped by air during the day, contained a veiled threat of what might occur if resistance continued.[31]

The question of when a commander may justifiably surrender is a difficult one. In theory, he must continue to fight as long as he can in any way damage or delay the enemy. But the advantage of a few more enemy casualties or one or two days' delay when balanced against the complete destruction of the defeated force is not always clear — especially to those who must die in the process. Also, a local commander is rarely authorised to surrender on his own initiative, so that if he does so he is guilty at the least of insubordination and at the worst of treason. Percival was of course under orders from Wavell to continue the struggle for as long as he was able. He had, indeed, just received a message from the ABDA commander authorising the last-minute escape of any 'bold and determined personnel', but nevertheless repeating his earlier order to 'fight it out to the end'.[32]

At the conference of the 13th Percival accepted his subordinates' view that a counter-attack would have no chance, but refused to surrender. He felt, he reported later, 'that the situation was undoubtedly grave but was not hopeless'.[33] Accordingly, he ordered the fight to go on.

The discussion then turned to the question of the final evacuation of non-essential personnel, since the naval command has already concluded that the night of the 13th would be the last chance for the remaining ships and smaller sea-going craft to leave. To avoid the brutal fate of the British nurses captured and horribly maltreated by the Japanese at Hong Kong, the Australian nursing sisters and hospital matrons had already left Singapore, and the group at Fort Canning quickly agreed that the remaining nurses and any other women should sail that night. A few selected staff-officers and technicians would also go. Unfortunately no one realised that the Japanese fleet, with strong air support, was now in a position to block further escape efforts. A number of the ships that left Singapore in its final days were intercepted, and captured or sunk. Many of the refugees were drowned, doomed to a slow death from starvation or disease on some desolate island, or tortured and murdered by the Japanese.

Late on February 13th, Percival sent Wavell a full report of the situation at Singapore, including the views of his subordinates on the advisability of capitulating and his own belief that resistance could last no longer than a day or two. 'There must come a stage', he concluded, 'when in the interests of the troops and civil population further bloodshed will serve no useful purpose'. Wavell's orders to fight on were being 'carried out, but under above circumstances would you consider giving me wider discretionary powers?'[34]

Bearing in mind Churchill's earlier very definite instructions, Wavell could only reply in the negative. The troops, he said, would 'continue to inflict maximum damage on enemy for as long as possible by house-to-house fighting if necessary'. He appreciated Percival's situation, but any delay or injury to the Japanese could have an important effect on the battle elsewhere.[35] To Churchill, Wavell reported what had occurred, but added his fear that prolonged resistance was doubtful.[36]

By the morning of the 14th, breaks in the water-mains had reduced the available water in Singapore to one or at most two days' supply. The Governor was seriously concerned about the possibility of an epidemic and cabled his fears to the Colonial Office in London. Percival reported this new danger to Wavell, who again ordered the defence to be continued. But by now, Japanese engineers had finally succeeded in repairing the causeway. Yamashita's heavy artillery and the rest of the Twenty-fifth Army tanks hastened across to support the attack. Although the Japanese were growing concerned about their heavy expenditure of artillery ammunition, the bombardment continued. Shells and bombs crashed down on Singapore in an increasing crescendo. A cloud of pitch-black smoke hung over the city and drifted out across the Japanese positions. 'Aerial bombing, artillery fire, and the oil tank explosions had created a hell's port'.[37]

All three Japanese divisions continued to attack. The bulk of General Nishimura's force pressed against the 2nd Malaya Brigade north-east of Kallang airfield, and also drove 11th Division troops back to within a few hundred yards of the Woodleigh pumping station, on which Singapore's water supply now depended. Further west, other Guards units attacking down Thomson Road forced a gap in the 18th

Division line, which had to be filled by a battalion withdrawn from the 11th Division. The Japanese 5th Division, meanwhile, supported by a fierce artillery bombardment — 'the artillery shells fell like rifle bullets', one Japanese noted in his diary[38] — attacked the left front of the British 18th Division. The 9th Brigade with tanks, drove a deep salient into Beckwith-Smith's line south of MacRitchie Reservoir before it could be halted.

General Mutaguchi's division, meanwhile, continued to attack the 1st Malaya Brigade in the area near the coast. Punishing artillery fire in the morning preceded a series of assaults which the defenders managed to beat off in desperate and bloody hand-to-hand fighting. Late in the afternoon, however, Mutaguchi attacked with all three infantry regiments, accompanied by tanks, and succeeded in forcing the brigade back, especially in the area along the shoreline.

In their advance, Mutaguchi's troops captured the British military hospital at Alexandra. They ignored an attempt by the staff to surrender and ran amok through the building, bayonetting doctors and patients — including one on the operating table. About 150 patients were herded into an adjoining building, jammed together tightly in small rooms without food or water, and in the morning executed. There was no apparent reason for this atrocity. One story has it that a retreating group of detached Indian troops may have fired from the hospital grounds, thus provoking the Japanese; but it seems more probable that Mutaguchi's men, having suffered heavy casualties in their attacks against the Australians and the 1st Malaya Brigade, were simply seeking revenge.[39]

While fighting raged almost everywhere else along the perimeter, the Australian sector was relatively quiet. The Japanese, having failed to crack Bennett's line earlier, were in no mood to try it again and were satisfied to shell and bomb the defenders. Nor did the Australians themselves take any offensive action. Indeed, because of a growing shortage of 25-pounder field artillery ammunition, Bennett ordered his artillery to fire only in defence of the Australian perimeter, and then only on specific and obvious targets. The Australian gunners thus had a clear view of General Mutaguchi's advance against the 1st Malaya Brigade to the south, but made no effort to put the Japanese under fire.

As the 1st Malaya Brigade was forced back during the afternoon, Bennett concluded that his perimeter would soon be by-passed and cut off by the Japanese advance. He cabled a report of his situation to Australian Army Headquarters in Melbourne, ending with this sentence: 'If enemy enter city behind us will take suitable action to avoid unnecessary sacrifices'.[40] By this, he explained later, he meant that if the Japanese overran Malaya Command headquarters in the city behind him 'it was my intention to surrender to avoid any further needless loss of life'.[41] Bennett was clearly authorised and entitled to communicate directly with the Australian authorities. And in the circumstances the timing of his surrender was probably wise, even though it violated Wavell's and Percival's orders. But Bennett failed to notify Percival of his intention − 'a most extraordinary procedure', as Percival later noted in a remarkably restrained piece of understatement.[42]

But now it made no difference. Although the Japanese made little further progress during the night, by Sunday morning, February 15th, the situation was hopeless. At 9.30 a.m., after attending Communion, Percival convened another meeting of his senior commanders and staff at his underground 'battle-box' in Fort Canning.* Each commander reported on the deteriorating situation in his area, and Percival's artillery officer announced that 25-pounder and light anti-aircraft shells were just about exhausted. The Japanese had captured, or were able to deny access to, the last depôts. There was also practically no more fuel. And while civilian food stocks were adequate, military rations were almost gone. Brigadier Simson, the engineer and civil defence officer, gave the dread news that only one day's water-supply was left, and that once this was consumed it would be several days before repairs could allow the water to start flowing again.

In the circumstances, said Percival, the defenders could either counter-attack to recapture the reservoirs and food depôts, and to push back the Japanese artillery, or they could surrender. Everyone present urged surrender and Percival concluded that he would have to capitulate. Indeed, he had little choice, for renewed Japanese attacks were further compressing the perimeter on the north and south-west.

During the conference or immediately thereafter Percival finally received the discretionary authority he had requested from Wavell. In London the previous afternoon, Churchill and the Chiefs-of-Staff had agreed that further efforts to hold out in the streets of Singapore could only expose the population to useless slaughter. They authorised Wavell to surrender whenever he judged further resistance futile. Wavell in turn cabled Percival† to continue fighting as long as the troops were capable

---

* The following description of events on February 15th is also based on Wild, Notes on the Capitulation of Singapore. Wild was present at this meeting and participated in the subsequent surrender negotiations.

† None of the available sources indicates exactly when, during the morning, Wavell's message reached Singapore. According to Brigadier Simson's recollection, however, Percival had already received it when he made his decision to surrender.

of harming the Japanese, but when it became clear that this was no longer possible Percival might surrender.[43]

Once Percival had made his decision, the group at Fort Canning discussed how to implement it. General Yamashita, in his call for surrender on the 11th, had instructed Percival to order a ceasefire and to send a 'parliamentaire' carrying a white flag and a Union Jack up the Bukit Timah Road. Percival decided to send a civil and military deputation to propose a 4 p.m. ceasefire, and to invite Japanese representatives to Singapore to discuss final terms. General Heath objected that Percival's emissaries could not make their way through the lines, talk with the Japanese, and get back by 4 p.m. He suggested that the ceasefire be delayed until 8 p.m. Percival, however, rejected this view. Orders went out to all formations to destroy codes and secret materials and cease fire at 4 p.m., but to retain personal weapons in case the Japanese refused to stop fighting before a final surrender agreement was reached.

The surrender deputation consisted of three men: Brigadier T.K. Newbiggin, Percival's administrative officer; Hugh Fraser, the Colonial Secretary; and Captain Cyril Wild, a III Corps staff-officer who spoke Japanese.[44] They left Fort Canning at 11.30 a.m. in an open car, a furled Union Jack and white flag in the back. After delays and detours to avoid blocked streets, they reached the point where Adam and Farrer Roads cross the Bukit Timah Road. This was the front line of the British 54th Brigade, marked by a heavily-mined and barbed-wired road-block. The three men got out of their car and, after explaining to a British patrol that they were not defecting to the Japanese, unfurled their flags and picked their way gingerly forward through the minefield.

About 600 yards further up the Bukit Timah Road, they met a patrol from Matsui's 5th Division. The Japanese relieved them of their pistols and conducted them to a small house near the road. There, while Wild tried desperately to explain their mission and to insist on being taken to Yamashita's headquarters, their hosts seemed more interested in taking pictures of the three emissaries than in doing anything to move matters along. Finally, after about an hour, Colonel Sugita and another staff officer reached the scene.

Brigadier Newbiggin handed Sugita a letter from Percival outlining his proposals for a ceasefire and for negotiations. Sugita ignored this, and gave Newbiggin a typewritten letter with a one-page appendix that he had prepared earlier in anticipation of this meeting. These documents contained instructions for Percival to follow 'in order that the Japanese Army commander may accept the surrender of your army'.[45] Percival was to meet Yamashita in Bukit Timah at 4.30 p.m. — according to Wild, the time was left blank and Newbiggin inserted it himself — and, meanwhile, British forces should immediately cease fire, lay down their arms, and remain in place. Captain Wild pointed out that the Japanese had not bound themselves to cease fire and hold in place, and that the British could hardly do so if there remained any danger of a renewed Japanese attack. But Sugita refused to discuss the matter. Since time was passing rapidly, Newbiggin decided not to press this issue.

Sugita produced a large Japanese flag and said it should be displayed from the top of the Cathay Building, the tallest in Singapore, as a signal that Percival had accepted the conditions and was coming to meet Yamashita. The Japanese officer then returned their pistols to the British emissaries. The three men were blindfolded and driven back to a point near the front line. They recrossed the minefield, found their car, and continued on to Fort Canning.

It was after 3 p.m. when Newbiggin and Wild reported to Percival. Newbiggin told Wild to take the flag to the Cathay Building, see that it was hung, and get back quickly so he could accompany Percival to Bukit Timah. Since III Corps Headquarters was in the Cathay Building, Wild asked if he should tell Heath anything further about the ceasefire time. In view of his conversation with Sugita, Wild was particularly concerned lest III Corps troops should lay down their arms and then be overwhelmed by a Japanese attack. But Newbiggin now simply told him that orders for a ceasefire had already been issued. The brigadier was referring to the earlier order to cease fire at 4 p.m., but Wild, still thinking about Sugita, assumed that new orders had gone out postponing the ceasefire. He was astonished therefore to discover at the Cathay Building that no such orders had arrived.

The telephone line between III Corps and Malaya Command was cut, so when Wild returned to Fort Canning he attempted to raise the matter with Newbiggin and Percival. Reiterating his fear of what might happen if the British disarmed themselves before final surrender terms were agreed upon, he tried to persuade the two senior officers to delay the ceasefire. By now, however, it was after 4 p.m., and probably too late to do anything about changing the ceasefire time. In any event, neither Newbiggin nor Percival paid any attention to Wild's anxious comments. Both were undoubtedly thinking of the difficult and humiliating meeting ahead.

The ceasefire, in fact, did not come at 4 p.m. Some of the British units stopped shooting at that hour, but the Japanese did not, and fighting continued for some time. In the III Corps area, Heath had directed a halt at 4 o'clock, but an hour later a staff-officer arrived from Fort Canning to tell him that Percival had not ordered a ceasefire. Heath then told his troops to resume firing. The next morning, according to Wild, the III Corps commander was astonished to be severely reproved by Percival for having stopped the fighting at 4 p.m. This confusion is perhaps understandable at a time of high tension, shock, and exhaustion on the part of nearly everyone. Fortunately, it seems to have made little real difference. But that it might have been tragic, as Wild believed, is clear. The three Japanese divisions did not actually halt their advance until early evening, after they received word of the final surrender.

The surrender took place at the Ford motor factory, just above Bukit Timah. It was well after the time set by the Japanese when the British delegation arrived: Percival, Newbiggin, Wild, and another staff officer. And it was close to 5.15 p.m. before Yamashita and half a dozen or more members of his own staff sat down with the British officers on either side of a long table.

A large number of descriptions of the surrender conference have been written, most of them based on accounts issued by the Japanese during the war. The latter are confusing if not misleading, but a recent publication of extracts from Colonel Sugita's diary helps somewhat to explain matters.[46] One thing is clear. Yamashita was in a hurry to end the battle. He was worried about his ammunition supply and about the continued ferocity of the British artillery fire. He now realised that Percival actually had more troops on Singapore Island than he did, and he was afraid that if the British commander discovered this he would decide to fight on. Yamashita also wondered whether Percival was trying to stall long enough for reinforcements to arrive, or to allow his troops time to occupy stronger defensive positions, or even to prepare a counter-attack. He was clearly unaware of the true condition and strength of the British forces, whatever their numbers, and of the shortages of water, food, ammunition, and other supplies. In any event, he felt he could take no chances.

Yamashita wanted to know two things right away: would the British surrender unconditionally, and if so how soon?

Sugita had already given Newbiggin a list of the Japanese require-ments as part of the original terms, and more specific written instructions were now handed to Percival. But there was no need to talk about these things now, said Yamashita. All details could be worked out later, after Percival had surrendered unconditionally. Percival, for

General Percival surrenders Singapore to the Japanese general, Yamashita, at 7 p.m. on 15th February

The Japanese march into Singapore after the surrender

his part, was equally anxious to end the fighting quickly. But he was unwilling to sign a surrender document without some guarantee for the safety of troops and civilians in Singapore.

So while Yamashita pushed for immediate capitulation, Percival pressed equally hard for some means of protecting disarmed soldiers and helpless noncombatants. When Yamashita asked if Percival would surrender, the British commander said he wanted to keep 1,000 men under arms to maintain order and prevent looting and rioting in Singapore. Yamashita said that the Japanese army would maintain order, Percival insisted on using his own troops, and the two began to repeat themselves. Finally Yamashita said that his forces had planned a night attack and would go ahead if Percival refused to surrender. Percival asked for a delay and repeated his request to maintain 1,000 armed troops. Yamashita again threatened to attack and Percival suggested a ceasefire while the other matters were being worked out. The Japanese interpreter at the conference was not particularly adept, and efforts by Wild and Sugita to assist him seem only to have made matters worse. At any rate, Yamashita's patience was becoming strained and it was at this point that he made his famous demand for a Yes or No answer. 'The time for the night attack is drawing near', he said. 'Is the British army going to surrender or not? Answer "Yes" or "No".' And he emphasized the words Yes and No firmly in English.[47]

With Yamashita's threat clear, Percival could hold out no longer. He agreed to surrender. But, having done so, he again raised the question of keeping 1,000 armed men in the city. And Yamashita, having gained his surrender, now agreed to Percival's request.

There remained one final point, the time of the ceasefire. Yamashita suggested 8.30 p.m. Percival wanted to wait until 10 o'clock to make sure that he had time to transmit the order to all of his forces. Yamashita said that the schedule for his planned attack would not permit such a delay. He would, furthermore, have to hold Percival and the Governor, Sir Shenton Thomas, as hostages if the 8.30 ceasefire time was not accepted. Percival gave in and agreed to Yamashita's demand.

At 6.10 p.m. on February 15th, after nearly an hour of frustrating and exasperating negotiation, Percival signed his name on the surrender document. Under its terms, the British forces surrendered unconditionally; all fighting would cease at 8.30 p.m.; British troops would remain in place and disarm themselves by 9.30, with the exception of a force of 1,000 armed men who would maintain order in Singapore. Neither Percival nor any other British officer received a copy of the surrender document nor a written list of the terms agreed to.

While Percival returned to Fort Canning to issue the last necessary orders, Yamashita and his staff celebrated their victory. The battle on Singapore Island had cost the Japanese 1,700 killed and 3,400 wounded, about as many casualties as they had taken in the entire drive down the Malayan mainland. But the capture of Singapore was a magnificent victory, symbolising the end of British power in the Far East. The officers at Twenty-fifth Army headquarters drank *sake* and raised their cups in a silent toast to the Emperor.

Inside the once-proud city, Percival cabled Wavell that he had been 'unable . . . to continue the fight any longer. All ranks have done their best and are grateful for your help'.[48] It was the last message to leave Singapore.

NOTES – Chapter 9

1. Malay Operations Record, p. 82. This discussion of Japanese plans and preparations is based on *ibid.*, pp. 82-93; ATIS, Malaya Campaign, pp. 72-79; Tsuji, *Singapore*, pp. 213-37; Disposition of Japanese Forces in Johore and Singapore Island Operation, in Far East Command, Special Studies, II, Tab 7; Southwest Area Air Operations, pp. 97-102; Potter, *Life and Death of a Japanese General*, pp. 75-79.

2. Bennett, *Why Singapore Fell*, p. 167; Wigmore, *The Japanese Thrust*, pp. 296-99; Kirby, *The Loss of Singapore*, pp. 370-71.

3. Information on Landing Craft Used in the Crossing of the Strait of Johore, in Far East Command, Special Studies, III-A, Tab 6.

4. Reasons for Failure of Japanese to Halt Reinforcement of Singapore by Sea, in *ibid.*, II, Tab 5.

5. Coombes, *Banpong Express*, p. 47.

6. Kirby, *The Loss of Singapore*, pp. 373-74; Wigmore, *The Japanese Thrust*, pp. 299-305; Percival, *Despatch*, pp. 1315-16; Coombes, *Banpong Express*, pp. 46-47; Attiwell, *Fortress*, pp. 163-64.

7. The account of the battle for Singapore in the remainder of this chapter is based primarily on the following sources. (1) British: Kirby, *The Loss of Singapore*, pp. 375-415; Wigmore, *The Japanese Thrust*, pp. 308-89; Percival, *Despatch*, pp. 1316-26; Percival, *The War in Malaya*, pp. 266-93; Bennett, *Why Singapore Fell*, pp. 173-96; Bhargava and Sastri, *Campaigns in South-East Asia*, pp. 314-57; Mackenzie, *Eastern Epic*, I, 383-404; Maltby, *Report*, pp. 1382-83. (2) Japanese: Malay Operations Record, pp. 93-101; ATIS, Malaya Campaign, pp. 79-99; Tsuji, *Singapore*, pp. 237-71; Southwest Area Air Operations, pp. 102-103.

8. Coombes, *Banpong Express*, p. 48.

9. J. Bowyer Bell, *Beseiged: Seven Cities Under Siege* (Philadelphia: Chilton Books, 1966), p. 300, n. 24; Attiwell, *Fortress*, p. 175.

10. For the 12th Brigade, see also Stewart, *History of the Argyll and Sutherland Highlanders*, pp. 102-16; Rose, *Who Dies Fighting*, pp. 124-46.

11. Malaya Command Operation Instruction No. 40, February 10th, 1942, App. K to Percival, *Despatch*.

12. See also Replies to Questions Concerning Japanese Forces at Singapore, in Far East Command, Special Studies, I, Tab 19.

13. ATIS, Malaya Campaign, p. 89.

14. Rose, *Who Dies Fighting*, p. 132.

15. On this point, see also Coombes, *Banpong Express*, pp. 49-50.

16. Major Cyril Wild, Notes on the Capitulation of Singapore, November 30th, 1945, p. 4. Wild was a captain at III Corps headquarters at this time. I am grateful to his brother, the Very Rev. John Wild for allowing me to use his personal memoir, and to Mr. Louis Allen for alerting me to it. This paragraph is also based on Wigmore, *The Japanese Thrust*, p. 289; Morrison, *Malayan Postscript*, p. 159; Barber, *A Sinister Twilight*, pp. 169-70.

17. Percival, *The War in Malaya*, p. 275.

18. Wavell to Prime Minister, February 11th, 1942, in Churchill, *The Hinge of Fate*, p. 101; Wavell, *Despatch*, p. 13.

19. Wavell, *Despatch*, p. 13.

20. Prime Minister to Wavell, February 10th, 1942, in Churchill, *The Hinge of Fate*, p. 100.

21. Bhargave and Sastri, *Campaigns in South-East Asia*, p. 325.

22. Wigmore, *The Japanese Thrust*, p. 349.

23. ATIS, Malaya Campaign, p. 89.

24. Wigmore, *The Japanese Thrust*, p. 353. Other, somewhat varying translations are in Tsuji, *Singapore*, pp. 252-53; ATIS, Malaya Campaign, p. 93; Attiwell, *Fortress*, pp. 221-22.

25. Bhargava and Sastri, *Campaigns in South-East Asia*, p. 335.

26. Tsuji, *Singapore*, pp. 253-54.

27. For the 9th Brigade, see also Diary of Pte. Yamashita, in ATIS, Current Translations, No. 45, p. 30, and diary of another 41st Infantry soldier in *ibid.*, No. 54, p. 30.

28. Wigmore, *The Japanese Thrust*, p. 366. See also Attiwell, *Fortress*, pp.

193-200; Morrison, *Malayan Postscript*, pp. 179-81; Glover, *In 70 Days*, pp. 204-15; Barber, *A Sinister Twilight*, pp. 208-18; Maxwell, *Civil Defence of Malaya, passim.*

29. Bennett, *Why Singapore Fell*, p. 183.

30. Maurice-Jones, *History of Coast Artillery*, p. 273.

31. Attiwell, *Fortress*, pp. 222-23.

32. Wavell to Percival, February 13th, 1942, in Churchill, *The Hinge of Fate*, p. 104.

33. Percival, *Despatch*, p. 1322.

34. Percival to Wavell, February 13th, 1942, in Churchill, *The Hinge of Fate*, p. 104.

35. Wavell to Percival, February 14th, 1942, in *ibid.*

36. Wavell to Prime Minister, February 14th, 1942, in *ibid.*, p. 105.

37. Malay Operations Record, p. 98.

38. Diary of Pte. Yamashita, in ATIS, Current Translations, No. 45, p. 30.

39. Attiwell, *Fortress*, pp. 213-16, 231-32.

40. Wigmore, *The Japanese Thrust*, pp. 374-75.

41. Bennett, *Why Singapore Fell*, p. 190; Wigmore, *The Japanese Thrust*, p. 375, n. 6.

42. Percival, *The War in Malaya*, p. 284.

43. Churchill, *The Hinge of Fate*, pp. 105-106; Bryant, *The Turn of the Tide*, p. 244. Barber, *A Sinister Twilight*, p. 263. See also Attiwell, *Fortress*, p. 220.

44. For Fraser's account see Barber, *A Sinister Twilight*, pp. 263-67.

45. Japan Defence Agency, *Mare Shinko Sakusen*, pp. 620-21; translation in Louis Allen, The Surrender of Singapore: The Official Japanese Version, *Durham University Journal*, LX (December 1967), pp. 1-6. Slightly different versions in Malay Operations Record, p. 99, and Tsuji, *Singapore*, pp. 266-67. See also Hattori, *The Greater East Asia War*, II, 64.

46. In Japan Defence Agency, *Mare Shinko Sakusen*, pp. 621-25; translated in Allen, The Surrender of Singapore, *loc. cit.*, pp. 2-6. See also brief extracts from Yamashita's diary in Potter, *Life and Death of a Japanese General*, pp. 88-90, and further indications of Yamashita's views in A. Frank Reel, *The Case of General Yamashita* (Chicago: Univ. of Chicago Press, 1949), pp. 53-55; Cmdr. Samuel S. Stratton, Tiger of Malaya, *United States Naval Institute Proceedings*, Vol. 80 (February 1954), p. 138; Swinson, *Four Samurai*, pp. 213-14.

47. Sugita's diary; see Allen, The Surrender of Singapore, *loc. cit.*, p. 3.

48. Kirby, *The Loss of Singapore*, p. 415.

10

After Seventy Days

The night of February 15th was quiet. For the first time in seventy days, the sounds of warfare were stilled in Malaya. The Twenty-fifth Army remained outside Singapore, while within the fallen city troops and civilians rested, waited, and wondered what would happen to them.

The next morning, the first Japanese entered Singapore. A few of Yamashita's staff-officers drove through the city and a special force of military police under General Kawamura, the 9th Brigade commander, set about establishing control. Yamashita held the bulk of his forces on the outskirts of Singapore. But lest there should be any misunderstanding on the part of the defeated British, he made a major demonstration with every tank in the Twenty-fifth Army – about 175 in all – through the streets of the city. Overhead, low-flying Japanese planes maintained constant patrol. Then the occupying forces set about establishing an administration. But the victory, coming a month sooner than expected, had caught Japanese military government officers by surprise. So until military administrators could reach Singapore, local British officials continued the job of running the city under Japanese direction.[1]

Meanwhile, a few were still attempting to escape. From Singapore south to Sumatra and Java, countless boats and small craft sought to slip through the close net of Japanese planes and warships. Aboard these fleeing vessels were not only private citizens but also officials and soldiers, many of the latter heeding the injunction of General Wavell that all those who could should make their way to safety by any means possible. Most however, were unaware of Wavell's blessing, and even among those who knew of it there was some confusion about exactly who was entitled to leave and who would have to stay As a result, many escape efforts were undertaken on individual initiative, and these and the escapes officially arranged, were often confused and disorganised. Unhappily many who set out hopefully to sea never reached their destination.[2]

One who did, but whose escape became a subject of great controversy, was the Australian, General Bennett. During the campaign, Bennett had proved himself a brave and inspiring commander who understood the importance of bold tactics and the necessity of an active defence. If his strong ego and tendency toward independent action sometimes made him imprudent, or if he occasionally over-estimated his troops, he still displayed a degree of vigour and imagination all too rare among the defenders. Yet his final act at Singapore did much to dim this lustre.

As early as the end of January, Bennett had considered the possibility of escape from Malaya. By the eve of Percival's surrender, he had made up his mind that he must get back to Australia with his eye-witness observation of enemy tactics, and a warning of the threat that Japan posed to his country. He and several of his staff-officers developed a plan and agreed to execute it. On the evening of February 15th, after the ceasefire but before he actually became a prisoner-of-war, Bennett handed over his command to his artillery commander and, with two others, made his move. The three left Singapore Island shortly after midnight aboard a Chinese junk, reached Sumatra, worked their way across the island, and were eventually flown to Java. Bennett landed in Australia on March 2nd, safe and sound after his difficult and dangerous journey. He was shocked to be received with coolness, if not hostility, by the military authorities in Melbourne, who felt very strongly that he should never have left his troops.

An official inquiry after the war concluded that Bennett's actions had been well-motivated but improper. It is difficult not to agree that there were others equally capable of reporting on Japanese tactics and that a commanding general's obligation to his men required Bennett to remain.[3]

The fate of those tens of thousands denied the mercy of escape was a bitter one. Delivered by ill fortune into the brutal hands of the Japanese, they had no choice but to follow orders, hope for the best, and steel themselves for the long, unhappy wait until death or liberation freed them from captivity.

On February 16th, the prisoners were brought together in various assembly areas round the edge of Singapore city. The next day, the 45,000 Indian troops were separated from the other captives and had to listen to speeches by Major Fujiwara and Captain Mohan Singh urging them to join the Indian National Army. Most of the Indians — exhausted, shocked, bewildered, and depressed — fell an easy prey to these exhortations or to later threats or applications of physical force. Now, or in the months that followed, they joined their compatriots who had earlier succumbed to Japanese pressure or coercion. Over five thousand, however, remained loyal to the British crown, despite continued cruel efforts by the Japanese to make them change their minds.

The lot of the British and Australian soldiers was somewhat different, but no less harsh. The Japanese ordered them to march to Changi Barracks, at the eastern tip of Singapore Island, taking ten days' rations with them. Percival objected that the men were in no shape to carry the food, and finally obtained permission to transport the rations in trucks. The movement took place on February 17th, under a scorching sun. Few Japanese were there to guard the prisoners, but in the heat and dust the weary troops made no effort to escape. In addition to the ration trucks, a number of other vehicles were commandeered by small groups of Britons or Australians without any interference from the Japanese. The Argylls, indeed, managed to get hold of enough trucks to carry the surviving members of the battalion, their proud piper at their head playing them all the way to Changi. But the bulk of the men had to walk, and the last tired groups did not reach their destination until the early hours of the 18th.[4]

Changi Barracks, a pleasant, wooded, somewhat rolling area near the water, was a former British garrison post with a number of large brick buildings and many smaller ones. It had been heavily bombed, but still offered a far more wholesome appearance than most World War II prisoner-of-war camps. It was to be home for the majority of the captives until their liberation more than three years later. Percival and other senior officers were moved to Formosa in the summer of 1942 and, two years later, to Manchuria, where they stayed until the end of the war. For those who remained at Changi, life was bitter. Crowded conditions, short rations, disease, and above all the cruelty of the guards — many of whom were Sikhs who had succumbed to the threats and blandishments of Fujiwara and Mohan Singh — caused many deaths. The Japanese moved thousands of prisoners from Changi in 1942 and 1943 to work on the infamous Burma-Thailand railway, where great numbers died before the survivors were returned to Singapore in late 1943 and early 1944. In all, many thousands perished in captivity, and those who lived would never be the same again.

What of the civilians who were in Singapore when Percival surrendered? The majority of the British were imprisoned in Changi Jail, where life was less painful than for the military captives in neighbouring Changi Barracks, but was still far from pleasant for most and sheer agony for many. The Malayans in Singapore were treated no better and no worse than captive people in other countries occupied by the Japanese during the war, while the Indians were encouraged to join the Indian National Army and did not suffer too greatly. The Chinese fell victim to the cruellest fate. Many were imprisoned and horribly illtreated. Hundreds, if not thousands, were summarily executed.[5]

The prisoners-of-war and the civilian captives looked back on the military campaign that led to their incarceration with a mixture of bitterness and incredulity. Those who had believed the tales of Singapore's impregnability, and who had listened to continued official statements about how the island would be held — listened, that is, until the explosion of Japanese bombs and the roar of artillery all but deadened their ears — were understandably angry at what they could only regard as deliberate and fatuous lies. The troops, especially those who had made the long, hard retreat down the Malayan peninsula, were particularly acrimonious.* 'The men blamed their officers for the disaster, junior officers blamed senior officers, and junior formations blamed senior formations'.[6]

In England and Australia, the criticism and shock were no less severe. The Australians, with the Japanese practically at their doorstep, blamed British leadership and the Indian troops. The Indians condemned the British civil and military authorities. The British found fault with their own commanders and chiefs-of-staff, with the Australian troops, and with the Prime Minister, Winston Churchill. General Wavell thought the trouble lay in training deficiencies and a lack of toughness and fighting spirit. Churchill himself was badly stunned, and months later was still trying to understand what had happened. He reproached himself and his advisers for not knowing about the weak defences on Singapore Island, but he stubbornly resisted the implication that he was responsible for the entire Malayan disaster. And he always steadfastly defended his own actions in allocating higher priorities for men and equipment to what he felt were more important theatres of war.[7]

The British defeat in Malaya may have had many causes. It is relatively easy, in reviewing the military campaign, to find mistakes, errors of commission or omission, that affected the course of battle. Yet it would be wrong to conclude that these should be blamed for the

---

* Much of the postwar literature about the campaign, especially that of a personal nature, contains ample evidence of this continuing bitterness, a sentiment rarely absent in defeat.

final outcome, or that if they had not occurred Singapore would not have fallen to the Japanese.

'The trouble', General Wavell noted two days after Percival's surrender, 'goes a long way back'.[8] He was referring to the sleepy Malayan atmosphere and its effect on peacetime training and tactical thought. But there were other long-term factors of even greater importance. The first was the British decision to drop the Anglo-Japanese alliance in favour of an Anglo-American alignment. When discarding as an ally the only major power in the Far East, which was at the same time the only nation capable of threatening British possessions in the Orient, Britain required some counter-weight to balance the loss. A strong Anglo-American alliance, backed by powerful military forces, and bases in the Pacific and South-east Asia, might well have done the trick. But the disarmament restrictions of the 1922 Washington Conference, and the disinclination of either the British or the American public to spend large sums of money on Far Eastern defences, effectively prevented the development of any reasonable military opposition to Japan. And the failure of Great Britain herself to transform Singapore into a powerful fortress, strongly garrisoned and supported by effective sea and air forces, left Malaya a hostage to fortune and a prey to Japanese ambition.

Although more than two decades passed between the end of the first World War and the beginning of the second, Great Britain was no better prepared to defend Malaya in 1939 than she had been in 1918. Indeed because of the growth of Japanese strength, she was probably less so, and, in the two remaining years before the Japanese struck, her relative strength declined still further. Like the United States, she would pay a bitter price for her unwillingness to build defences.

The twenty-seven months between the outbreak of war in Europe and the start of hostilities in the Pacific witnessed a growing disparity between Britain's ability to defend Malaya and Japan's capacity to seize it. The conflict in Europe and the Mediterranean effectively tied down British land, sea, and air forces, hindering further reinforcement of Malaya and focusing British attention on the danger nearer home. The fall of France not only increased the immediate threat to England and gravely extended the tasks of the British fleet, but it also opened French Indo-China to Japanese occupation – and Japan's establishment of air and naval bases in Indo-China doomed the weak Malayan defences. Given the relatively short Japanese lines of communication and the increased range of modern aircraft, British strength in Malaya was clearly incapable of meeting this threat. Then, at a time when

Malaya cried loudest for reinforcements, Britain's burden at home was heaviest. Not only did she stand alone against Germany and Italy, but after June 1941 she had to send vital equipment to support her new Russian ally, and to deploy vast numbers of men and quantities of material to defend her key positions in the Mediterranean and the Middle East.

The decisions to try to keep Russia in the war, and to defend the Middle East at the expense of the Far East, can only be criticised on the assumption that England herself could have stood if Russia and the Middle East had fallen. This was a risk that the British government was understandably unwilling to take. The threat in the Orient was still potential, while the danger at home was real.

In December 1941, then, British Far Eastern land, sea, and air forces were inferior to those of the Japanese. For practically the first time in her history, Great Britain would be forced to wage a distant military campaign without a clear command of the seas. Nor was she in any position to dispute with her enemy for control of the air. This was her weakest point. Without sufficient airpower, neither the presence of large bodies of troops nor the arrival of a British battlefleet could have saved Malaya and Singapore.

Yet if Malaya was doomed by British strategic weaknesses in the Far East, could Japanese victory have been delayed by better tactical decisions once the war had begun? The answer seems to be yes, but not by much.

The abortive *Matador* plan might have set back Japanese timing. Alternatively, it might have allowed General Yamashita to destroy Percival's army in forward positions and in detail. The latter, in effect, is what happened. The unfortunate siting of the British airfields, and the necessity of disposing troops to defend them, forced Percival to scatter his units and to oppose the Japanese with piecemeal defences. The absence of British seapower, moreover, left the long Malayan coastal flanks open to amphibious assault, and Percival had to maintain strong forces in Johore lest the Japanese should land behind him. He also faced the dilemma of trying to keep the enemy as far to the north as possible, without at the same time losing so many troops that he would be unable to defend positions further south. Without effective air support, with no tanks, with poorly trained troops and inexperienced officers, and with questionable intelligence, it is in many ways surprising that Percival held northern Malaya for as long as he did.

Yet a ruthless early decision to abandon northern Malaya and make a stand further down the peninsula might have delayed the Japanese for as long, and at a lower cost to the defenders.[9] It would have spared III Corps its slow, punishing retreat and the grim, debilitating effects of steady pressure, constant movement, and lack of sleep. Certainly fewer casualties in northern Malaya — the preservation of the 11th Division, for example — might have permitted a more prolonged defence in Johore.

Part of the credit for whatever delay was imposed on the Japanese must go to the courageous British flyers who fought a losing battle against overwhelming odds. Despite their inferior numbers, they diverted Japanese airpower and kept General Sugawara from concentrating on more direct support of Yamashita s troops. Had the Japanese been free to use their airpower as they should have, the British defeat on the ground would surely have been swifter and more devastating.

Admiral Phillips also rates applause for courage. That his ships should not have been at Singapore in the first place without air cover, or that they should have been swiftly withdrawn after the war began, were matters beyond his control. But to say that he himself should not have made the effort to interfere with Japanese landing operations, whatever his lack of support from the air, is a conclusion that ignores centuries of British naval tradition, and the undeniable fact that with a little luck Phillips might have caused the enemy considerable damage. Since the *Prince of Wales* and the *Repulse* would probably have been lost anyway, once London had failed to order their immediate escape, it was better to make the effort and go down fighting than to suffer the ignominious fate of being sunk at anchor in Singapore Harbour, or while attempting to flee from the area later on.

General Percival, having lost his air and sea support, could now only hold out in the hope that enough reinforcements might arrive in time to avoid ultimate defeat. But the quality of the ground reinforcements that could reach him quickly was poor, and there were not enough modern aircraft available to turn the tide. He thus had to fight the decisive battle for Johore with inadequately prepared troops and, in accordance with Wavell's orders, in dispositions that do not appear to have been the most effective. That the battle did not result in an even greater disaster for the defenders was due less to any British actions than to Japanese failure to make the most of their gains.

With Johore lost, the fall of Singapore was inevitable. Percival may fairly be criticised for not doing more about the northern defences of the island, and for undue preoccupation with the danger of an assault against the north-east coast. Yet the defence of Singapore against an attack from the mainland clearly lay in Johore, either along General

Dobbie's proposed, but unbuilt, line or by means of ground and air action to stop the Japanese advance. Prepared positions on the north shore of Singapore Island might have delayed, but surely could not have prevented, the Japanese victory. But even so, Percival's troop dispositions would seem to merit criticism. Here, General Wavell must share the initial blame. Having overruled Percival's planned dispositions in Johore, he then acquiesced in the deployment on Singapore, even though he believed that Percival was wrong. After the Japanese landed, however, Percival himself was at fault in failing to shift troops rapidly to the obvious point of danger. Once General Yamashita had landed tanks it probably made little difference, but swifter reaction by Percival to the enemy landings might have delayed, if only temporarily, the inevitable.

There are a few other points that always seem to arise in any discussion of the Malayan campaign. The first is the old *canard* about the Singapore guns that pointed in the wrong direction. That they did no such thing is less important than that they represented an outmoded concept of defence and that by the beginning of World War II they were already an anachronism. The development of modern aircraft and effective bombing techniques greatly reduced the value of coast artillery. The Singapore guns, even in the best of circumstances, would have been of limited use against an attack either from land or from the sea. And certainly, lacking adequate target observation and more suitable ammunition, the Fixed Defences added little to the island's ability to withstand assault from Johore. They caused trouble and inflicted casualties, but had they indeed faced the wrong way it would scarcely have made any difference.

Another point frequently criticised is the failure of the British to arm the native population of Malaya and use them to offset their own numerical weakness. This might have been a practical idea had it been implemented earlier as part of a major plan to build strong defences in Malaya. A well-trained Malayan army, supported by powerful British air and sea units and backed by a force of regular British troops, might well have been just the thing to defend Malaya. But in the short and all too ineffective period of preparation on the eve of war, there was neither the equipment with which to arm local forces nor sufficient time nor means to train them properly. What was needed in Malaya was not necessarily more troops, but rather better troops and more and better arms and equipment. Two dozen squadrons of modern aircraft, or a regiment of tanks, would have proved far more valuable than any native force raised at the last moment.

Small numbers of local troops might have been used with good effect as guerrillas or 'stay-behind' parties. A few of these did operate under the effective leadership of men like Colonel Chapman, and the British made some effort to develop ties with a growing Chinese communist guerrilla movement in Malaya. But these endeavours were limited and far less effective than they might have been. Concentrated guerrilla attacks on the long, exposed, Japanese lines of communication could undoubtedly have hampered Yamashita's advance; whether this delay would have saved Singapore is questionable, but it might well have extended its life.[10]

In any review of the abortive British defence of Malaya, the figure of General Percival emerges as the most critical. Both Brooke-Popham and Wavell, despite their superior rank, played limited roles, as did Pulford and Phillips, Heath and Bennett. It was Percival who made most of the major decisions, to whom the troops in the field and their commanders looked for leadership, and who alone was in a position to exercise the forceful, imaginative, and indeed ruthless command that more than anything else, might have prolonged the defence of Singapore. But Percival was not that sort of a man. A knowledgeable and experienced officer, solidly grounded in the fundamentals of warfare, familiar with Malaya and the problem of defending it, he appeared to lack those outstanding qualities that the situation demanded: aggressiveness, firmness in the face of adversity, the capacity to make and enforce unpopular decisions, and the ability to arouse men to perform great deeds. Only these qualities could have developed a sense of urgency and matched the powerful and imaginative tactics of the Japanese.

If the result had been a delay of several weeks in the fall of Singapore, would this have significantly affected the progress of the war? Wavell seemed to think so. A month, he felt, would have allowed additional reinforcements to reach Malaya, and a simultaneous build-up of strong allied air forces in the Indies; sufficient to half the Japanese and provide a line from which to launch a counter-offensive.[11]

This view is attractive but not persuasive. The Japanese had already seized major portions of the Indies by the end of January, and few of the forces assigned to Malaya were scheduled to participate in subsequent operations to the south. Had Singapore proved stubborn, the Japanese would simply have by-passed it — as they did the determined defenders of the Philippines — and continued with their planned invasions elsewhere. Their overwhelmingly superior naval and air forces could easily have crushed any allied effort to regain control of the sea and sky in the ABDA area. Whatever additional troops reached

Singapore would probably have been lost in the end. A more realistic view might indeed be that as soon as Singapore seemed to be doomed, all reinforcements should have been shifted to Burma to halt the Japanese advance there. This action had been discussed in London, but never implemented. In the cold light of hindsight, it would seem the more effective course.

The abortive defence of Malaya cost the British Empire approximately 125,000 troops killed or captured. This figure is somewhat less than the number given in the official British histories of the campaign, which is accepted by most other sources; but it appears to be more in accord with the evidence.[12] An earlier decision to accept the loss of Singapore could have saved many thousands of men to fight elsewhere and would probably not appreciably have speeded the Japanese victory in Malaya.

British losses, of course, also included the *Prince of Wales* and the *Repulse* and almost all the aircraft present in Malaya on December 8th or brought in as reinforcements; a total of at least 250 planes. The two ships might have been saved by a swift decision in London to withdraw them once they had failed as a deterrent. Aircraft losses probably could not have been avoided in any reasonable way.

Any view of the fall of Singapore that concentrates exclusively on British weaknesses and mistakes does an injustice to the ability of the Japanese. From start to finish, they planned and executed the Malayan campaign with a high degree of skill, and they made very few mistakes. General Yamashita demonstrated coolness, imagination, and determination. With no choice, until the final weeks, but to use his army in piecemeal fashion, he managed to bring tactically superior forces to bear at decisive points and to maintain almost constant pressure on his foe. He made far better use of limited resources than did Percival, and he exploited his superiority to the utmost. If he blundered in failing to prevent the evacuation from Johore, the fault was probably more General Sugawara's than his. The 3rd Air Group did an excellent job in destroying British airpower and, in the main, of supporting the Twenty-fifth Army advance. But it was not effective in cutting British lines of communication nor in preventing reinforcements from reaching Singapore. In the latter failure, it was joined by the naval 22nd Air Flotilla. All credit goes to Admiral Matsunaga's fliers for sinking the *Prince of Wales* and the *Repulse*; but it is still difficult to understand the success of British reinforcement in the face of such overwhelming Japanese air superiority.

The Japanese, nevertheless, fought a magnificent campaign, completing it a month sooner than the 100 days they thought would be necessary. The fact that the Twenty-fifth Army suffered less than 10,000 casualties — 3,507 killed, 6,150 wounded[13] — clearly attests their skill. Losses in the 3rd Air Group were proportionately higher. Enemy action and operational accidents accounted for 331 planes, while personnel losses exceeded 500.[14] Casualties in the 22nd Air Flotilla and in the naval surface forces are unknown, but were apparently light.

For the Japanese, the conquest of Malaya and Singapore was a great strategic, economic, psychological, and political victory. Militarily, they destroyed large enemy forces at small cost and gained unchallenged entry into the Indian Ocean, the fine Singapore naval base for their fleet, forward airfields for their planes, and ample protection for the flanks of their advances south and west. At Singapore itself they captured great stocks of weapons and equipment, although the British successfully destroyed most of the Fixed Defence guns, leaving among the larger weapons only a single 15-inch gun and two 6-inch pieces that could be repaired.[15] Economically, Japan now possessed more than a third of the rubber and over half the tin being produced in the entire world, vital assets in a major war. Once she had captured the resources of the Indies, she would have gained all that she had gone to war for. And, finally, psychologically and politically the capture of the supposedly impregnable bastion of Singapore dealt a heavy blow to British prestige, destroyed the myth of Western invincibility, and constituted an important step in Japan's bid for the leadership of Asia.

Each Japanese gain was an equal loss for Great Britain. Deprived of the Singapore base, British air and sea power was pushed back as far south as Australia and as far west as Ceylon and, for a while, to the coast of Africa. Calcutta was useless as a port and the whole eastern shore of India lay exposed to Japanese sea power. The raw materials of Malaya that now filled the holds of Japanese transports could no longer support the British war effort. Even greater than these physical losses was the shock to Britain's Pacific allies. Australia, New Zealand, China, Burma, and India shuddered at the great defeat and wondered at their wisdom in placing faith in England. The United States, despite its own disaster at Pearl Harbour, still fought on in the Philippines, and Americans made invidious comparisons between Corregidor and Singapore. For Great Britain itself, the fall of Singapore was a blow that shook the very foundations of the Empire; its consequences might be compared to the defeat at Yorktown just over a century and a half earlier, when Lord Cornwallis surrendered to George Washington.

It is any wonder that the Japanese exulted? In Tokyo, on the morning of February 16th, the Emperor summoned his chiefs-of-staff and gave them a special Imperial Rescript commemorating the great victory and expressing gratification at the sacrifices and achievements of those who had destroyed the vaunted British fortress. The next day, Imperial Headquarters announced that henceforth Singapore would be known as *Shonan*, or 'Southern Light'. February 18th was designated 'First Victory Day' in Japan, an occasion for public celebration. Poems and songs commemorating the triumph quickly appeared. One well-known poet compared the Japanese termination of the long British rule over Singapore to burning flames that purged away more than 120 years of evil. A colourful and unrestrained marching song described the capture of Singapore in bloody tones, proclaiming in one stanza:

> We have won, we have won, we have reduced it!
> The virile roar of righteousness, echoing in the haunted jungle and
> winding through crocodile-infested creeks, breaks into the
> enemy's stronghold.
> Ah! This deeply stirring victory!
> Singapore has fallen![16]

Perhaps the simplest words of all and those most full of meaning were written in his diary by a Japanese machine-gunner outside Singapore city on the evening of February 15th:

> Since landing at the Malaya front line, seventy days of restless
> pursuit and attacking have finally come to an end.[17]

NOTES – Chapter 10

1. Malay Operations Record, pp. 101-102; Percival, *Despatch*, p. 1326; Tsuji, *Singapore*, pp. 272-74; Coombes, *Banpong Express*, p. 56; Potter, *Life and Death of a Japanese General*, p. 91; Barber, *A Sinister Twilight*, pp. 287-88.

2. Wigmore, *The Japanese Thrust*, pp. 383-89; Maxwell, *Civil Defence of Malaya*, pp. 121-26; Barber, *A Sinister Twilight*, pp. 259-61, 269-71, 301-309.

3. Bennett, *Why Singapore Fell*, pp. 193-219; Wigmore, *The Japanese Thrust*, pp. 273, 377-81, 383-85, 659-52. Legg, *The Gordon Bennett Story*, is a sympathetic defence of Bennett. (It is significant that when General MacArthur – a military leader of far greater value to the Allied cause, who knew at least as much about Japanese tactics as Bennett – escaped from the Philippines, he left only after receiving specific orders to do so from the President of the United States. Morton, *Fall of the Philippines*, pp. 353-59.)

4. Percival, *The War in Malaya*, p. 307; Wigmore, *The Japanese Thrust*, pp.

382-83, 511-12; Mackenzie, *Eastern Epic*, I, 403-404; Malay Operations Record, p. 102; Khan, *I.N.A. & Its NETAJI*, pp. 17-24 and *passim*; Durrani, *The Sixth Column*, p. 62 and *passim*; Coombes, *Banpong Express*, pp. 56-58; Stewart, *History of the Argyll & Sutherland Highlanders*, pp. 116-17.

5. Wigmore, *The Japanese Thrust*, Part III; Percival, *The War in Malaya*, chap. xxii; Coombes, *Banpong Express*, Parts II-III; Barber, *A Sinister Twilight*, Part III; Stewart, History of the *Argyll & Sutherland Highlanders*, App. IV; James Leasor, *Singapore: The Battle That Changed the World* (Garden City: Doubleday, 1968), pp. 255-57.

6. Wigmore, *The Japanese Thrust*, p. 511.

7. Churchill, *The Hinge of Fate*, pp. 49-50, 155-56; Khan, *I.N A. & Its NETAJI*, pp. 6-9; Bryant, *The Turn of the Tide*, pp. 9, 22, 242, 245; Kennedy, *The Business of War*, pp. 196-97; Kirby, *The Loss of Singapore*, pp. 388, 468; Moran, *Churchill: Taken from the Diaries of Lord Moran* (Boston: Houghton, Mifflin, 1966), pp. 29-30; Eade (ed.), *Churchill's Speeches*, pp. 63-64. Churchill's general defence of his role is implicit throughout his account of the Far East campaigns in *The Grand Alliance* and *The Hinge of Fate*.

8. Wavell to Chiefs of Staff, February 17th, 1942, in Kennedy, *The Business of War*, p. 198.

9. For suggestions along this line, see Col. A.O. Robinson. The Malayan Campaign in the Light of the Principles of War, *Royal United Services Institution Journal*, CIX (August, November 1964), pp. 224-32, 325-37.

10. Chapman, *The Jungle is Neutral*, especially chaps. iv-v, is a strong argument for the value of 'stay-behind' parties in Malaya.

11. Wavell to Chiefs of Staff, February 17th, 1942, in Kennedy, *The Business of War*, pp. 197-98.

12. The official histories agree that British strength in Malaya on December 8th, 1941, totalled 88,600 men, consisting of 19,600 British, 15,200 Australians, 37,000 Indians, and 16,800 local troops. They also agree that total losses in the campaign were 138,708 men, including 38,496 British, 18,490 Australians, 67,340 Indians, and 14,382 local troops. Kirby, *The Loss of Singapore*, pp. 163, 473; Wigmore, *The Japanese Thrust*, pp. 102, 382; Bhargava and Sastri, *Campaigns in South-East Asia*, p. 357. The additional 19,000 British and 3,000 Australian troops are clearly accounted for by reinforcements that reached Singapore during the campaign. The decrease of 2,000 in the number of local troops remains unexplained. But the increase of over 30,000 in the number of Indian troops seems to be an error. Indian reinforcements consisted of the 45th Brigade on January 3rd, the 44th Brigade plus 7,000 individual replacements on January 22nd, and probably about 1,000 more men on February 5th, amounting to a total of no more than 15,000 troops, or half the number suggested by the official histories. Deducting the difference of 15,000 Indian troops from the official total of nearly 139,000 leaves a figure of roughly 124,000. Adding the mysteriously vanished 2,000 local troops raises the total to about 126,000. In support of this figure is General Percival's statement that 'the total number of officers and men who took part in the campaign on the British side was a little over 125,000'. Percival, *Despatch*, p. 1328. Japanese sources vary in their estimates, but none sets the total of British forces killed and captured at anything

higher than 120,000. Japanese estimates, also, of the number of enemy killed and captured on the Malayan mainland range from 13,000 to 25,000. Adding these to the maximum of 100,000 troops Percival had on Singapore in early February gives at most 125,000. Tsiji, *Singapore*, pp. 38, 214, 270; 'Malay Operations Record', pp. 80, 101; *Communiques Issued by the Imperial General Headquarters, From December 8th, 1941 to June 30th, 1943* (Tokyo: Mainichi Publishing Co., 1943), pp. 46, 55, 60, 69; ATIS, 'Malaya Campaign', pp. 66, 102, 104.

Weighing all the evidence, 125,000 would seem to be about the proper total. The number of troops in Malaya Command killed in action is less clear. Kirby, *The Loss of Singapore*, p. 473, sets this at a maximum of 8,000 (out of 138,000), but the Japanese sources cited above indicate that the actual figure may have been as high as 15,000 or possibly even higher (out of 125,000).

13. Malay Operations Record, pp. 80, 110; Tsuji, *Singapore*, p. 271.

14. Southwest Area Air Operations, pp. 103-107.

15. Report on Installations and Captured Weapons, pp. 4-70.

16. *Shingaporu wa Kanraku Su!* (Singapore Has Fallen!), in ATIS, Current Translations, No. 16, January 25th, 1943, p. 42; *Communiques Issued by Imperial General Headquarters*, pp. 53-54; ATIS, Malaya Campaign, pp. 99, 101; Butow, *Tojo*, p. 416; Donald Keene, Japanese Writers and the Great East Asia War, *Journal of Asian Studies*, XXIII (February 1964), p. 214.

17. Diary of Pvt. Yamashita, in ATIS, Current Translations, No. 45, p. 30.

Appendix

MAJOR FORCES PARTICIPATING
IN THE MALAYAN CAMPAIGN

BRITISH

Far East Command (to January 3rd, 1942)
 Air-Chief-Marshal Sir Robert Brooke-Popham (to December 27th, 1941)
 Lt.-Gen. Sir Henry Pownall (to January 3rd, 1942)

ABDACOM — General Sir Archibald Wavell

 Malaya Command — Lt. Gen. Arthur Percival

III Indian Corps — Lt. Gen. Sir Lewis Heath

9th Indian Division — Maj. Gen. A.E. Barstow (killed January 28th, 1942)
 8th Brigade — Brig. B.W. Key (to January 10th, 1942)
 22nd Brigade — Brig. G.W.A. Painter

11th Indian Division — Maj. Gen. D.M. Murray-Lyon (to December 23rd, 1941)
 6th Brigade — Brig. W.O. Lay (to December 23rd, 1941)
 15th Brigade — Brig. K.A. Garrett (to December 23rd, 1941)

28th Indian Brigade — Brig. W. St. J. Carpendale (to December 23rd, 1941)

8th Australian Division — Maj. Gen. H.G. Bennett
 22nd Brigade — Brig. H.B. Taylor
 27th Brigade — Brig. D.S. Maxwell

18th British Division — Maj. Gen. M.B. Beckwith-Smith
 53rd Brigade — Brig. C.L. Duke

54th Brigade – Brig. E.H.W. Backhouse
55th Brigade – Brig. T.H. Massy-Beresford

12th Indian Brigade – Brig A.C.M. Paris

44th Indian Brigade – Brig. G.C. Ballentine

45th Indian Brigade – Brig. H.C. Duncan (killed January 20th, 1942)

Singapore Fortress – Maj. Gen. F. Keith Simmons
1st Malaya Brigade – Brig. G.G.R. Williams
2nd Malaya Brigade – Brig. F.H. Fraser

Far East Command, Royal Air Force – Air Vice Marshal C.W.H. Pulford

Eastern Fleet – Admiral Sir Tom Phillips (killed December 10th, 1941)
Vice Adm. Sir Geoffrey Layton

JAPANESE
Southern Army – Field Marshal Count Hisaichi Terauchi

Twenty-fifth Army – Lt. Gen. Tomoyuki Yamashita

5th Division – Lt. Gen. Takuro Matsui
9th Infantry Brigade – Maj. Gen. Saburo Kawamura
11th Infantry Regiment – Col. Tsunahiko Watanabe
41st Infantry Regiment – Col. Kanichi Okabe
21st Infantry Brigade – Maj. Gen. Eikichi Sugiura
21st Infantry Regiment – Col. Noriyoshi Harada
42nd Infantry Regiment – Col. Tadao Ando

18th Division – Lt. Gen. Renya Mutaguchi
23rd Infantry Brigade – Maj. Gen. Hiroshi Takumi
55th Infantry Regiment – Col. Hiroshi Koba
56th Infantry Regiment – Col. Yoshio Nasu
114th Infantry Regiment – Col. Hisashi Kohisa

Imperial Guards Division – Lt. Gen. Takuma Nishimura
Infantry Group – Maj. Gen. Takashi Kobayashi
3rd Battalion, 3rd Guards Regiment

4th Guards Regiment — Col. Kentaro Kunishi
5th Guards Regiment — Col Takeo Iwaguro

3rd Tank Group

3rd Air Group — Lt. Gen. Michio Sugawara

Southern Force — Vice Adm. Nobutake Kondo
Main Body — Vice Adm. Nobutake Kondo
Southern Expeditionary Fleet — Vice Adm. Jisaburo Ozawa
22nd Air Flotilla — Rear Adm. Sadaichi Matsunaga

Bibliography

DOCUMENTS AND REPORTS

Brooke-Popham, Air Chief Marshal Sir Robert. *Despatch: Operations in the Far East, from October 17th, 1940 to December 27th, 1941.* May 28th, 1942. Supplement to the *London Gazette* of January 20th, 1948.

Layton, Vice-Admiral Sir Geoffrey. *Despatch: Loss of H.M. Ships* Prince of Wales *and* Repulse. December 17th, 1941 Supplement to the *London Gazette* of February 20th, 1948.

Maltby, Air Vice-Marshal Sir Paul. *Report on the Air Operations During the Campaigns in Malaya and Netherlands East Indies from December 8th, 1941 to March 12th, 1942.* July 26th, 1947. Third Supplement to the *London Gazette* of February 20th, 1948.

Percival, Lieut.-General A.E. *Despatch: Operations of Malaya Command, from December 8th, 1941 to February 15th, 1942.* April 26th, 1946. Second Supplement to the *London Gazette* of February 20th, 1948.

Southwest Pacific Area, Allied Translator and Interpretor Section (ATIS). Filed in National Archives Records Branch, Washington National Records Centre, Suitland, Md.:

    (a) *Bulletin No. 747.* February 24th, 1944.

    (b) Current Translations. Nos. 16 (January 25th, 1943); 27 (April 19th, 1943); 45 (June 1st, 1943); 54 (June 14th 1943); 57 (June 26th, 1943); 64 (July 13th, 1943); 106 (March 20th, 1944).

    (c) Enemy Publications. No. 6, *Hawaii-Malaya Naval Operations*, May 27th, 1943; No. 278, *Malaya Campaign 1941-1942*, January 11th, 1945.

Supreme Commander for the Allied Powers, ATIS. In National Archives Records Branch: Research Report No. 131, *Japan's Decision to Fight*, December 1st, 1945.

U.S. Army Forces, Far East. Japanese Monograph Series. In Office of the Chief of Military History, Department of the Army, Washington, D.C.:

(a) No. 24, *History of the Southern Army, 1941-1945.*

(b) No. 31, *Southern Area Air Operations Record (1941-1945).*

(c) No. 45, *History of Imperial General Headquarters Army Section* (Revised Edition).

(d) No. 54, *Malay Operations Record, November 1941-March 1942.*

(e) No. 55, *Southwest Area Air Operations, November 1941-February 1942.*

(f) No. 68, *Report on Installations and Captured Weapons, Java and Singapore, 1942.*

(g) No. 103, *Outline of Administration in Occupied Areas, 1942-1945.*

(h) No. 105, *General Summary of Naval Operations, Southern Force.*

(i) No. 107, *Malaya Invasion Naval Operations* (Revised Edition).

(j) No. 116, *The Imperial Japanese Navy in World War II.*

(k) No. 156, *Historical Review of Landing Operations of the Japanese Forces.*

(l) No. 177, *Thailand Operations Record.*

U.S. Congress, Joint Committee on the Investigation of the Pearl Harbour Attack. *Pearl Harbour Attack.* 39 Pts. Washington: U.S. Government Printing Office, 1946.

U.S. Department of the Army. *Reports of General MacArthur.* 2 Vols. Washington: U.S. Government Printing Office, 1966.

U.S. Far East Command, General Headquarters, Military History Section, Japanese Research Division. *Special Studies.* 5 Vols. 1951-1960. In Office, Chief of Military History, Dept. Army.

U.S. Strategic Bombing Survey (Pacific). *Interrogations of Japanese Officials.* 2 Vols. Washington: U.S. Government Printing Office, 1946.

U.S. Strategic Bombing Survey (Pacific). *Japanese Air Power.* Washington: U.S. Government Printing Office, 1946.

Wavell, General Sir Archibald. *Despatch by the Supreme Commander of the ABDA Area to the Combined Chiefs of Staff on the Operations in the South-West Pacific, January 15th, 1942 to February 25th 1942.* (August 1942.) London: His Majesty's Stationery Office, 1948.

Wild, Major Cyril H.D. *Note on the Capitulation of Singapore.* November 30th, 1945. Copy in author's possession, courtesy of the Rev. John H.S. Wild.

BOOKS

Ash, Bernard. *Someone Had Blundered: The Story of the* Repulse *and the* Prince of Wales. London: Michael Joseph, 1960.

Attiwell, Kenneth. *The Singapore Story*. London: Transworld, 1961.

Barber, Noel. *A Sinister Twilight: The Fall of Singapore 1942*. London: Collins, 1968.

Barclay, Brigadier C.N. *On Their Shoulders: British Ceneralship in the Lean Years, 1939-1942*. London: Faber and Faber, 1954.

Bell, J. Bowyer. *Beseiged: Seven Cities Under Siege*. Philadelphia: Chilton Books, 1966.

Bennett, Lieut. Gen. H. Gordon. *Why Singapore Fell*. Sydney: Angus and Robertson Ltd., 1944

Bhargava, K.D., and K.N.V. Sastri. *Campaigns in South-East Asia, 1941-1942*. Official History of the Indian Armed Forces in the Second World War, 1939-1945. Calcutta?: Combined Inter-Services Historical Section, India & Pakistan, 1960.

Braddon, Russell. *The Naked Island*. London: Laurie, 1952.

Brereton, Lewis H. *The Brereton Diaries: The War in the Air in the Pacific, Middle East and Europe*. New York: William Morrow and Company, 1946.

Brown, Cecil. *Suez to Singapore*. New York: Random House, 1942.

Bryant, Arthur. *The Turn of the Tide: A History of the War Years Based on the Diaries of Field-Marshal Lord Alanbrooke, Chief of the Imperial General Staff*. London: Collins, 1957.

Butler, J.R.M. *Grand Strategy*: Vol II, *September 1939-June 1941*. History of the Second World War: United Kingdom Military Service. London: Her Majesty's Stationery Office, 1957.

Butow, Robert J.C. *Tojo and the Coming of the War*. London: Oxford University Press, 1961.

Caidin, Martin. *The Ragged, Rugged Warriors*. New York: Ballentine Books, 1966.

Cain, Lieutenant Commander T.J., as told to A.V. Sellwood. *H.M.S. Electra*. London: Frederick Muller Limited, 1959.

Chapmen, F. Spencer. *The Jungle is Neutral*. London: Chatto and Windus, 1949.

Churchill, Winston S. *The Second World War*: Vol. II, *Their Finest Hour*; Vol. III, *The Grand Alliance*; Vol. IV, *The Hinge of Fate*. London: Cassell & Company, 1949-1951.

Clutterbuck, Brigadier Richard L. *The Long Long War: Counterinsurgency in Malaya and Vietnam*. London: Cassells, 1967.

Communiques Issued by the Imperial General Headquarters, From December 8th, 1941 to June 30th, 1943. Tokyo: Mainichi Publishing Co., 1943.

Coombes, Major J.H.H. *Banpong Express.* Darlington: Wm. Dresser & Sons, [1948].

Craven, Wesley Frank, and James Lea Cate. (Eds.). *The Army Air Forces in World War II*: Vol. I, *Plans and Early Operations, January 1939 to August 1942.* London: Cambridge University Press, 1948.

D'Albas, Andrieu. *Death of a Navy: Japanese Naval Action in World War II.* London: Robert Hale & Co. Ltd., 1957.

Donahue, Flight Lieutenant Arthur G. *Last Flight from Singapore.* London: Macmillan, 1944.

Duff Cooper, Alfred. *Old Men Forget: The Autobiography of Duff Cooper (Viscount Norwich).* London: Rupert Hart-Davis, 1953.

Durrani, Lt. Col. Mahmood Khan. *The Sixth Column.* London: Cassell and Company, 1955.

Eade, Charles (Ed). *Winston Churchill's Secret Session Speeches.* New York: Simon and Schuster, 1946.

Farago, Ladislas. *The Broken Seal: The Story of Operation Magic and the Pearl Harbour Disaster.* London: Barker, 1967.

Gallagher, O.D. *Retreat in the East.* London: Harrap, 1942.

Gill, G. Herman. *Royal Australian Navy, 1939-1942.* Australia in the War of 1939-1945, Series 2, *Navy*, Vol. I. Canberra: Australian War Memorial, 1957.

Gillison, Douglas. *Royal Australian Air Force, 1939-1942.* Australia in the War of 1939-1945, Series 3 *Air*, Vol. I. Canberra: Australian War Memorial, 1962.

Glover, Edwin Maurice. *In 70 Days: The Story of the Japanese Campaign in British Malaya.* 2nd ed. London: Frederick Muller Ltd., 1949.

Greenfield, Kent Roberts (Ed.). *Command Decisions.* Washington: Office of the Chief of Military History, 1960.

Grenfell, Captain Russell, R.N. *Main Fleet to Singapore.* London: Faber & Faber, 1951.

Gwyer, J.M.A., and J.R.M. Butler. *Grand Strategy*: Vol. III, *June 1941-August 1942.* History of the Second World War: United Kingdom Military Series. London: Her Majesty's Stationery Office, 1964.

Hashimoto, Mochitsura. *Sunk: The Story of the Japanese Submarine Fleet, 1941-1945.* London: Cassell & Company, 1954.

Hasluck, Paul. *The Government and the People, 1939-1941.* Australia in the War of 1939-1945, Series 4, *Civil*, Vol. I. Canberra: Australian War Memorial, 1952.

Hattori, Takushiro. *The Complete History of the Greater East Asia War.* 4 Vols. Tokyo: Masu Publishing Co., 1953. Unpublished translation by U.S. Army Forces, Far East, 500th Military Intelligence Service Group, on file in Office, Chief of Military History, Dept. Army.

Hayashi, Saburo, in collaboration with Alvin D. Coox. *Kogun: The Japanese Army in the Pacific War.* Quantico, Va.: The Marine Corps Association, 1959.

Higham, Robin. *Armed Forces in Peacetime: Britain, 1918-1940, A Case Study.* London: Foulis, 1963.

Hough, Richard. *Death of the Battleship.* New York: Macfadden-Bartell Corporation, 1965.

Ike, Nobutaka (trans. and Ed.). *Japan's Decision for War: Records of the 1941 Policy Conferences.* Stanford: Stanford University Press, 1967.

Ito, Masanori, with Roger Pineau. *The End of the Imperial Japanese Navy.* London: Weidenfeld & Nicolson, 1963.

Iwaguro, Takeo. *Seiki no Shingun: Shingaporu no Sokogeki.* (*March of the Century: The Assault on Singapore*) Tokyo: Shio Shobo, 1956.

Japan Defence Agency, War History Section. *Mare Shinko Sakusen.* (*Operations of the Malaya Campaign*) Tokyo: Asagumo Shimbunsha, 1966.

Kemp, Lieutenant-Commander P.K. *Key to Victory: The Triumph of British Sea Power in World War II.* Boston: Little, Brown and Company, 1957.

Kennedy, Major-General Sir John. *The Business of War.* London: Hutchinson, 1958.

Khan, Maj-Gen. Shahnawaz. *My Memories of I.N.A. & Its NETAJI.* Delhi: Rajkamal Publications, 1946.

Kin, David George. *Rage in Singapore.* New York: Wisdom House, 1942.

Kirby, Major-General S. Woodburn, *et al. The War Against Japan*: Vol. I, *The Loss of Singapore.* History of the Second World War: United Kingdom Military Series. London: Her Majesty's Stationery Office, 1957.

Leasor, James. *Singapore: The Battle That Changed the World.* London: Hodder & Stoughton, 1968.

Legg, Frank. *The Gordon Bennett Story.* Sydney: Angus and Robertson, 1965.

Liddell Hart, Captain Sir Basil, and Barrie Pitt (Eds.). *History of the*

Second World War. 8 Vols. London: Purnell & Sons, Ltd., 1966-1969.

Macintyre, Donald. *The Battle for the Pacific.* London: Batsford, 1966.

Mackenzie, Compton. *Eastern Epic*: Vol. I, *September 1939-March 1943: Defence.* London: Chatto & Windus, 1951.

Matloff, Maurice, and Edward M. Snell. *Strategic Planning for Coalition Warfare, 1941-1942.* 'United States Army in World War II: The War Department.' Washington: Office of the Chief of Military History, Department of the Army, 1953.

Maurice-Jones, Col. K.W. *The History of Coast Artillery in the British Army.* London: Royal Artillery Institution, 1959.

Maxwell, Sir George. *The Civil Defence of Malaya.* London: Hutchinson & Co., Ltd., [1944?]

McKie, R.C.H. *This Was Singapore.* London: Robert Hale Limited, 1950.

Meskill, Johanna Menzel. *Hitler and Japan: The Hollow Alliance.* New York: Atherton Press, 1966.

Miller, Eugene H. *Strategy at Singapore.* New York: The Macmillan Company, 1942.

Moran, Charles McM. Wilson. *Churchill: Taken from the Diaries of Lord Moran.* Boston: Houghton Mifflin Company, 1966.

Morison, Samuel Eliot. *History of United States Naval Operations in World War II*: Vol. III, *The Rising Sun in the Pacific, 1931-April 1942.* London: Oxford University Press, 1950.

Morrison, Ian. *Malayan Postscript.* London: Faber & Faber Limited, 1942.

Morton, Louis. *The Fall of the Philippines.* United States Army in World War II: The War in the Pacific. Washington: Office of the Chief of Military History, Department of the Army, 1953.

Morton, Louis. *Strategy and Command: The First Two Years.* 'United States Army in World War II: The War in the Pacific.' Washington: Office of the Chief of Military History, 1962.

Okumiya, Masatake, and Jiro Horikoshi, with Martin Caidin. *Zero.* London: Cassell & Company, 1957

Owen, Frank. *The Fall of Singapore.* London: Michael Joseph, 1960.

Percival, Lieut.-General A.E. *The War in Malaya.* London: Eyre & Spottiswoode, 1949.

Playfair, Giles. *Singapore Goes Off the Air.* London: Jarrolds, 1944.

Pogue, Forest C. *George C. Marshall*: Vol. II, *Ordeal and Hope, 1939-1942.* New York: The Viking Press, 1966.

Potter, John Deane. *The Life and Death of a Japanese General.* New

York: The New American Library, 1962.

Reel, A. Frank. *The Case of General Yamashita.* London: Cambridge University Press, 1950.

Richards, Denis, and Hilary St. George Saunders. *Royal Air Force, 1939-1945*: Vol. II, *The Fight Avails.* London: Her Majesty's Stationery Office, 1954.

Rose, Angus. *Who Dies Fighting.* London: Jonathan Cape, 1944.

Roskill, Captain S.W. *The War at Sea, 1939-1945*: Vol. I, *The Defensive.* History of the Second World War: United Kingdom Military Series. London: Her Majesty's Stationery Office, 1954.

Sakai, Saburo, with Martin Caidin and Fred Saito. *Samurai.* London: New English Library, 1969.

Schroeder, Paul W. *The Axis Alliance and Japanese-American Relations, 1941.* London: Oxford University Press, 1958.

Smyth, Brigadier Sir John. *Before the Dawn: A Story of Two Historic Retreats.* London: Cassell & Company Ltd., 1957.

Stewart, Brigadier I. MacA. *History of the Argyll & Sutherland Highlanders, 2nd Battalion: Malayan Campaign, 1941-1942.* London: Thomas Nelson and Sons Ltd., 1947.

Swinson, Arthur. *Four Samurai: A Quartet of Japanese Army Commanders in the Second World War.* London: Hutchinson, 1968.

Thompson, Wing Commander H.L. *New Zealanders with the Royal Air Force*: Vol. III, *Mediterranean and Middle East, South-East Asia.* Official History of New Zealand in the Second World War, 1939-1945. Wellington: War History Branch, Department of Internal Affairs, 1959.

Toland, John. *But Not in Shame: The Six Months After Pearl Harbour.* London: Gibbs & Phillips, 1962.

Tsuji, Colonel Masanobu. *Singapore: The Japanese Version.* London: Constable, 1962.

Weller, George. *Singapore Is Silent.* New York: Harcourt, Brace and Company, 1943.

Wigmore, Lionel. *The Japanese Thrust.* Australia in the War of 1939-1945, Series 1, *Army*, Vol. IV. Canberra: Australian War Memorial, 1957.

Wohlstetter, Roberta. *Pearl Harbour: Warning and Decision.* Stanford: Stanford University Press, 1962.

Woodward, Sir Llewellyn. *British Foreign Policy in the Second World War.* History of the Second World War. London: Her Majesty's Stationery Office, 1962.

ARTICLES

Allen, Louis. The Surrender of Singapore: The Official Japanese Version, *The Durham University Journal*, LX (December 1967) No. 1, pp. 1-6.

Barclay, Brigadier Cyril N. The Fall of Singapore: A Re-appraisal, *Army*, April 1968, pp. 44-53.

Barclay, Brigadier Cyril N. The Indian Army, *Army*, July 1967, pp. 52-58.

Croizat, Col. Victor J. Japan Drives Southwest, *Army*, June 1967, pp. 65-73.

Dedman, J.J. Defence Policy Decisions Before Pearl Harbour, *The Australian Journal of Politics and History*, XIII (December 1967) No. 3, pp. 331-46.

Esthus, Raymond A. President Roosevelt's Commitment to Britain to Intervene in a Pacific War, *The Mississippi Valley Historical Review*, L (June 1953) No. 1, pp. 28-38.

Falk, Stanley L. Japanese Strategy in World War II, *Military Review*, XLII (June 1962) No. 6, pp. 70-81.

Falk, Stanley L. Organization and Military Power: The Japanese High Command in World War II, *Political Science Quarterly*, LXXVI (December 1961) No. 4, pp. 503-18.

Gunther, John. Singapore – A Warning to Japan, *The Saturday Evening Post*, June 18th, 1938, pp. 10-11, 90-94.

Hayes, Lt. J.O.C., R.N. The Withdrawal to Singapore Island, *The Army Quarterly*, XLV (November 1942) No. 1, pp. 107-13.

Keene, Donald. Japanese Writers and the Greater East Asia War. *Journal of Asian Studies*, XXIII (February 1964).

Lanza, Col. Conrad H. Malaya, *The Field Artillery Journal*, XXXIV (August 1944) No. 8, pp. 521-29.

Lewis, E.R. Dreadnought, *United States Naval Institute Proceedings*, XCII (January 1966) No. 1, pp. 120-21.

Minnigerode, H. Gordon. Life Grows Grim in Singapore, *National Geographic Magazine*, LXXX (November 1941) No. 5, pp. 661-86.

Mlaker, Lieut. Colonel. Singapore – British Naval Base, in *Militärwissenschaftliche Mitteilungen*, May 1941, translated and digested in *Military Review*, XXI (October 1941) No. 82, pp. 52-53.

Parkinson, C. Northcote. The Pre-1942 Singapore Naval Base, *United States Naval Institute Proceedings*, LXXXII (September 1956) No. 9, pp. 939-53.

Price, Willard. America's Enemy No. 2: Yamamoto, *Harpers Magazine*,

CLXXXIV (April 1942) No. 1103, pp. 449-58.

Robinson, Colonel A.O. The Malayan Campaign in the Light of the Principles of War, *Royal United Service Institution Journal*, CIX (August, November 1964) Nos. 635, 636, pp. 224-32, 325-37.

Sansom, Sir George. The Story of Singapore, *Foreign Affairs*, XXII (January 1944) No. 2, pp. 179-97.

Singapore, *The Times*, London, October 14th, 1940, reprinted in *United States Naval Institute Proceedings*, LXVII (February 1941) No. 2, pp. 262-65.

Stratton, Lt. Cdr. Samuel S. Tiger of Malaya, *United States Naval Institute Proceedings*, LXXX (February 1954) No. 2, pp. 137-43.

Swinson, Arthur, with Major Tokuji Morimoto and Matsuya Nagao. The Conquest of Malaya *History of the Second World War*, Eds. Captain Sir Basil Liddell-Hart and Barrie Pitt (8 Vols. London: Purnell and Sons Ltd., 1966-1969).

Tolley, Rear Admiral Kemp. Cruise of the *Lanikai, Shipmate*, XXX (January 1967) No. 1, pp. 2-6.

Tolley, Rear Admiral Kemp. Divided We Fell, *United States Naval Institute Proceedings*, XCII (October 1966) No 10, pp. 37-51.

Tolley, Rear Admiral Kemp. The Strange Assignment of the USS Lanikai, *United States Naval Institute Proceedings*, LXXXVIII (September 1962) No. 9, pp. 71-83.

Thompson, Virginia. The Landward Side of Singapore, *Pacific Affairs*, XIV (March 1941) No. 1, pp. 21-34.

Ward, Robert E. The Inside Story of the Pearl Harbour Plan, *United States Naval Institute Proceedings*, LXXVII (December 1951) No. 12, pp. 1271-83.

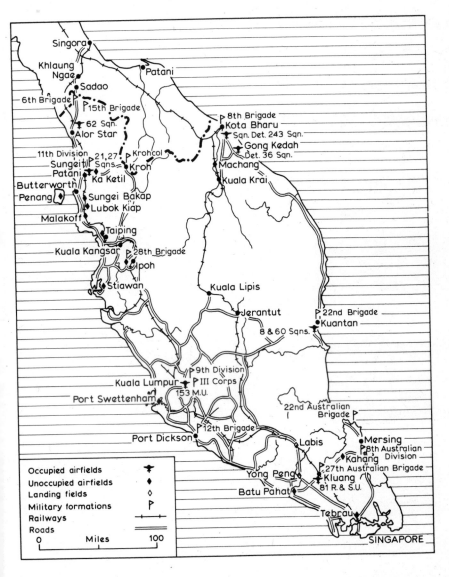

Dispositions of Formations, early December 1941. On Singapore Island were 34, 36, 100, 205, 243, 453 and 488 Squadrons, 4 Anti-Aircraft Co-operation Unit, a Photographic Recconnaissance Unit, 151 Maintenance Unit, and 1st and 2nd Malaya Brigades.

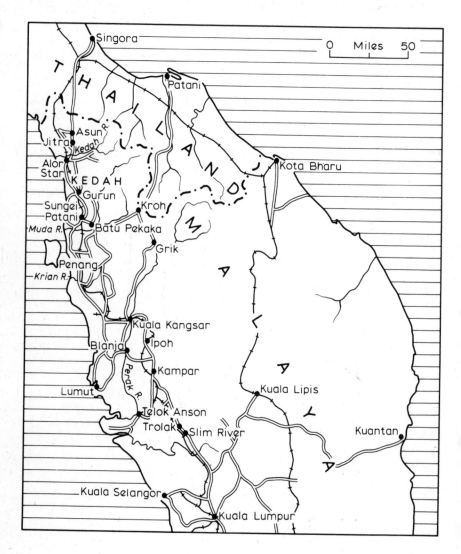

Northern Malaya

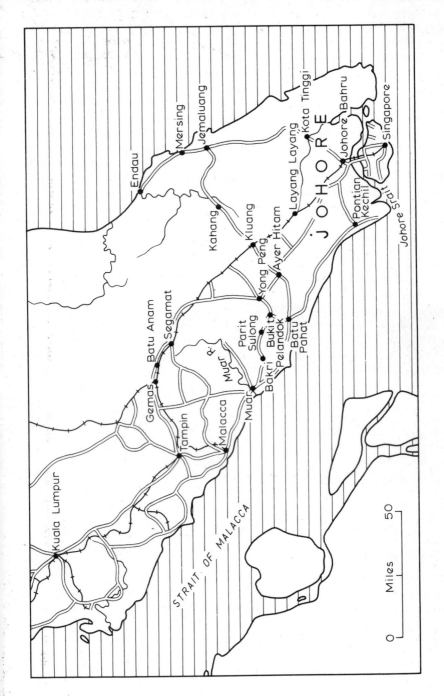

Southern Malaya

Singapore Island

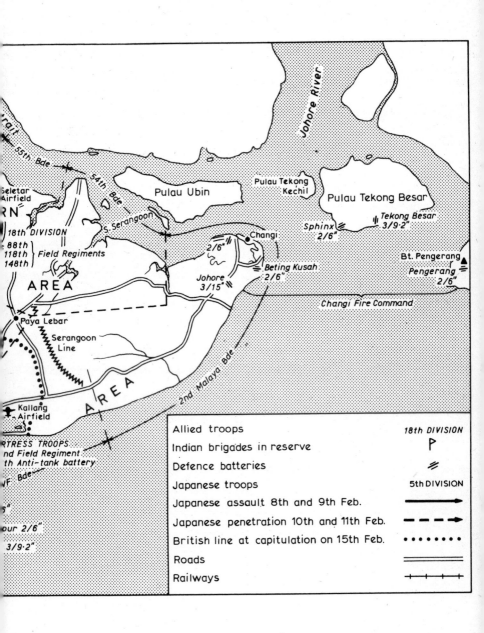

Pulau Ubin

Pulau Tekong Kechil

Pulau Tekong Besar

Johore River

Strait

55th Bde

54th Bde

Seletar Airfield

S. Serangoon

RN

18th DIVISION
88th
118th Field Regiments
148th

AREA

Paya Lebar

Serangoon Line

AREA

Kallang Airfield

RTRESS TROOPS
nd Field Regiment
th Anti-tank battery

F Bde

5"

our 2/6"

3/9·2"

2nd Malaya Bde

Changi

2/6"

Johore
3/15"

Beting Kusah
2/6"

Sphinx
2/6"

Tekong Besar
3/9·2"

Bt. Pengerang

Pengerang
2/6"

Changi Fire Command

Allied troops	18th DIVISION
Indian brigades in reserve	P
Defence batteries	⚡
Japanese troops	5th DIVISION
Japanese assault 8th and 9th Feb.	⟶
Japanese penetration 10th and 11th Feb.	- - - ⟶
British line at capitulation on 15th Feb.	• • • • • • •
Roads	═══
Railways	+++++

Index